POLITICAL

LIFE

POLITICAL
LIFE

WHY PEOPLE GET INVOLVED IN POLITICS

BY ROBERT E. LANE

THE FREE PRESS OF GLENCOE, INC.

A DIVISION OF THE CROWELL-COLLIER PUBLISHING COMPANY

SECOND PRINTING AUGUST 1961

Copyright © 1959 by The Free Press, a corporation

Printed in the United States of America

DESIGNED BY SIDNEY SOLOMON

LIBRARY OF CONGRESS CATALOG CARD NO. 58-6485

TO HELEN

Acknowledgments

MY FIRST DEBT is to the many scholars whose theoretical work and special studies have contributed ideas and evidence for this analysis. The dead cannot communicate their protests. The living can, and I hope they will.

I wish to acknowledge the assistance of the Fund for the Advancement of Education whose support permitted me to study for a year at the Yale Institute of Human Relations. The Social Science Research Council provided, through a Faculty Research Fellowship, time for me to complete this work before launching into a further study of the personal meanings of politics. At the Center for Advanced Study in the Behavioral Sciences I found a congenial atmosphere for discussion, writing, and reflection on many phases of political life. While there, I had many opportunities to draw on the wisdom and special knowledge of Morris Rosenberg. Wilbur Schramm gave me useful assistance in thinking through the problems treated in Chapter 19. Raymond Wolfinger, at an early stage in the writing, helped me with the historical and other sections. Angus Campbell and the Survey Research Center at Michigan kindly provided me with unpublished material of great usefulness. And to my editor, Jeremiah Kaplan, I am indebted for a steady judgment and a remarkably effective blue pencil.

From these and other sources I have received the truth. For error I alone am to blame.

Robert E. Lane

YALE UNIVERSITY
MARCH 1958

CONTENTS

Contents

Part I

---

*The Growth and Defense
of Popular Government
in America*

CHAPTER 1

An Approach to the Study of Political Life

So UNIVERSAL has the influence of government become in the great Western republics at mid-century, that few areas of life remain unaffected. Trivial things, like the price of a movie, and momentous destinies of nations threatened with incineration from the sky are at stake in the political decisions of the time. Particularly in those nations with free speech and the secret ballot, the people, informally as a series of publics and formally as the electorate, exercise some influence over these decisions. They not only vote, but in their discussion of public issues they create, or at least reflect, a "climate of opinion"; they exercise pressure in petitioning the government; they comprise the human reserve whence came the grass roots leaders of party, state, and nation. Or at least some of the people do and are these things.

Who are these members of the public? Through what channels do they exercise their influence? Under what conditions does the public become thus "engaged" in politics? What personal qualities do the active members of the public possess? And when is democracy safe in their keeping?

Since the publication of Merriam and Gosnell's *Non-Voting* in 1924,[1] and the series on citizenship edited by Merriam in the late twenties and early thirties,[2] considerable work has been done on popular participation—and non-participation—in politics. The earlier analyses of voting statistics have been supplemented by the kinds of survey studies associated with the names of Lazarsfeld, Berelson, and Campbell. These studies have given us insight into the way such demographic factors as religion, age, education, region, and income have affected electoral behavior; they have examined a variety of

1. Charles E. Merriam and Harold F. Gosnell, *Non-Voting* (Chicago: University of Chicago Press, 1924).

2. The summary volume is Charles E. Merriam, *The Making of Citizens, A Comparative Study of Methods of Civic Training* (Chicago: University of Chicago Press, 1931).

attitudes toward issues, parties, candidates, and various community groups; they have investigated the ways in which an individual's associates may influence his decisions; and they have provided valuable information on the effect of the media on the electorate.[3] To the evidence presented in these major studies must be added the contributions of many special investigations of letter writing, lobbying, electioneering, and campaigning. Taken all together, these present a comprehensive picture of political life at the grass roots. Beyond this, there have been a number of studies of political motivation dealing with the part that personality factors play in political decisions. Lasswell, Almond, Adorno and associates, Reisman, and others have, on the basis of case histories as well as broader attitude studies, attempted to analyze the needs that are met by political beliefs and behavior.

This book represents an effort to bring together and synthesize these various kinds of data and interpretation. However, the studies just referred to are special studies, presenting the data and interpretations arising from the examination of a few persons, a single community, or a single election. It is useful to supplement their findings with material of another kind: Studies of small groups (including the family), community life, the content and influence of the media, ethnic life in America, social class, occupational mobility, and income distribution contain many additional clues to electoral and civic behavior. We have, then, broadened the range of explanation to include the material from these various sources. Throughout our investigations we have been fortunate in that much unpublished and uninterpreted data has been made available to us for analysis.[4]

In Part I of this book we discuss the history of electoral participation in the United States and outline some of the arguments and theories advanced in support of enlarging the electorate. Part II focuses upon analysis of the ways in which the public participates in the political process. In Part III we analyze the motives and attitudes of the political participant, thus presenting, in one sense, a picture of political man. The analysis in Part IV deals with the influence upon political activity of the groups that men belong to and the communities they live in. In Part V we deal with several of the important social institutions which impede or encourage political participation. And in Part IV we discuss the social and political consequences of several patterns of political participation.

Three limitations upon the scope of this book must be acknowledged; two of these are the limitations of time and place. The evidence on which the hypotheses are grounded is (except for Chapters 2 and 3) largely confined to the

---

3. Two reviews, interpretations, and contributions to this literature may be found in Samuel J. Eldersveld, "Theory and Method in Voting Behavior Research," *Journal of Politics, 13* (1951), pp. 70-87; and Seymour M. Lipset, Paul F. Lazarsfeld, Allen H. Barton, and Juan Linz, "The Psychology of Voting: An Analysis of Political Behavior," in Gardner Lindzey, ed., *Handbook of Social Psychology* (Cambridge, Mass.: Addison-Wesley, 1954), pp. 1124-70.

4. In particular, I wish to thank Angus Campbell of the Michigan Survey Research Center, Morris Rosenberg, and Wilbur Schramm for making mimeographed and manuscript material available for this study.

present time and to the United States. Perhaps the hypotheses are true of other times and places; we hope they have this broader generality. The time limitation is imposed by the lack of appropriate special studies to extend the period covered. The limitation of place is—let us face it—due to the difficulty of making informed judgments of a social and psychological, as well as political, nature on events in unfamiliar cultures. The third limitation is imposed upon the behavior studied: this is a study of the ways people engage in the political process, not of their political preferences. It deals with how, when, and why people do the following things: vote, electioneer, contact public officials, go to political meetings, contribute to political parties, read and listen to political material, talk politics, and join quasi-political associations. It does not deal with the reasons they are Republicans, liberals, internationalists, or opposed to these views. The virtue of these limitations is that homogeneity of time, place, and behavior, while narrowing the scope of the interpretation, increases its validity.

NOTE ON A MODEL FOR ANALYZING ELECTORAL BEHAVIOR

We shall deal with three groups of phenomena: the political behavior of the public, the attitudes and personality qualities relevant to this behavior, and the environmental influences which affect the political participation of the public. How are these three kinds of phenomena related? Here we have borrowed a model which has had its most extensive use in learning theory,[5] but which has been applied to the analysis of labor-management relations,[6] the administration of a war-relocation center,[7] and electoral behavior in an American community,[8] among others. It is a simple model (indeed, in a mathematical sense, it is no model at all), having only three elements: S (stimulus), O (organism or individual), and R (response). Expressed as S→O→R, it merely means that a selected response, guided by a series of predispositions and traits, follows (is caused by) some external event perceived as a stimulus by the individual. Although, in this form, it appears to mean that the initiative for a response must come from some change in the environment, we do not mean to exclude the possibility of a purely psychic change leading to a re-

5. See Clark Hull, *Principles of Behavior* (New York: Appleton-Century-Crofts, 1943), pp. 1-49. It should be noted that learning theorists have generally preferred to limit their discussion to what is directly observable, that is, the stimuli and the responses, minimizing speculation on what must be inferred, the contents of the "O". Various notations are in use in this model, with a tendency among learning theorists to use "little s" and "little r" in place of the O.

6. F. J. Roethlisberger, *Management and Morale* (Cambridge, Mass.: Harvard University Press, 1941), pp. 18-22.

7. Alexander H. Leighton, *The Governing of Men* (Princeton: Princeton University Press, 1945), pp. 83-88.

8. Bernard R. Berelson, Paul F. Lazarsfeld, and William N. McPhee, *Voting* (Chicago: University of Chicago Press, 1954), p. 278.

sponse, that is, a response where S is constant. This may happen through the resolution of psychic tensions unrelated to environmental factors, although usually the environment provides some cue to trigger this resolution.

In our analysis, then, the R refers to the types of political behavior described in Part II and represents, collectively and individually, the dependent variables. The O refers to the psychological attributes of the individual discussed in Part III, and represents one set of independent variables. The S refers to the social or environmental factors discussed in Parts IV and V and represents the other set of independent variables. All together, and with great simplification, these relationships may be expressed diagrammatically as in Figure 1.

FIGURE 1.—Paradigm for the Study of Electoral Behavior.

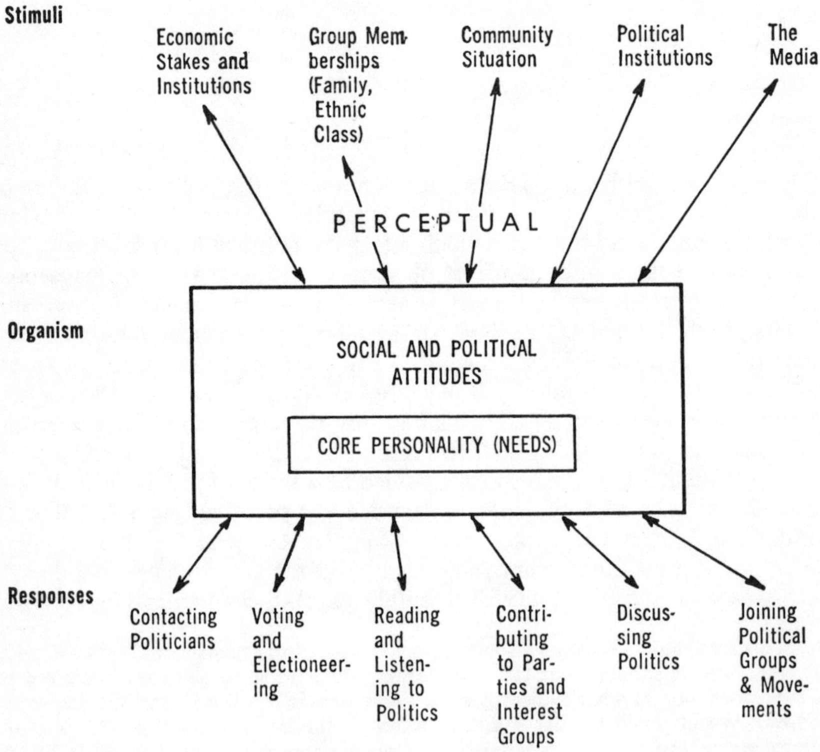

Four things should be noted about this diagram. In the first place, the relationship between the environmental stimuli and the person is chiefly a perceptual one, which means that all of the varieties of distortion, over-simplification, and selective attention which characterize perception apply here.

It should be noted, in the second place, that this is a snapshot, not a motion picture; it is a diagram of one moment in time. Over a period of time, of course, many of the environmental pressures are internalized and become, in different form, part of the attitudinal and personality structure. In the third place, note that the relationships indicated by the arrows are reciprocal; each response *may* have an internal effect as well as an external effect, each perception *may* have an effect on the thing perceived as well as on the perceiver. Fourth, it should be stated explicitly, although obvious enough on the face of it, that these are illustrative selections of variables, not in any sense a complete roster of political stimuli or political responses.

CHAPTER 2

The Historical Background: How Americans

Won the Franchise and the Use They Made of It

Since the electoral behavior we will analyze has roots in the past, it is useful to examine the laws and behavior which have left their mark upon the present.[1] Although "conceived in liberty," and emerging from a struggle against "taxation without representation," the constituent legislatures of the

---

1. There are many excellent studies of the growth of the franchise in Europe and the United States. See, for example, Charles Seymour, *Electoral Reform in England and Wales* (New Haven: Yale University Press, 1915); Charles Seymour and Donald Paige Frary, *How the World Votes* (Springfield, Mass.; C. A. Nichols, 1918), 2 vols.; James Bryce, *Modern Democracies* (New York: Macmillan, 1921), 2 vols.; Harold F. Gosnell, *Democracy, The Threshold of Freedom* (New York: Ronald, 1948), and *Why Europe Votes* (Chicago: University of Chicago Press, 1930); Alfred de Grazia, *Public and Republic* (New York: Knopf, 1951); James Hogan, *Elections and Representations* (Cork, Ireland; Cork University Press, 1945); George Burton Adams, *A Constitutional History of England* (New York: Holt, 1921); Georges D. Weil, *Les Elections Legislatives Depuis 1789* (Paris: Ancienne Librairie Gerner Bailliere et Cie., F. Alcan, 1895); Charles Seignobos, *Histoire Politique de l'Europe Contemporaine* (Paris: A. Colin, 1897); G. Lowes Dickinson, *The Development of Parliament During The 19th Century* (London: Longmans, Green, 1895); John R Seager, *Registration of Voters Under The Reform Act, 1918* (London: P. S. Ring, 1918). On American developments specifically, see Albert E. McKinley, *The Suffrage Franchise in the Thirteen Colonies in America* (Boston: Ginn, 1905); John B. McMaster, *The Acquisition of Political, Social and Industrial Rights of Man in America* (Cleveland: Imperial Press, 1903); James Bryce, *The American Commonwealth* (New York: Macmillan, 1910), revised edition; Kirk H. Porter, *A History of Suffrage in the United States* (Chicago: University of Chicago Press, 1918); Richard P. McCormick, *The History of Voting in New Jersey* (New Brunswick, N. J.: Rutgers University Press, 1953); Dudley O. McGovney, *The American Suffrage Medley* (Chicago: University of Chicago Press, 1949); and various specialized histories of women and Negro suffrage. V. O. Key summarizes some of this material in his *Politics, Parties and Pressure Groups* (New York: Crowell, 1952), 3rd ed.

[8]

several American states offered their citizens only a limited franchise.[2] In contrast to the doctrines of Samuel Adams, Tom Paine, and Thomas Jefferson, the limitations of the franchise seem to be the salient feature; in contrast to the then prevailing and subsequent electoral laws in France and England the breadth of the franchise seems most notable. The second of these two contrasts seems more significant, however, as we examine the immediate post-revolutionary history of electoral expansion in the United States, an expansion which may be viewed as a two-phase process. First, from the end of the Revolution to the time of the Mexican War the main struggle focused on the franchise of native white American males. In the process, the principle of universal white male suffrage was clearly accepted and the logic for other extensions was established for future use. From 1845 onward, the problems of electoral participation by aliens, Negroes, and women have occupied the center of the stage.

EXPANDING THE ELECTORATE THROUGH CHANGES
IN THE LAW

The peculiar origins of the United States have left their mark on electoral reform as on other aspects of history. Among these are the theocratic Puritan beginnings, the commercial nature of some of the first colonial adventures, the freehold system of land tenure, the lack of a feudal tradition, and, of course, the frontier. We note, in connection with the first of these elements the peculiar emphasis placed on orthodox belief in early colonial and even some post-revolutionary electoral requirements. Thus many members of minority religions were excluded from the ballot and an oath of religious belief was often required before a man was allowed to vote. Yet, for proper perspective, it should be noted that France also required a religious oath at several points in her series of stormy electoral changes. Also, of course, the exclusion of the unorthodox is often prompted by what may be called "normal xenophobia," not necessarily associated with Puritanism. This generalized xenophobic pattern, in contrast to attacks on purely religious deviants, is illustrated by the complaints of the colonial writer who protested that "Jews, strangers, sailors, servants, and Frenchmen" could vote under the terms of the laws in his state.[3]

But the more important limitations dealt with property qualifications. Immediately before the revolution, seven of the thirteen colonies maintained an uncompromising landed property qualification on voting, while the other six permitted a person to substitute either evidence of personal property or a tax payment as a prerequisite for admittance to the franchise. The record of

---

2. Factual data for the following discussion is taken chiefly from K. H. Porter, *op. cit.;* C. Seymour and D. F. Frary, *op. cit.;* A. de Grazia, *op. cit.;* R. P. McCormick, *op. cit.;* and V. O. Key, *op cit.* The interpretation of the data, of course, should not be attributed to these authors.

3. Quoted in K. H. Porter, *op. cit.,* p. 5.

FIGURE 2.1.—Duration of Property and Taxpaying Qualifications.

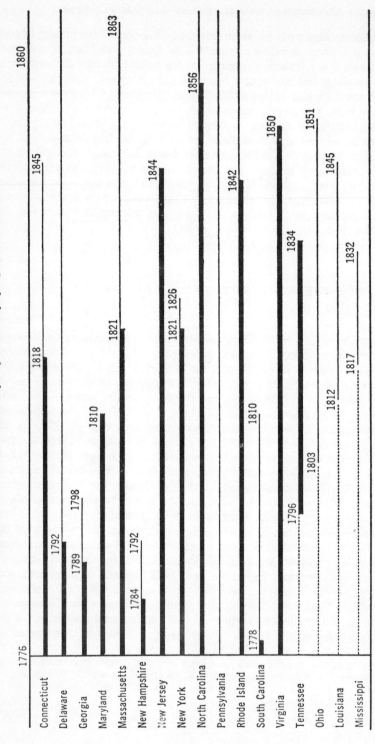

Notes to Figure 2.1. Heavy lines indicate duration of property qualification. Broken lines represent period prior to the states coming into the Union.

Vermont and Kentucky came into the Union in 1791 and 1792 respectively and Indiana in 1816, but without property or taxpaying qualifications. After Mississippi, in 1817, no state came in with a property or taxpaying qualification.

SOURCE: Kirk H. Porter, "A History of Suffrage in the United States" (Chicago: University of Chicago Press), 1918.

franchise reform during the first sixty years of the nation's history is made up of the erosion of these requirements. Promptly after the war eight of the thirteen colonies modified their property and tax requirements, although only Pennsylvania abolished property requirements altogether (retaining a tax provision), and none did away entirely with all economic means tests. Slowly, under the pressure of prosperous urban individuals, real property qualifications were broadened to include personalty requirements as alternative forms of wealth, which, in turn, were superceded by more lenient provisions based upon payment of taxes. In any event, party organization was a more significant factor in affecting turnout than the severity of property requirements.[4] When, in the end, some of these tax requirements were abandoned, it appeared that their restrictive effect was minimal. Thus when New York abandoned the tax-paying requirements for complete adult manhood suffrage in 1827, the electorate was increased by only 1 per cent.[5] As may be seen in Figure *2.1*, by 1845 property restrictions on the right to vote were almost extinct, and by the end of the Civil War only four states retained the much more moderate tax requirements. In some places persons who did not meet these requirements were permitted to substitute service in the militia, or work on local roads as an alternative. The abortive efforts during the 1930's to limit the franchise of persons on relief on the basis of ancient pauper laws, and the continuation of a poll tax in several southern states represent the vestiges in the modern period of early property or tax requirements.

The effort to impose or strengthen property requirements turned out to be inadequate in the face of the many campaigns to weaken or destroy such requirements. Yet conservatism in this area was supported by powerful forces. The fact that many of the early settlements were established by commercial companies, some of whose members were stockholders, made participation in government analogous in many ways to participation in the control of a business firm. As a consequence, property requirements seemed a peculiarly appropriate condition for the privilege of voting,. In the second place, the Calvinistic ethic of the Puritan culture placed special premiums on economic possessions as the tangible evidence of spiritual worth. Men marked by success in wordly affairs were thought particularly fit to govern.

In addition to these factors with a unique basis in American history, there were the more usual arguments identifying propertied people as more stable, more intelligent and better educated, less prone to passion, more interested in the public well-being, and (oddly enough), less devoted to special interests. Furthermore, it was argued that while the government protected everyone's life and liberty, it also protected property, and therefore the man with property had a greater stake in government. In some instances this led to the suggestion that a property qualification might be imposed on those voting for the upper house of the state legislature, evidently under the presumption that the Senators would look out for property rights, while other representatives would take care of life and liberty.

---

4. See R. P. McCormick, *op. cit.*, p. 84.
5. C. Seymour and D. P. Frary, *op. cit.*, vol. I, p. 232.

Yet in spite of the strength of "vested interests," and the reinforcement they received from certain unique forces in American life, economic qualifications for the vote quickly withered away. There were several reasons for this, the most important being the special situation created by the emergence of new states in the West. Thus in this sense, as in others, the frontier has been said to have encouraged "the development of political democracy as a habit and the American as a unique political creature."[6] Whether or not this statement is exaggerated, it is undoubtedly true that the conditions of frontier life, including the relative lack of class distinctions, the requirement that *all* settlers work together to defeat the Indians and, more importantly, the forces of nature, and the lack of traditional leadership patterns combined to add to ideological convictions a situational urgency for a wider democracy.[7] Of all the new states admitted to the union only Tennessee imposed a property qualification upon the franchise, and after Mississippi (in 1817) no state entered the union with even a tax-paying qualification.

The consequence, and to some extent the intent, of these more liberal voting requirements, is said to have been to attract settlers into the freer states —although from the standpoint of mid-twentieth century it seems doubtful that many people actually chose their destination with electoral provisions in mind. In any event the Eastern states became concerned and, in response to the competitive appeal of their Western rivals, also gave up their economic restrictions on the vote. But even without this Western pressure other forces were at work which would have promoted universal manhood suffrage at an early point. Among these were the cogent reiterations of American versions of the European ideological arguments, arguments based on the rights of man given special impetus by the Declaration of Independence and the terms of conflict of the American Revolution. Furthermore, the widespread ownership of property, largely in the form of homesteads, made extension of the franchise a less hazardous operation because relatively fewer people were added when the property requirements were modified. As Louis Hartz has pointed out, the lack of the experience of feudalism in the United States is a central feature of our history,[8] and the failure of class lines to be rigidified at the beginning of the industrial revolution deprived the opponents of universal suffrage of a certain esprit, a common bond, and an ingrained elitist ideology which would have strengthened their resistance. Although the current state of electoral interest in politics does not suggest it, on the whole it seems true that Americans were more politically minded and more ready for the franchise than their counterparts in Europe. Speaking of the French, for example, Seymour and Frary remark, "The slight interest taken in the voting privilege, as indicated by the large number of abstentions is the salient characteristic of elections during the Revolutionary period."[9] And, in England, after the Re-

---

6. Stanley Elkins and Eric McKitrick, "A Meaning for Turner's Frontier, I: Democracy in the Old Northwest," *Political Science Quarterly*, 69 (1954), p. 324.

7. *Ibid.*, p. 325.

8. Louis Hartz *The Liberal Tradition in America* (New York: Harcourt, Brace, 1955).

9. C. Seymour and D. P. Frary, *op. cit.*, p. 317.

form Act of 1832, "there were many qualified electors who did not care to have their names in the list" of registered voters, partly, it appears, for business reasons.[10] Finally, we note the earlier development of public education in the United States, and the consequent emergence of a substantial public who were exposed to civic appeals and literate enough to read the daily press. For all of these reasons, the extension of the franchise to free white males was relatively quick and even painless in the United States.[11]

With the passing of property qualifications, provisions began to appear in state constitutions restricting voting on the basis of sex (it having been previously taken for granted that women would not vote), race, and nationality, and additional precautions against voting by the incompetent and the transient. Of the three major problems centering on aliens, Negroes, and women, the alien issue was the first real center of attention and controversy.

A certain chauvinism, plus fears of the political consequences of bloc voting by the ignorant and pliable, led the Eastern states to impose restrictions aimed at newly arrived immigrants. Immigrants were a major source of labor for new industries in these states and, therefore, were likely to congregate in the cities. Inevitably, this created apprehensions about the emergence of a voting proletariat. This combination of attitudes in the Eastern states tended to contribute to their longer retention of property qualifications and to stricter literacy and residence requirements for everyone. When these restrictions were finally modified, direct restrictions on naturalized, as contrasted to native-born, citizens were attempted. Massachusetts, for example, required naturalized citizens to wait two years from the date of their citizenship before they could vote, regardless of how long they had lived in their voting district up to that time. Discriminatory residence restrictions for naturalized citizens were also attempted, but none of these provisions endured for long, again partly because of competitive pressure from the West.

The attitude toward aliens in the newer states of the Great Lakes and Ohio Valley regions was very different. These states showed great eagerness to attract new settlers and were willing to offer easy voting laws as an enticement. Wisconsin, for example, permitted aliens to vote if they would declare their intention to become citizens; other states followed along in this direction, although few relaxed customary restrictions so thoroughly as did Wisconsin. The usual practice was to give the vote to aliens a year or two after they had declared their intention to seek naturalization.

Negro voting became a problem of some consequence in the North, and particularly the border states, in the 1830's and '40's. Half a dozen Northern states adopted measures prohibiting Negroes from voting, or imposed special tax and property restrictions on them, although an equal number of states, principally in New England, took no action against Negro suffrage. In the Southern states Negro voting presented less of a problem at this time, since

---

10. Ivor Bulmer-Thomas, *The Party System in Great Britain* (London: Phoenix, 1953), p. 13.

11. For a discussion of the dilemma of the propertied middle classes in this process, see A. de Grazia, *op. cit.*, pp. 244-51.

free Negroes usually tended to migrate north, and slaves, of course, were not considered eligible (although they formed a modified basis for apportionment of Congressmen). The border states, with the highest proportion of free Negroes, were most diligent in restricting Negro voting, generally prohibiting it outright; and newly admitted states in the Middle and Far West did the same. Such states as Wisconsin, which had been so eager to permit aliens to vote, refused to permit Negro suffrage under any circumstances.

The Civil War, of course, caused a revolutionary upheaval in Negro voting patterns. The Fifteenth Amendment explicitly (and the Fourteenth implicitly and by intent) prohibited the denial of the vote to anyone on the basis of his race. This seems to have settled the question in the North, but it did no such thing farther south. The state governments which were established in the South immediately after the war, controlled as they were by previously dominant elements, imposed complete prohibition on Negro suffrage. The reconstruction regimes which quickly succeeded them completely reversed this stand, and Negroes were given full suffrage. One of the conditions under which the southern states were readmitted to the Union was their acceptance of the Fourteenth Amendment guaranteeing "equal protection of the laws." However, as soon as Federal troops left, the southerners set about to disfranchise the Negro, a task made easy by the Negro's political apathy and lack of experience in politics. Where necessary, southern whites employed violence and intimidation, often through the Ku Klux Klan, and at other times persuasion, fraud, or simply social pressure.

Once they regained control of their state governments, the native whites were able to dispense with most of these violent methods, and resort to other devices, some of which are discussed below.[12] Such extra-legal measures, supported by the lenient stand of the Federal courts, were continued for about twenty years, until the southern states began to rewrite their constitutions to make legal, and constitutional, provision for denying the vote to Negroes without excluding (too many) whites. In the end, legal provisions, discriminatory administration of the laws, threats of violence and economic pressure, combined to deny southern Negroes the right to vote, a right which they have not yet attained in many areas.

The southerners were aided in their endeavors by the Federal courts, which ruled that it was necessary for a Negro to prove that he was being excluded from the polls *on grounds of color,* rather than for any other reason.[13] The Supreme Court further ruled that "it is not an offense against the laws of the United States to prevent a citizen, white or black, from voting at a state election, by violence or otherwise."[14] Thus unless the Negro could prove that his race was the ground for exclusion from the polls, he had no case. And the allegation by an election official of any other reason for his refusal to let a Negro vote was usually accepted by the courts.[15] Furthermore, the Court took

---

12. See pp. 315-17 below.

13. *United States v. Reese,* 92 U.S. 214 (1876).

14. *United States v. Amsden,* 10 Biss, 283 (1881).

15. K. H. Porter, *op. cit.,* p. 202.

the position that it would not issue orders which it could not enforce, and refused to interfere in "administrative" interpretations of literacy or "good character" as these applied to Negroes seeking the electoral franchise.[16] On the other hand, the Court declined to accept the "grandfather clause" which (in the Oklahoma version) would have enfranchised illiterates who had been eligible to vote in 1866 or who were lineal descendants of 1866 voters.[17]

During the twentieth century the white primary was the main device for disfranchising Negroes and, although this was successfully attacked in several versions,[18] it was finally declared constitutional.[19] This victory for the white primary was short-lived, however, for after intimating the mortality of this opinion in the *Classic* case,[20] the Court finally decided in *Smith v. Allwright* that primaries were elections and protected by the Fourteenth and Fifteenth Amendments.[21]

During the history of this prolonged struggle, which is in a particularly acute phase in mid-twentieth century, the arguments employed to support the case for equal extension of the franchise to the Negro embrace those familiar to equalitarian liberals and advocates of the universal franchise generally.[22] Those opposed to the extension of the franchise to the Negro, however, consider certain features of the dispute exceptional. In the first place, there is the problem presented by the radical change in status—equality of voting status not just of a subordinate class, but of an inferior caste. In the second place, racial sentiments of the order here at work are not penetrable by new information or cognitive reorganization; their roots often lie beyond the reach of the rational mind. In the third place, the abrupt character of the division between white and Negro, with no such intermediate groups as are present in economic gradations to shift their support now to one side and now to another, has reduced the possibility of gradual change. Fourth, unlike any other similar problem of extension of the franchise, this one has been aggravated by war thus adding new grounds for resistance to Negro (Northern) pressure. Finally, as in many such situations, attitudes have become embedded in a network of one-party institutions which have created safe constituencies where vested interests tend to resist Negro voting for personal reasons. All these and many more historical, institutional, and attitudinal forces give special strength to the resistance to extending the franchise to the Southern Negro.[23]

The issue of women's suffrage appeared on the national scene in the late 1840's when a number of women launched a widely reported campaign to

---

16. *Giles v. Harris,* 189 U.S. 475 (1903).
17. *Guin v. United States,* 238 U.S. 347 (1915).
18. *Nixon v. Herndon,* 273 U.S. 536 (1927); *Nixon v. Condon,* 286 U.S. 73 (1932).
19. *Grovey v. Townsend,* 295 U.S. 45 (1935).
20. *United States v. Classic,* 313 U.S. 299 (1941).
21. *Smith v. Allwright,* 321 U.S. 649 (1944).
22. See below, pp. 26-37.
23. For a history of Negro voting see Paul Lewinson, *Race, Class and Party* (New York: Oxford University Press, 1932); C. S. Mangum, Jr., *The Legal Status of the Negro* (Chapel Hill: University of North Carolina Press, 1940).

secure the vote for their sex. Prior to this there had been several isolated cases of female voting rights, including the inadvertent inclusion of women in the franchise in New Jersey in both the Constitutions of 1776 and 1797, a situation quickly changed by the legislators at the turn of the century when a few women attempted to exercise their voting rights. With the exception of such incidents as this, and the growing practice of allowing women to vote in school elections, women were not permitted to vote in the United States until the territory of Wyoming extended the privilege to them in 1869. Although three other Western states provided female suffrage in the nineteenth century, it was not until the Progressive movement gave impetus to their cause in 1910 that other states, mainly Western, admitted women to the general vote. Finally, of course, the matter was settled on a national basis in 1920 by the Nineteenth Amendment.[24]

The controversies surrounding the extension of the vote to women dealt in part with the special qualities which were thought to inhere in the "fair sex," the "weaker sex," "men's better half," and so forth. Opponents pointed to the dependence of women on men (or to their alarming independence), the unfortunate changes in role which such worldly interest implied, the unsuitability of the female temperament to the nature of the decisions required, the consequent altered relations between the sexes if such a trend were to continue, and the bad effect upon church and home. Distilling and brewing interests were particularly alarmed because of the association of women with prohibition; corporate interests feared radical tendencies; and political bosses trembled over the expected impact of female reformist zeal. On the other hand, advocates of women's franchise, men as well as women, claimed that in addition to the logic of natural rights and equalitarianism in general, the unique qualities of women would sweep corruption from the scene, enhance provision for children, and liberate women from their undeserved subordinate position. On the whole it seems probable that the eventual success of female suffrage was more a product of the gradual change in the general status of women than of the intellectual merits of the controversy waged in such heated fashion.

CHANGING PATTERNS OF ELECTORAL TURNOUT

If such is the nature of the history of the expanding franchise, what of the use of these rights? Tocqueville, who commented on the highly political na-

24. See *The History of Women Suffrage,* six volumes, New York: Volumes I-III were edited by Elizabeth C. Stanton, Susan B. Anthony, and Matilda J. Gage; Vols. I and II were published by Anthony in 1881; Vol. III was published by Anthony in 1886; Vol. IV was edited by S. B. Anthony and Ida H. Harper and published in 1902 by Anthony; Vols. V and VI were edited by I. H. Harper and published by the National American Woman Suffrage Association in 1922. The periods covered by these volumes are: I, 1848-61; II, 1861-76; III, 1876-85; IV, 1883-1900; V, VI, 1900-20.

ture of the American people,[25] and Bryce, who commented on the political apathy of the American people,[26] represent polar views of the extent of participation in the nineteenth and early twentieth centuries. Taken at face value, it appears that participation, or at least involvement in politics, declined during this period; but possibly the observers were wrong, or possibly qualitative changes might account for their different impressions. One might investigate the quantitative aspects of their views, insofar as voting can be taken as an index of participation, relating the total vote to the population over the time period indicated. We have done this in Table 2.1 and Figure 2.2.

For the reasons indicated in the Notes to Table 2.1, comparison of voting totals to population totals are of limited usefulness because they reflect both legal rights and popular interests. They do indicate, however, and this is important, what proportion of the total population may be said to be sharing in national policy-making at the electoral level at any one time. In spite of Tocqueville's impression that a very large number of Americans were immersed in politics, these data show the limitations of this interpretation. Only 10 to 12 per cent of the population voted in the presidential elections of the 1830's, which, to be sure, is certainly more than were voting in France from 1815 to February 1848. But only thirteen years after the first edition of *Democracy in America* appeared in Paris, French elections (1848) were attracting 64 per cent and, in one case, 84 per cent of the electorate to the polls —and the electorate included all male citizens twenty-one and over in pos-

---

25. "It is difficult to say what place is taken up in the life of an inhabitant of the United States by his concern for politics. To take a hand in the regulation of society and to discuss it is his biggest concern and, so to speak, the only pleasure an American knows. This feeling pervades the most trifling habits of life; even the women frequently attend public meetings and listen to political harangues as a recreation from their household labors. . . . In some countries the inhabitants seem unwilling to avail themselves of the political privileges which the law gives them; . . . But if an American were condemned to confine his activity to his own affairs, he would be robbed of one-half of his existence. . . ." Alexis de Tocqueville, *Democracy in America* (New York: Knopf, 1945), Vol. I, p. 250, Phillips Bradley edition.

26. Bryce finds politics in the United States, as contrasted to Europe, more concerned with trivia and minutiae and hence less interesting to able young men who might otherwise be attracted to public life. This state of affairs was notable for forty years or more following the Civil War, but in his 1910 edition he finds that more able men are being attracted to politics. On political discussion, he says: "The citizen has little time to think about political problems. Engrossing all the working hours, his avocation leaves him only stray moments for this fundamental duty. It is true that he admits his responsibilities, considers himself a member of a party, takes some interest in current events. But although he would reject the idea that his thinking was done for him, he has not leisure to do it for himself, and must practically lean upon and follow his party. It astonished me in 1870 and 1881 to find how small a part politics played in conversation among the best educated classes and generally in the cities." James Bryce, *The American Commonwealth* (New York: Macmillan, 1910), Vol. II, p. 291.

session of civil right.[27] Although these figures lend themselves to various interpretations, greater political interest in the United States relative to that of other countries is not clearly established.

A second feature of note is the general growth of the participating electorate, with significant declines only in the 1840's, the post-Civil War period, turn of the century and first decade of the twentieth century, and the 1940's. On the other hand, as later analysis will show, the increases from 1912 to 1924 were due almost wholly to changes in electoral laws, not to increased interest in politics. Whatever the reason it is significant that generally speaking, decade by decade, over the course of American history, a constantly increasing proportion of the population has registered its preference in national elections.

In the third place, bearing out the above observation, the different effects on turnout of legal changes is seen in three time periods. In the first period of rapid increase, 1824-40, the influence of an additional number of states with popular choice of presidential electors, combined with the more modest effect of the relaxation of economic qualification on the franchise, is clearly revealed. In the second period, from 1840 to 1916, further relaxation of economic restrictions has little effect, and, as we know from the history of the times, the enfranchisement of the Negro had only sporadic and minimal influence. In the third period it is apparent that the enfranchisement of women was a move with greater influence on the proportion of the population admitted to the franchise (though not on the complexion of the vote) than that of any other legal change in the period at least from 1832 on.

Since we are interested not only in the number of people who participate in elections but also in the proportion voting of those eligible for the vote, we must search other data for these relationships. Questions of motivation and social pressure, apart from considerations of legal standing, are involved here. Early figures on this aspect of participation are not available on a national scale, but the data from 1856 to 1952 are presented in Table 2.2 and Figure 2.3.

With the qualifications stated in the Notes to Table 2.2, we may study these data in the light of relevant events in American history, searching for such general factors as may be at work in the electoral process. First, reviewing the record, it appears that a major slump took place after the Civil War, probably partly because of "war fatigue" and partly because the Democratic candidate in 1868, Horatio Seymour, had little appeal and, like Horace Greeley in 1872, suffered from the stigma incurred by the Democrats during

---

27. The figures on the percentage of electorate voting are given in Charles Seymour and Donald P. Frary, *op. cit.,* Vol. 1, pp. 350-51. Weil quotes a government proclamation of the period as follows: "La loi electorale provisoire que nous avons faite est la plus large qui, chez aucun peuple de la terre, ait jameis convoqué le peuple à l'exercice du suprême droit de l'homme, sa propre souveraineté. L'élection appartient à tous sans exception. A dater de cette loi, il n'y a plus de prolétaires en France. . . . Il n'y a pas un citoyen qui puisse dire à l'autre: Tu es plus souverain que moi. — Contemplez votre puissence, préparez-vous a l'exercer et soyez digne d'entrer en possession de votre règne." Georges-Denis Weil, *op. cit.,* p. 170.

TABLE 2.1.—The Relation of Total Vote for President to Total Population (Minus Slaves) 1824-1952.

Year	Total Population (minus slaves) (000 omitted)	Total Vote for President (000 omitted)	Percentage Total Vote of Total Population	Comments
1824	9,386	356	3.8	gradual
1828	10,228	1,155	11.3	withdrawal
1832	11,733	1,218	10.4	of tax and
1836	12,936	1,498	11.6	property
1840	14,633	2,411	16.5	qualifi-
1844	17,082	2,699	15.8	cation for
1848	18,202	2,872	15.8	voting;
1852	21,707	3,144	14.5	minimal
1856	24,258	4.054	16.7	importance
1860	27,559	4,680	17.0	1848-60.
1864	34,863	4,019	—	
1868	38,213	5,716	—	Voting
1872	41,972	6,466	15.4	total for
1876	46,107	8,431	18.3	United States
1880	50,262	9,219	18.3	only, 1864.
1884	55,379	10,050	19.0	No popular
1888	60,496	11,392	18.8	vote counted
1892	65,666	12,150	18.5	for 4
1896	70,885	13,813	19.5	Southern
1900	76,094	13,965	18.4	states,
1904	82,165	13,524	16.5	1868.
1908	88,709	14,887	16.8	
1912	95,331	15,031	15.8	Female
1916	101,966	18,529	18.2	suffrage in
1920	106,466	26,705	25.1	transition
1924	114,113	29,022	25.4	for states
1928	120,501	36,879	30.6	in the union
1932	124,840	39,814	31.9	1892-1916.
1936	128,053	45,648	35.6	
1940	131,970	49,901	37.8	Complete
1944	138,083	47,974	34.7	female
1948	146,631	48,794	33.3	suffrage
1952	157,022	61,552	39.2	from 1920 to date.

SOURCES: Bureau of the Census, "Historical Statistics of the United States, 1789-1945" (Washington, D.C.; 1949), pp. 27, 289-90; Bureau of the Census, "Statistical Abstract of the United States; 1955 76th ed. (Washington, D. C.; 1955), p. 13; Charles A. Titus, "Voting Behavior in the United States" (Berkeley, Calif.; University of California Press, 1935), p. 55; Election statistics after 1932 are from: George Gallup, "The Political Almanac" (New York; B.C. Forbes, 1952), p. 53; and Earl Rockwood and Lyle O. Snader (Clerk of the House), "Statistics of the Presidential and Congressional Election of November 4, 1952" (Washington, D.C.; U.S. Gov't. Printing Office, 1953), p. 55.

Notes to Table 2.1. The analysis of turnout as a proportion of total population presents certain difficulties: (1) We must assume that the proportion of adults to total population does not vary so much as to alter the general configuration of the electoral record, an assumption which must take into consideration the known changes in infant mortality balanced by the increase in longevity over the period. (2) The figures for 1824 and 1828 are not strictly comparable to the other figures because in 1824 six states, and in 1828 two states, did not provide for popular election of presidential electors (and South Carolina did not give up legislative selection of presidential electors until after the Civil War). (3) The eligible electorate varies from year to year until roughly 1876, due to changes in qualifications based on property, tax payment, citizenship, color (for free Negroes), residence, and sex.

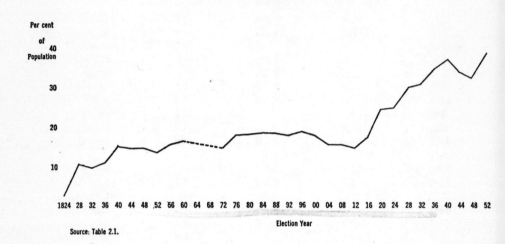

FIGURE 2.2—Per cent of Total Population Voting in
Presidential Elections, 1824-1952

Source: Table 2.1.

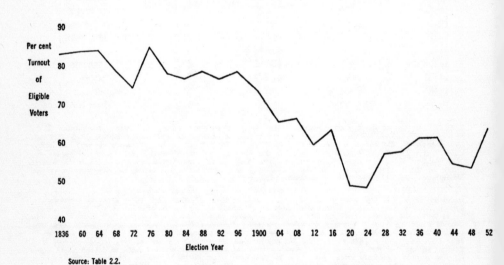

FIGURE 2.3.—Per cent of Eligible Voters Voting in
Presidential Elections, 1856-1952.

Source: Table 2.2.

TABLE 2.2
Votes Cast per 1,000 Voting Population, 1856-1952.

A. 1856-1876

Year	Voting population	Votes cast for President	Votes cast per 1,000 voting population	Comments
1856	5,022	4,194	835	Exclusion of the
1860	5,555	4,677	842	South in 1864 gives
1864	4,743	4,025	849	more weight to relatively more
1868	7,208	5,725	794	urban and industrial
1872	8,633	6,466	749	states. Compare another war year,
1876	9,799	8,413	858	1944.

B. 1880-1932

1880	11,740	9,208	784	
1884	13,110	10,050	767	
1888	14,475	11,392	787	
1892	15,900	12,150	764	
1896	17,450	13,813	792	
1900	18,970	13,965	735	Woman suffrage
1904	20,580	13,524	658	in transition
1908	22,440	14,887	663	1892-1916.
1912	25,040	15,031	600	
1916	29,060	18,529	637	
1920	54,060	26,705	493	
1924	59,200	29,022	491	
1928	64,340	36,879	574	
1932	69,000	39,814	578	

C. 1936-1952

1936	73,700	45,648	619	
1940	80,260	49,901	621	Low soldier vote
1944	85,800	47,974	551	affects 1944
1948	91,200	48,794	535	turnout.
1952	96,800	61,552	636	

SOURCES: Data for Part A, 1856-1876, are from Arthur M. Schlesinger and Erik M. Eriksson, "The Vanishing Voter," New Republic, 40 (1924), p. 167. Data for Part B, 1880-1932, are from Charles H. Titus, "Voting Behavior in the United States" (Berkeley: University of California Press, 1935), p. 55. Data for Part C, 1936-1952, are from Bureau of the Census, "Historical Statistics of the United States, 1789-1945" (Washington, D.C.; 1949), pp. 32, 288-90; Earl Rockwood and Lyle O. Snader (Clerk of the House), "Statistics of the Presidential and Congressional Election of November 4, 1952" (Washington, D.C.; 1953), p. 55; and George Gallup, "The Political Almanac" (New York; Forbes, 1952), p. 53.

Notes to Table 2.2. Although the precise basis of the Schlesinger and Eriksson figures is not known, they probably represent estimates of the population age twenty-one and over minus slaves and those disfranchised by property and citizenship qualifications. Data on the Civil War period presumably include only the Northern states. Although not clearly defined, "voting population" in Titus' data presumably refers to all male citizens twenty-one or over and all female citizens twenty-one or over in states where they were eligible to vote. This was the basis of our own calculations providing data on the post-1932 period. Analysis of Gallup's figures reveals the inclusion of non-citizens.

the war years. Following the peak of excitement in the 1876 election, produced partly by the scandals then being uncovered in the Grant administration, and by the restiveness touched off by the panic of 1873, the country settled down to a relatively stable period of political interest and participation lasting almost twenty years. From 1900 to 1920, however, a steady and marked decline of participation is apparent, relieved only by the relative increase in 1916, when, again, an issue of considerable magnitude affected public interest. With the advent of woman suffrage on a national scale in 1920, and, therefore, the inclusion in the eligible electorate of a number of people unaccustomed to the franchise, the rate of participation reaches its nadir, although of course this should not be interpreted to mean that there was necessarily a loss of interest on the part of the general public. From 1928 to 1940 there is a rapid increase in the turnout, partly no doubt, because of the increasing use of the franchise by women, but also because of the intense interest (attraction and repulsion) in Al Smith's candidacy, and then again because of the interest in Franklin D. Roosevelt once his views had become known to the electorate. The increase in turnout between 1932 and 1936, moreover, also reflects both an increased interest in a range of issues covered by the phrase "New Deal" and the newly emphasized class alignment. We say newly "emphasized" because, although the main basis for group coalitions had generally been geographic prior to this time, there is some evidence that in the Jacksonian elections urban class alignments played an important part,[28] as they also did in the 1928 election.[29] There were no presidential elections during the period of American participation in the First World War, but during the Second World War the 1944 election reveals a low rate of electoral participation, partly because of the number of men serving in the armed forces and the low soldier vote, and partly because of preoccupation with other matters and a general agreement as to the way the war should be conducted. As with the first presidential post-war election after the First World War, the first election after the Second World War shows a low rate of participation, attributable as much to the lack of "appeal" of the candidates[30] as to any possible "war fatigue." Finally, due to both the enormous appeal of a successful and popular general, and to the feeling of stalemate over the Korean war, the 1952 election shows the highest rate of participation since 1916.

---

28. See Arthur M. Schlesinger, Jr., *The Age of Jackson* (Boston: Little Brown, 1945), pp. 334-49; Edward Pessen, "Did Labor Support Jackson?: The Boston Story," *Political Science Quarterly*, 54 (1949), pp. 262-74, followed by a rebuttal by Robert T. Bower in the same journal, 55 (1950), pp. 441-44. On the whole, it seems that labor did support Jackson.

29. See V. O. Key, Jr., "A Theory of Critical Elections," *Journal of Politics*, 17 (1955), pp. 3-18; Samuel Lubell, *The Future of American Politics* (New York: Harper & Brothers, 1951), pp. 34-41.

30. See Angus Campbell and Robert L. Kahn, *The People Elect a President* (Ann Arbor, Mich.: Survey Research Center, 1952).

POLITICAL INVOLVEMENT: THE LESSONS OF HISTORY

Several generalizations, relating to sectional versus class conflict, the effect of candidate appeal, and the relationship of issues to turnout, are suggested by these data. The most striking feature of the over-all picture is the persistent decline in the proportion of eligible voters making use of the franchise from 1896 to 1924. This trend appears to be independent of the periodic fluctuations in turnout from one election to the next, or at least seems to result from different causes. The plateau of participation from 1876 to 1896 was, in the first place, sustained by the sectional tensions associated with the Civil War, when the bloody shirt was flourished frequently as the symbol of the great conflict between North and South.[31] Then, as the Civil War faded as a sectional issue, it was succeeded by the East-West split dramatized by the free silver fight. In the 'eighties and 'nineties party coalitions aligned the rural, debtor, and Democratic West and South against the urban, creditor, Republican East. The parties represented broadly opposed interests and causes, and were supported as such in each area. After 1896, however, growing industrialization, urbanization, concentration of wealth, and increased immigration, began to break up the Republican solidarity of the East.[32] At the same time, some alleviation of economic discontent and a growth of commercial centers reduced the tendency of the West to make the sectional struggle the center of politics. With the parties presenting less sharp choices of policies, say Schlesinger and Eriksson, voter interest dropped off.

While this explanation minimizes the appeal of the Progressive movement and the "New Freedom" (which were in large part middle-class movements), it obviously needs to be revised in light of the politics of the New Deal era. From 1932 onward, there has been a tendency to emphasize class interests in politics and to make the differences between them more meaningful. However, even with this modified class conflict, voting has not regained the high level of the late nineteenth century. The advent of female suffrage is one reason for this slump, but another may be the more equivocal incentive to political participation in class as opposed to sectional conflict. In the United States sectional conflict tends to produce greater turnout for several reasons. For lower-class individuals, there is an implicit humiliation in acceptance of their relatively lower status, and hence a reluctance to participate in politics on a basis which emphasizes this lower status. An objective appraisal of one's interests is often distasteful and frequently not necessary. Both the

31. Arthur M. Schlesinger and Erik M. Eriksson, "The Vanishing Voter," *New Republic, 40* (1924), pp. 162-67.

32. For a discussion of the effect of urbanization in shifting political conflict from a sectional to a class basis, see Arthur N. Holcombe, *The New Party Politics* (New York: Norton, 1933) and *The Middle Class in American Politics* (Cambridge, Mass.: Harvard University Press, 1940).

reality of mobility and the illusions of classlessness fostered by American society contribute to the ease with which a person can avoid seeing politics in terms of socio-economic status. Failing to perceive these socio-economic ties to political life, a person may well regard a non-sectional political alignment as relatively meaningless. Moreover, class conflict, because it involves geographical neighbors, is more unpleasant in many respects than is sectional conflict, which, within the local community, has uniting, rather than divisive tendencies. One application of this is in the matter of "commercial tenuousness" which will be discussed later in greater detail.[33] Briefly, this is a description of a situation where a businessman depends upon goodwill to the extent that he will hesitate to express his political beliefs for fear of antagonizing some of his customers. Commercial tenuousness obviously has a dampening effect upon expressions of class conflict. On the other hand, sectional conflict does not raise such questions of neighbor against neighbor—the enemy being out of commercial, financial, and social range—and hence enemies can be attacked without fear of the consequences from outraged customers and friends. To repeat, within the local community, class conflicts are divisive, while sectional conflicts are not, and, indeed, tend to have centripetal effects, in the same way wars do.

A second generalization—which we shall partially reject—attributes the major reason for variation in turnout to the instrinsic features of the candidates' personalities. This is an element of the more general theory of "resonance" between leaders and followers, that is, a belief that the characterological needs (moralistic, aggressive, etc.) of a group of followers are "satisfied" by the personality of the leader. There is no doubt but that this force is operative and that candidate appeal includes some such element.[34] Moreover, it is probably a force somewhat independent of issues—but not nearly so independent of issues as has been supposed. Let us consider some historical problems associated with an excessive reliance upon this view as the basis for variations in turnout. One of these relates to the difference in apparent appeal of the same leader: Grant in 1868 and 1872, Roosevelt in 1932 and 1936, and, for a losing candidate, Bryan in his three elections. (On the other hand, note the identical turnout in Cleveland's two winning elections and also in the two FDR elections in 1936 and 1940, after he was better known and before we were in the war.) These considerations are, of course, only suggestive inasmuch as *two* major candidates are involved in each election.

Another such difficulty has to do with special features of public personality which are said to be especially appealing. If here one refers to a special resonance with the common man in the sense of mirroring the common man's own qualities, we cannot fail to note not only the appeal of the patrician Roosevelt, but also the marked increase in turnout in 1916 when the contest was between a reserved professor and an upper-class lawyer. Furthermore, on these grounds, how can we account for the poor drawing power evident in

---

33. See p. 324.

34. See, for example, Fillmore H. Sanford, "Public Orientation to Roosevelt," *Public Opinion Quarterly*, 15 (1951), pp. 189-216.

Bryan's last two campaigns? The Great Commoner had lost none of his capacity for identification with the man in the street, but he never again could rouse the country as he had in 1896.

One key to Bryan's differential appeal lies in the area of the campaign issues. In 1896 Bryan found in the silver issue a symbol of the desires and resentments of the agricultural West. To the dissatisfied, free coinage of silver was the solution to all their problems. Bryan's background, personality, and abilities were perfectly suited to exploit such an issue and thus bring him into close contact with the common man. But after 1896 free silver lost its political appeal, and, as Hofstadter says, "Bryan's political career after 1896 was a long, persistent search for an issue comparable in effect to free silver."[85] One can only conclude from such evidence that candidate appeal is closely related to the issues of the time; the two interact to produce varying degrees of interest, depending upon their inter-relationship with each other and with the public mood.[86] Candidates are appealing and issues are electrifying only with respect to the nature of the public involved and the time of the election under analysis. Hence it may be said of Eisenhower, not that intrinsic features of his personality have a capacity to stir the electorate at any time, but rather that in 1952 and 1956 "For a great many voters, it was a happy combination of the man and the hour."[87]

As for the nature of the issues which seem most closely associated with a higher turnout, it is normally true that domestic and economic issues attract the greatest attention. Slavery, reconstruction, free land, monetary policies including the monetization of silver, tariff, control of trusts, labor, social security, relief, all seem to have been historically more salient than foreign policy. And current survey material in the last twenty years reinforces this impression of the greater weight given by the public to domestic issues.[88] But the impact of wars upon electoral turnout seems nevertheless to be significant:

In general these data support the hypothesis that turnout tends to be high on the eve of wars and lower in post-war periods. This pattern has a certain logic. Periods just prior to major wars (not the Spanish-American war) are likely to be times of crisis, with problems of foreign policy and defense becoming salient and pressing. The issues attendant upon such crises tend to draw voters to the polls. The slumps in turnout generally associated with post-war elections can perhaps be partially accounted for by the natural letdown and diminution of interest which follow such periods of sustained participation. In fact, the evidence suggests that it is generally difficult to maintain political enthusiasm and emotion and that a relaxation of tension, sometimes accompanied by a reaction against the party which conducted the war (1918

35. Richard Hofstadter, *The American Political Tradition* (New York: Knopf, 1948), p. 193.

36. A. M. Schlesinger and E. M. Eriksson, *op. cit.*, p. 163.

37. A. Campbell and associates, *op. cit.*, p. 176.

38. See Herbert H. Hyman and Paul B. Sheatsley, "The Current Status of American Public Opinion," *National Council for Social Studies Yearbook*, 21 (1950), pp. 11-34; reprinted in Daniel Katz and associates, *Public Opinion and Propaganda* (New York: Dryden, 1954), pp. 33-48, especially pp. 35-36.

TABLE 2.3.—The Impact of War on Electoral Turnout.

Turnout in Presidential Elections

Four American Wars	Election prior to outbreak of war	Election after conclusion of war
Civil War	slightly **higher** in 1860 than in 1856	markedly **lower** in 1868 than in 1864 or 1856
Spanish-American War	markedly **higher** in 1896 than in 1892	markedly **lower** in 1900 than in 1896 or 1892.
World War I	markedly **higher** (reversal of trend) in 1916 than in 1912	markedly **lower** in 1920 than at any previous time (but woman suffrage accounts for most of this decline)
World War II	sustained **high** in 1940 compared to 1936 and before	markedly **lower** in 1944 and 1948 than in 1940 or 1936.

* Because the 1952 election occurred during a period of truce in the Korean War, and hence is partially a war-year election, the Korean War is omitted from this table.

and 1920, 1946), is inevitable in politics. People get tired of politics, and, being quick to lose interest, are more difficult to arouse no matter how appealing the candidates or how exciting the issues.

The above discussion suggests a conclusion which is a major theme of this book: few political events have single causes; different and often interrelated factors account for any single phenomenon. Thus candidates, issues, the public mood, party dispositions, and numerous other points must be considered in order to post a theory which adequately accounts for historical fluctuations in level of electoral participation.

In summary, therefore, we may say:

The proportion of the population voting has increased almost continuously from the period of the Revolution to the present.

The proportion of the eligible voters making use of their franchise declined from the post-Civil War election of 1876 to 1928 when the trend (interrupted by the war) was reversed and this proportion shows a tendency to increase.

Historically, periods of sectional conflict in the United States (North against South, East against West) have experienced greater electoral turnout than periods of class conflict

Although the personal qualities of a candidate exert great influence on popular interest in politics, these qualities are dependent for their effect upon the issues associated with the candidate and the political mood of the public at the time.

The politics of pre-war periods attract popular interest and participation in public affairs; the politics of post-war periods fail to attract such interest and participation.

CHAPTER 3

The Argument over Popular Government and

the Social Conditions of the Rise of Democracy

SOME OF THE TERMS OF THE ARGUMENT

IN THE AMERICAN discussion over the extension of the franchise, both sides accepted the premise that "Governments were instituted among men, deriving their just powers from the consent of the governed." But the next question, the nature of man, was disputed. In the language of the times, the question of the "virtue" of the man in the street had to be resolved. Those who argued for extended franchise assumed that men were "good" in the sense that they were willing to accord to others the same rights and privileges, and attribute to them the same needs, that they themselves experienced. This is the central meaning of the more favorable views of man in nature apparent in Locke and Rousseau. Such is the basis of the idea of the "general will," and of the Lockian social contract, although it may be noted that this "goodness" is not necessarily included in the Adam Smith or Bentham formula. Hamilton (or Madison) referred in *Federalist 49* to the "virtue" of the people as a cause for the successful transformation from colonial status to self-government. And Jefferson argued for the feasibility of democracy on the grounds that men have consideration for the welfare of others and have the capacity to restrain themselves.[1]

On the other hand, in the Debates on the Federal Convention, Gouverneur Morris and others argued against an extended franchise because men were venal and those without property would sell their votes to those who could buy them, a situation that Jefferson also thought not unlikely, although less

---

1. See the discussion of Jefferson's views in Avery Craven, *Democracy in American Life, A Historical View* (Chicago: University of Chicago Press, 1941), especially pp. 34-35.

dangerous if the electorate were large enough.[2] Furthermore, the Federalist abounds with references to "party spirit," "faction," and other evidences of a fear that men might falter in their virtue and become self-seeking in their use of the franchise.[3] Neither in the United States nor in Britain were the advocates of extended franchise convinced that men would always employ the vote for the common good; hence in the United States the checks and balances, provision for indirect elections, and the cautious approach to universal suffrage.

A second issue turned on the reasonableness or rationality of man. Out of the stream of European liberalism came the view that "Man is, in principle at least, everywhere and in every condition, able, if he wills it, to discover and apply rational solutions to his problems."[4] But in the framing of the Constitution and the argument over its adoption there were constant doubts about whether "reason" or "passion" would prevail. "The reason of man, like man himself, is timid and cautious when left alone . . . . " If the people were asked to settle disputes among the three departments of government, "The *passions* . . . not the *reason,* of the public, would sit in judgment. But it is the reason, alone, of the public, that ought to control and regulate the government."[5] Thus the capacity for rational behavior is present in man, but it must be nurtured and cannot always be relied upon.

The way to nurture both reason and virtue was through education, a view which implies that man is educable or plastic. Jefferson argued for the general education of the public on these grounds, but noted that while all were educable up to a point only the more able students should be selected for higher education.[6] Somewhat later Robert Owen and James Mill were making even greater claims for the power of education to prepare the people for their parts in a democratic system of government.[7]

On the whole, the proponents of democracy in the United States were optimistic but cautious about the nature of the public in which power was to

---

2. For Morris' discussion see the August 7, 1787 debate on suffrage as reported in "Madison's Notes" in Max Farrand, ed., *The Records of the Federal Convention of 1787,* 4 vols. (New Haven: Yale University Press, 1937), p. 202. Jefferson discusses the problem of the corruptibility of man in his *Notes on the State of Virginia* (Philadelphia: Prichard and Hall, 1788), pp. 211 and 267ff.

3. Compare: "Party feeling is probably far more a survival of the primitive combativeness of mankind than a consequence of conscious intellectual differences between man and man." Sir Henry S. Maine, *Popular Government* (New York: Holt, 1886), p. 31.

4. Isaiah Berlin, "Political Ideas in the Twentieth Century," *Foreign Affairs, 28* (1950), p. 357.

5. Alexander Hamilton or James Madison, "Federalist No. 49," in Edward M. Earle, ed., *The Federalist* (New York: Modern Library edition, 1937), p. 329.

6. See Jefferson, *op. cit.,* pp. 267-69.

7. See Robert Owen, *A New View of Society* (Glencoe, Ill.: The Free Press, undated, facsimile reproduction of the 3rd ed., 1817), p. 19; James Mill, *Essay on Government, Jurisprudence, Liberty of the Press and Law of Nations,* Philip Wheelwright, ed. (Garden City, N. Y.: Doubleday, Doran, 1935). Although public elementary education was established relatively early in the nineteenth century in the U.S., it was not until 1870 that Great Britain passed her first public elementary education law.

be vested—more cautious and reasonable than British or continental spokesmen of the same period. In contrast to these views, others like Gouverneur Morris in the Federal Convention and Chancellor Kent in the New York Convention of 1821 argued that man was selfish, weak, and passionate. Kent said:

There is a tendency in the poor to covet and share the plunder of the rich; in the debtor to relax or avoid the obligation of contracts; in the majority to tyranize over the minority, and trample down their rights; in the indolent and profligate to cast the whole burthens of society upon the industrous and the virtuous; and there is a tendency in ambitious and wicked men, to inflame these combustible materials.[8]

Thus the proponents of an enlarged franchise and their opponents argued over certain features of the social order but agreed on many others. They agreed upon the desirability and possibility of a government of laws and not of men, that is, roughly in the rule of law. They were both embued in the American spirit of progress, although they foresaw different destinies for the American nation. There was no question over the merits of free private enterprise, an enterprise system which was facilitated by the social revolution accompanying the war of Independence.[9] In the later phases of the argument, prior to the Civil War, both parties ignored the growing problems of the squalid life of the mill worker, child labor, and slavery.[10] Democracy in the sense of an enlarged franchise seemed unrelated to these issues which later were to become the burden of the arguments over the content of a democratic society.

On the role of government, some of the opponents of an enlarged franchise, such as Hamilton, took a mercantilist position; while proponents, like Jefferson and Jackson, believed in minimum government. The advocates of extended franchise were, partly because of their Western and frontier backgrounds, more nationalist and isolationist; their opponents felt stronger ties with Europe. The advocates of an enlarged franchise were, of course, more equalitarian, carrying out the changes in the status system which had begun in the American Revolution. Advocates of a broader base for the electorate, such as Thomas Paine and Henry Clay in America and Bentham in England, argued for a system whereby the responsibility of the elected official to the electorate was close and immediate, so that his interests would be congruent with popular interests of his constituency; their opponents argued for longer terms and indirect elections. Basically, the issues were drawn between those who preferred a hierarchical arrangement of the social order, and those who did not.

The grounds on which the argument for enlarged participation rested often turned on moral rather than functional questions. The distinction rests upon whether an argument claims that the exercise of the franchise is, in some way, desirable or justified in itself, or whether it is desirable because of certain

---

8. *Reports of the Proceedings and Debates of the Convention of 1821,* N. H. Carter, W. L. Stone, and M. T. C. Gould, eds. (Albany: 1821), pp. 219*ff.*

9. See J. Franklin Jameson, *The American Revolution Considered as a Social Movement* (Princeton: Princeton University Press, 1926).

10. Craven, *op. cit.,* pp. 66-67.

consequences which follow. Aristotle, it will be recalled, argued in the latter vein, while the theorists of the eighteenth century were more likely to take the former view.

At the dawn of American history John Cotton contended that God did not ordain democracy "as a *fitt* government *eyther* for church or commonwealth."[11] But theology lost its primacy and natural law and natural rights became the basis for the moral arguments. The Virginia Declaration of Rights (Williamsburg, 1776) stated: "That elections of members to serve as representatives of the people in assembly, ought to be free: and that all men having sufficient evidence of permanent common interest with, and attachment to the community, have the right of suffrage. . . . " Thirteen years later across the ocean the Declaration of the Rights of Man and Citizens (Versailles, 1789) held:

Law is the expression of the general will. All Citizens have the right to take part personally or by their representatives in its formation. . . . All citizens being equal in its eyes, are equally eligible to all public dignities, places, and employments, according to their capacities. . . .

All the citizens have the right to ascertain, by themselves or by their representatives, the necessity of the public tax, to consent to it freely, to follow the employment of it, and to determine the quota, the assessment, the correction, and the duration of it.

Behind these views of the natural rights of man was a revision of the relationship between God and man. "The individual instead of the state or prince was now deified and endowed with imprescriptable rights."[12]

However persuasive the morality of the natural rights view, the logic was defective (if men, why not women?) and the practice aberant. Indeed, as Justice Story commented, "the right of voting, like many other rights, is one which, whether it has a fixed foundation in natural law or not, has always been treated in the practice of nations as a strictly civil right, derived from and regulated by each society according to its own circumstances and interests."[13] By the 1830's even the liberals, like Lieber, were abandoning the natural rights doctrine.[14]

A variation on the natural right to vote is the position that the right may be earned, not by demonstrating competence, but rather by sacrifice for the nation. This was a position advanced in the interest of the veterans of the War of Independence during the early debates on suffrage and today it is argued that those over eighteen should have the right to vote because they are liable to be called into the military service at that age.

A reversal of the moral obligation ends in the argument that employment

---

11. Thomas Hutchinson, *History of the Colony of Massachusetts-Bay* (Boston: T. & J. Fleet, 1764), Vol. I, pp. 497-98.

12. Carl L. Becker, *Modern Democracy* (New Haven: Yale University Press, 1941), p. 25.

13. Joseph Story, *Commentaries on the Constitution of the United States,* 3 vols. (Boston: Hilliard, Gray and Company, 1833), Vol. II, p. 55.

14. Francis Lieber, *Manual of Political Ethics,* T. D. Woolsey, ed. (Philadelphia: Lippincott, 1792); *On Civil Liberty and Self-government,* T. D. Woolsey, ed. (Philadelphia: Lippincott, 1891).

of the franchise and participation in policy-making is a duty which the individual owes to the state. In return for what he receives (what may roughly be called civilization), he owes his service and energy to society. In the nineteenth century "Arguments about the relative degree of the obligation of the individual to society and *vice versa* filled the air."[15] With variations this is seen in the philosophy of T. H. Green, and earlier, in the views of society announced by the Utopian socialists. As in all things, Marx and Engels in the *Manifesto* reinterpret this to mean obligations to class, and the defectors are referred to as "social scum." The end result of such lines of thought is, of course, a compulsory vote, comparable to compulsory military service, which Belgium adopted in 1893.

However, most arguments supporting extended political participation, and implicitly even the moral arguments, are based upon some pragmatic consideration or some expected benefit or loss which will emanate from an extension of the franchise. Those theories which dealt with the social benefits of enlarged participation often took their cues from natural harmony and utilitarian doctrines. The pursuit by each individual of his own interest in politics, as in economics, would, according to these doctrines, lead to the greatest good for the greatest number. Other varieties of social consequences turn on the fate, not of the total society, but of the excluded groups. Only if they were equipped with the means of self-defense—the vote—would they be able to share in the benefits of government and, also, be able to ward off the predatory attacks of government. Others argued for extended franchise not because it would promote the general welfare or protect the underdog, but because it would provide a more stable form of government. As Bryce notes, it is not in its wisdom so much as in its strength that popular government excells others.[16] It commands the obedience of a larger portion of the community, and is flexible enough to meet new needs as they arise. A somewhat similar argument is expressed by those who maintain that widespread participation is desirable largely because it enables government institutions to function more smoothly and serve the people more adequately. Bryce summarizes these arguments as follows:

> Every man is the best judge of his own interest, and therefore best knows what sort of government and what laws will promote that interest. . . .
> Two men are presumably better able than one to judge what is for the common good. Three men are wiser still, and so on. . . .
> Individual men may have selfish aims, possibly injurious to the community, but these will be restrained by the other members of the community whose personal aims will be different. . . .

---

15. Berlin, *op. cit.*, p. 355. Compare J. F. S. Ross: "There has been endless talk of the right to vote, and very little of the duties and responsibilities that the electoral function carries with it." *Elections and Electors* (London: Eyre & Spottiswoode, 1955), p. 35 (original in italics).

16. James Bryce, *The American Commonwealth* (New York: Macmillan, 1910), vol. II, p. 263. Compare Sir Henry Maine, "popular governments of the modern type have not hitherto proved stable as compared with other forms of political rule . . . they include certain sources of weakness which do not promise security for them in the near or remote future." *Op. cit.*, pp. 52-53.

As every man has some interest in the well-being of the community, a part at least of his own personal interest being bound up with it, every man will have a motive for bearing his share in its government, and he will seek to bear it, so far as his personal motives do not collide therewith.

Inequality, by arousing jealousy and envy, provokes discontent. . . .

Hence equality in political rights, while it benefits the community by opening to talent the opportunities of rendering good service, tends also to peace and good order.

To sum up, government by the whole people best secures the two main objects of all Governments—Justice and Happiness, Justice because no man or class or group will be strong enough to wrong others; Happiness, because each man, judging best what is for his own good, will have every chance of pursuing it. The principles of liberty and equality are justified by the results they yield.[17]

Against views of this character a group of spokesmen ranging from Gouverneur Morris and Chancellor Kent to Sir Henry Maine and W. E. H. Lecky, believed that extended influence for the poor would mean the plunder of the rich. Others, like Fisher Ames, feared that a democratic government would inevitably stir up the passions of the voters who are generally lacking in the powers of self-control.[18] Emile Faguet abroad, and Ralph Adams Cram in America, have argued that popular rule is government by the incompetent and particularly that the masses prefer to select as leaders mediocre men like themselves.[19] Indeed the lack of leadership became a central theme of the anti-democratic theorists. Maine argued that leadership is an exercise of the will, and since the public has no will it can exercise no leadership.[20] For those who rejected such leaders as came forward in a democracy a variety of principles for leadership selection were available. Irving Babbitt advocated selection according to demonstrated strength of character;[21] others have argued for some such principle as the inner sense of mission (charisma). But most of those who oppose popular influence look to some form of traditional leadership for relief. All have maintained that excessive democracy threatens the stability and natural order of society, an order which is properly hierarchical in its arrangement.

As for the consequences to the individual of his sharing in the electoral determination, several views are relevant. Ross has stated that "the exercise of the franchise is a means to an end, and that end is not the individual advantage of the elector but the political welfare of the whole community."[22] But of course communities may be thought to gain as do their constituent members. This would be true of Franklin's argument in the Federal Convention of 1787 that to impose new restrictions on the suffrage "would depress

---

17. James Bryce, *Modern Democracies*, 2 vols. (New York: Macmillan, 1921), Vol. I, pp. 44-45.

18. *Works of Fisher Ames*, Seth Ames, ed. (Boston: Little, Brown, 1854), p. 394.

19. Emile Faguet, *The Cult of Incompetence*, translated by Beatrice Barstow (London: Murray, 1911); Ralph Adams Cram, *The End of Democracy* (Boston: Marshall Jones, 1937).

20. Maine, *op. cit.*, p. 88.

21. Irving Babbitt, *Democracy and Leadership* (Boston: Houghton Mifflin, 1924).

22. Ross, *op. cit.*, p. 35.

the virtue and public spirit of our common people."[23] It would also apply to Tocqueville's view that individuals in a democracy, in contrast to a monarchy, have released within them new stores of creative energy.[24] It would be true of J. S. Mill's position that participation in electoral decisions is a broadening and moralizing experience.[25] And it would be true of John Dewey's opinion that because people take their image of themselves from their social situation, only those who have some measure of social power can have the self-confidence for the full development of their potentialities.[26]

The achievement of universal adult suffrage was accomplished and persists in the face of a steady flow of criticism, not only from those who believe that popular rule is undesirable but also from those who believe it is impossible and hence that democratic forms are a sham. Among those who believe that popular rule is at least deceptive in that it gives the illusion of power to groups who do not in fact exercise power, some, like Gouverneur Morris, stated, as mentioned earlier, that the people would sell their votes to others and hence the purchasers of the vote, not the sellers, would be represented;[27] thus Sir Henry Maine argued that a group of "wire-pullers" or bosses, would exercise the true power;[28] and James Burnham and the Marxists maintained that political power could not be divested from economic control in the modern state.[29] In recent times, Robert Michels' formulation of the "iron law of oligarchy" represents a classic statement of the impossibility of democratic control of leaders in institutions which purport to be democratic.[30]

Granted the possibility of popular influence through democratic processes, the boundaries for admission to the electorate required definition: which class of people might and which class might not exercise this privilege? Seymour and Frary suggest an historical progression in this classification marked by four stages: citizenship, property, universal membership in the state, and privilege and duty granted by law.[31] The first of these, membership in the state is denoted by a selective status of "citizen." This was the chief basis for voting membership in the Athenian democracy and it is, in a sense, paralleled in the treatment of non-metropolitan areas by the great empires of Rome, and in Britain in the seventeenth and eighteenth centuries. The controversy over the granting of the franchise to aliens in the United States illustrates this

---

23. Farrand, *op. cit.*, p. 204.

24. Alexis de Tocqueville, *Democracy in America*, Phillips Bradley, ed. (New York: Knopf, 1945), Vol. II, pp. 136-139.

25. John Stuart Mill, *Representative Government*, reprinted in Mill, *Utilitarianism, Liberty and Representative Government* (New York: Dutton, 1910), p. 217.

26. John Dewey, "The Ethics of Democracy," Philosophical Papers, Ann Arbor, 1888, quoted in John D. Lewis, "The Elements of Democracy," *American Political Science Review, 34* (1940), p. 469.

27. Farrand, *op. cit.*, p. 202.

28. Maine, *op. cit.*, p. 30.

29. See James Burnham, *The Managerial Revolution* (New York: John Day, 1941), p. 59.

30. Robert Michels, *Political Parties*, translated by Eden and Cedar Paul (Glencoe, Ill.: Free Press, 1949).

31. Charles Seymour and Donald Paige Frary, *How the World Votes*, 2 vols. (Springfield, Mass.: C. A. Nichols, 1918), pp. 1-15.

principle; the imputation of non-citizenship to Negroes by Southern white officials is a more glaring example. Often underlying these views on citizenship are concepts of racial superiority, such as those of John W. Burgess on the political superiority of the "Teutonic race" or Madison Grant's theories of Nordic superiority.[32] Aristotelian views on innate character have their modern incarnation here.

A second basis of classification is the possession of property, often, as with many of the "founding fathers," revealing a preference for landed property. This classification frequently implies that persons of property have a stake in society greater than those without such property and therefore have a clearer claim to a voice in social policy. Or it is said that only those with property have "a sufficient attachment to the community" to be entrusted with the vote.

A third determinant may be found in the idea that the class of people to be admitted to participation includes all adults who have not forfeited their right by commission of crime or demonstrated incapacity. In this view voting is an appropriate attribute of adult membership in the human race, and nothing less. It is, in short, a natural right.

The fourth stage provides a functional basis for inclusion and exclusion, not as a right, but as a means of applying the provisions of the constitution. The franchise is to be given to those who can use it. On this basis literacy, age, length of residence in a community, all become relevant criteria for granting or withholding the office of "voter."[33]

Underlying these schemes of classification, and running through the history of the struggle for the universal franchise, certain common themes are apparent. The problem of citizenship or membership in the state involved *in-group out-group* feelings based less on economic lines than on ethnic, race, culture, and nationality differentiation. The central question with respect to property and tax classifications turned on the *policy consequences* of admission and the safety of a certain specified order of society. Related to both of these types of classification, but more apparent in discriminatory features dealing with education, literacy, and maturity, is the theme of *competence*. Underlying age and sex limitations were doubts about the "radicalism" or the "religious or moral orientation" of the prospective voters. But substantial questions also arose with regard to the more general question of competence. Who seeks admission? Whom will the admitted favor? Can they perform their duties adequately?

The decisions to be made by those who are allowed to participate in political life have always been, in some manner, subject to contention. *Should the*

---

32. John W. Burgess, *Political Science and Comparative Constitutional Law* (Boston: Ginn & Co. 1890), Vol. I, pp. 44-45; Madison Grant, *The Passing of the Great Race,* 4th ed. (New York: Scribner's, 1922).

33. James Bryce seems to argue that in England the third and fourth stages are reversed in order. "In England, the argument generally accepted in 1870 that fitness for the exercise of the suffrage should be a precondition to the grant of it was in 1918 tossed contemptuously on the dustheap of obsolete prejudices, because a new generation had come to regard the electoral franchise as a natural right." *Modern Democracies,* Vol. I, p. 49.

electorate choose the President directly, or should he be elected by Congress, or by an electoral college. In the Federal Convention of 1787, oddly enough, Gouverneur Morris argued for popular elections, Colonel Mason for legislative election, and Madison, Gerry, and others for indirect election by electors chosen in the several states according to several principles. *Should they elect the members of the Senate directly,* or through their state legislatures? Not until 1913 and the passage of the seventeenth amendment was this matter finally settled for all states in favor of direct popular elections. *Should they elect judges?* In *Federalist No. 78,* Hamilton argued for judges independent from popular control, but within a few years (1812, Georgia; 1832, Mississippi) state and local judges were chosen through popular elections in several states. *Should the people elect administrators* (as contrasted to executives)? Today the long ballot everywhere attests to the strength of this misguided belief. *Should the people make laws?* In the twenty-year period from 1898 to 1918 twenty American states adopted initiative and referendum provisions for ordinary legislative matters; since then, no further provisions have been adopted.

The degree and channels of influence appropriate for the public has by no means been settled, although many of the solutions to the issues mentioned are so imbedded in law and custom that controversy over them seems moot. Disagreement over the proper place of public opinion polls in policy making;[34] the drift from town meetings, to representative town meetings, to strictly representative forms of local government; the movement back to longer terms of office and to a short ballot in many areas; and the tendency to rely more on line departments and less upon the quasi-autonomous citizen boards in state and local government all bespeak a modern hesitancy to invest the public with responsibilities and decisions which once were thought appropriate for them.

But reservations about popular control of public affairs have deeper roots than a preference for modest institutional reform or a rehearsal of a Burkian attack on the mandate theory of representation. Moreover, most of the current criticism of popular rule does not emanate from the enemies of democracy, but rather from its saddened friends. It deals in part with the capacities of the people to make wise decisions in their own interest, the strength of their desire to participate in government, and the nature of the benefits they derive therefrom. On the basis of clinical research and public opinion polls, students of democratic government have concluded that the electorate is wanting both in vital information and in rational pursuit of enduring self-interest; the tasks have exceeded the capacities of the public to perform them.[35] Thus Walter

---

34. See Lindsay Rogers, *The Pollsters* (New York: Knopf, 1949).

35. Berlin, *op. cit.,* discusses this irrationalist interpretation of democratic choice as a feature of the modern emphasis on (and desire to relieve) the agony of choice. In what may be considered a reply to this article, or at least to the general alarm about the rise of irrational forces in politics, Wishy counters with the proposition that we are suffering from over-rationalism, that is, principles and demands carried to their *logical* extreme. Without further specification of the meaning of "rationality," a tricky word at best, neither position seems to be coming to grips with real problems. See Bernard W. Wishy, "Is There a Revolt Against Reason," *Political Science Quarterly, 71* (1956), pp. 242-56.

Lippmann, continuing a line of argument he began so brilliantly in *Public Opinion* some thirty-five years ago, states that a central cause for the breakdown of democratic governments in modern times has been that "the assemblies and the mass electorates have acquired the monopoly of effective powers" and do not know how to use them. They have usurped the proper functions of the executive and, for the return of political health, the electorate must assume a more modest posture in government.[36]

Erich Fromm, although he favors widespread social participation, has cast doubt upon men's desire for the burdens which such participation implies. Freedom implies choice, participation implies responsibility, and under stress the majority of the people may find choice painful and responsibility too weighty a load. Apathy, withdrawal, conformity, "pseudo-willing" result.[37] Even the social consequences of minimal participation are said to be beneficial. Moderates have claimed that political indifference is positively useful to the functioning of democracy in that it facilitates the ease of compromise and adjustment among competing factions.[38]

It is said that the masses have not gained through their new political power because the sources of their trouble are not political but economic. Democracy is a mask for plutocracy, and the plutocrats remain entrenched in power.[39] Thus the long struggle to enfranchise the masses of men has, so far, come to no avail; the franchise is useful only as it offers leverage to attack the real citadel of power, corporate wealth.

We have sampled, and little more, the arguments which have accompanied the struggle for broader political participation in the modern period. We approach our analysis, then, at a time when a phase of democratic history in the West seems to have come to an end. This is not to say that democracy has been permanently established, of course, but rather that in Western Europe and America—wherever democracy is established—the franchise is legally granted to all adults, with only minor and technical qualifications. As a consequence, a discussion which focuses on the question of rights now seems somewhat antiquarian, and a discussion which speculates as to the results of the granting of these rights must be squared with experience to be meaningful. As Ross says:

. . . it has been tacitly assumed, at least by those who have pressed for the widening of the franchise, that once the man or woman had received the vote all would be well: he or she would know by instinct how to use it. These are lament-

---

36. Walter Lippmann, *The Public Philosophy* (Boston: Little, Brown, 1955), p. 57.

37. Erich Fromm, *Escape from Freedom* (New York: Rinehart, 1941).

38. Bernard R. Berelson, Paul F. Lazarsfeld, and William N. McPhee, *Voting* (Chicago: University of Chicago Press, 1954), pp. 314-15.

39. This idea is curiously at the confluence of three streams of thought. The first, liberal democracy, is illustrated by Becker, who says that "economic forces . . . brought about an increasing concentration of wealth and power in the hands of the fortunate few, and thereby nullified, for the majority of people, many of those essential liberties which provide both the theoretical justification and the necessary conditions for the practical success of democratic institutions." (*Op. cit.*, p. 61.) The second element in this confluence is contributed by Mosca and Pareto, both of whom identify democracy with plutocracy. And the third element, of course, is the Marxian interpretation of bourgeois democracy as a complex of institutions manipulated by the capitalist class.

ably inadequate views, and there is much need for their reconsideration and revision.[40]

SOME CONDITIONS FACILITATING
THE EXPANSION OF SUFFRAGE

Some of the social conditions associated with the extension of the franchise are so generally significant that they can be regarded as prerequisites for any elective form of government at any point in history; some are limited to the modern period but seem to be closely associated with the suffrage movement in many Western countries; some are associated only with the American experience. Thus "living on the raw American continent greatly simplified the social structure, gave wider freedom to men and forced a greater self-reliance upon them."[41] Still other social conditions are important forces for only one group—the propertyless, or the Negro, or women. We shall now focus largely on some of the important conditions of the growth of the suffrage in the modern period in the West. One condition has been said to be "a certain economic security," by which is meant material prosperity,[42] and indeed the rise of democracy does seem correlated with the rise of economic standards of living. Whether this is a necessary condition, however, may soon be tested in the development of a broad franchise in the so-called underdeveloped countries. And it should be observed that when the United States, a poor country at the time, pioneered in democratizing the franchise the poorest sections within the country (the frontier) were in the forefront of this development. Indeed, in Turner's phrase, "The most important effect of the frontier has been the promoting of democracy here and in Europe. . . . "[43] Upon reflection it seems that the necessary economic conditions are of another character. As Gosnell has suggested, like Harrington before him, in order for political expression to be meaningful, the economy must provide some degree of economic independence for those granted the franchise.[44] And for the system of government based upon a broad franchise to endure, there must be a general lack of economic frustration, or at least the possibility of achievement consonant with aspiration. It is these facets of the economy, rather than the standard of living it provides, which are important conditions of popular government.

A second socio-economic condition has been said to be the presence of social mobility. "Mobility invites and fosters comparisons of status, and the difference between the right to vote and the lack of that right is conspicuous";

40. Ross, op. cit., p. 35.
41. Craven, op. cit., p. 41.
42. Becker, op. cit., p. 12.
43. Frederick Jackson Turner, "The Significance of the Frontier in American History," Address delivered at the forty-first annual meeting of the State Historical Society of Wisconsin, December 14, 1893 (Madison: State Historical Society of Wisconsin, 1894).
44. Harold F. Gosnell, Democracy, The Threshold of Freedom (New York: Ronald, 1948), pp. 21-22.

immobility not only minimizes this comparison but prevents exposure to the kinds of stimuli which increase the demand for the franchise.[45] This condition is not a necessary one, however much it has facilitated the universal franchise movement in modern times, as the experience of European countries has shown.

Historically, war has been associated with the growth of the franchise, as in the case of the foreign wars leading to the French Revolution, the American Revolution, the enfranchisement of women in France following the Second World War. War, then, is a third social factor associated with broader franchise, although, of course, it is hardly a necessary one.

The demand for participation in government, and the success of such participation, does not come without some kind of relevant democratic experience for a leadership group. The Puritan churches in England are said to have performed this service for the British people;[46] the early American church government and the communal life of the frontier provided useful experience for groups who subsequently were enfranchised in the United States. The failure of the French revolution to establish a continuing stable popular government may be partially attributed to the lack of democratic cadres trained in churches or other social institutions. The failure of the post-Civil War experience with Negro voting has, in part at least, the same origin in lack of experience. Thus a fourth force making for stable expansion of the electorate is the presence of leadership training in the techniques of democracy for members of excluded groups.

There is some evidence to indicate that, in order to succeed, demands for the extension of the suffrage must correspond to the economic advantage of some powerful and rising social class or group. This is most obviously the case with respect to the rising commercial classes everywhere; and it may be said that the generally more formidable status of women in the twentieth century made of this group an equivalent "powerful and rising social class." That class, then, with its organizations, ideology, and group morale, becomes the vehicle of the movement for the extended suffrage. Yet, however much the proposition may hold for these groups, there are other groups for which it is misleading and the proposition is valid only in conjunction with the one which follows.

In a situation where some are excluded from the vote, factions within the voting elite seek allies outside of the admitted group and so exercise pressure for a broader franchise. It has been a matter of observation in the United States and elsewhere that the extension of the right to participate in selecting political leaders is often produced less by the demands of the excluded than by the manipulation of the party leaders.[47] Usually, of course, both of these things happen: leaders of the excluded and their friends among the voting

---

45. *Ibid.,* pp. 20-21.

46. A. D. Lindsay, *The Modern Democratic State* (London: Oxford University Press, 1943), pp. 115-21.

47. Elmer E. Schattschneider, *Party Government* (New York: Rinehart, 1942), p. 48.

groups join forces in the name of some high principle for their mutual political gain. It is these combinations which produce the "organized agitation" that are a prime condition for the growth of the suffrage, including "monster mass meetings and threats of revolt" such as those preceding the British Reform Bill of 1832, "Dorr's Rebellion" in Rhode Island, and the hunger strikes of the militant suffragettes.[48]

It has been said that agreement on certain fundamentals is a prerequisite for democratic growth or even for its survival. In rebuttal it is argued that fractionation of belief such that fundamental disagreements do not cumulate and polarize is an equally solid basis for popular rule.[49] Populations with homogeneous and heterogeneous beliefs have each extended the franchise and hence perhaps the question of "basic bliefs" turns on another point. We would say that the feasibility of bringing new groups into the sphere of political influence will depend upon the degree of alienation of the groups, that is, their commitment to their friends, communities, and nation as groups to which they properly belong.

Finally, we may consider certain facilitating modes of thought, among which is the tendency for legal thinking to generalize from the particular instance to all similar instances—an institutional embodiment of what Parsons calls universalistic, as contrasted to particularistic, thinking. Emphasis upon material values ("taxation without representation") may be associated with the growth of the suffrage, as Gosnell asserts,[50] but certainly the abolitionists who advocated that the Negro be equal in political as in other rights, and the woman suffragists who gained little material reward, and the development of democratic experience in the synods and councils of Protestant churches in England and the United States does not argue the necessity of a materialistic mode of thought. Other modes of thought which are more likely to be facilitating conditions for the growth of the franchise include the doctrine of individual responsibility for one's own fate in life (with only limited belief in the efficacy of prayer), modestly equalitarian views of society, concepts of honor which do not embrace violence, and lack of any dogma too precious to be challenged to open debate or changed by peaceful election.

Briefly, then, we may say that enlarged popular participation in government is encouraged by the following conditions:

> The widespread distribution of property, particularly landed property.
> Economic achievement generally consonant with economic aspiration.
> Widespread social and geographic mobility.
> Wars requiring mass participation and mass sacrifice..
> Training in democratic procedures by the elite of an excluded group.
> Growing self-consciousness, power, and status of an excluded group; their willingness and capacity to engage in organized agitation.
> Political advantage for one (or both) contending enfranchised factions in

---

48. Gosnell, *op. cit.*, pp. 28-30
49. See Carl J. Friedrich, *The New Belief in the Common Man* (Boston: Little, Brown, 1942).
50. Gosnell, *op. cit.*, p. 26.

sponsoring the admission of new voters.

Minimal social alienation in the society.

Tendencies to generalize and extend the application of moral principles.

COMPARISON OF THE HISTORY OF SUFFRAGE

IN FRANCE, ENGLAND, AND THE UNITED STATES

Some of the idiosyncratic features of the American experience, as well as the features it holds in common with other Western countries, are revealed by comparison with the political histories of England and France.[51] These may be viewed in the light of less frequent electoral participation in the United States today, in contrast to participation in Europe.

While universal male (white) suffrage was generally established in the United States by the late 1840's, the British electoral laws, even after the important 1867 reform, retained some restrictions, and the French did not establish male suffrage in meaningful elections until 1875 (with a few brief exceptions). Women were admitted to the franchise on the same terms as men in the United States in 1920, and in some states much earlier. In England, although most women were admitted to the vote in 1918, they were somewhat discriminated against until after World War II. Women were not permitted to vote in France until after the liberation in 1944. Thus one point of contrast is the earlier victory in America of those seeking extension of the right to vote.

In the United States there seems to have been markedly less concern about the radicalism or instability of youth. Except for recent proposals to *lower* the age of the franchise to eighteen, in the United States twenty-one was everywhere considered an appropriate age, in contrast to various higher age levels in force in England and France during the last 150 years. Political conservatives, it should be noted, were almost always the ones in favor of higher age limits. The suggestion of a greater tendency toward radicalism among European youth falls in line with the view that political intensity in young people arises from a need to revolt against parents, a need which has been observed to be less urgent in the United States than in Europe.[52]

The history of the struggle for the franchise in England, and to a lesser extent in the United States, shows a linear progression from a narrow to a broader franchise, in contrast to the French irregular extension and retraction of the right to vote. Narrowed in 1791, the franchise in France was broadened in 1792, slightly narrowed in 1795, broadened (but made less meaningful) in 1799, further restricted in 1802, greatly narrowed in 1814, greatly broad-

---

51. The data underlying these comparisons are derived in part from the histories of the struggle for the franchise in England and France in Charles Seymour and Donald P. Frary, *How the World Votes* (Springfield, Mass.: C. A. Nichols, 1918), Vol. I, Chapters III-VIII, and XV-XVIII. See also Footnote 1, Chapter 2, above.

52. See Eric H. Erikson, *Childhood and Society* (New York: Norton, 1950), p. 277. But note that the "disowning" of parents, if not actual rebellion, is a common pattern among the children of immigrants in America.

ened in 1815, returned to the 1814 provisions following Waterloo, broadened in 1830-31, greatly broadened in 1848, narrowed in 1850, and so forth. The chief area of vacillation in the United States has been legislation dealing with aliens, a point of interest since ethnic problems represent a politically sensitive area in this country.

In all three countries controversy has arisen over the secret ballot, with conservatives, who have regularly used their economic power and prestige to influence tenant and worker votes when these could not be kept secret, taking high moral positions in favor of the open ballot.

The preferences of conservatives for extending the franchise to rural, as contrasted to urban populations, has varied among the several countries. French conservatives have feared the influence of Paris and other large cities and made administrative arrangements to limit urban influence. On the other hand, although the apportionment arrangements in England favored the rural constituencies, in this period there have been provisions requiring *higher* property qualifications in the country as contrasted to the borough constituencies. In the United States Jeffersonianism and subsequent economic conservatism has favored rural over urban constituencies, chiefly through malapportionment, but the fear of the frontier and so-called agrarian radicalism has colored this preference so that American conservative attitudes toward rural voting have often been less sanguine than the attitudes of European conservatives.

As to the effectiveness of the votes cast, several comparisons are notable. The malapportionment of American and British constituencies and the Constitutional arrangements of the United States have tended to give some votes much greater weight than others. This malapportionment was substantially corrected in Britain in the 1890's but remains a serious problem in the United States. In France the problem seems in general to have been less acute. In both France and the United States the use of indirect elections was employed to limit the influence of the electorate, and in France a series of graduated property requirements ensured that at every higher stage of the process the electoral bodies would include only persons of higher rank and greater fortune. In the United States the growth of parties tended to do away with the "indirection" of presidential elections at an early point, and senators were increasingly elected by popular ballot until the seventeenth amendment made direct popular election universal. In France, but only rarely in Great Britain and never in the United States, the government *qua* government intervened in the election campaigns to indicate the preferred candidates and to threaten those who did not vote for them. Under these circumstances, as in the Nazi and Communist plebiscites, the vote was often meaningless and people stayed away from the polls in great numbers (something impossible in the dictator's plebiscites).

Of these three countries, only in the United States today (but only in a section thereof), is a class of adults systematically deprived of the franchise by threat, social sanction, and administrative irregularity.

Reviewing these contrasts reinforces the notion that the struggle for universal adult suffrage has been both quicker and easier in the United States—with the single important exception of the Negro. The result of this relatively easy victory may be reflected in the American public's relative casualness toward participation in politics. Thus:

Political participation will tend to be greater among those groups and in those countries where the struggle to win the franchise has been more strenuous.

Part II

The Political Expression
of the American Public

CHAPTER 4

Who Takes Part in Elections

and What Do They Do?

As we have seen from our brief historical reviews, broadening the franchise did not always lead to increased *rates* of participation. We turn now to an analysis of political participation in America today. This clearly means more than voting; indeed, in some areas of politics voting is a minor feature of the public's participation in the political process. A letter to a congressman, a contribution to a candidate's campaign chest, support of a lobby, even just being a member of a political audience—these, too, form essential features of popular participation in the American democracy. We want, then, to know three things about such behavior: (1) *What* is the nature of such participation? (2) *Who* are the participants? (3) *Why* do they do it? This chapter and the two which follow deal with "what" and "who."

VOTING IN ELECTIONS

Members of the American electorate are given many important responsibilities in our scheme of government. Consider the choices they were required to make in 1956. In seventeen states the electorate was asked to express a preference among their party's aspiring presidential nominees—and then, in all of the states, the electorate was asked to choose among the candidates themselves. Forty-two states had primary contests for state office in that year (all states have some provision for direct primaries and nine states have provision for run-off primaries if the initial primaries are not conclusive). All but six of the states elected state legislators in 1956 and most of them elected both state senators and representatives. All forty eight states elected members of the national House of Representatives; thirty one elected United States Senators; thirty states elected Governors. The electorate in some states was also required to choose a number of state officers. Thus in North Dakota, in 1956, the electorate had to select the following:

Governor
Attorney General
Secretary of State
Treasurer
Auditor
Commissioner of Agriculture and Labor
Commissioner of Insurance
Public Service Commissioner
Tax Commissioner
Superintendent of Public Instruction
Judge of the Supreme Court

At the County level, there are County Commissioners, Sheriffs, Judges to be elected. There are some 50,000 school districts in the United States most of which have elected officers, and many other special districts also with elected officers. Municipalities generally require the election of a mayor and a council, the councils varying in size from three to fifty (Chicago). About one-third of the cities with a population of over 5,000 require the election of a Treasurer. Approximately one-quarter elect a Clerk, others elect Assessors, City Attorneys, and other officers.[1]

Finally, the electorate is often asked to settle important policy questions. In one recent two-year period, a few of the problems submitted for electoral consideration included: poll tax modifications, restoring the rights of Indians to vote, establishing a presidential preference primary, governor's salaries, frequency of meeting for the state legislatures, innumerable bond issues, the regulation of dredge mining, veterans preferences, the sale of liquor to Indians, the admission of women to jury service—and many others.[2] Of course no single member of the electorate must decide all these issues—but the individual voter is likely to find himself called upon to express his official preference among many men for many offices, and on several issues of varying importance.

VOTING IN ELECTIONS

The formal nature of the election will create situations with quite different meanings for the electors. First, consider the difference between voting on issues and voting for people, that is, referenda and constitutional amendments on the one hand and the election of candidates on the other. The whole complex of personal attraction (and repulsion) is a feature of the election of can-

---

1. *Municipal Year Book 1957.* (Chicago: International City Managers' Association, 1957), Vol. 24, p. 76.
2. *The Book of the States, 1956-57* (Chicago: Council on State Governments, 1956), Vol. XI, p. 133.

didates but not of the referendum. Secondly, the difference between primaries and elections in two-party areas offers a distinction between a contest where a well-worn and familiar (party) loyalty is usually called into play and one where this is not present. Or, finally, consider the difference between local elections and national elections. The tangible material rewards at stake in the local election, combined with a more clear-cut ethnic appeal, evoke responses very different from the broader and more policy-oriented appeals involved in national elections. The voting in elections for aldermen or constable may represent popularity contests when these elections are separated from other elections; they may merely represent exercises in party loyalty when these offices are part of a long list of offices to be filled at a general mayoralty election. In this sense, although the marking of the ballot may be the same in every case, the type of election will, in large measure, structure the types of attitude, knowledge, and skills associated with electoral participation.

Yet the act of voting, however it may differ in the above respects, will almost universally require certain qualities of the voter. We refer to these here because such requisite qualities represent a kind of threshold which an individual must be able to pass before he can exercise the franchise; they sift the population for "culls" although not all non-voters are "culls" in this sense, by any means. In the first place, voting should be understood as an *act* involving an expenditure of energy and time, the coordination of muscles and mind, scheduling the event among other events, and partaking of the nature of a positive act in other ways. Second, voting requires a *decision;* perhaps a decision on a very low level of decisiveness, but nevertheless a positive commitment to one side or the other (with ticket splitters committing themselves more to individuals than parties). Third, the voting decision implies a certain *relatedness to society,* an awareness of surroundings, a listening to radio and reading of the newspaper, an awareness that *this* Tuesday is election day. Fourth, a voting decision usually implies the *implementation of an emotion.* The emotion may be fear of non-conformity, a partisan loyalty to a symbol or group, a dedication to a program, but whatever it is, the act of voting goes beyond the stage of merely experienced feeling. The person who cannot do this, remains to "stew in his own juice." Finally, the voting act is an *affirmation,* an interpretation that democracy is not a sham; the votes are counted, they do make a difference.

Some of these "threshold factors" along with many other social and psychic forces are reflected in the analysis of non-voting in 1948 and 1952 by various demographic groups, as revealed in Table *4.1.* This table tells a familiar story: non-voting is generally higher among women, the youngest eligible age group, negroes, rural communities, non-union members, lower status (income, education, occupation) groups, and Southerners. Of all the states, Mississippi and South Carolina had the lowest rate of participation; of several occupations, service workers had the lowest rates of electoral participation.[3]

3. Gordon M. Connelly and Harry M. Field, "The Non-Voter—Who He Is, What He Thinks," *Public Opinion Quarterly, 8* (1944), pp. 175-87.

TABLE 4.1.—Relation of Demographic Characteristics to Non-Voting in 1940, 1948, and 1952.

Demographic characteristics	Per Cent of Group Non-Voting Election year		
	1940	1948	1952
Sex			
Male	25%	31%	21%
Female	39	41	31
Age			
21-34		44	32
35-44		34	24
45-54		25	21
55 and over		37	23
Religion			
Protestant		42	32
Catholic		21	15
Jewish		—	—
No religion		—	—
Race			
White	32	34	21
Negro	64	64	67
Type of community			
Metropolitan areas	25	17	21
Towns and cities	32-35	37	27
Rural areas	39	59	32
Education			
Grade School		45	38
High School		33	20
College		21	10
Occupation of head of family			
Professional and managerial	22	25	12
Other white collar		19	19
Skilled and semi-skilled		29	26
Unskilled	40	50	40
Farm operators	39	58	33

These relations do not hold true everywhere, of course, and indeed they are spurious in the sense that some third intervening variable, such as education, may cause the apparent differences in the rate of voting. A few of the areas where such third factors are operating will be perceived at once; others may be revealed by studies in which such third factors were controlled.

Since education, income, and urbanization are among the most significant social forces affecting non-voting, one would naturally examine these factors to see if they might account for other relationships, or exaggerate or conceal "true" relationships.

Age. Probably part of the reason why the younger group votes less than the middle group is their relatively lower income, although their relatively higher education would tend to increase turnout. Other reasons connected with age differences are certainly also at work, however. Among these are the

Demographic characteristics	Per Cent of Group Non-Voting Election year		
	1940	1948	1952
Trade union affiliation of head of family			
Member		27%	23%
Non-member		38	27
Income			
Under $2,000		54	47
$2,000—2,999		39	32
$3,000—3,999		26	24
$4,000—4,999		25	17
$5,000 and over		18	12
Region			
Northeast		—	16
Midwest		—	15
South		—	51
Far West		—	23
Ethnic background (non-native born)			
Scandinavian		—	17
German		—	20
English-Scotch		—	19
Irish Catholic		—	5
Italian		—	11
Polish		—	13
Generation time in America (Omits Negroes)			
First (Foreign born American citizens)			
Second		—	19
Third		—	14
Fourth or more		—	16
Fourth or more		—	29

SOURCES: For 1948 and 1952: Angus Campbell, Gerald Gurin, Warren E. Miller, "The Voter Decides" (New York: Row, Peterson, 1954), pp. 70-4, 76, 77, 78; for 1940, Gordon M. Connelly and Harry H. Field, "The Non-Voter—Who He Is, What He Thinks," Public Opinion Quarterly, 8 (1944), pp. 175-87.

fluidity of occupational interests, greater geographic mobility, less clearly defined reference and membership groups, greater emphasis on entertainment, and lower frequencies of home ownership.

Religion. The Catholic population tends to be both more urban (therefore in a higher voting milieu) and poorer (therefore in a lower voting group). Consequently there is no clear evidence in these data on the effect of religious affiliation or even ethnic grouping on the turnout. In the city of Delaware, Ohio, where class voting rates are much more equal and, of course, everyone is urban, there was virtually no difference between Catholic and Protestant turnout in 1948.[4]

Race. Negro participation is depressed by external pressures and customs in the South, and by the lower income strata to which most Negroes everywhere belong. It is increased by the urbanization of the Northern Negro, but,

4. Ben A. Arneson and William H. Eells, "Voting Behavior in 1948 as compared with 1924 in a Typical Ohio Community," *American Political Science Review, 44* (1952), pp. 432-34.

since two-thirds of the Negroes live in the South, the urbanization factor will be much the smaller of the influences.

Type of Community. Metropolitan areas are more heavily immigrant, ethnic, Catholic, and Jewish; most of these groups have a higher than average voting rate. Hence the higher rate in Metropolitan areas will be a product of the presence of these groups—just as the voting rates of these groups will be influenced by their urbanization.

Income and Education. Both of these elements are forces associated with higher voting rates, and each has an influence on voting independent of the other, as illustrated in Table *4.2.*

**TABLE 4.2.—Percentage Voting in 1944 Presidential Election
by Education and Income.**

Education	Income		
	Upper Quarter	Middle Half	Lower Quarter
College	87%	76%	70%
High School	83	68	54
Grade School	83	67	54

SOURCE: Connelly and Field, "The Non-Voter—Who He Is, What He Thinks," "Public Opinion Quarterly, 8" (1944), pp. 179-80.

First, note that with reference to education it is college education that makes the difference in every income group; the high school and grade school groups being almost identical in their participation rates. More importantly, income and status roles are much more important than education: those with maximum income but minimum education scoring 83 per cent while those with maximum education but minimum income scoring only 70 per cent.

Although it is easy enough to get figures on the changing proportion of the total population voting over the years, data on the changing proportions within each group are not so readily accessible. Three sources of information, . however, give us clues as to what is happening to this phase of participation: the above comparative figures for 1940, 1948, and 1952, a study covering three elections in New York City, and a comparison between 1924 and 1948 voting rates in identical groups in Delaware, Ohio.[5]

On the whole the following changes seem to be taking place:

Increases:
Negroes both in the North and South have greatly increased their rate of voting.
The foreign born population has greatly increased its rate of voting.
Women have so increased their rate of voting that when education level is

---

5. Angus Campbell, Gerald Gurin, Warren E. Miller, *The Voter Decides* (Evanston, Ill.: Row, Peterson, 1954), pp. 70-74; Gerhart Saenger, "Social Status and Political Behavior," *American Journal of Sociology, 51* (1945-46), pp. 103-13; Arneson and Eells, *op. cit.*

controlled they come rather close to voting in the same proportions as men.[6]
In Northern cities their voting rate approximates or exceeds the white rate.[7]
The most poorly educated group (no schooling) have greatly increased their
voting rate.

Jews have increased their rate of voting since the 1920's.[8]

Decreases

Farmers and others in agricultural occupations have decreased their voting rate.

Young voters (21-29) have decreased their rate of voting.

People in certain trades closely associated with government, such as railroad
and traction and public service employees, have decreased their rate of voting.

One other question arises, not with respect to the incidence of non-voting
in different groups, but with regard to the proportion of people who never
vote: those who do not merely skip a particular election, but skip all elections.
Unfortunately, we do not have data on the nature of this group—only its
size. Warren Miller, in a discussion of the political profile of the electorate,
finds that 10 per cent of the electorate old enough (age twenty-nine and over)
to have voted in the presidential elections of 1944, and 1952 failed to vote in
any of these elections.[9] Another interpretation by Samuel Eldersveld of a
study which includes all ages, estimates that 17 per cent of the electorate have
never voted.[10]

In reviewing this material, we find certain general relationships as well as
information on the history and the incidence of voting behavior in society.
Some of our conclusions may be set forth as follows:

The act of voting in different situations, although identical in form has different meanings and evokes different motives for the electors according to whether it
involves (a) a choice of issues (referendum) or of men (elections), (b) a primary
or inter-party election, (c) a local or national election, (d) a contest between men
known "personally" to an elector or men known, if at all, largely through some
identifying labels, etc.

The act of voting partially defines the electorate in imposing certain minimum
requirements on the voter: energy and time for going to the polls, capacity to
decide among conflicting claims, sufficient relatedness to society for awareness of
the election, capacity to implement emotional predispositions, an affirmative view
of the electoral process.

On the basis of relatively short-term and localized evidence, it seems probable
that, as contrasted to twenty-five years ago, the following groups vote more frequently: foreign-born, women, Negroes, Jews, and least well educated. The following probably vote less frequently: farmers, youth, persons in government-related
occupations.

---

6. This inference is supported by data in Louis Harris, *Is There a Republican Majority?* (New York: Harper, 1954), p. 107.

7. See Donald S. Strong, "The Rise of Negro Voting in Texas," *American Political
Science Review, 42* (1948), pp. 510-22.

8. Saenger, *Loc. cit.*

9. Warren E. Miller, *The Political Profile of the American Electorate,* (Ann Arbor,
Mich.: Survey Research Center, undated) p. 10.

10. Samuel J. Eldersveld, "The Independent Vote: Measurement, Characteristics,
and Implications for Party Strategy," *American Political Science Review, 46* (1952),
p. 739.

At mid-century, on a national basis, non-voting was higher in the following classes of people: women, youth, Protestants, rural, Negro, lower income, less skilled occupations, less well educated. Southern. These incidences of non-voting are misleading, however, since overlapping third factors often account for the higher incidence of non-voting in a given group.

WORKING IN ELECTIONS

Electoral machinery is most effective when the professional politicians, the people whose livelihood and/or status depends primarily upon their political activity, are assisted by a group of amateurs who work side-by-side with the professionals. Democratic theory presumes such a group of voluntary parti-cipants, and civic groups promote the amateur at the expense of the profes-sional whenever possible. What do these campaign workers do? Who are they?

Defining the group of amateurs or volunteers is not easy. Ostrogorski divided those active in politics into two groups, officers and privates, on the basis of whether or not they held official positions.[11] Bryce refers to an Inner Circle and an Outer Circle, the first comprising not only those who have jobs, but also those who want them, and the second comprising all the others (thought to be a "purer" group).[12] More recently, De Grazia has divided the "politists," that is, those who are "particularly occupied with the political process" into roughly four groups: party officials, civil servants, interest group leaders, and amateurs (lawyers, union leaders, etc.)[13] Another classi-fication refers to "functionaries," including campaign managers, party offi-cials, and candidates; "key figures" in the campaign efforts other than the above; and "steady workers" who are the active workers of the lower eche-lon.[14] Finally, Berelson and his associates conceive of the politically active group in an election as divided into "top party leaders," "party workers," "lay enthusiasts," and the "grass roots" group.[15]

Although not quite congruent with this last classification, our own is roughly similar. Here we focus upon the bottom three levels: (a) precinct leaders, ward captains, town committeemen or others with official, but rela-tively low level, party positions; (b) volunteer workers, without title or position, who take part in political campaigns; and (c) "opinion leaders" or

---

11. M. Ostrogorski, *Democracy and the Party System in the United States* (New York; Macmillan, 1910), pp. 164-65.

12. James Bryce, *The American Commonwealth* (New York: Macmillan, rev. ed., 1910), Vol. II, pp. 56, 62, 67.

13. Alfred de Grazia, *The Elements of Political Science* (New York: Knopf, 1952), p. 83.

14. Charles R. Nixon and Dwaine Marvick, "Active Campaign Workers: A Study of Self-Recruited Elites," Paper delivered at the American Political Science Association Convention, September, 1956 (mimeographed).

15. Bernard R. Berelson, Paul F. Lazarsfeld, Paul N. McPhee, *Voting* (Chicago: University of Chicago Press, 1954), p. 169.

"persuaders" who talk politics and carry on the informal educational work of a campaign in an unorganized and private capacity.

The work to be done at each of these levels will vary from the selection of candidates to run for office to the handing out of leaflets at a street corner. Elsewhere there are detailed accounts of the work of the precinct leader which reveal the services he may perform for his constituency, including ceremonial functions, assistance in interpreting the machinery of government, bartering of favors for votes, even intimate personal counseling in certain situations.[16] The volunteer group, by and large, renders other kinds of services to the party and the constituencies. Among these would be preparing registration lists, promoting publicity, arranging neighborhood "coffee-klatches" for a local candidate, speaking to a special language group, arranging a TV party to hear a national candidate, ringing doorbells, taking a friend to the polls, working on a mailing, and so forth. For many people this is not particularly interesting work, but there are those who agree to do it, some willingly, others reluctantly to satisfy an obligation. We shall discuss the work of political opinion leaders below.[17]

Interpreting the relative sizes of these various groups has been a speculative activity until recently;[18] current estimates are based on somewhat more accurate information. The precinct leaders probably number some 250,000 nationally, or about .25 per cent of the potential electorate.[19] As for the volunteer workers, in a survey after the 1954 election the American Institute of Public Opinion estimated from their sample that some 5,000,000 persons have served in this capacity, or a little less than 5 per cent of the electorate at that time (AIPO, 2/28/55). The opinion leaders (persons who feel that others come to them for information) were found, in two studies of moderate-sized urban communities, to comprise 21 per cent (Erie County, Ohio) and 23 per cent (Elmira, N.Y.) of the adult population.[20] If these proportions held for the nation at large, this group would include about 22,000,000 people in the 1950's. Since one national sample found 27 per cent "talking to people and trying to show them why they should vote for one of the parties or candi-

---

16. See, for example, Harold Gosnell, *Machine Politics: Chicago Model* (Chicago: University of Chicago Press, 1937), pp. 27-50; Sonya Forthal, *Cogwheels of Democracy, A Study of the Precinct Captain* (New York: William Frederick Press, 1946), pp. 39*ff.*

17. See pp. 90-92 below.

18. Ostrogorski (*op. cit.*, p. 166) estimated that there were about 50,000 members of the most important committees and about 1,000,000 members of other committees active in electoral work. Bryce (*op. cit.*, p. 63 *n*) took the number of national, state, and local offices, allowed one "expectant" for each office, and divided this latter estimate by half to take care of those who "work with no special eye to office". By means of this calculation he arrived at the figure of 250,000 active political workers around the turn of the century.

19. Hugh A. Bone, *Grass Roots Party Leadership, A Case Study of King County, Washington,* (Seattle: Bureau of Governmental Research and Services, University of Washington, 1952, mimeographed), p. 31.

20. Paul F. Lazarsfeld, Bernard R. Berelson, Hazel Gaudet, *The People's Choice* (New York: Columbia University Press, 2nd ed., 1948), p. 50; Berelson and Associates, *op. cit.*, pp. 109-14.

dates,"[21] this figure may be approximately accurate. Finally, of course, there is the mass of the electorate who are the main target for the communication network.

The middle group, the volunteer workers who are the present focus of attention, are a shifting group, some active in one election and some in another. One study by Elmo Roper asked, "In the last four years have you worked for the election of any political candidate by doing things like distributing circulars or leaflets, making speeches, or calling on voters?" About 11 per cent of the national sample said that they had done things of this sort over the four-year period.[22] Since this is about double the group who said that they had worked in the one 1954 congressional election, it appears that many of the volunteer workers must work in only some of the elections. Thus, in addition to a reliable core of workers available for all elections, there is also an irregular group which is mobilized on certain occasions but not on others. And this fluidity is characteristic not only of volunteer workers but of official precinct committeemen as well.[23]

But this group which is called upon to work in elections hardly exhausts the possibilities. Figure *4.1*, taken from the AIPO study of the 1954 election shows a surprising reservoir of party workers who have never been brought into action. Even after an appropriate allowance for the difference between promise and delivery has been made, this suggests a much more *actively* interested public than has been supposed to exist. Taken at face value, it would appear that about 22 per cent of the eligible electorate are willing to electioneer for the political parties or candidates of their choice. The different political roles of the two sexes, too, are clearly illustrated in these data where only about half as many women as men actually do voluntary political work— a more marked difference than is apparent in voting ratios. But also note that among those not now serving as volunteers approximately the same number of women (8.1 million) as men (8.3 million) indicated that they would like to work, suggesting that some of the low participation is due to resistance of the party leaders; probably based upon the presumed lower effectiveness of women volunteers. Finally, it appears from the same survey that the average coverage per volunteer worker in a typical congressional election is only six or seven people.

As for the groups in the population that feed these crops of amateur politicians, it is almost impossible to generalize. However, three principles seem clear. First, occupations such as law, real estate, undertaking, and insurance, which offer their members advantages derived from political activities, are likely to be over-represented.[24] Second, certain ethnic groups, such as the Irish, which find in their cultures reinforcement for political activity, tend also to be somewhat over-represented. Beyond these relatively well-known prin-

---

21. Campbell and associates, *op. cit.,* p. 30.

22. Julian L. Woodward and Elmo Roper, "Political Activity of American Citizens," *American Political Science Review, 44* (1950), p. 874.

23. See William E. Mosher, "Party and Government Control at the Grass Roots," *National Municipal Review, 24* (1935), pp. 15-18.

24. See Gosnell, *op. cit.,* pp. 27-50.

FIGURE 4.1.—Numbers of People Who Worked in the 1954 Congressional Campaigns and Would Like to Work in Election Campaigns, by Sex and Political Party.

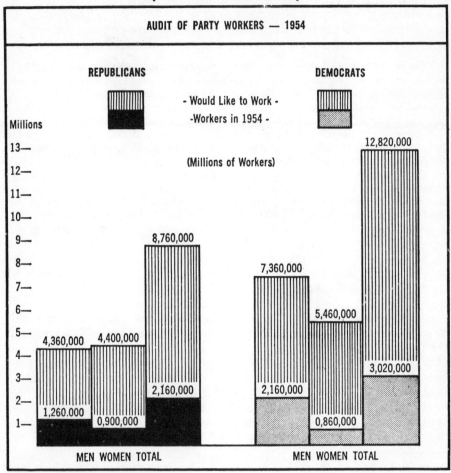

SOURCE: AIPO release dated March 13, 1955.

ciples, however, there is a more general principle of majority group over-representation, that is the over-representation of a salient constituency characteristic among the volunteers and precinct leaders. Thus, in a farming district, it seems to be true that, proportionate to the district population, farmers are over-represented in the corps of political activists;[25] in a neighborhood where one ethnic group predominates, the proportion of political activists from this ethnic group tends to be larger than the proportion of this group in the district

25. Leon Weaver, "Some Soundings in the Party System: Rural Precinct Committeemen," *American Political Science Review, 34* (1940), pp. 76-84.

population;[26] and it seems to be the case that in a relatively prosperous and well-educated area, such as Kings County, Washington, the precinct leaders, and probably also their volunteer helpers, are, in contrast to other areas, markedly better educated and more prosperous than the rest of the population.[27] Since this principle is also apparent in the selection of candidates, it should occasion no surprise that it holds true in the corps of political activists.

In reviewing this material, one may summarize, tentatively as follows:

The classification of types of campaign workers may be based on level of influence and nature of duties, differentiating (a) top leadership, (b) grass roots committeemen, (c) campaign volunteers, (d) and opinion leaders.

The proportion of the adult population involved in these several levels are: (a) top leadership, unknown, (b) precinct committeemen 0.25 per cent, (c) volunteers in any one election, 5 per cent, (d) opinion leaders, 22 to 27 per cent. The volunteer group includes fewer than those who are willing so to serve, particularly among women, and is rather fluid.

The principle of majority over-representation among political campaign workers, with and without official positions, may be stated as follows: The group of political activists in a district will tend to possess any characteristic which is regarded as politically salient by the largest self-conscious group in the community in greater proportion than is to be found in the general community population.

FINANCIAL CONTRIBUTIONS

A financial contribution to a party or candidate comprises a unique form of participation, involving, as it does, the possession of "surplus" resources.[28] While other forms of participation demand the sacrifice of time, and possibly, of energy, financial contributions do not require these forms of sacrifice, but instead involve sacrifices of "goods and services foregone," and may be measured in terms of things given up in order that the contribution may be made to the party or candidate. As with other market phenomena, interpersonal comparisons in these respects are hard to make and likely to be invalid. The degree of sacrifice implied by a contribution of a specified sum is proportion-

---

26. H. Gosnell, *op. cit.*

27. H. Bone, *op. cit.*

28. Here we omit entirely the discussion of policy in controlling campaign contribution. On this subject see Louise Overacker, *Presidential Campaign Funds* (Boston: Boston University Press, 1946); Overacker, *Money in Elections* (New York: Macmillan, 1932); and Overacker, "Presidential Campaign Funds, 1944," *American Political Science Review, 39* (1945), pp. 899-925. A summary of national and state laws may be found in *Election Law Guidebook*, 1952, Senate Document No. 97, 82 Cong., 2 Sess. Two recent inquiries into expenditures in elections are presented in "Investigation into the 1950 Ohio Senatorial Campaign," *Hearings before the Senate Committee on Rules and Administration*, 82 Cong., 2 Sess.; "Senator from New Mexico," *Hearings before the Senate Committee on Rules and Administration*, 83 Cong. 1 Sess. together with Subcommittee *Report* on these hearings, 83 Cong., 2 Sess.; and "1956 Presidential and Senatorial Campaign Contributions," *Hearings before the Senate Committee on Rules and Administration*, 84 Cong., 2 Sess., Parts 1 and 2.

ate less to the size of the gift than to the income of the giver, for, as is well recognized in the principles of progressive taxation, the utility of the marginal 10 per cent of his income to a rich man is usually less than the marginal 10 per cent of a poor man's income (although this may not be the case in a minority of instances). For these reasons the size of the contribution, or even the ratio of contribution to income, cannot serve as a measure of intensity of motivation and this phase of the problem must be left for more refined psychological interpretation.

Who are the individuals who contribute to the financing of political parties? Pollock, in an earlier study, divides the sources of party funds into three groups: friends of the party, office-holders, and candidates; the first is voluntary, the latter two combine assessment and voluntary giving.[29] Unfortunately, these categories tend to overlap, for the "friend" of the party may be a person who aspires to be a candidate or office holder, and the candidate may contribute partly because he is a friend of the party and what it stands for and partly for his own advancement. Nevertheless, the classification according to whether or not a person has or seeks government office, which is the heart of Pollock's division, has some utility. Furthermore, following the Hatch Acts of 1940 and 1941, it is undoubtedly true that the proportion of funds coming from assessed office holders and candidates has declined and the proportion coming from "friends" has therefore increased.

Another method of classifying the sources of campaign funds has been attempted by Overacker in her series of studies, in this case by the financial interest of the donor. Overacker is more concerned with the effect of the donations than with the motives of the donors, but her data reveal the percentages of contributions from several occupational interests. Computations from Overacker's 1932 figures show that of the large (over $5,000) contributions given to each party in 1928, bankers and brokers gave about a quarter, manufacturers gave about a fifth, mining and oil interests and railroads and public utilities each gave between 6 per cent and 7 per cent of the total gifts.[30] Each of these interests, except the railroad and utilities group, contributed substantially more to the Republican party than to the Democratic party.

Since the 1930's the importance of bankers and brokers for both Democrats and Republicans has declined and the importance of the manufacturing group, particularly government contractors, has increased. There has also been a sharp decline in the contributions from the business community to the Democratic party and a substantial increase in union financial support for the Democrats, a support which changed greatly in form but far less in amount after the passage of the Smith-Connelly Act and the Taft-Hartley Act. There has also been a decline in importance of the single large donation subsequent to the Hatch Act, which imposed a $5,000 limit on individual donations to any one political organization,[31] although this limit could be circumscribed, as seen in Table 4.3.

---

29. James K. Pollock, *Party Campaign Funds* (New York: Knopf, 1926), p. 113.

30. Overacker, *Money in Elections*, p. 162.

31. Overacker, "Presidential Campaign Funds, 1944," p. 916.

TABLE 4.3.—Contributions to Party Organizations by Members of Selected Families, January 1—November 1, 1956.

Number of Donors	Family	Total Amount
14	Rockefeller	$100,500
7	Mellon	99,150
32	Dupont	88,300
4	Pew	46,000
7	Reynolds	41,250*
4	Vanderbilts	33,800
1	Weir	11,000
		$420,000

* Contributed to the Democratic Party—all other funds went to the Republican party.

SOURCE: Interim Report on 1956 Presidential and Senatorial Campaign Studies, Subcommittee on Privileges and Elections of Senate Committee on Rules and Administration, 84 Cong. 2 Sess. (mimeographed, 1956), p. 9.

This total of $420,000 given by the seven families contributing the largest sums, should be compared to the total cost of the campaign, estimated to be about $140 million in 1956;[32] it is a relatively small fraction of this amount.

Although corporations are forbidden to make financial contributions to political parties, the officers of these corporations may do so. Therefore by examining the business connections of the heavy donors some inferences are possible about the business advantages of political favors anticipated in return for the gifts. Following this line of reasoning the Senate Subcommittee on Privileges and Elections found some concentration in the petroleum industry which they associated with the disposal of tidelands oil; some concentration among government contractors, and among directors of the American Iron and Steel Institute. But only one out of 218 Directors of the National Association of Real Estate Boards, one of the most powerful lobbies in Washington, made a contribution over $500 to a political party organization, and none of the board members of the American Medical Association gave sums of this size in spite of their current concern about socialized medicine.[33] One reason for this, of course, is political prudence—and the fact that there are ways of giving which are impossible to trace—but with big, as with little donors, economic motives, in the sense that the donors give in anticipation of commensurate economic rewards, comprise only a small part of the motivational pattern. Indeed, a glimpse into another, non-economic form of reward is shown in the high proportion of ambassadors appointed in the years from

32. Testimony of Alexander Heard, *1956 Hearings* (see Footnote 28), p. 10.
33. *1956 Hearings, op. cit.,* Part 2, p. 531.

1952 to 1956 from the ranks of heavy Republican donors, as revealed in the Committee hearings.[34]

The declining percentage of party funds coming from office-holders and candidates, and from the very large donations prevalent up until the 1940's, suggests that other sources have supplied funds for electioneering. We said earlier that corporations cannot make gifts to political parties, but this does not mean that they are unable to employ their resources to advance political objectives. In good faith and perfect legality they may:

1. Pay salaries and wages of officers and regular employees while engaged in political activity.
2. Publish opinions and arguments of a political nature, expressed as the the views of the corporation, in any house organ or other printed document circulated at the expense of the corporation.
3. Purchase radio and television time or newspaper space for the presentation of the corporation's political views.
4. Use any other means of expressing the political views of the corporate management, publicly or privately.
5. Encourage people to register and vote and disseminate information and opinion concerning public issues without regard to parties or candidates.[35]

And that isn't all. Perhaps without sanction of the law, but with slim chance of legal difficulty, the management of a corporation or trade association may divert funds to political purposes as follows:

1. Make use of the advertising or entertainment funds of trade associations for political contributions.
2. Place advertisements in political publications through public relations firms or advertising agencies.
3. Make contributions in kind to political candidates (make available to them without pay the use of offices, airplanes, etc.).
4. Permit the padding of expense accounts with the understanding that political contributions should be made out of the padded amounts.
5. Pay or repay bonuses with the explicit or tacit understanding that part of such remunerations shall be spent in campaign contributions.[36]

Examination of the financial contributions of financial and elite groups at the national level tends to obscure some of the characteristics of the givers which may be seen in the detailed study of a smaller area. The authors of the 1948 Elmira study for example, describe a central elite of that city in a series of concentric circles. At the heart of the circle is, what they term, the "old guard," the dozen owners of the large, locally owned, businesses and banks.

---

34. For example, President Eisenhower's nominee for Ambassador to Ceylon, Maxwell H. Gluck, testified before the Senate Foreign Relations Committee on July 2, 1957 that he did not know the name of the Prime Minister of Ceylon, could not pronounce the name of the Prime Minister of India, but had given between $20,000 and $30,000 to the Republican party in 1956. (*New York Times*, 8/1/57).

35. Interim Report on 1956 Presidential and Senatorial Campaign Studies (see Source for Table 4.3), p. 18.

36. *Ibid.*, pp. 18-19.

In the 1948 campaign, eight members of this group made contributions averaging around $200 each. Surrounding this group there is an "inner circle" of about fifty important business and professional families who belong to elite clubs and sit on the important charity boards. Of this group, twenty nine persons made contributions averaging $65.00 each. The outer circle of the elite is made up of the managers of absentee owned industry, more recently arrived in Elmira, less firmly rooted and less well integrated in the community, although, because they control large resources, still powerful. Not one of this group made a contribution to the local Republican party (two contributed to the Democrats).[37]

Many of the other businessmen and lawyers in town, men who could not qualify as members of the elite, made contributions to the Republican party in smaller average sums, but very few contributed to the Democrats. As a group, the tavern keepers were the only important local business contributors who seemed Democratically oriented.

Businesses and businessmen, candidates and office holders, represent only part of the financial resources of political parties; there remains the mass of party adherents and sympathizers. As yet the dues systems prevalent in Europe have not taken hold in the United States, but more people of moderate means are making a larger number of contributions. Although the actual number of people contributing to the parties at campaign time is obscure because of vagaries in the reporting system, Overacker reports that "many more persons contributed to the financial support of the parties in 1928 than in 1924."[38] Almost thirty years later, Paul Butler, Chairman of the Democratic National Committee, continued in the same vein, "we are broadening the base of our political contributions." As evidence he showed that the number of contributions to the Democratic National Committee in 1952 was three times as large as in 1948, and in 1956, when he testified, the number of contributors promised to be twice as large as in 1952. These are not large contributions— the average in 1956 was $2.04. Moreover, the 1956 figures were given on October 10th before "Dollars for Democrats Day" when, so it was said, 500,000 workers were scheduled to go from door to door collecting small contributions for the Democratic Party.[39] Something similar was planned by the Republican Party.

In 1955 the American Institute of Public Opinion (3/4/55 release) asked a national sample of the American people whether, during the last year, they had been asked to contribute and whether they did contribute to a political party (national, state, or local). The AIPO concluded from the answers of their sample that individuals in almost five million families, split evenly between Republicans and Democrats, said that they had been asked to contribute and about half that number had done so. Of those asked, the Democrats were slightly more likely to give than were the Republicans.

Furthermore, on the basis of the answers to an additional question: "If you were asked to give, would you contribute $5.00 to the campaign fund of

37. Berelson, et al., *op. cit.*, pp. 154-60.
38. Overacker, *Money in Elections*, p. 13.
39. *1956 Hearings*, p. 396.

the political party you prefer" it appears that nearly 16 million families (about a third of the eligible families in the United States) might be willing to contribute this sum. At least, discounting those who might falter when actually approached for the gift, there appears to be a large untapped reservoir of financial participation which requires only a proper machinery for enlistment.

In some ways, the natural collection agency for working-class political contributions are the trade unions, which are themselves forbidden by the Taft-Hartley Act from making contributions out of their general treasuries. Most union members giving under these circumstances, however, are hardly aware that they are making a political contribution—they think of it as a contribution to the union. In some large metropolitan unions, about 25 per cent of the members contribute in this way.[40] Furthermore, the unions themselves may legally employ their own funds for certain political purposes. They may and do:

1. Systematically organize drives for registration of voters.

2. Carry out a systematic program of political education (including the organization of schools where political questions are discussed), and the compilation and distribution of voting records.

3. Exercise the right of free speech by expressing their views on political questions in print and by means of television and radio and otherwise.[41]

Although the individual contributions to political parties collected by union officers are relatively small, and the general union contributions to advance the interests of their candidates and favored issues are only moderate, they serve as a counterpoise to the financial weight of the business interests.

Whether these new techniques for popular financing of campaigns will be adequate to the task has yet to be determined. The cost of election campaigns increased 60 per cent from 1940 to 1952, but this should be contrasted to an increase in the cost of living of 90 per cent in the same period and an increase in national income of 240 per cent.[42] Evidently, in terms of constant dollar values and in relation to increasing purchasing power, the price of politics, perhaps the demand for politics, has declined over this period.

In summary, then, we may report certain hypotheses with some suggestive evidence to support them:

The larger a person's income, the more likely he is to give to a political party or to other public organizations because (a) he is a more visible target to money raisers, (b) his stakes in public policy may be more direct and easily seen, (c) the sacrifices entailed in making the contribution are smaller (on the theory of diminishing marginal utility of money).

Regardless of income, persons with interests more affected by public policy (tariff, regulation, subsidy) are more likely to contribute to a political party or other public organization than those less affected.

Those with membership in an inner circle of a community characterized by (a) long residence, (b) ownership of important community resources, and (c)

---

40. Arthur Kornhauser, Albert J. Mayer, and Harold L. Sheppard, *When Labor Votes* (New York: University Books, 1956), p. 125, 125n.

41. *Interim Report on 1956 Presidential and Senatorial Campaign Studies*, pp. 17-18.

42. Testimony of Alexander Heard in *1956 Hearings*, p. 10.

interlocking organizational relationships, will contribute more to political parties than those with membership only in groups where any of these factors is weaker.

Changing patterns of contributions indicate less campaign support from office holders and very large donors and increasing support from union members and small party supporters or candidate supporters. Of the latter about half of those asked to give report giving; but only a third of those who say they are willing to give have been asked to give.

Beyond these hypotheses, however, some speculative ideas regarding the comparative rates of giving in communities with equal resources may be set forth as follows:

Proportional rates of financial participation (ratio of income to political contribution at each income level) in any community are directly and positively related to the closeness of electoral victories over a period of time.

Proportional rates of financial participation are positively related to ethnic and class tension in a given community, where these groups are considered rivals for power.

The greater the density of population the smaller the proportion of persons at the upper income level contributing to the local party organization and the larger the proportion of persons at the lower income level contributing to the *local* party organization; but, *the greater the density of population the larger the proportion of persons at the upper income level contributing to NATIONAL political organizations.*

The stronger the party organization and, therefore, the more efficient the solicitation, the higher the proportional rates of financial participation in any given community.

CHAPTER 5

Who Tries to Influence Public Officials

and How Do They Do It?

PERSONALLY PETITIONING PUBLIC OFFICIALS

"THE RIGHT OF THE PEOPLE peacefully to assemble, and to petition the Government for a redress of grievances" is guaranteed by the Constitution. But who exercises this right and how is it done?

Petitioning public officials in a face-to-face contact requires certain qualities of the petitioner and certain opportunities which help to define the group that engages in this form of political behavior. In the first place, unlike voting, it is an interpersonal act and, therefore, an act inhibited by shyness or other difficulties in relating to people. In this sense it is also different from letter writing where the contacts take place at a distance. It involves getting close to people with power and therefore is attractive to those who are power seekers.[1] An effective petition implies a sufficient knowledge of politics to inform a person whom it is worth seeing.

Personally petitioning public officials takes place within a social hierarchy such that those higher in the hierarchy will have easier access to higher officials and will feel freer to see them or write to them.[2] It often implies a bargain whereby a citizen will offer something—a vote, a financial contribution, or a promise to refrain from "making trouble"—in return for the official action he seeks.

But, in spite of the fact that almost all contacts imply these conditions, official contacts represent some additional factors. Consider two aspects of

---

1. See Fillmore Sanford, *Authoritarianism and Leadership* (Philadelphia: Stephenson Brothers, 1950).

2. "A person of higher social rank than another originates interaction for the latter more often than the latter originates interaction for him," George C. Homans, *The Human Group* (New York: Harcourt Brace, 1950) p. 145.

personal contacts with officials at local and national levels. William Foote Whyte reports on a series of personal contacts in Cornerville (a metropolitan area) which may be paraphrased as follows:[3]

Some corner boys were playing softball in a small park. Some of the more powerful hitters occasionally drove the ball over the wall bounding the lot and against the building across the street. Several windows were broken. . . . The park commissioner ruled that no boys over sixteen should be allowed to play softball in this lot and asked the Cornerville captain to take action. The captain spoke to the sergeant and the sergeant broke up a hotly contested game one Sunday afternoon.

Sam Franco, the leader of one of the corner gangs, had been organizing a soft-ball league, which was to include sixteen teams. . . . He talked with an older man who had met the park commissioner. The park commissioner attended a near-by church. Sam and his friend waited for him outside and asked if his department could erect a wire-netting extension to the wall so that the building would be protected. He said that he had no appropriations and could do nothing for them. A few days later they sought to talk with him again, but he said, "I don't want to have anything to do with you," and brushed past them. Franco then enlisted the help of Mr. Kendall, the head of boys work at Cornerville House, who went to see the local Alderman, Mr. Fiumara, with little effect. Sensing that the politician did not see the potential voting strength involved in the softball organization, Mr. Kendall took some of the team captains to see Fiumara in person. At this point things began to happen.

Now consider a few of Congressman Dirksen's appointments in 1943 as described by a reporter for *Fortune* who spent a day in his office.[4]

His first visitor, after a less-experienced Congressman seeking advice, was a Chicago business man [who] . . . wanted to talk about home loan financing. (Dirksen is trying to kill HOLC) and also about rent control on commercial properties in connection with a bill pending before the House Banking Committee. . . . On the heels of the banker came a distiller's representative, worried about the recent newspaper story that liquor consumption was to be cut 99 per cent for the duration [of the war]. . . . Next visitor was a college trustee worried about what would happen to the college unless the Army or Navy selected it for one of their training programs.

And so it went, throughout the day. Many of the visitors were other congressmen, public officials, or official lobbyists, but many of them were also "merely" constituents.

The Cornerville group and Dirksen's visitors are from two entirely separate populations, with different skills, needs, and means of access to officialdom. Certainly it is true that while the second group are among the letter writing public, the first group, except for the social worker, are probably not. It is also probably true that while Dirksen's visitors also contact officials on the local level,[5] the Cornerville group do not contact officials on the national

---

3. William Foote Whyte, *Street Corner Society* (Chicago: University of Chicago Press, 1943), pp. 247-49.

4. "Congressman: A Case History," *Fortune*, 27 (April, 1943), pp. 80, 177.

5. In "Aurelia" persons who were rated as influential in foreign affairs were also influential locally. See Kenneth P. Adler and Davis Bobrow, "Interest and Influence in Foreign Affairs," *Public Opinion Quarterly*, 20 (1956), pp. 89-101.

level. Thus, there are two groups of petitioners: local only, and national and local. The demographic characteristics of the two groups to be read into the above accounts point to the obvious conclusion that the first group is relatively low on income, education, and occupational scales, while the second group is relatively high.

This inference based on common sense and the two cases mentioned above is further borne out, at a somewhat rarified level of society, by a study of persons designated by members of an upper-class suburb as "influential" in foreign affairs, and others designated merely as "interested."[6] Although both groups were in the $10,000 and up income bracket, the "influentials" were substantially more prosperous than the "interested." Their respective patterns of personal contact and letter writing may be seen in Table 5.1.

TABLE 5.1.—Some Channels of Influence Used by Foreign Policy "Influentials" and "Interested."

Influence Channel Used	Influentials (N=39)	Interested (N=99)
Write media executives	15%	10%
Talk to media executives	10	0
Write Congressmen	38	35
Talk to Congressmen	33	0
Write executive branch	8	12
Talk to executive branch	10	1

SOURCE: Kenneth P. Adler and Davis Bobrow, "Interest and influence in Foreign Affairs," "Public Opinion Quarterly, 20" (1956), p. 96.

Although writing to persons thought able to affect policy is approximately equally frequent in the two groups, talking directly to such persons comes only with very high rank—and motivation. The relation between income and letter writing may be roughly linear, but, between income and talking directly to decision-makers, the relation is positively accelerated at the "wealthy" end of the scale.

At the national level there is a presumption that contacting officials is more frequent among representatives of group interests: bankers, distillers, small colleges. At this level people rarely speak for themselves and somewhat less rarely for only their own firm when they approach an official; often the relationship takes on the character of an ambassadorship from a larger group, either informal or formal. In this sense, then, the petitioners emerge as designated or informal leaders of special interest groups of all kinds. This is less likely to be true at the local level where personal favors are a subject of negotiation. Even at the local level, however, there is an objective as well as a subjective difference between asking for something for a group and asking for something for oneself. "The interaction necessary in the hierarchy in

---

6. *Idem.*

order to obtain community improvements differ from those which are required for personal favors."[7]

The nature of the request then has an effect upon the relationship between petitioner and petitioned; so does the selection of the person or group petitioned. The citizen has a choice: he may approach the administrative branch of government; he may approach a member of the legislature in an informal manner; he may present his case in a formal hearing, when such hearings are available. The petitioner at a hearing is likely to represent some formal group, although, in the Eightieth Congress, for example, some sixty persons appeared before the House Judiciary Committee as single individuals representing no one but themselves.[8] Unless they are invited by the Committee, which is not infrequent, such individuals must indeed be zealous, fond of public attention, and highly political in orientation and intensity of interest.

As to the choice between petitioning a bureaucrat and a legislator in the privacy of their offices (or over the impersonal telephone lines), such a choice will be affected in part by whether the expansive person-oriented style of a legislator or the more inhibited task-oriented style of the bureaucrat is more congenial to the petitioner.[9] Both legislative and administrative branches develop special patterns in their receptivity and resistance to pressure, but the administrative departments must develop standards and techniques for getting the job done which tend to exclude accommodation to certain types of pressure.[10] In either event, pressures from relatively lower strata in society require a kind of organization and coordination which those at the more exalted levels do not require.

But status is only one of many qualities which affect the nature of contacts with congressmen. The manner in which it is done is also important. A threatening tone or lack of subtlety may be fatal. Consider the following comment made by a congressman, referring first to business representatives:[11]

When these guys wine you and dine you this way, they never see you about anything in particular. It's just to get acquainted. I simply couldn't begin to name a list of all the industries that have done this to me, milk, dirt farmers too—everybody but labor. There I think labor makes a mistake. God knows I'm not working for more of it; I'm tired to death from it all; but labor groups ought to do it. They don't. They have a chip on their shoulder. . . . But what will labor do? Send in a delegation and threaten you so you want to vote against them, so you will show them you aren't the man to be intimidated. They're crude as hell.

Or a lofty moral tone and unsympathetic manner such as is said to be

---

7. Whyte, *op. cit.,* p. 246.

8. W. Brooke Graves, *Administration of the Lobbying Regulation Provisions of the Legislative Reorganization Act of 1946* (Washington, D.C.: Library of Congress Legislative Reference Service, 1950). Not much is known about the individuals who exercise their right to petition on their own behalf since they are not required by law to register —even though a few do.

9. Robert K. Merton, "Bureaucratic Structure and Personality," *Social Forces, 18* (1940), pp. 560-68.

10. See Whyte, *op. cit.,* pp. 249-50.

11. Frank Bonilla, "When is Petition 'Pressure!' " *Public Opinion Quarterly, 20* (1956), p. 46.

characteristic of the League of Women Voters also brings criticism. Partly, however, this is because all groups without clear economic stakes in a policy dispute are viewed with skepticism by legislators.[12]

In summary, one might hypothesize:

Political participation through petitioning officials in person is related to the possession of social skills, the desire to be close to "greatness," and some knowledge (awareness) of political life.

Participation through personally petitioning governmental officials is related to class status in the following ways: (1) Those of lower socio-economic status are more likely to contact only local officials, while those of higher socio-economic status may contact both local and state or national officials. (2) Those of lower socio-economic status require greater organization and effort for an audience with an official or to secure an equivalent effect upon that official than those of higher status. (3) Contacting national officials, at least on foreign policy matters, is a positively accelerated function of wealth and social position.

Petitioning public officials is differentiated according to whether the *objective* is (a) a personal favor (selfish interest), (b) a group favor involving some interest group, or (c) a community or national cause. Personal favors are likely to be more numerous at the local level and to be directed to the legislative branch.

Petitioning public officials is differentiated according to the *person or group petitioned* as follows: (1) Those who prefer public attention and are openly and intensely political prefer public hearing. (2) Those who prefer warm interpersonal relations and mutual obligations prefer private conferences with their legislative representations. (3) Those who are task-oriented and want to deal with a case on its merits prefer conferences with administrators.

Petitioning public officials is differentiated according to the *manner* of contact. Subtlety enough to keep congressional super-egoes quiet, lack of belligerence or threat, avoidance of references or suggestions of morality in favor of stressing "hard," i.e., group economic interests, make contacts more effective.

WRITING LETTERS TO OFFICIALS

Writing or wiring a congressman, the mayor, or some administrative official such as the chief of the Division of Farms and Markets requires, at the lowest level, certain skills of spelling and punctuation (however casual), and familiarity with paper and pencil. It can be done alone or collectively, on one's own initiative or under inspiration from another, on a postcard in a few words, or at length. The policy consequences are remote and difficult to appraise. Thus, certain intrinsic factors tend to limit and select the letter writing public. Who are they?

Sources: The potential letter writing public is substantial, at least according to people's own estimates of their "willingness" to write. The number of people who would be *willing* to write their congressmen periodically ranges over time (1943-1945) from a half to almost three-quarters of the adult

12. *Ibid.,* pp. 46-7.

public;[13] those who have "ever thought they'd *like* to write a letter to their congressman or government official" amount to 46 per cent (1943) of the population; while those who have ever written or wired their congressman or senator amount to about a seventh (14 per cent of the population (1946).[14] Apparently there is a substantial gap between the wish and the act, with those limiting factors mentioned above taking their toll of this potential public, bringing it down from about a half to a seventh of the population.

As in almost all acts of political participation, and particularly with respect to those less frequently performed, socio-economic status and education are important conditioning factors. Nationally, the relationship of these factors to letter writing may be seen in Table 5.2.

TABLE 5.2.—Per cent of Group Writing Letters to National Government Officials, by Occupation and Education.

("Have you ever written or wired your Congressman or Senator in Washington," AIPO 5/2/46).

	Yes	No
National total	14%	86%
By occupation		
Business and professional	32	68
White collar	17	83
Farmers	12	88
Manual workers	7	93
By Education		
College	35	65
High School	15	85
Grammar school or no school	9	91

SOURCE: Hadley Cantril, ed., "Public Opinion 1935-1946 (Princeton: Princeton University Press, 1951), p. 703.

In addition to this general (but not universal) difference in patterns of letter writing by socio-economic groups, there is a very substantial difference in letter writing practices among the three religious groups, with the Jewish population tending to write far more letters than Catholics or Protestants.[15] Here, as with other activities such as club-joining, ethnic subcultures place their stamp upon the "appropriate" areas of participation for an individual, providing stimuli, skills, and conventions in one area or another. Moreover, it is probable that the concentration of letter writing in upper status and selected ethnic groups is exaggerated by the use of "plural voting" in this mailbag ballot box. From the finding that 13 per cent of the public had, in

13. Hadley Cantril, ed., *Public Opinion 1935-1946* (Princeton: Princeton University Press, 1951). p. 703.

14. *Ibid.*, pp. 702-703.

15. Gerhart H. Saenger, "Social Status and Political Behavior," *American Journal of Sociology, 51* (1945), p. 105.

the late 1940's, written one or more times to a public official, and 7 per cent had written two or more times, one might conclude that, just as with joining organizations or exposure to the media, the "repeaters" account for a substantial portion of the activity.[16]

We have no accurate historical record of letter writing, as we do of voting, yet from such evidence as is available it is clear that the average daily flow has increased substantially during the twentieth century. At the turn of the century it is estimated that the White House mail averaged about 100 letters a day, gradually increasing until the period of our entry into World War I when the rate increased to about 800 a day. During the period of "normalcy" under Harding and Coolidge the rate dropped down to about 400 a day, increasing again in the depression during Hoover's administration to between 600 to 800 a day. Following Hoover, a somewhat cold and uninviting personality, at best, the White House mail again increased substantially. Except for a decline toward the end of F. D. Roosevelt's administration, Roosevelt's daily average has been estimated as between 4,000 and 8,000, but the daily mail varied greatly as indicated by the fact that on one day President Roosevelt received 150,000 pieces.[17]

In relation to the historical changes in rate of voting, this record reveals several interesting contrasts. As a voluntary act for which everyone is eligible, letter writing would be more likely to parallel changes in public interest in voting rather than changes in those eligible to vote, although it would be affected by the latter. Consequently it is interesting to note the steady growth of letter writing during the 1900-1920 period when the proportion of eligible voters voting declined. No doubt this is due in part to the fact that women were writing letters before they could vote (although women write fewer letters than men), but it also reflects the rising standard of education which is more closely related to letter writing than to voting.

In the second place, it appears that letter writing is a form of participation more sensitive to events (particularly depressions and wars or threat of war) than is electoral turnout. Its range of fluctuation during the Roosevelt years shows a peak day, with something close to twenty-five times the mail of an average day, during a period when the proportion of eligible voters voting fluctuated only a few percentage points from an average of 59 per cent for the four elections, with a peak of 62 per cent in 1936. This is, of course, understandable in view of the *immediate* and *specific* nature of the letter writing response, as well as the possibilities of growth of an activity normally performed by only a small fraction of the electorate. In the third place, over the years the mail *trend* reveals a much greater increase than is apparent in voting, due again to increased education, and no doubt, to the multiplying effect present in plural voting through the mailbag.

These comparisons, moreover, raise the question of whether letter writing is in any sense an alternate form of participation in relation to voting in elec-

16. Julian L. Woodward and Elmo Roper, "Political Activity of American Citizens," *American Political Science Review*, 44 (1950), pp. 872-85.

17. Leila A. Sussmann, "FDR and the White House Mail," *Public Opinion Quarterly*, 20 (1956), pp. 9, 5n, 6n.

tions, or whether, as seems more probable, it is a supplement to voting. Some evidence that letter writing *may* be done by those who do not vote is found in the fact that, on one occasion, of 100 letters to a Senator from a particular city, only thirty-three were from people registered to vote.[18] But this is unusual, and is only likely to occur at all with what is called "inspired" mail, that is, mail sent at the behest of an active pressure group, rather than self-originated mail.

The substantial portion of the congressional mail which is inspired in this way by interested parties means that there is a tendency toward a concentration of sources. Dexter estimates that four large firms may "easily have stimulated 40 per cent or more of all mail received by all Congressmen in 1954 [opposing] . . . reciprocal trade."[19] On the other hand, the League of Women Voters, favoring greater reciprocal trade, is estimated to have produced "probably three-fourths" of the (much lighter) mail received by congressmen reflecting this view.[20]

Much of the mail, therefore, comes either from businessmen or from organized labor—but particularly businessmen. It is a curious feature of the mail, however, highlighting the low policy orientation of the American political party official, that almost no mail dealing with the tariff issue was received from county chairmen of the parties[21]—although further examination of the kind of mail found in Dirksen's mail bag (see below) might show many requests for patronage and favors from these political sources.

Content: The kind of letter received, of course, can vary almost infinitely. *Fortune* reports on Dirksen's mail as follows:[22]

Congressional mail falls into six classes: (1) letters asking for help in getting a job or military commission or in dealing with some government agency; (2) those asking for information; (3) those asking the Congressman to vote for or against a specific bill; (4) those offering the writer's opinions on various aspects of current affairs; (5) those asking for a donation to some organization or cause; (6) requests for handouts from government and social agencies.

Some examples of non-issue mail include:[23]

The relatives of a Navy man recently killed in action asking if the Congressman could run over to Annapolis to be present at the opening of the sailor's safe-deposit box and sign an affidavit on its contents.

A judge, asking Dirksen to help get a forty-two year old constituent out of the Army.

A woman, announcing: "We are in need of information concerning production in the world."

A constituent wanting a job as guard in one of the government buildings.

---

18. Lewis A. Dexter, "What Do Congressmen Hear: The Mail," *Public Opinion Quarterly*, 20 (1956), p. 17.
19. Dexter, *ibid.*, p. 19.
20. *Ibid.*, p. 20.
21. *Ibid.*, p. 21.
22. *Fortune, op. cit.*, p. 180.
23. *Ibid.*, pp. 180, 183.

A proud Peorian who requested the Congressman to see if he could get a U.S. warship named Peoria.

As for mail dealing with issues and requesting the legislator (or President) to take a specified stand, several studies reveal something of its content. In the first place, many important issues evoked almost no mail response, among these, in the 1955 session, were mutual aid programs for Europe and Asia, the Housing Act of 1955, and restriction of wheat and cotton acreage.[24] Even the Japanese treaty received very little attention in the mail.[25] On the other hand, the reciprocal trade legislation evoked a very considerable amount of mail in that year, and, of course in other years such crucial steps as the military service bills have raised a flood of letters to Congress.[26] Much of the mail, however, is misguided. It deals with measures not before the Congress, it comes too late to do any good, it makes proposals which are technically impossible, the meaning is obscure, and it is misinformed. As Dexter says, after reading thousands of letters on the subject, "I have hardly ever seen a letter which indicated any technical mastery of reciprocal trade legislation. The few people who have such mastery would probably go and see the appropriate people rather than write letters."[27] The content of the mail is expressive, rather than informative. As in the public opinion polls, in writing letters people are willing to express opinions (and to go to some trouble to do so) without much information to support their views.

Other aspects of the content of the mail are revealed in a study of the Senatorial mail on the Burke-Wadsworth bill, mentioned previously.[28] On the whole, this analysis shows, the letters were rather even-tempered discussions of one's own predicament if the measure were passed. They were not likely either to cite authority or to claim that they were speaking for a vast public, nor were they likely to refer to the position of the Senator, certainly not in a threatening way. Most of the authors probably did not know what the Senator's views on the bill were. Only the letters from upper-status correspondents referred to national welfare or some ideological goal; the lower-status groups said simply what they thought should be done and supported this with references to their personal (often economic) situation. On the other hand, the mail on reciprocal trade, being largely from businessmen, cloaked an obvious self-interest in broad generalizations on national welfare to a much greater extent.[29]

To Whom: Within the legislative branch, there seems to be no discrimination in selecting those members of Congress who are members of important

---

24. L. A. Dexter, *op. cit.,* p. 19.

25. Bernard C. Cohen, "Political Communication on the Japanese Peace Settlement," *Public Opinion Quarterly,* 20 (1956), p. 36.

26. See Rowena Wyant, "Voting via the Senate Mailbag, Part I," *Public Opinion Quarterly,* 5 (1941), pp. 359-82; and R. Wyant and Herta Herzog, "Voting via the Senate Mailbag, Part II," *Public Opinion Quarterly,* 5 (1941), pp. 590-624.

27. L. A. Dexter, *op. cit.,* p. 21.

28. Wyant and Herzog, *op. cit.,* pp. 590-613.

29. L. A. Dexter, *op. cit.,* p. 19; F. Bonilla, *op. cit.,* pp. 42-43.

committees in contrast to those who are not.[30] Most letter writers write to "their own" senators or congressmen.[31] There is some evidence, however, that at least on one issue—the Japanese treaty, there were substantial differences in the nature of the communications (from individuals as well as interest groups) directed to the Executive Department and the legislature. Thus Cohen says, "In the case of the Japanese peace settlement, members of the Executive and the Congress received somewhat different images of 'public opinion' on the treaty, because different groups and individuals communicated different things to them at different times."[32] Although both Congress and the Department of State found the public generally apathetic on the issue, allowing the government a free hand, so to speak, members of Congress, compared to the Executive branch, heard more opposed views, more general statements of broad orientation and less technically informed arguments, and more statements referring to sovereignty, Nationalist China, and aid to Communism. Moreover these views were more likely to be communicated in face-to-face expression than was true of views expressed to the Executive branch. On the other hand, the Executive branch heard more about such tangible practical aspects as rearmament, fisheries, claims, and the effect of the treaty on the Japanese economy, more favorable, or at least balanced, opinions, and received these more often in written form. The ideologically-oriented groups and individuals were more likely to go to Congress; the more tangible, practical interests were more likely to go to the Executive branch. Whether this is a general pattern or not, remains to be seen, but there is some evidence that this is due to the focus of power in the Department of State in treaty making; on matters where Congress has the power for prescribing the detail of legislation, the tangible and specific representations may be made to congressmen.[33]

Writing to the President, as compared to both the administrative agencies and departments under him and Congress, may fulfill needs rather different from those satisfied in other cases. The President is a father figure in a way legislators seldom are, and letter writers may turn to him for vague, undefined help, or in order to complain of some general situation, or merely as a means of assuaging a general anxiety. Nor are such expressions useless; on the contrary, Louis Howe states that such letters received particular attention during Roosevelt's term in office.[34] But they may be less likely to refer to specific policies or to refer to matters directly in the news. Furthermore, status aspirants may naturally turn to what seems to them the highest authority, and may cherish a reply on White House stationery rather more than a reply from a legislator's office. As we shall see later, the turnout is almost always greater in elections for a chief executive than for any legislative offices,[35] and the similar psychic forces of dependency and need for vicarious power, as

30. L. A. Dexter, *op. cit.*, p. 23.
31. Wyant and Herzog, *op. cit.*, p. 599.
32. B. Cohen, *op. cit.*, p. 27.
33. *Ibid.*, p. 38.
34. Cited in L. Sussman, *op. cit.*, p. 13.
35. See p. 318.

well as the social forces focusing attention on the executive office, may be at work in both cases.

When Do People Write? Historically, as we have noted, the mail flow is likely to be greater in times of depression, national emergency, and war. Thus, just prior to our entry into the Spanish war, McKinley's mail swelled greatly;[36] at the time of the great Coal Strike of 1902 Theodore Roosevelt received an increased number of letters, and the increase in mail under FDR was at least partly due to the great depression of the thirties.[37] People write when an organized campaign is set on foot to "let your congressman know how you feel," as during the Burke-Wadsworth bill discussion in the late thirties. On the other hand, of those who reported having written to their congressmen or senators in 1946, two-thirds claimed to have initiated the move themselves,[38] although this no doubt exaggerates the spontaneity of the letter writers, and varies greatly with the content of the letters. People write when the chief executive appeals to the public to support him against a recalcitrant legislature. Thus, as Governor of New York State, Roosevelt appealed to the people over the heads of a reluctant legislature and ". . . the results were immediate. Mail came flowing into Albany, most of it in support of the Roosevelt position and most of it addressed to the working level of the legislature."[39] Later, as President, he employed the same device with such effect that legislators came to know that it was he, rather than they, who had "first claim" on the voters' allegiance. Perhaps this situation was duplicated for a time under the Eisenhower administration.

From such evidence and interpretation as has been presented certain facts and relationships appear probable.

Political participation through letter writing is related to (a) verbal skills and personal familiarity with written expression, (b) a capacity to crystallize the desire to write into a decision to write, (c) upper occupational and educational status, (d) membership in a subcultural group with appropriate cultural norms (Jews), (e) clear-cut economic stakes in specific governmental decisions (businessmen), (f) membership in organizations with stakes in legislative policy. Letter writing on policy issues is not associated with official position in the party organizations.

Over the past fifty years the number of letter writers has grown, proportionate to the population, faster than the per cent of eligible voters voting (on the basis of White House mail). In the short run, letter writing is more sensitive to national crises than is the rate of voting; over periods of a few decades the rate of letter writing sometimes follows trends opposite those followed by voting rates. Although "inspired" mail may come from non-voters, most letter writers are also voters.

Because much mail is written at the behest of organized groups there is often a concentration of letters from a given specific "sociological area" (principle of social focus). Another kind of concentration is promoted by the fact that much mail on a variety of subjects comes from "repeaters" (principle of plural voting).

36. L. Sussmann, *op. cit.*, p. 9.
37. *Idem.*
38. Hadley Cantril, *op. cit.*, p. 703.
39. Grace Tully, *FDR—My Boss* (New York: Scribners, 1949), p. 82, quoted in L. Sussman, *op. cit.*, p. 14.

Analysis of the content and timing of the Congressional mail on several issues reveals (a) greater responsiveness to issues with direct and immediate importance to a group as contrasted to issues with long-run and indirect importance, (b) general lack of knowledge of the substance of the issue, the congressman's position on the issue, the procedures required for enactment of a bill. The mail tends to consist of even-tempered statements of the author's plight, largely in economic terms, selectively supplemented by welfare rationalizations.

The selection of executive department or legislative targets for issue-oriented mail will depend upon (a) the respective powers of the two branches generally and on the specific matter involved (treaties being executive-centered, legislation, appropriation, etc., being legislative-centered); (b) ideological balance between the two branches; (c) the greater receptivity and sense of welcome afforded by the legislative branch; (d) the greater organized facility for inviting and receiving statements available in the legislative branch; and (e) personal needs for generalized reassurance from the President. The consequence of these differences may mean discrepant images of public opinion on a policy matter.

Letter writing is a function of (a) a sense of crisis such as is precipitated by war, civic disturbance, or depression, (b) the organization and sensitivity of interest groups, (c) formal appeals for support by the chief executive or other public figure, (d) apparent "warmth" or receptiveness of the chief executive or other addressee, (e) the sense of political efficacy of a given interested group on a given topic at a given time.

MEMBERSHIP IN POLITICAL ORGANIZATIONS

Although a person may belong to certain groups because of birth (family and ethnic groups), or because of choices relevant to other goals (occupation), there are many other groups that a person consciously decides to join because the group, as such, offers him certain advantages. We refer here to unions, business organizations, fraternal groups, recreational clubs, veterans organizations, farm groups, and, of course, political clubs. Joining these groups has political significance in several senses. For one thing, in joining them the individual is giving his support, intentionally or otherwise, to the organizations' *political activities,* whatever these may be. Where parties are weak, as in the United States, supporting these group political activities has special political significance. Second, joining the group opens up *channels of communication* between the individual and certain elites which often are used for transmitting political messages and attitudes. These may be two-way channels of communication such that the individual receives "the word" from association leaders and also, in turn, communicates his grievances to them. And, in the third instance, joining a political organization may be a deliberate means of advancing the political goals of the individual. In this case it is a means of *personal political expression.*

The American public is said to be made up of "joiners" and indeed there has long been evidence of a proliferation of voluntary organizations throughout the country of every possible type and description.[40] At the community level, one study shows 357 associations for a town of 17,000.[41] At the national and regional levels, the number of trade and professional associations, to cite only one kind, grew from around 1,000 in 1920 to about 3,000 in 1941.[42]

How political are these organizations? In what way is an organization political? Clearly, there are marked differences between a bowling club and a political club and these differences will undoubtedly be associated with the effect of the organization upon (1) the political process and (2) the political interests and motives of the individual members. In loose terms, one might establish a kind of rough dimension according to the degree of political content of an organization on which we could fit some of the data gathered in recent national studies:[43]

Belong to a political club or political organization (1952)	2%
Belong to an organization that sometimes takes a stand on housing, better government, school problems or other public issues (c1948)	31%
Belong to a formal organization of any kind (1952)	64%

The number of people belonging to strictly political clubs or organizations, however, is, like most political activity, distributed unevenly throughout the United States. On the whole, it seems much higher in metropolitan areas (10 per cent of the population of New York belonged to organizations in 1944), and, unlike voting, tends to be higher among Catholics than among Jews, no doubt a reflection of ethnic subcultural values. Compared to other forms of "joining," moreover, there is very little tendency for upper-income people to join political clubs in greater proportions than those on a lower income level.[44] And for a good reason: "Many of the activities of political clubs are identical with those of the social clubs."[45] Since the middle classes have other social clubs to take care of these interests, the political club, with a neighborhood basis and no pretensions of exclusiveness, fills a social as well as a political purpose for the working class urban dweller. Thus joining such an organization may be a political act in the sense that it is prompted by a

---

40. See A. De Tocqueville, *Democracy in America,* Phillips Bradley edition (New York: Knopf, 1945), Vol. II, p. 106.

41. W. Lloyd Warner and Paul S. Lunt, *The Social Life of a Modern Community* (New Haven, Yale University Press, 1941), p. 303.

42. Leroy W. Marceron and Calvert J. Judkins, *Selected Trade Associations of the United States* (Washington, D.C.: U.S. Dept. of Commerce, 1935); Calvert J. Judkins, *Trade and Professional Associations of the United States* (Washington, D.C.: U.S. Government Printing Office, 1952).

43. A. Campbell and associates, *The Voter Decides* (Evanston: Row, Peterson, 1954), p. 30; J. Woodward and E. Roper, *op. cit.,* p. 874; Survey Research Center, Ann Arbor, Michigan, unpublished material, 1952.

44. G. Saenger, *op. cit.,* p. 105.

45. Roy V. Peel, *The Political Clubs of New York City* (New York: Putnam's, 1945), pp. 127-28.

concern about elections, candidates, or issues, or even patronage, but it may not be.

The political nature of organizations that take stands on issues (so that this feature is sufficiently important to be recalled by respondents) varies from time to time. A business association, like the Connecticut Manufacturers Association, reveals, through the content of its journal, a steadily declining interest in government and politics from 1937 to 1946 (omitting the war years) and an increasing interest in the problems of production.[46] On the other hand, a steady rise in the political interests of unions (particularly since the passage of the Taft-Hartley Act) during this same period may be noted.[47] By and large it seems to be true that the closer the attachment of the individual to such an organization, the more he adopts the organization's political line and reveals an over-all political involvement.[48]

As for other formal associations, their political effects will be noted chiefly in increasing the opportunities for political discussion and other political stimuli. In this connection, the homogeneity of the organization is important. Persons in organizations which are socially homogeneous are more likely to talk politics, since, under these circumstances, it is a less divisive topic. And, when there is such talk, the consequences are likely to be the reinforcement of political predispositions, a phenomenon which tends to increase political interest and emotion.[49] Since, in most areas, social class and ethnic membership are related to political preference, one may consider inter-class and inter-ethnic groups as less political in their content and effect than other groups. Of interest in this connection is the finding in Yankee City that even though three times as many people belonged to large associations (membership over eighty) as to small ones (twenty or under), very few associations included all classes (in a six-class system) and, of course, even fewer included only one. Most of the associations were composed of two and three adjacent class memberships. Similarly, about half of the associations were limited to only one religious group—Protestant only 35 per cent, Catholic only 11 per cent, Jewish only 3 per cent, and Greek Orthodox only 1 per cent—the remainder combining these groups in different patterns and only 5 per cent being totally inclusive.[50] The social "bridging" function of associations and their politicizing function are, we suggest, inversely correlated.

Answers to the question of who joins these various formal associations across the nation is provided by some unpublished material gathered by the Survey Research Center in their 1952 election survey. Table 5.3 gives a pic-

46. See Robert E. Lane, *The Regulation of Businessmen* (New Haven: Yale University Press, 1954), pp. 53-54.

47. See Fay Calkins, *The CIO and the Democratic Party* (Chicago: University of Chicago Press, 1952).

48. A. Kornhauser and associates, *op. cit.*, pp. 150-52.

49. An illustration of the influence of political disagreement in inhibiting political conversation with others in the same organization is seen in the fact that in the United Automobile Workers Union in Detroit fewer Eisenhower supporters talked politics with co-workers than did Stevenson supporters. A Kornhauser and associates, *When Labor Votes* (New York: University Books, 1956), p. 77.

50. W. L. Warner and P. S. Lunt, *op. cit.*, pp. 346, 349.

ture of the demographic correlates of participation in formal associations. A few of the relationships shown in this table may be quickly observed. Belonging to associations is more closely associated with education and income than any other factor, a relationship also supported by other studies.[51] Farmers, probably because of their more isolated situations, are not good joiners; the young and the elderly are less likely to belong to many associations than are the people in their middle years. Although joining is related to urbanization, the size of the city doesn't make much difference; in spite of their lower educational and economic status, Negroes are more likely to belong to several organizations than are whites;[52] sex doesn't make much difference; New England and the Midwest are the areas of high association membership.

But if the United States has proliferated associations, and membership in these associations is widespread, one should not overlook the fact that many people belong to no groups at all and many more belong only to one.[53] In the Survey Research Center Study 36 per cent of all respondents belonged to no organizations whatsoever, and this is a low estimate compared to the information from certain metropolitan centers (where memberships are usually greater).[54]

It would not be appropriate to conclude this brief review of the type of political behavior we have called "joining groups" without some reference to the social movement. By and large this is distinguished by (a) the development of an ideology or a substantial part thereof, (b) an organizational framework which, if it includes a political party (like the Socialist party) is not limited to the party, and (c) an enduring quality which carries it beyond the transitory appearance of a fad or an *ad hoc* group.[55] Such movements are usually peripheral to the main political events in the American low tension scheme of things, but even on the periphery they exercise influences and, in times of crisis, they may be of overwhelming importance for certain segments of the population. Here we only note their existence as special cases of political associations with high political content, high intensity of emotion, and various degrees of social influence throughout the society.

---

51. W. L. Warner and P. S. Lunt, *op. cit.*, p. 329; Paul F. Lazarsfeld, Bernard R. Berelson and Hazel Gaudet, *The People's Choice*, 2nd ed. (New York: Columbia University Press, 1948), p. 145.

52. See also, Gunnar Myrdal, *An American Dilemma* (New York: Harper & Brothers, 1944), Vol. 2, pp. 952-55.

53. See Bernard Barber, "Participation and Mass Apathy in Associations," in Alvin W. Gouldner, ed., *Studies in Leadership* (New York: Harper & Brothers, 1950), p. 483.

54. Mirra Komarovsky, "The Voluntary Associations of Urban Dwellers," *American Sociological Review, 11* (1946), 686-98.

55. For discussion of social movements in various contexts, see: Theodore Abel, "The Pattern of a Successful Political Movement," *American Sociological Review, 2* (1937), pp. 347-52; Hadley Cantril, *The Psychology of Social Movements* (New York: Wiley 1941); Rudolf Heberle, *Social Movements, An Introduction to Political Sociology* (New York: Appleton-Century-Crofts, 1951); Harry W. Laidler, *Social Economic Movements* (New York: Crowell, 1948); Seymour M. Lipset, *Agrarian Socialism, The Cooperative Commonwealth Federation in Saskatchewan* (Berkeley and Los Angeles: University of California Press, 1950); Robert Michels, *Political Parties*, translated by Eden and Cedar Paul (Glencoe, Ill.: Free Press, 1949); Werner Sombart, *Socialism and the Social Movement*, translated by M. Epstein (New York, E. P. Dutton, 1909).

TABLE 5.3.—Some Demographic Correlates of Social Group Participation.

Demographic Variables	Total Number of Group Memberships					
	Two or More	One	None	Not ascertained	Total	Number of cases
Sex						
Male	35%	33%	32%	—	100%	240
Female	32	28	39	1	100	302
Race						
White	33	30	37	*	100	487
Negro	37	32	31	—	100	54
Age						
Under 30 years	23	33	43	1	100	92
30-44 years	40	33	26	1	100	198
45-59 years	36	30	34	—	100	141
60 years and over	27	24	49	—	100	103
Education						
Grade school	21	32	47	—	100	219
High school	37	32	31	*	100	242
College	58	22	19	1	100	80
Income						
Under $2,000	18	21	60	1	100	102
$2,000—4,999	31	35	34	—	100	299
$5,000 and over	53	26	20	1	100	131
Occupation of Head						
Professional and managerial	51	26	23	—	100	118
Other white collar	32	35	31	2	100	51
Skilled & semi-skilled	33	32	35	—	100	147
Unskilled	21	36	43	—	100	56
Farmers	25	33	40	2	100	67
Region						
Northeast	36	34	30	—	100	129
Midwest	39	29	31	1	100	198
South	25	29	46	—	100	149
Far West	29	30	39	2	100	66
Type of Community						
Metropolitan areas	35	31	34	—	100	147
Cities and towns	35	30	35	*	100	311
Open country	26	30	43	1	100	84

* Less than one-half of 1 per cent.

SOURCE: Survey Research Center, University of Michigan, Ann Arbor, Michigan. Based on a national sample, 1952.

Briefly, then, we may say:

Joining associations may be thought to be political in three senses: (1) It supports the pluralistic bases of political power and group representation. (2) It opens up a two-way channel of political communication between memberships and elites. (3) It is a means of expressing personal political interests.

The "politicalness" of an organization may be roughly graded according to the proportion of time and interest devoted to political content. Three points along this continuum would be represented by (a) political clubs, (b) (quasi-political) organizations that take stands on public issues, (c) other organizations. Outside this classification, and of varying degrees of importance, are the social movements.

Joining all such organizations generally follows the demographic pattern established for voting with the following exceptions: (1) Joining political clubs is not related to income and is more prevalent for Catholics than Jews. (2) Membership in formal associations of unspecified kinds is higher among Negroes than among whites. (3) Women are almost as likely to join associations as men.

Since an individual's purpose in joining a group and the purpose of the group may be at variance, the act of joining a political organization may or may not be related to a desire to achieve some political purpose, i.e., policy goal, electoral victory, or patronage reward.

For quasi-political organizations, the more attached a member is to the association, the more politically involved he is likely to be.

The more homogeneous the ethnic and status composition of an association, the more likely it is to have a high political content.

CHAPTER 6

Political Discussion: Who Listens to What?

Who Talks to Whom?

Even when members of the public are not voting, or electioneering, or communicating with public officials, they may yet be politically operative. As members of an audience whose opinions and beliefs are respected, or, if not that, perhaps feared by politicians, they shape public policy. Their casually expressed responses guide political leaders sensitive to public opinion—as does the uneasy anticipation of those responses which may remain unexpressed. The public is a sounding board for policy; the *audience function* of the electorate is a significant one, particularly in the United States.

This audience engages in discussion not as a cosmic Vox Populi but in small groups, among friends, in the home, the market, the factory. Such discussion serves to anchor each man's opinion in the culture of his life station. It is a form of reality testing. Without it public opinion tends to be hallucinatory, bloodless, and inoperative. We turn, then, to an analysis of how the electorate functions as an audience and how its members become engaged in political discussion. A concluding section deals generally with the political activists and the passivists, the doers and the listeners.

READING, VIEWING, AND LISTENING TO POLITICS

The media blanket the political market: television owners spend an average of two and a quarter hours a day "viewing" the passing scene; non-television owners spend two hours a day listening to the radio; five-sixths of the population read a newspaper regularly, and three-fifths of the population read

[80]

at least one magazine regularly.[1] The media are like the air we breathe—we are immersed in them and inhale their contents almost unconsciously. Exposure to them is, of course, politically significant chiefly insofar as the content of the media is political, although one should not minimize the shaping of political values by fiction, crime news, and human interest stories. At election time about half of the average newspaper front page is devoted to political and public affairs news and about an eighth of radio broadcast time is devoted to news and public affairs. As might be expected, between elections the news becomes less political and more general. Television, for example, devotes from 5 to 8 per cent of its time to news and public affairs between elections.[2] Although crude, these proportions suggest that the person with moderate exposure to the content of the media will be exposed to some political material relevant to his civic role.

Exposure of this nature may reflect an active search for political information or it may be accidental, "coming across" the material without intending to. Both of these have their impact upon the observer, but the second is more widespread than the first; more people run across political news than seek it out.[3] In the second place, reading the newspaper may mean a scanning of headlines only, or an actual reading of the news stories. A substantial proportion of the news readers in each community where studies have been made, are, as it turns out, merely headline readers, passing on to the comics, sports, or woman's page where their true interest lies.[4] People expose themselves to different numbers of media. Therefore, in the third place, we might say that there are the single medium and the multi-media exposed. About an eighth of the population in 1952 were exposed to but a single medium (and about 6 per cent were non-exposers), the rest being multi-media exposed.[5] Finally, in this short illustration of various kinds of exposure, we may say there are the consumers and the retailers of news, that is, those who listen and learn for their own benefit or amusement or to relieve their boredom, and

1. These data and other figures on the characteristics of the general newspaper, radio, television, and magazine audience come from the following sources: American Institute of Public Opinion, *Release,* July 12, 1945; Angus Campbell and Charles A. Metzner, *Public Use of the Library and other Sources of Information* (Ann Arbor, Mich.): Institute for Social Research, 1950), pp. 47-60; United States Department of Agriculture, *Extension Service Circular 490—1953;* Bureau of the Census, Housing and Construction Reports, *Housing Characteristics,* Series H-121, No. 1, 1955.

2. See pp. 276-7. The content and effectiveness of the media is discussed further in Chapter 19. The present discussion focuses on the nature of the audience.

3. Bernard R. Berelson, Paul F. Lazarsfeld, William N. McPhee, *Voting* (Chicago: University of Chicago Press, 1954), p. 244.

4. An early report on readership habits may be found in Walter Lippmann, *Public Opinion* (New York: Macmillan, 1922). More recent confirming evidence is available in Survey Research Center, *Interest, Information and Attitudes in the Field of World Affairs* (Ann Arbor, Mich.: Survey Research Center, 1949, mimeographed); Wilbur Schramm and David M. White, "Age, Education, and Economic Status as factors in Newspaper Reading: Conclusions," in W. Schramm, ed., *The Process and Effects of Mass Communications* (Urbana, Ill.: University of Illinois Press, 1954), pp. 71-73.

5. Angus Campbell, Gerald Gurin, Warren E. Miller, *The Voter Decides* (Evansville, Ill.: Row Peterson, 1954).

those who report and talk about what they have heard.[6] The most active of these are the opinion leaders, about which more later.

The more education a person has the more likely he is to read magazines and books, but he is not more likely to listen to the radio and only a little more likely to go to the movies.[7] These latter mass media—radio and movies —can, therefore, address "their own," that is, the masses, with relatively pure mass culture. As for newspaper reading, the college educated person is not much more likely to be exposed to the daily press, but is more likely to read more than one newspaper, and, moreover, is more likely to read the paper for what it contains by way of information on public affairs. This is in contrast to the scanning of the paper for "entertainment, sensational news, and pictorial material" by the less well educated, for whom, apparently, the news has less value and makes less sense.[8] Incidentally, at the very bottom of the educational level, about a third of those who never completed grammar school never see a newspaper. As for television, although at one point (1953) the college educated were less likely to have sets than the high school educated, today one may assume that television, in urban communities at least, is almost as universal as the newspaper and radio. Furthermore, reliance on TV for campaign information is about the same at different educational levels, although the better educated are more likely to supplement television viewing with reading matter. Radio, on the other hand is more likely to be the favored medium of the poorly educated (1952). Finally, magazines are, to some extent, media with a primary appeal to the better educated groups, particularly the college educated.[9]

Now the better educated, generally, although not universally, are also better off financially and have more prestigeful occupations. Therefore, as we examine the data we find that what we have said of the better educated is also generally true of those who can be said to have higher socio-economic status, although there are a few differences (there is no decline in picture and cartoon reading and there is an increase in society and sports perusal as income increases—but not as education increases).[10] But if one culls from this better educated, wealthier group a special elite of those with national influence, particularly in foreign affairs, it appears that some new reading and listening patterns emerge. Persons in this group actively seek information, rather than merely receiving what is available. They read books and out-of-town papers

6. See Robert K. Merton, "Patterns of Influence: A Study of Interpersonal Influence and of Communications Behavior in a Local Community," in Paul F. Lazarsfeld and Frank N. Stanton, *Communications Research, 1948-1949* (New York: Harper and Bros., 1949); pp. 180-219.

7. See Paul F. Lazarsfeld and Patricia Kendall, *Radio Listening in America* (New York: Prentice-Hall, 1948), pp. 9-10; A. Campbell and C. A. Metzner, *op. cit.*

8. W. Schramm and D. M. White, *op. cit.*, pp. 72-73.

9. These statements represent an interpretation of complex and partially conflicting evidence in Angus Campbell, Gerald Gurin, and Warren E. Miller, "Television and the Election," *Scientific American, 188* (1953), pp. 47-48; Morris Janowitz and Dwaine Marvick, *Competitive Pressure and Democratic Consent* (Ann Arbor, Mich.: University of Michigan Institute of Public Administration, 1956), pp. 60-61.

10. W. Schramm and D. M. White, *op. cit.*, p. 73.

and rely on these to a much larger extent. In this group the radio-TV audience disappears almost to the vanishing point, at least insofar as reliance for foreign affairs interpretation is concerned.[11] In combination, these findings on education and elite groups will lead us to various conclusions: To one person they may suggest that there is a kind of democracy of the media—something for everyone. To another they will imply an unfair class advantage for the upper status and income groups. A third person may feel that managers and leaders of the society are those who are most fit for these positions because they are the more informed and the better equipped.

Geographically, of course, newspapers and radio, and now, perhaps, television cover the nation from coast to coast. Yet the homogeneity is not complete because of the relatively greater reliance upon radio in the rural areas and in the South—although in these places television may soon challenge the radio (and perhaps already has). In such places, it appears, the newspapers are of less significance in conveying political news.[12] Whether this is because of an "income effect" or "educational effect," or because the newspaper is less readily available and less prompt in delivery, or for some other reason is uncertain. However that may be, there are unexplored reasons here for the prevalence of hillbilly music or the persistence of "old fashioned oratory" in the South.

As for sex differences in listening habits, one is not surprised to learn that women are more likely than men to prefer radio to newspapers and to derive more political news from that source.[13] No doubt there are deeper reasons, but the fact that women can do their housework with the radio turned on while men can scarcely ever listen to the radio while on the job has something to do with the case. It is more surprising, however, to find that women are almost as likely as men to read the articles and editorials on "government and political activity."[14] Nor is age irrelevant to political exposure, at least when it comes to the content of newspaper reading. As Schramm and White point out, "There are noteworthy declines of reading of comics and sports with age, noteworthy increases in the reading of public affairs news and editorials. Editorials, which are near the bottom in the ten to twenty bracket, are second only to news pictures in the over sixty bracket."[15] Evidently a life of work outside the home, with its responsibilities, social contacts, and training in the relevance of political "abstractions" enhances the individual's interest in public policy.

Now it may be true that each of several social groups has, so to speak, its own medium and even its special content, but it is also true that there is considerable overlap in the audiences. Indeed, at least two investigations have

---

11. See Kenneth P. Adler and Davis Bobrow, "Interest and Influence in Foreign Affairs," *Public Opinion Quarterly, 20* (1956), pp. 89-101.

12. A. Campbell, G. Gurin and W. Miller, "Television and the Election," p. 47.

13. *Ibid.*

14. *Readership Dimensions of The Newspaper,* Research Division, University of Minnesota School of Journalism, March 1948, p. 14. This is a study of readership of a Minneapolis morning paper, Feb. 21-26, 1948. The sample size was 833.

15. W. Schramm and D. White, *op. cit.,* p. 71.

found that if a person is exposed to one medium he is more likely to be exposed to others as well, and if he is "high" in listening and reading political material at one time, he is also more likely to be "high" at another time.[16] Although we do not find this stated anywhere, the simplest way of thinking of these overlapping audiences is in terms of a (Guttman) scale such that exposure to (though not necessarily reliance on) the less popular medium is inevitably associated with exposure to the more popular medium: TV viewing, newspaper reading, magazine reading, book reading. Radio and movies are out of this scale, because they have no clear relationship to further exposure activities.

The personal qualities of the readers and listeners—the political audience —suggest a hopeful theme that runs through the body of literature on political behavior. On the whole, in contrast to non-readers and non-viewers, they are a better informed group, more self-confident, more self-aware, and less neurotic, as well as better educated.[17] This is more true of the reading and viewing public than the radio public, but it is generally true across the board. They are more likely to know their party's program and to support it; they are more likely to vote and so to put it across. Nor are these qualities artifacts due to the higher status and education of the "exposed"—they tend also to be true within status ranks. As Janowitz and Marvick note, people with these several qualities are less susceptible of manipulation, are more likely to judge for themselves where their true interest lies than has sometimes been supposed, although the personal resistances to such manipulation may still be rather weak.[18]

Looking now at the media, rather than the audiences, we see that each has its special effectiveness. Leaflets and mailing, if these may be called media, seem generally ineffective: people cannot remember whether they received them or not and even if they do, they evoke minimal responses. Magazines are said to be effective, not only because they reach the better educated and hence presumably the leaders who pass along their messages, but also because of their special group appeal. They come, as it were, as friendly and familiar spokesman for a point of view, or a profession, or a special group which already has the ear and support of their recipients. Television is said by more people (1952) to be the "most important source" of news than any other medium and is considered more trustworthy than the newspapers (at least in urban labor groups). By and large, it has won its place at the expense of radio, not newspapers and magazines. The radio, like television, but not like the newspapers or magazines, personalizes its message—the message comes from an individual with whom the listener and viewer can establish, if only in fantasy, some kind of personalized relationship. And the newspaper, while not the "most important source," is the most widespread source of informa-

---

16. Paul F. Lazarsfeld, Bernard Berelson, and Hazel Gaudet, *The People's Choice,* 2nd ed. (New York: Columbia University Press, 1948), p. 122; B. Berelson, *et al., op. cit.,* p. 242.

17. M. Janowitz and D. Marvick, *op. cit.,* pp. 62-66; B. Berelson and associates, *op. cit.,* p. 243.

18. *Ibid.,* p. 62.

tion and has the largest coverage.[19] Political ideas are conveyed in many ways to many strata of the population; or, put differently, there are tastes and habits in reading and listening which lead to a variety of political exposure in the course of a day. Finally, lest the motive for reading and listening and viewing political material be confused with the social, political, or civic purposes achieved, we may turn for a moment to an examination of some of the personal functions performed by these activities. Thus, a man reads the paper or listens to the news on radio and television to provide material with which to increase his prestige, either as he barters this in conversation or as he imagines himself in a statesman's shoes. He reads and listens because he needs the information to get along in his job or with his family, or, if he doesn't need it for this, he may, nevertheless, feel anxious if he isn't *au courant,* or doesn't know the score—or the ropes. He reads and listens to get some respite from the anxieties of the day: politics is said to be dull, but for some it is a hobby or a fantasy. People escape into politics from family or other worries, just as they escape from politics when the political area creates nervous tension. Political material gives meaning to inescapable events which are more threatening when they are uninterpreted than when interpreted in some kind of framework.[20] Reading and listening and viewing will serve these various needs for the citizens of a democracy if, as in our society, the material is made "easy" and readily available.

Reviewing these data and interpretations of the nature and incidence of exposure to political material in the media, we suggest the following hypotheses.

Exposure to political material may be classified according to (a) the intent and interest of the person exposed, (b) the superficiality or depth of the reading or listening, (c) the number of media to which a person exposes himself, and (d) the use to which it is put: consumption or retailing.

Exposure to political material generally increases with status (income, occupation, education); the leaders of society are the most exposed and, therefore, the most likely to be informed on general political developments.

Exposure to political material is generally greater in those with personality qualities which make for more effective, self-confident social human beings.

Each medium has a characteristic audience and characteristic effectiveness: The newspaper has the widest coverage and greater effectiveness in the middle and upper status than in other groups. Television with an inter-class appeal is more likely to be trusted than the press and is generally more likely to be cited as the most important source of campaign news. Radio reaches into the South and the

---

19. On the effectiveness of these various media see, in addition to Chapter 19 below, Joseph T. Klapper, "The Comparative Effects of the Various Media," in Wilbur Schramm, ed., *The Process and Effects of Mass Communication* (Urbana, Ill.: University of Illinois Press, 1954); Arthur Kornhauser, Albert J. Mayer, and Harold Sheppard, *When Labor Votes* (New York: University Books, 1956), pp. 78-84.

20. Bernard Berelson, "What 'Missing the Newspaper' Means," in Paul F. Lazarsfeld and Frank N. Stanton, eds., *Communications Research, 1948-49* (New York: Harper & Bros., 1949), pp. 111-29; Ralph O. Nafziger, Warren C. Engstrom, and Malcolm S. MacLean, Jr., "The Mass Media and Informed Public," *Public Opinion Quarterly, 15* (1951), pp. 105-14.

rural regions and, more than the press, personalizes its messages. Magazines are most effective with college educated groups in contrast to others, and have a persuasiveness based upon special interests shared with their readers.

Exposure to political matter satisfies a range of human needs not confined to the advancement of political goals.

POLITICAL DISCUSSION

The political content of conversation varies enormously from place to place and time to time. Tocqueville noted a very high political content in the conversations around him;[21] more recent commentators have been likely to note its absence, particularly in the conversation of the "upper classes." Andrew Carnegie commented in 1886, "One hears more political discussion at a dinner in London than during the whole season in New York or Washington," attributing this partly to a greater consensus in America on the nation's fundamental laws.[22]

In spite of these comments, however, political discussion of one sort or another is almost universal today in the United States. Some 83 per cent of the people in Elmira and 78 per cent of the United Automobile Workers in Detroit report that they engaged in political discussion during the 1948 and 1952 campaigns.[23] Furthermore, even between campaigns, there is substantial discussion of matters with political relevance. In "Midwest Community A" between 70 and 80 per cent of the population report discussing "public affairs."[24] Stimulated by the media, and often motivated by their own partisan feelings, the American public does, in some fashion, engage in political discussion.

The nature of this discussion is, of course, varied and complex for it reflects the personal qualities of the participants to an unusual degree, as well as the many situations in which they find themselves and the varied topics which are present in the news. A brief analysis of the nature of political discussion, then, might proceed to examine (a) the topics, (b) the situation, and (c) the participants of such discussion. As for the topics of political discussion, it seems clear that, by and large, these reflect the content of the media, although not with the same emphasis chosen by the editor. In a sense, therefore, we may characterize political discussion in the first instance as *reactive,* rather than as a spontaneous expression of personal problems. Political discussion serves as a distorted mirror of the media.

We may go farther than that, I think, and outline some of the principles

21. Alexis De Tocqueville, *Democracy in America,* Phillips Bradley edition (New York: Knopf, 1945), Vol. I, pp. 248-49.

22. Andrew Carnegie, *Triumphant Democracy* (New York: Scribners, 1886), pp. 471-72.

23. Berelson and associates, *op. cit.,* p. 102n; A. Kornhauser and associates, *op. cit.,* p. 77.

24. George Belknap and Ralph Smuckler, "Political Power Relations in a Mid-West City," *Public Opinion Quarterly,* 20 (1956), p. 78.

which guide this selective reaction to political news as reflected in the media. Four of these may be set forth as follows:

The general public (a cross section of the population) will tend to talk more about politically important people than about issues.[25]

The public will tend to talk more about the concrete than about the abstract elements of politics.

The public will tend to talk more about domestic affairs than about foreign affairs.

The public will tend to talk disproportionately (compared to the press) about the violation of moral norms in public life (scandal).

The last of these "principles" is in line with another, larger, and more inclusive theory of "rumor." Political rumor dealing with "secret deals," corruption, and patronage "payoffs" is in many ways similar to rumor in wartime and partakes of the "hate-fear-wish" trichotomy which was found to be salient in such rumors.[26] This kind of content would, according to the theory, be higher in periods of stress, such as campaign periods, for those with partisan views on political matters.[27] Undoubtedly, in America, where political involvement is low, political discussion has fewer of these rumor characteristics than does European politics.

Judging from what is known of the participants and circumstances of political discussion, however, the most substantial "theme" in political discussion will be the reciprocal expression of agreed upon political cliches and stereotypes.[28] It is rewarding to express them both because one thereby shows that he is in the appropriate subculture and role position and because one's audience reacts with flattering expressions of agreement. It is rewarding to hear such opinions expressed because of the common bond established—through the confirmation of one's own "opinion" or the opportunity for agreeing with the spokesman. Even rumors which, through a process called "assimilation" are often forced to serve the communicators' prejudices and stereotypes, conform to this pattern.

One further point on the "topics" of political discussion should be made, a point related to the manipulation of stereotypes. There is a difference between what may be called the manifest topic and the latent topic. The manifest topic refers to the denotative meaning of the words and phrases used. But not infrequently the purpose of the conversation, the topic salient in the conversationalists' minds is something quite different, as when the message conveyed is "I know important people" (the name-dropper), or "You don't know as much about this as you thought you did," (gamesmanship), or "I

25. In this respect discussion will exaggerate an emphasis already present in the media. See LeRoy C. Ferguson and Ralph Smuckler, *Politics in the Press, An Analysis of Press Content in the 1952 Senatorial Campaign* (East Lansing, Mich.; Michigan State University, 1954), pp. 27-45.

26. See Robert H. Knapp, "A Psychology of Rumor" *Public Opinion Quarterly, 8* (1944), pp. 22-37.

27. See Gordon W. Allport and Leo Postman, "An Analysis of Rumor," *Public Opinion Quarterly, 10* (1946-47), pp. 501-17.

28. See Berelson and associates, *op. cit.*, pp. 106-109.

dislike radicals so don't you talk like one." In an important sense these latent topics are the significant themes of political discussion, however little they appear in survey analysis. Probably the latent topics will be relatively more important among the less well educated and the personally insecure.

As for the situations which provoke political discussion, we know not only that political discussion is greater in periods of political campaigns than in other periods, but also that political discussion increases both in amount and intensity as the campaign progresses.[29] Inasmuch as political discussion is a reflection of press treatment (with some feedback, of course), it will follow the crises in foreign affairs, race conflict, partisan conflict in the legislature, and other headline making events. Furthermore, there is a fatigue principle or a pressure toward closure which, if the matter "drags on too long," will bring discussion to a terminus whether or not the event is concluded.[30] Finally, it is certainly clear from several community studies that opportunity has a lot to do with political discussion: the person who has more community contacts, more organizational memberships, and more leisure is likely to be a greater political talker.[31]

The situation in which political discussion takes place determines not only the extent, but also the character of the discussion. For example:

Political discussion in groups or organizations where politics is "group relevant," that is, a salient feature of group or organizational goals, will tend to be more consensual than in groups where politics is not group relevant.[32]

Dominance in political discussion between persons occupying different social roles will pass to the person whose role is related to the topic of the discussion: Women more often assume the lead in discussion of local, particularly educational, affairs, men in the discussion of foreign affairs and economic policy.[33]

Political rumor will increase in proportion to the importance of the subject to the public *times* the ambiguity of the evidence pertaining to the topic.[34]

More is known about the characteristics of the relationship between political conversationalists than about the circumstances which promote and inhibit discussion. Summarizing some of the evidence one can again suggest certain principles along these lines:

During a political campaign people are more likely to talk politics with people who agree with them on their vote decisions than with those who disagree with them.[35]

On the other hand, this principle does not reverse itself; agreement on vote

---

29. *Ibid.*, p. 30; Kornhauser and associates, *op. cit.* pp. 216-17.

30. See Gordon W. Allport and Janet M. Faden, "The Psychology of Newspapers: Five Tentative Laws," *Public Opinion Quarterly, 4* (1940), pp. 687-703.

31. Berelson and associates, *op. cit.*, pp. 111-12.

32. Stanley Schacter, "Deviation, Rejection, and Communication," *Jouranl of Abnormal and Social Psychology, 46* (1951), pp. 190-207. A report on a replication of this study on a different population is available in Richard M. Emerson, "Deviation and Rejection: An Experimental Replication," *American Sociological Review, 19* (1954), pp. 688-93.

33. James G. March, "Husband-Wife Interaction Over Political Issues," *Public Opinion Quarterly, 17* (1953-54), pp. 461-70.

34. Allport and Postman, *op. cit.*, p. 503.

35. Berelson and associates, *op. cit.*, p. 106.

decision is not, by itself, associated with political discussion. Evidently, agreement serves as a facilitating factor in the presence of some other stimulus to discussion.[36] This principle has a corollary which helps to explain some apparent discrepancies in the data:

Talking politics is different from, and much more frequent than, efforts at political persuasion.

This comes to light when one notes that although 78 per cent of a sample of the UAW in Detroit reported that they talked politics, only about half that number stated that they talked to people in an effort "to help get their candidate elected."[37] In response to a question on this latter kind of discussion in a national survey, only 27 per cent of the population stated that they talked to people "to try to show them why they should vote for one of the parties or candidates."[38]

One reason why political discussion is likely to take place between people who agree with one another is that, like other interaction, it tends to take place in socially homogeneous groups: within the family, within the same occupational strata, and, to some extent, within ethnic boundaries.[39] Since these group memberships are all related to political outlook, it is not so surprising that consensual discussion is the most usual kind.

What happens, however, when political conversation takes place across group lines? In almost all such situations there are status differences which tend to affect the outcome: men have higher status in our society than women; older people generally have higher status than younger persons; upper socio-economic groups have greater status than lower ones. The evidence suggests that:

1. The lower status partner tends to initiate more such cross-status political conversations than the upper-status partner[40] (in spite of Homan's report that higher-status people are more likely to initiate interaction in cross-status situations).
2. The lower status person is more likely to report agreement with the upper-status person than is the higher-status person to report agreement with the lower-status person.[41]
3. The lower-status person is more likely to remember and value the conversation than the upper-status person.

With reference to the socio-economic status differences, we are reminded of Riesman's discussion of the "conversations across the railroad tracks," where the point of view is expressed that a two-way and relatively tolerant communication takes place.[42] Examination of the Elmira data confirms that this is indeed the case, and that, in point of fact, the middle proposition above,

36. *Ibid.*, p. 108.

37. Kornhauser and associates, *op. cit.*, pp. 77, 125. See also Woodward and Roper, "Political Activity of American Citizens," *American Political Science Review*, 44 (1950), p. 874.

38. Campbell and associates, *op. cit.*, p. 30.

39. Berelson and associates, *op. cit.*, p. 105.

40. *Ibid.*, p. 104*n*.

41. *Ibid.*, p. 107.

42. David Riesman, *The Lonely Crowd* (New Haven, Conn.: Yale University Press, 1950), pp. 257-60.

while suggestive, is somewhat tenuous. There is only a slight degree of difference (75 per cent to 65 per cent) in the tendency of people in one socio-economic class to report agreement with those in the other, and both see much more agreement than disagreement.

Opinion Leaders. We have noted that there is a difference between the talkers and the persuaders, but there is one further stage which involves not only the effort to persuade but also being sought after for political opinions— or at least having the feeling that one is sought after. Bales distinguishes between those who seek and those who give orientation—here we mean the orientation givers.[43] In order to discover something about the differences between those who generally give political orientation, both the Erie County study and the Elmira study posed questions on this point: "Has anyone asked your advice on a political question recently?" (Erie County, 1940); and "compared with the people you know, are you more or less likely than any of them to be asked your views about politics?" (Elmira, June, 1948).

Those who seek orientation may be roughly said to be the following: wives seek political orientation from their husbands but not vice versa; in cases of inter-generational discussion the younger are more likely to go to older people for orientation; in discussion between people of different status, the lower-status seeks guidance from the upper-status person.[44]

The reverse side of the picture, the giving of political advice, is also suggested by the above data, but there are additional complications. There are certain people in every occupational stratum who generally give more orientation than they receive and/or are actively engaged in political persuasion. In the Erie County and the Elmira studies these people are termed opinion leaders. The two studies show the following distribution of opinion leaders by occupation.

Such a list raises the question of the social forces which turn a person into an opinion leader, or at least make it easy for him to be one. Put this way, it appears that being an opinion leader is an involuntary act, a product of place and position. That this is not wholly incorrect is suggested by the Elmira study, which shows that the following characteristics are associated with opinion leadership, *whether or not a person is interested in politics*:

1. Belonging to two or more organizations
2. Male sex
3. Know party workers
4. Talk politics outside the family

Thus, being placed in the role of a more knowledgeable person (male), being confronted with more opportunities to see people (belonging to more organizations), having some slight pipeline of party gossip (knowing a party worker), and being in a milieu where politics is talked about all combine to make for opinion leadership.[45]

---

43. For a basic analysis of the forms of interaction in certain kinds of discussion, see Robert F. Bales, *Interaction Process Analysis* (Cambridge, Mass.: Addison-Wesley, 1950).

44. Berelson and associates, *op. cit.,* pp. 102-106; March, *op. cit.*

45. Berelson and associates, *op. cit.,* p. 112.

TABLE 6.1.—Occupational Distribution of Opinion Leaders.

Erie County		Elmira	
Occupation	Per cent Opinion Leaders	Occupation	Per cent Opinion Leaders
Professional	35	Professional & Managerial	31
Proprietary, managerial	25		
Clerical	33	White collar	18
Commercial, sales	44		
Skilled workers	35	Skilled workers	27
Semi-skilled workers	32		
Unskilled workers	23	Semi- and unskilled	
Farmers	15		
Housewives	13	workers	22
Unemployed	15		
Retired	35		

SOURCE: P. F. Lazarsfeld and associates, "The People's Choice" (New York: Columbia University Press, 1948), p. 50; Berelson and associates, "Voting" (Chicago: University of Chicago Press, 1954), p. 377.

Situationally, the opinion leader has other distinctions. He is slightly better off than his following, and slightly better educated. These differences are slight, otherwise he would lose his capacity to be "one of the boys" and thus have their trust and confidence. And within the broad classifications of middle and working class, it will be seen in the above figures that the professional and managerial group supplies more opinion leaders than does the white collar clerical group; among the working class, the skilled workers supply more opinion leaders than do the semi- and unskilled workers.

But of course opinion leadership is much more than a product of situation and slightly superior status. It is also a product of greater interest, and the greater information and more clear-cut orientation with which this is associated. Opinion leaders on every educational level

are more interested in an election

have more information

are more exposed to the media

know more about the candidates' positions

feel that they have more influence on elections.

Thus there is a real reason for people to seek their advice and guidance, and for them to offer it and engage in persuasive activities. And, too, there is evidence that the influence of the opinion leaders may be to assist others to become more consistent in their orientation. On several issues (such as the Taft-Hartley Act, 1948), it has been shown that the opinion leaders more generally understand and support their party's position.[46]

---

46. *Ibid.*, pp. 111-14. For differences between "advisers" and "talkers" see Robert E. Aggar and Vincent Ostrom, "The Political Structure of a Small Community," *Public Opinion Quarterly, 20* (1956) pp. 81-89. Superior information alone will not make a person an opinion leader—see Elihu Katz and Paul F. Lazarsfeld, *Personal Influence* (Glencoe, Ill.: Free Press, 1955), p. 275.

In summary, then, we may consider the following hypotheses to be suggested by the evidence:

The political content of conversation varies according to place and class (it is higher in upper class England than in upper class United States; and according to time (it is lower in the United States in the twentieth century than it was in the early nineteenth century); according to the closeness of an election (more people talk politics in October than in June of an election year. Calendar elections give a regular periodicity to political conversation.

The content of political conversation will tend to emphasize (a) persons as contrasted to issues, (b) concrete events as contrasted to issues or principles, (c) domestic affairs as contrasted to foreign affairs, (d) the cliches and stereotypes of politics, (d) scandal, (f) media-stimulated topics as contrasted to self-initiated topics.

Political discussion will include latent content dealing with implications about the conversationalists and their emotions as well as manifest content referring to the topics discussed. The latent content will tend to increase with personal insecurity and decrease with amount of education.

Political discussion will increase generally with national and international tension, and media emphasis on politics; for any individual or group it will increase with exposure to most forms of interpersonal contact. It will decrease on any given topic according to a "natural" cycle of interest and fatigue.

Many more people talk politics than seek to persuade others of their point of view. Most "talkers" do not see themselves as contributing to the campaign effort of their party or candidate. Most political discussion is consensual and this is at least partly because it takes place in homogeneous age, status, and religious groups.

Political conversation across status lines is (a) usually initiated by the lower-status partner, (b) usually produces more statements of agreement from the lower-status partner, though the difference is small enough and the agreement is high enough to indicate a mutuality in the "conversation across the tracks."

Opinion leadership (giving political orientation to persons in personal contact) is (a) related to opportunity to acquire special knowledge and influence, (b) role positions which makes the leadership appropriate, including, (c) slightly higher education and income within a social stratum, and (d) greater personal interest and feelings of effectiveness.

POLITICAL ACTIVITIES: SPECIALIZATION AND GENERALIZATION

We have reviewed the kinds of popular political activity most frequently found in American democracy and have discussed briefly for each type of activity the nature of the behavior, its incidence among several social groups, and, where the information was available, its growth or decline. All of the activities, of course, vary in frequency and nature over time, with elections giving a kind of periodicity for most of them; and such events as international tension and war, economic recession and inflation, great changes in population, stimulating enhanced activity of the several kinds. Secularly, one might say that a growing proportion of the population has participated in the political activities described since the turn of the century and perhaps for a longer period. Certainly the letter writing, organization-joining, petitioning, listening, and "viewing" activities have increased in frequency and broadened in their population bases. Voting among the eligible has increased irregularly since 1920. On the whole it seems clear that more people, proportionate to the population (or even more men proportionate to the male population), engage in more political activities today than has been true for at least fifty years. That this has taken place without a parallel increase in emotional investment in politics is one of the more significant political phenomena of the time.

Looking broadly at the research findings in terms, not of change, but of contemporary incidence in the population—who is doing what—certain generally familiar relationships stand out. In the first place, there is a high degree of concentration of these activities in certain strata of the population. They are almost all related to socio-economic status so that there is a heavy overlap between the economic and professional leaders of society and the politically active group variously called "politists," "gladiators," or "activists." This is true for income, occupation, education, or other measures of socio-economic status. This does not mean, of course, that others are excluded—it only means that they are underrepresented in this active and influential group.

The other general relationships are equally familiar: men are more likely to be politically active than women, although this difference is growing smaller all the time. Within limits, older people are more likely to be politically active than younger people—except for certain kinds of activity such as joining associations where the middle years seem to bring forth greater activity. Nationality and religious differences are likely to vary according to the activity examined; Negro-white differences are not clear-cut. In the North Negroes vote as often as whites in their own income brackets, and belong to more organizations, but are less active in other ways. Regionally, one finds the South low in almost all forms of political activity—and the Northeast generally high.

If we examine the constellations of activity, not by historical periods nor by incidence in the population, but by patterns of associated activity, some new insights emerge. In the first place the fact that some activities are more general in the population than others suggests that there is a kind of latent structure in the pattern of political behavior. Is there an order in these various kinds of behavior such that everyone performing a less frequent act is overwhelmingly likely to have performed the next more frequent act? Experimental work along these lines shows that there is such a pattern for some populations for the following kinds of behavior:[47]

If a person electioneers he is almost certain to attend party meetings.

If a person attends party meetings he is almost certain to be among those who contact public officers and other political leaders.

If a person contacts public officers and leaders he is almost certain to be a member of some politically oriented (though not strictly political) association.

---

47. Frederick H. Harris, Jr., "A Study of Political Participation in Two North Carolina Counties," *Research Previews, 3,* (1955), pp. 1-7, issued by the Institute for Research in Social Science, Univ. of North Carolina (mimeographed).

If a person is a member of such an association he is almost certain to be a voter.

Notice that the relationship is a one way affair in the sense that voting, for example, does not imply membership in a quasi-political group and so forth. Also, it should be observed that this latent structure was found to hold true for one of two counties studied but not for the other. Patterns of associated behavior, then, vary from place to place. Also, certain kinds of activity did not fit this pattern: contributing funds, talking politics, and reading and listening to political material.

This reveals one kind of order in the pattern of political behavior, but the data also suggests another: "passive" exposure to political material forms a kind of "spectator" syndrome which is somehow different from the more active forms of behavior. Evidently there are those who are content to follow the news and, indeed, may be "interested" in politics and public affairs but have no inclination or capacity to do anything about it. Following our discussion of the difference between talking politics and attempting to persuade others, one might say that these people would also be the talkers but not the persuaders, a feature of their behavior which is also suggested by other studies.[48]

Voting itself seems to lie somewhere between the active and passive forms of political involvement. In some studies it is considered a separate form of behavior between the spectators and the activists, in others it is included in the spectator forms,[49] and in the latent structure study given above it appears to be the "lowest" element of the activist forms. No doubt it represents all three in the sense that for some people voting is a purely conventional and emotionally neutral activity, for others it is an important civic duty, while for still others it represents a means to a desired political end.

In review, then, we may say:

The ratio of political activists to the general population, and even the ratio of male activists to the male population, has generally increased over the past fifty years, but this has not been accompanied by rising intensity of emotion.

Political participation is a function of status, education, age, male sex. It is lowest in the South. Race, religion, and national-origin are complexly related to political activity of various specific kinds.

There is a "latent structure" pattern in most populations such that those who perform certain less frequent political acts are almost certain to perform *all* the more frequent acts. From least to most frequent these acts are: electioneering, attending party meetings, petitioning public officials, belonging to quasi-political associations, and voting.

Two constellations of participation seem to represent different psychic and social forces: (1) passive spectator behavior—the consumption of politics; (2) active participation designed or at least resulting in political change of some order. The act of voting represents a kind of mid-point between these two constellations.

---

48. See W. S. Robinson, "The Motivational Structure of Political Participation," *American Sociological Review, 17* (1952) pp. 151-56.

49. See Lester Milbrath, "Personality and Political Participation," a paper delivered at the annual meeting of the Southern Political Science Association, Gatlinburg, Tenn., November 9, 1956.

Part III

Political Man

CHAPTER 7

Why is the Study of Human Nature Important

for the Study of Electoral Behavior?

POLITICAL SCIENCE has always had to come to terms with the nature of man, the political animal. Plato (*Republic*) dealt with the problem of instilling in youth the qualities of character necessary for effective citizenship; Aristotle (*Politics*) remarked on the necessity of fitting the constitution of a city state to the character of the people; Hobbes (*Leviathan*) dealt with the question of national character and personality, under the heading "the interiour beginnings of voluntary motions commonly called the passions; and the speeches by which they are expressed;" and John Stuart Mill wrote:

. . . political machinery does not act of itself. As it is first made, so it has to be worked by men, and even by ordinary men. It needs not their single acquiescence, but their active participation; and must be adjusted to the capacities and qualities of such men as are available.[1]

These capacities and qualities are themselves articulated elements of a total personality system, the whole man. Allport puts it this way:

The political nature of a man is indistinguishable from his personality as a whole, and . . . his personality as a whole is not the sum-total of his specific reactions, but rather a congruent system of attitudes, each element of which is intelligible only in the light of the total pattern. A man's political opinions reflect the characteristic modes of his adjustment to life.[2]

Today this is a common view: ". . . ideology regarding each social area must be regarded as a facet of the total person and an expression of more central

---

1. John Stuart Mill, "Representative Government," in *Utilitarianism, Liberty, and Representative Government* (New York: Dutton, 1910, Everyman ed.), p. 177.

2. Gordon W. Allport, "The Composition of Political Attitudes," *American Journal of Sociology, 35* (1929-30), p. 238.

('subideological') psychological dispositions,"[3] and "look far enough into the origins of any opinion and one will find not just an opinion but a sample of how the holder of that opinion copes with his world."[4]

The answers to these questions about the nature of man color, perhaps even determine, a person's attitude toward alternative political systems. As we have seen, those who argue that man is educable, pacific, self-reliant, and rational are likely to be democrats; those who view man as instinct-ridden, belligerent, a creature of the mass-mind, and irrational, are likely to prefer some other political system. In one sense men's political behavior has demonstrated with rich variety that he is at different times everything that has been said about him on either side.

In a less global sense, the inquiry into the nature of man contributes to an understanding of political behavior within the democratic framework. Explanations of political decisions which rely wholly upon analyses of the social environment, while they may have high predictive value, neglect a vital link: they never explain why an individual *responds* to the environment the way he does. Such purely external analysis tends to presume that two individuals behaving in the same way in a given situation are responding identically. But as seen from the inside out, from the point of view of the individuals, the forces to which they respond may be quite dissimilar. For example, our analysis shows that persons rated as authoritarians according to one attitude scale, vote in about the same proportions as those rated as equalitarians. But the equalitarians respond to a sense of civic duty, to conscience, while the authoritarians respond to the pressure of their social groups to act conventionally, and possibly also to a desire to exercise a small degree of political power.[5]

Without knowing the attitudes on which a decision is based, the observer may generalize in a wholly wrong direction. In 1948 when political scientists predicted a Dewey victory on the basis of early surveys on attitudes toward the *candidates,* they were wrong partly because underlying *party* loyalties were for many people more salient than candidate preferences.[6] The opposite mistake, the misinterpretation of party loyalties as conclusive when a dramatic candidate in fact was perceived as the more salient feature of the election, occurred in 1952.[7] In a deeper sense, the phenomena of Communist party

---

3. T. W. Adorno and associates, *The Authoritarian Personality* (New York: Harper. 1950), p. 207.

4. M. Brewster Smith, Jerome S. Bruner, and Robert W. White, *Opinions and Personality* (New York: Wiley, 1956), p. 40.

5. Robert E. Lane, "Political Personality and Electoral Choice," *American Political Science Review, 49* (1955), pp. 173-90.

6. For a discussion of this and related problems, see Frederick Mosteller and associates, *The Pre-Election Polls of 1948* (New York: Social Science Research Council, 1949); Bernard R. Berelson, Paul F. Lazarsfeld, and William N. McPhee, *Voting* (Chicago: University of Chicago Press, 1954), pp. 253-76.

7. American Institute of Public Opinion, Release, Nov. 3, 1952. For confirming evidence see Angus Campbell, Gerald Gurin, and Warren E. Miller, *The Voter Decides* (Evanston, Ill.: Row, Peterson, 1954), pp. 165-77.

membership in the 1929-1940 depression, was misinterpreted as a function of economic deprivation, when, in fact, in the United States the party members, perhaps triggered by general economic failure, were dealing with the problem of acculturation, social adjustment, and the expression of a generalized hostility.[8]

If a purely social and external analysis has trouble "explaining" the behavior of those who do in fact behave in the expected direction, how much more difficult it is for such analysis to explain the deviants. If one finds that increased exposure to the media during election time is associated with higher rates of participation, one can, in a sense, explain the higher participation by the greater stimuli and the interest they arouse. But what shall the analyst do with those who were equally exposed and who failed to participate? A fruitful analysis must rely upon a psychologically informed interpretation of the meaning of exposure to different people.

The control over behavior given by a knowledge of the psychological processes at work in any situation is much greater than may be provided merely by a knowledge of the situation and the response. For example, while the study of the followers of nativist agitators through an analysis of the ideological themes presented and the membership of their various organizations gives a picture of what is happening in this area of politics, it gives very little idea of how it may be controlled. But if some insight is available into the psychic needs of the followers which are served by such agitation,[9] then an approach is possible through alternate means of satisfying those needs, or through reducing these needs by increasing other life satisfactions, or through giving self-insight to these audiences feeding on delusion, or in some other way.[10] Only when the intervening psychological variables are explored and brought into the analysis can many social problems (such as authoritarian politics, ethnic prejudice, or intolerant "Americanism") be brought under control.

In order not to overstate the case, let us be explicit on the limitations of psychological forces in political analysis. Some situations so clearly structure behavior; some roles leave so little room for personal choice; and some social norms are so unambiguous that personal differences have little effect upon behavior. On the other hand some situations afford considerable "scope" for personality to affect behavior. Among these are the following:

Situations where reference groups have politically conflicting points of view.

Situations at the focus of conflicting propaganda.

Current situations which for any individual are in conflict with previous experience.

---

8. See Gabriel Almond, *The Appeals of Communism* (Princeton: Princeton University Press, 1954).

9. See Bruno Bettelheim and Morris Janowitz, "Reactions to Fascist Propaganda—a Pilot Study," *Public Opinion Quarterly, 14* (1950), pp. 53-60.

10. See T. W. Adorno, "Democratic Leadership and Mass Manipulation," in Alvin W. Gouldner, ed., *Studies in Leadership* (New York: Harper, 1950), pp. 418-38.

Situations where social roles are ambiguous, strange, and unfamiliar.

Some types of behavior are less likely to offer scope for the expression of personal differences. These would, by and large, include the more conventional items, such as voting, expressing patriotic opinions, and accepting election results as final, at least temporarily. On the other hand, those types of expression which are more likely to reveal the idiosyncratic features of personality include:

Selection of the grounds for rationalizing a political act.

Selecting topics for political discussion.

Selecting types of political behavior over and above voting.

Expression of the probable consequences of participation.

Holding particular images of other participants.

Styles of personal interaction in political groups.

In the following discussion, then, we search first into the basic motives or drives which induce a person to play a political role, analyzing how these drives are harnessed to politics. We then seek to characterize the most important attitudes of "political man" in twentieth century America. By and large this discussion deals with the ordinary voter, the Democrats and Republicans of modern America, rather than the eccentric, the radical, the alienated man on the fringes of democratic politics.

CHAPTER 8

What Conscious Needs are Served by

Participation in Political Life?

ECONOMIC, SOCIAL, AND INTELLECTUAL NEEDS

OF WHAT USE to a man is his politics? As Graham Wallas points out, it is unfruitful to say that men in politics are self-interested. That only leads to the further question: which interests? He criticizes the over-rational approaches of the utilitarians, and deals instead with the political expression of such "impulses" as affection, fear, laughter, the desire for property, the "fighting instinct," "suspicion, curiosity, and the desire to excel."[2] Lasswell concurs in the impulse theory, but believes that their expression in politics represents a displacement from areas of private life.[3]

Another possible approach is through the study of values: Which values do men pursue through political instruments? Lasswell suggests that these values are: power, wealth, well-being, skill, enlightenment, affection, rectitude and respect—and it is true that men do seek these values in politics[4]. It is said that men join social movements because some object, person, or idea has become "ego-involved"—and this idea of the extension of the self to include selected

1. This is the Benthamite formula. Even the critics of Bentham, like Macaulay, assumed that men adapted their politics to serve conscious self-interest. "When we see the actions of a man, we know with certainty what he thinks his interest to be," quoted in Graham Wallas, *Human Nature in Politics* (Boston: Houghton Mifflin, 1909), p. 22. On this see David Riesman's discussion of "self-interest: death of a motive," in his *Faces in the Crowd* (New Haven: Yale University Press, 1952), p. 33.

2. Wallas, *op. cit.*, pp. 21-38.

3. Harold D. Lasswell, "Psychopathology and Politics," reprinted in *The Political Writings of Harold D. Lasswell* (Glencoe, Ill.: Free Press, 1951), pp. 74-77.

4. Harold D. Lasswell, *The World Revolution of Our Time* (Stanford, Cal.: Stanford University Press, 1951), p. 6.

features of society is useful⑤ Smith, Bruner, and White believe that men develop their political opinions to meet three needs: (1) to understand the world and to control events, (2) to get along well with others, and (3) to express psychic tensions.[6]

While all of these views are partially true, and frequently useful, it has served our purposes to develop the following grammar of political motives. These are the needs served by men's political activity.

1. Men seek to advance their economic or material well-being, their income, their property, their economic security through political means.
2. Men seek to satisfy their needs for friendship, affection, and easy social relations through political means.
3. Men seek to understand the world, and the causes of the events which affect them, through observing and discussing politics.
4. Men seek to relieve intra-psychic tensions, chiefly those arising from aggressive and sexual impulses, through political expression.
5. Men seek power over others (to satisfy doubts about themselves) through political channels.
6. Men generally seek to defend and improve their self-esteem through political activity.

These are not mutually exclusive motives, they are overlapping and leave lacunae, but they are "real" in the sense that their connection with political acts can be traced, and they are at the focus of attention of those who have discussed human nature in politics in the last thirty or forty years.

POLITICS AND THE PURSUIT OF ECONOMIC GAIN

Here lies the substance of the older economic interpretations of politics: a man adopts those opinions and undertakes those activities which advance his material well-being. He protects his property by an interest in governmental economy implemented by a contribution to the local taxpayers' research bureau. He advances his security (certainty of income) by writing a letter to the President urging an extension of social security for the self-employed. He votes for a candidate because that candidate seems to be "for people like me"—a motive which combines many elements but includes the hope that the voters' economic interests will be favored. There is no doubt that, along with the political pursuit of other needs, men pursue economic gain through political activity.

Conceptualization in this area is clouded by certain irrelevancies which

---

5. Hadley Cantril, *The Psychology of Social Movements* (New York: Wiley, 1941); Muzafer Sherif and Hadley Cantril, *The Psychology of Ego-Involvements* (New York: Wiley, 1941).

6. M. Brewster Smith, Jerome Bruner, and Robert White, *Opinions and Personality* (New York: Wiley, 1956), p. 41; see also Smith, "The Personal Setting of Public Opinions: A Study of Attitudes Toward Russia," *Public Opinion Quarterly, 11* (1947), pp. 516-23.

confuse the issue. Problems regarding the relation of the "cultural superstructure" to the economic basis of society, dialectical materialism in history, rationality of economic choice, etc., must be set aside as only tangential to the study of economic needs served by political activity. What is needed at this point is something less ambitious, a classification of the nature of the gratifications to be achieved by political pursuit of economic gain.

Perception of Economics in Politics: From survey material there accumulates evidence that relatively few people believe that national elections will "affect me personally"—only three out of ten in 1944.[7] Observers and interpreters of the political scene, relying on more impressionistic material, have come to the same conclusion. "We must not ignore the fact that political involvement may supply the individual with . . . the practical gratification of satisfying some material need. But psychologically speaking, the less obvious 'meanings' of politics are probably more influential in determining political behavior."[8] The articulation in the mind of the individual voter of economic life and political affairs is loose. But it is not altogether missing, and it takes devious routes.

One reason for this low perception is the individualized means whereby men in America satisfy their needs. If a man wants housing, lower prices, or other material satisfactions, he generally tries to gratify these needs individually by shopping around in the existing market, rather than through political organization. As one Ithaca citizen said, "I don't think politics or election results will or do affect my own life very much. Regardless of who is in power, I'll keep my job and my home."[9] Even Tocqueville noted something of this sort when he said, "The discharge of political duties appears to them [Americans] to be a troublesome impediment, which diverts them from their occupation and business. These people think they are following the principle of self-interest, but the idea they entertain of that principle is a very crude one. . . ."[10] Thus, in at least one crucial respect, the interpretation of economic man in the political arena is different from the view of the species in the marketplace. The relations of his acts to his needs in politics are even more obscure than usual to him.

Level of Economic Need: Economic theory tells us that the more money a person has, the less will each additional dollar contribute to his total satisfaction; money, like everything else, has a diminishing marginal utility. That is, for those with more money a 10 per cent increase in spendable income has less utility than has a 10 per cent increase for those with less, although the range within which this is true has never been specified. In any event, one cannot account for political activity on this basis since such activity shows

7. Gerhart H. Saenger, "Social Status and Political Behavior," *American Journal of Sociology, 51* (1945), p. 104.

8. Morris Rosenberg, "The Meaning of Politics in Mass Society," *Public Opinion Quarterly, 15* (1951), p. 8.

9. Morris Rosenberg, "Some Determinants of Political Apathy," *Public Opinion Quarterly, 18* (1954-55), p. 363.

10. Alexis de Tocqueville, *Democracy in America,* The Henry Reeve Text, edited by Phillips Bradley (New York: Knopf, 1945), p. 141.

a positive correlation with income. The less money a person has, the less likely he is to pursue economic or any other gain through political activity. The possibility exists, however, that the economic rewards of politics are more salient for the lower income groups: to the extent that they are interested at all in politics, they may see it more in economic terms. There is some evidence that this is true from a study of public attitudes toward Roosevelt, in which personal economic gain was more salient for the lower income groups than for the middle income groups.[11] This relatively greater salience of personal economic gain and loss for lower income groups is also supported by analysis of values in senatorial mail on the conscription issue. Here it was found that while 32 per cent of the low income group referred to conscription in terms of its effect upon their economic situation, only 16 per cent of the high income group made this kind of reference. The high income group was, on the other hand, much more likely to refer to "freedom," or civil liberties, or other generalized social values.[12] This greater focus of interest on personal-economic problems in lower income groups not only reflects greater marginal utility of money but also lower interest in general policy matters, lower capacity for handling abstractions, and generally lower horizons of knowledge and awareness.

There are, on the other hand, reasons for believing that lower income groups, instead of relating their economic well-being to political decisions more closely than others, in fact are less likely to perceive this relationship. At least in 1944 fewer lower status than upper status people expected the presidential election of that year to affect them personally.[13] And for a very good reason. Businessmen receive more individualized benefits from government: contracts, tariffs, tax abatements, etc. For them, therefore, there is an opportunity to relate personal gain to individual effort. Others, and especially workers, receive benefits only as members of larger groups and therefore see the rewards of effort as more tenuous and less probable. Under these circumstances, the salience of personal economic stakes in political decisions would be greater for businessmen (and to some extent farmers) than for urban laborers and white collar workers. Thus, there are both theoretical and empirical reasons for believing that the political perspectives of lower income persons have a higher than average economic content and reasons for believing the opposite.

From these findings, combined with our evidence, given below,[14] that electoral turnout is not in the least related to economic depression, it seems clear that level of income, awareness of economic implications of political decisions, and individualized incidence of economic benefit are so intertwined as to make a *general* relationship between economic need and political participation unlikely.

---

11. Fillmore Sanford, "Public Orientation to Roosevelt," *Public Opinion Quarterly*, *15* (1951), pp. 189-216.

12. Rowena Wyant and Herta Herzog, "Voting via the Senate Mailbag, Part II." *Public Opinion Quarterly*, 5 (1941), p. 607.

13. G. H. Saenger, *op. cit.*, p. 104.

14. See below, pp. 329-30.

Reference Groups and the Perception of Economic Need: Almost everyone is better off than someone he knows and worse off than someone else. Almost everyone has unfulfilled desires which might be fulfilled if he had greater income. How, then, does he determine, in his own mind, whether he is underprivileged or privileged, whether he is economically deprived or not. Of course, such a determination is a complex matter to which personality variables make a contribution, as do a host of circumstantial factors. Among these factors, however, the location and relative wealth of the individual's significant reference groups make considerable difference. In the armed services it was found that a person's estimate of his deprivation depended upon whom he compared himself with. If he was behind the lines overseas, his sense of deprivation was greater if he compared himself with others back home, and less if he compared himself with those in the front lines.[15] The perception of economic deprivation undoubtedly follows the same pattern. Those who compare themselves with parents who were or are less well off, or with their own status in their years of apprenticeship, may be less likely to perceive politics as a means of satisfying economic needs. Those who compare their status with more prosperous college friends, or with the image of exaggerated success their parents held out to them, may see everything, including politics, in terms of their economic needs.

Self and Group: Most, but not all, political decisions which re-allocate resources affect selected classes of the population: importers, owners of natural gas wells, the unemployed, and so forth. Thus, when a person appraises politics in terms of the satisfaction of his economic needs, he is confronted with a group gain or loss and his perception of the group, and his identification or disidentification with the group, will color his attitudes toward the politico-economic decisions involved. When Beard reports that of the members of the Constitutional Convention of 1787, "The overwhelming majority of members, at least five sixths, were immediately, directly, and personally interested in the outcome of their labors at Philadelphia,"[16] a mixture of motives is apparent: loyalty to the class of men who were involved and satisfaction in the group gain along with the personal satisfaction in the individual's own gain.

Individual economic gain from political activity, of course, still persists in the form of patronage positions, assured contracts, or legal protection. In this form, however, the sanctions of the society tend to be brought to bear upon the individual, for the difference between group gain and individual gain usually coincides with the boundaries of what is loosely called political morality. With respect to individual gain, then, the desire for economic gain must be strong enough to cross the threshold imposed by concepts of unethical practice and hence a stronger economic orientation is likely to be implied.

---

15. Robert K. Merton and Alice S. Kitt, "Contributions to the Theory of Reference Group Behavior," in Merton and Paul F. Lazarsfeld, eds., *Studies in the Scope and Method of "The American Soldier"* (Glencoe, Ill.: Free Press, 1950), pp. 42-70.

16. Charles A. Beard, *An Economic Interpretation of the Constitution of the United States* rev. ed. (New York: Macmillan, 1948), p. 149.

When considering the decisions of group members on group-related issues, not only ethics but conflicting group memberships and political beliefs must be considered. In a study dealing with public attitudes toward government personnel problems, it was found that veterans were only slightly more in favor of veterans' preference provisions than were the general public.[17] Similarly, college educated respondents were only a little more favorable than respondents with less education to preference for educated persons in government hiring policies. Herring points out that cultural items favoring equality of opportunity interfere here with the college graduates' self-interest.

Economic Values as Instrumental to Other Values: One of the great difficulties in the kind of politico-economic analysis which has prevailed in this area of politics and economics is the illusion of economic gain as a terminal value. Beyond certain minima, economic gain is inevitably associated with prestige and status, self-validation called "success," opportunities for assertion against others, autonomy from disliked persons, tasks, or situations, and so forth. What gives economics its power to command such energy as is invested in the pursuit of gain is often its instrumental value as a means to some other objective. Money buys more than commodities; it buys psychic gratifications of all sorts—although never so completely as the money-seeker thinks it will. The pursuit of income through politics, then, may be preliminary or auxiliary to the gratification of other needs mentioned in this section.

The Dynamics of Politico-Economic Pursuits: We have said that money and wealth often become libidinized, so to speak, because of their instrumental values. There are two ways in which this investment of wealth with high priority may be achieved. Society may do it by making certain equations between income and success or income and prestige. In some instances, as may be seen in the favored position of the middle-class child in public schools, income and morality tend to be equated[18]—a hideous perversion of the Calvinist doctrine first applied to the Puritan adult. Thus, social transfusion of value takes place, creating economic needs where there were none before.

The second method is the psychic process of displacement or generalization which will be discussed more systematically below. We need not accept, nor deny, the identification of thrift and miserliness with early training in cleanliness, though there is considerable case material to support this view. But considering only the processes of displacement in the mature adult, we may find that an individual substitutes pursuit of economic gain for the pursuit of sex objects, or of aggressive activity forbidden by the society. In this latter regard there are social gains, as Keynes notes in remarking that it is better for a man to tyrannize over his bank account than over other people.[19] We shall discuss below Lasswell's formula for political displacement, but we may note here that one might express this displacement in the economic sphere in similar terms: private emotions displaced onto an economic object

17. E. Pendleton Herring, "How Does the Voter Make Up His Mind " *Public Opinion Quarterly*, 2 (1938), pp. 32-33.
18. August de B. Hollingshead, *Elmtown's Youth* (New York: Wiley, 1949).
19. John Maynard Keynes, *The General Theory of Employment, Interest, and Money* (New York: Harcourt Brace, undated [c. 1936]), p. 374.

and rationalized into an economic theory equals Economic Man. The explanation of the pursuit of economic needs through political activity, then, might examine the terms of the rationalization (human nature requires the profit motive), or the economic object (oil wells, pensions), or the private emotions (a desire to defeat the father in cross-generational competition). Out of such material, in the abundant society, are fashioned economic drives which may be pursued through political participation at every level.

That they are so pursued needs little documentation. Perhaps it is most clearly seen in the stakes of the ward leader or precinct committeeman. In King County, Washington, about an eighth of the group worked for the government and therefore had economic stakes in electoral outcomes; in Elmira, New York, about a third of the ward leaders were in this position.[20] The precinct and ward leaders in Chicago in the late thirties and forties freely admitted their economic interests in their political work, and in Detroit volunteer workers included "several hundred paid workers" in 1952.[21] On certain kinds of issues, notably the tariff, the mail tends to emphasize economic self-interest or thinly disguised generalizations about the welfare of those whose jobs are jeopardized by low tariffs.[22] And in the various analyses of financial contributions to campaign funds, the economic self-interest of the contributors is stressed by most authors on the subject.[23]

In summary, then, we may say:

Political participation in pursuit of economic needs is impeded by the obscure relation of political decisions to the gratification of these needs. Paradoxically, this obscurity may be more characteristic of the American political system, where economic orientation is said to be high, than other cultures.

Political participation to satisfy economic needs is unrelated to level of income in the American culture.

Political participation to satisfy economic needs is related to the perception of needs mediated by the selection of reference groups.

Political participation to satisfy economic needs is usually associated with group gain or loss and the gratifications involved are related to attitudes toward the group. Where the gains and losses from political activity are individual, rather

---

20. Hugh A. Bone, *Grass Roots Party Leadership: A Case Study of King County* (Washington, Seattle: University of Washington, 1952, (mimeographed): Bernard R. Berelson, Paul F. Lazarsfeld, William N. McPhee, *Voting* (Chicago: University of Chicago Press, 1954), p. 164.

21. H. Gosnell, *Machine Politics, Chicago Model* (Chicago: University of Chicago Press, 1937); Sonya Forthal, *Cogwheels of Democracy, A Study of the Precinct Captain* (New York: William Frederick Press, 1946); Peter J. Turano, *Organization and Operation of the Democratic Party in Wayne County, Mich.* (Ann Arbor, Mich.: Edwards, 1953, (paper bound), p. 103.

22. Lewis A. Dexter, "What Do Congressmen Hear: The Mail," *Public Opinion Quarterly,* 20 (1956), pp. 16-27; Frank Bonilla, "When is Petition Pressure? *Public Opinion Quarterly* 20 (1956), pp. 39-49.

23. James D. Pollack, *Party Campaign Funds* (New York: Knopf, 1926), pp. 113, 126, Louise Overacker, *Money in Elections* (New York: Macmillan, 1932), pp. 169-93; V. O. Key, *Politics, Parties, and Pressure Groups,* 3rd ed. (New York: Crowell, 1952), pp. 537-42.

than group, the culture usually attributes some immorality to the transaction and hence motivation must be strong enough to overcome this cultural stigma.

Economic needs motivating political participation are usually instrumental to the gratification of some other psycho-social needs, such as status, power, or self-validation.

The investment of economic goals with emotional intensity is a product of (a) cultural equations between economic success and other values, and (b) the displacement onto economic objects of emotions and drives arising from unconscious needs and wishes of the individual.

SOCIAL ADJUSTMENT

Political interests and activity may facilitate easy interpersonal relations, and so satisfy a person's needs for social adjustment. Common political beliefs lay the groundwork for sharing equivalent emotions of anger, sympathy, and distress; common interests improve the opportunities for small talk; common activities create bonds of friendship. Politics may offer to the lonely man new opportunities for association with others—the excuse may be politics, the need may be fear of isolation. In short, political interests and activity may "lubricate" social relations and create opportunities for association in many areas.[24]

The effect of political disagreement is just the reverse. Interests or attitudes which diverge from those held by a person's friends may cause him to withdraw from politics and turn his attentions elsewhere. It is possible, at least, that one reason for American political apathy is that American political preferences frequently cut across class, religious, and ethnic lines so that without a clear orientation on the attitudes of one's social groups, the expression of political opinions offers risks of social friction rather than opportunities for social adjustment.

How strong is the need for agreement! The "strain toward agreement" (for most, but not all, people), and the fear of disagreement has been examined in experiments and field observations for over twenty years.[25] Persons viewing *together* an illusory movement of a fixed point of light give estimates of movement within a narrow range, whereas when persons view the illusion *separately,* there is a much broader range of reported movement. Furthermore, those who have established a standard in viewing the illusion alone, adjust their standard when they hear the reports of others in a second trial so that their standards come closer to the group norms.[26] Opinions on relative lengths of real objects, where there is no illusory effect, are subject to group pressure in such a way that many people will refuse the evidence of their senses in order to avoid an isolated opinion—although when given even a small minority with which to agree they become much more resistant to this

---

24. See Rosenberg, "The Meaning of Politics in Mass Society," pp. 6, 11.
25. See Theodore M. Newcomb, "The Prediction of Interpersonal Attraction," *American Psychologist,* 11 (1956), pp. 575-86.
26. Muzafer Sherif, *The Psychology of Social Norms* (New York: Harper, 1936).

pressure.[27] College students who are oriented toward the college group adopt the favored attitudes of the college community;[28] members of a cooperative housing project have been shown to adjust their views on Russia to what they conceive to be the group mode.[29]

The facts of the situation seem clear. But the private meanings of these acts of opinion adjustment for social purposes may differ in each individual. Among these meanings, perhaps the instrumental need of the group's support for some personal project or goal, say election to office, is the most "objective." Other such needs turn directly upon the manner in which interpersonal relations are interpreted by the individual himself. Fear of conflict may be the motivating force in the politicization of a non-political person in a political group. Or social adjustment may serve as a needed counterweight to a nagging sense of personal inadequacy, perhaps as a reminder that one's private idiosyncratic behavior does not cut one off from other people as much as is sometimes feared. Whatever it is, it has a private meaning deriving from the individual's experiences and personality structure.

To some extent, perhaps, the problem of adequate integration in a human group is universal: all adults have experienced in some manner the "separation anxiety" which comes with growing up.[30] But in different societies this expresses itself in different ways. The mode of life and cultural pressure of the times creates, among most Americans, a need to "get along" with other people in a superficially harmonious manner but without deep personal emotional commitments.[31] This is the "other-directed" person, low in affect and high in facile competence in interpersonal relations. In a sense, this is a corollary to Lewin's diagnosis of American personality—a relatively small core of private "self" surrounded by a larger area of public "self" which is exposed to view and not so easily hurt. (This is in contrast to the German personality where the public area is much smaller and the private area larger).[32] The needs which such personality constellations reveal in abundant measure are adjustment needs; not the need for personal integrity, not the need for propitiating a stern super ego, but the need to get along socially without friction.

Horney makes this point in her discussion of the relation between culture and neurotic symptoms in the present era. She says, "One of the predominant

27. Solomon E. Asch, "Effects of Group Pressure upon the Modification and Distortion of Judgments," reprinted in Dorwin Cartwright and Alvin Zander, eds., *Group Dynamics* (Evanston, Ill.: Row, Peterson, 1953), pp. 151-62.

28. Theodore M. Newcomb, *Personality and Social Change* (New York, Dryden, 1943).

29. Raymond L. Gorden, "Interaction between Attitude and the Definition of the Situation in the Expression of Opinion," *American Sociological Review, 17* (1952), pp. 50-58.

30. See Sebastian de Grazia, *The Political Community* (Chicago: University of Chicago Press, 1948).

31. Riesman, *op. cit.*

32. Kurt Lewin, *Resolving Social Conflicts* (New York: Harper & Bros., 1948), pp. 1-31.

trends of neurotics of our time is their excessive dependence on the approval and affection of others," a condition partly attributable to the highly competitive terms of existence in a laissez-faire industrialized society.[33] If this is true, group life will reflect these mutual demands for affection, or at least acceptance, to an unusual degree. The social adjustment function of politics will, in such a period, serve needs which have been culturally intensified.

The history of the past four hundred years is a history of increasing "individuation," the destruction of the primary group bonds of the individual.[34] This is true of the individual's family connections, religious connections, his class and status connections, his occupational connections, and, with the kind of mobility in America, the ties which bind him to a town or region. It is also true of political connections, particularly in America where "independence" is so highly valued. Fromm believes that man cannot endure such negative freedom, the loosening of old institutional bonds, and he seeks constantly to establish new ones which will relate him to his friends and his work and his beliefs either in a "positive" autonomous manner, or, failing that, in a destructive or dependent manner. Many persons do not have the capacity to make such bonds for themselves, to create a relationship which was once created ready made in the order of things. For them political life may serve acute needs for social adjustment and integration.

Toward whom does a person need to adjust? Authoritarians seek adjustments with people of higher status and power, content to ignore those with relatively less of these qualities. In much the same manner the ethnocentric, the snob, and often the merely insecure, define their adjustment needs in such a way that much of the population is excluded. The question of social adjustment is intricate in detail and specific in content for each individual.

We have suggested that such social adjustment needs may lead people to join political parties—although they may also lead them to avoid joining where this might antagonize others who are important. In a similar manner, the need for social adjustment, the need to make friends and keep their friendship on an easy frictionless plane, may lead them to join other organizations and to contribute to the political process in this way. Indeed the pluralistic basis of American politics may be dependent upon the prevalence of acute social adjustment needs in the population. Joining organizations and seeking friends, in turn, will lead to political discussion where this is not divisive, the kind of discussion referred to above as a reinforcement of mutually agreed upon views. Furthermore, social adjustment needs may lead to other forms of political behavior, such as financial contributions to parties. For some doners to political parties, the salient motive is to be a "good fellow" combined with a fear of the impression which refusing to "go along with the boys" may make upon friends and acquaintances.[35] Similarly, for party

---

33. Karen Horney, *The Neurotic Personality of Our Time* (New York: Norton, 1937), pp. 35, 284.

34. Erich Fromm, *Escape from Freedom* (New York, Rinehart, 1941).

35. Overacker, *op. cit.*, pp. 169-95.

workers, door to door canvassing may be a "social event" whose primary meaning lies in the increased rate of visiting and gossiping.[36]

In summary, then, the following hypotheses reflect the ideas set forth.

Participation is a function of the individual's need for social adjustment with others in his community, although such adjustment has a variety of idiosyncratic meanings and functions for each person.

In all societies, some common ends and directives contribute to the mental health of the members of that community; hence behind the adjustment function there lies the powerful pressure towards consensus in some significant areas of life.

Persons brought up in the American culture are more likely to employ their participation as an aid to social adjustment than persons socialized in other Western cultures.

Gemeinschaft politics (particularly totalitarian movements) serve as especially suitable vehicles for participation for those with social adjustment needs arising from feelings of alienation.

Historically, the individualization or atomization of persons in society has tended to leave unsatisfied the drives for social adjustment, leaving available a powerful unfulfilled need for political movements.

Participation based upon the need for social adjustment will be differentiated according to the nature of the adjustment needs toward (a) people of differing status and power, (b) inclusively or exclusively defined groups.

Periods of crisis for societies, as for individuals, are likely to produce a "regressive" mode of satisfying social adjustment needs in politics.

THE NEED TO UNDERSTAND

"On *a priori* grounds one might suppose that a person's attitudes toward any topic serve the important function of sorting out his world of experience into a predictable order that can provide the background for an orderly existence."[37] An understanding of political events is a tool for living, an instrument whereby other goals are achieved. But, more than that, there is satisfaction in understanding which does not depend upon its utility in achieving further goals. "Quite apart from the pressure of particular emotions, we continually seek to extract meaning from our environment. There is, so to speak, intellectual pressure along with the emotional. To find a plausible reason for a confused situation is itself a motive. . . ."[38] An interest in public affairs and opinions about the world around us serves this motive and represents a response to this pressure. The results may be grotesque, as Lippmann's discussion of stereotypes suggests, but it is the very need to understand that partially accounts for the oversimplified image which causes "Mrs. Sherwin of Gopher Prairie" to think of a world war in terms of a personal duel.[39]

36. Berelson and associates, *op. cit.,* p. 165.
37. Smith, *op. cit.,* p. 521.
38. Gordon W. Allport and Leo Postman, "An Analysis of Rumor," *Public Opinion uarterly, 10* (1946-47), p. 503.
39. Walter Lippmann, *Public Opinion* (New York: Macmillan, 1922), p. 8.

The pressure to have opinions on remote political topics is not just the vestige of days when opinions and influence went hand in hand. It is not just social pressure; it is, even for the ignorant, internal and personal.[40]

The nature of the "meanings" extracted from the environment varies. In a study of attitudes toward Russia, some people were more projective than others in their interpretation of events, making the meanings and opinions serve their wishes; others did not.[41] Some seek syntheses of many variables in an over-all world view, and nothing short of a comprehensive ideology is satisfactory. Others extract extremely limited meanings. As shown in recent studies, rational arguments are assimilated by some individuals relatively easily; others are blocked in their understanding of such arguments by over-riding emotional needs. Furthermore, persons fearful that their interpretations, if stated aloud, will reveal their ignorance, will be inhibited from exercising their curiosity and asking questions about politics.[42]

The basis of this curiosity, like its products, has many facets. Animal psychologists, finding that rats who have satisfied all of the so-called "basic" drives (hunger, thirst, sex, relief from pain, etc.) may still be active, have included curiosity as an additional drive. This interpretation would give the phenomenon a biological basis. Good maternal care is said to be the basis for developing curiosity, and therefore educability, in the human child. Freud found sexual curiosity to be the beginning of intellectual curiosity. And it is said that "High school and college foster an abstract orientation and an involvement in the superpersonal. Hence educated people feel at home in the company of political ideas which partake of the abstract."[43] No doubt all these factors (and many more) may explain differential efforts to extract meaning from the political environment.

What does this pursuit of meaning lead people to do in the political sphere? People who seek to satisfy this need are undoubtedly more attentive to the media and are relatively well informed. An example of this behavior is the following response from a person who was deprived of his daily paper by a strike of newspaper dealers.[44]

I don't have the details now, I just have the results. It's almost like reading the headlines of the newspaper without following up the story. I miss the detail and the explanations of events leading up to the news. I like to get the story behind the news and the development leading up to—it's more penetrating. . . . I like to analyze for myself why things do happen and after getting the writers' opinions of it from the various newspapers, in which each one portrays the story in a different manner, I have a broader view and a more detailed view when I formulate my own opinion.

40. David Riesman and Nathan Glazer, "The Meaning of Opinion," *Public Opinion Quarterly, 12* (1948), pp. 631-48.
41. Smith, *op. cit.*, pp. 516, 521.
42. Rosenberg, "Some Determinants of Political Apathy," p. 353.
43. Rosenberg, "The Meaning of Politics in Mass Society," p. 7.
44. Bernard R. Berelson, "What 'Missing the Newspaper' Means," in Paul F. Lazarsfeld and Frank N. Stanton, eds., *Communications Research, 1948-49* (New York: Harper and Bros., 1949), pp. 111-29.

Does the pursuit of meaning lead beyond this to active political behavior? One study of the factors associated with participation in grass roots civic meetings on a college campus shows that both a superior academic record and a capacity for critical thinking (as measured by a special test) were positively related to such participation.[45] This does not necessarily mean that going to civic or political meetings was prompted by the need to think through a problem, but this is at least a possible interpretation.

In a broader sense, it seems to have other results. In one analysis the pursuit of meaning forms one of the two most important psychological bases for participation in social movements (the other being the need for self-esteem).[46] It is reflected in almost all the interviews and psychoanalytic material dealing with Communists and former Communists.[47] Thus it seems to be a feature of both modal and deviant politics, of both active and "spectator" political participation.

Although political opinions may be functional, they may be dysfunctional as well. Ignorance has psychic utility too, and there are at least five circumstances in which a man will cling tenaciously to ignorance of public affairs. The first of these, *conflict-avoidance ignorance,* is illustrated by the businessman who remarked that he preferred not to study economics because it might undermine his faith in a system with which he had to work. Such a businessman is, of course, in a position similar to the Catholic who permits his reading to be guided by the Index, or a Communist who studies only Marxist social science. All of them are avoiding mental conflict before it begins to work upon them, rather than wait and, possibly, withdraw from the painful conflict after it has been initiated.

The second variety of useful ignorance exists when a person has discovered some tension relief in a belief which would be threatened by new knowledge, a variety which may be thought of as *cathartic ignorance.* For those to whom Red Russia has provided a legitimate target for the discharge of hostile emotions, a scientific treatment of the Soviet Union must be threatening—not because such a treatment would not provide evidence to feed their hatred, but the balanced tone of the discussion would suggest that their emotional investment was inappropriate. Similarly, the anti-intellectualism of the ethnocentric serves to ward off any study of ethnic relations which would jeopardize his, to him, useful hostilities. The very term selected by the anti-aliens of the 1850's—"Know-nothings"—although chosen for another reason, reflects a frame of mind where ignorance is positively valued.

In the third place, those who defend the *status quo* do not need to go to the trouble of producing evidence about it to the same extent as those who propose a reform. If this is an economic conviction they can rest upon the assumption that the challenger must make the case. If it is a psychic conviction that whatever is is best, inquiry is dangerous and should be suppressed.

45. Everett K. Wilson, "Determinants of Participation in Policy Formation in a College Community," *Human Relations, 7* (1954), pp. 287-312.

46. Cantril, *op. cit.,* pp. 53-77.

47. Gabriel Almond, *The Appeals of Communism* (Princeton: Princeton University Press, 1954).

"A man who is prone to identify himself *a priori* with the world as it is has little incentive to penetrate it intellectually and to distinguish between essence and surface."[48]

A variation of this view, and an additional set of reasons for ignorance, is suggested by the fact that political affairs, for many people, meet few direct and urgent needs; they are "remote from the direct concerns of daily life."[49] Thus the person who is immersed in getting along in his own world from day to day avoids the political. His own private status quo, like the larger social status quo, does not require him to be politically informed. This kind of drive to exclude political information from what is learned may be termed *apathetic ignorance.*

Fourth, political views may alienate friends, neighbors, customers, and group members, as we have noted before. Better then, not to hold them. Ignorance from such a motive may be termed *socializing ignorance* (about which, more later). And a fifth situation, where ignorance of public affairs serves some personal function, occurs when the drive to politicize men and saturate their lives with community, partisan, or social meaning becomes fatiguing and a person experiences the longing to privatize his life. This suggests a kind of *privatizing ignorance.*[50]

To summarize these views on the pursuit of meaning, the following hypotheses may be set forth:

Political participation and involvement are products of the need for meaning, both as a source of satisfaction in itself and as a means of satisfying other needs.

The pursuit of meaning is said to be based on (a) a physiological drive apparent in animals, (b) early socializing experiences and particularly the treatment of sexual curiosity, (c) education and other experiences awakening interests and developing skills for handling abstractions.

The pursuit of meaning leads to exposure, attention, and absorption of knowledge (with feedback effects) and, in some circumstances, to civic and political participation.

The reverse of the pursuit of meaning, clinging to ignorance, serves other needs: (a) avoidance of knowledge which might create internal conflict (conflict-avoidance ignorance), (b) avoidance of knowledge which might deprive a person of needed tension-releasing opinions (cathartic ignorance), (c) apathy about knowledge which fulfills no useful purpose (apathetic ignorance), (d) avoidance of knowledge which would disrupt social relations (socializing ignorance), and (e) evoidance of knowledge in order to protect interest and attention in other, and private affairs (privatizing ignorance).

---

48. T. W. Adorno and associates, *The Authoritarian Personality* (New York: Harper & Bros., 1950), p. 658.

49. Rosenberg, "Some Determinants of Political Apathy," p. 363.

50. Ernst Kris and Nathan Leites, "Trends in Twentieth Century Propaganda," in Geza Roheim, ed., *Psychoanalysis and the Social Sciences* (New York: International Universities Press, 1947), pp. 393-410.

CHAPTER 9

How Are Unconscious Needs Expressed in Politics?

IN THE PREVIOUS CHAPTER we examined certain personal needs which are frequently directed into political channels. These are needs, which in some form, are likely to be recognized by the conscious mind and often explicitly stated. Of course they need not be conscious. Society puts a premium upon rationalizations of all personal needs in terms of the general welfare or the public interest. In addition, the individual may prefer not to examine his needs for social adjustment or his need for increments of goods and services for these may raise painful thoughts in his mind. But they are distinguishable from the needs discussed in this chapter not only in their substance, but also on the grounds of accessibility to consciousness.

THE RELIEF OF INTRA-PSYCHIC TENSIONS

An important function served by political participation is the relief of intra-psychic tensions. We do not mean here the conflicts at a more or less conscious level between identification with this or that reference group, or between pursuing one conscious goal or another.[1] Rather, we are dealing with conflicts which occur, partially at least, at the subconscious level, conflicts between impulse and control mechanisms, or between conflicting impulses, or between the unconscious super-ego and the rational mind.

In the first place, such conflicts may tend to produce a withdrawal from politics and almost complete self-absorption rather than political interest and participation. For example, those who rate high on a simple index of neuroticism ("I often find myself worrying about the future," "A lot of people

---

1. For an adaptation of learning theory to psychic conflict in humans see John Dollard and Neal E. Miller, *Personality and Psychotherapy* (New York: McGraw Hill, 1950), pp. 352-68.

around here ought to be put in their place," etc.) tend to listen to and read about politics less than others.[2] Certainly this is a possible solution for the person in conflict. But even if he does adopt a position of withdrawal in his general "social cathexis" this may not mean a political withdrawal. "Insofar as inner conflict does lead to withdrawal tendencies, it does not necessarily follow . . . that those objects that constitute the staple of public opinion studies will necessarily lose cathexis."[3] In other words, a person fatigued by inner conflict may withdraw from family life but endow political interests with increased attention. If, as so often happens, the inner conflict is closely connected with family life (and here the sex theme is particularly important), withdrawal from family life will be rewarding and immersion in politics will provide a plausible excuse. In such a situation, inner conflict produces a withdrawal in one sphere and displacement of emotion into another sphere. This seems to be true of many of the Communists whose case histories have been analyzed by social scientists.[4] In these instances, moreover, withdrawal from the party was often a subsequent event of psychic origin occasioned by the subsidence of the internal conflict.

When the inner conflict is expressed by social (as contrasted to familial) withdrawal, participation is, of course, bound to be a casualty of the conflict. Indifference to politics may be the result of a "major expenditure of energy on internal emotional struggles."[5] Corroborating evidence on this theme is provided by clinical studies revealing the utter fatigue of many neurotic individuals. At this point, moreover, the theory of psychic conflict joins company with a theory of the withdrawal tendencies of the individual who is cross-pressured by his various group memberships or other social forces. Withdrawal is, of course, only one of the many possible responses to such a situation, but, when it does occur, it may be that the social conflict involved in cross-pressures is reinforced by, or is even congruent with, internal psychic conflicts.

There is some evidence to show that, in fact, the politically apathetic individual, more than the participant, is likely to be someone who suffers from intra-psychic conflict and, as a consequence, tends to fear any searching self-examination.[6] A study of college students, contrasting those who were interested in national and local politics and intended to participate in political activities after college with those who were not interested and didn't expect to be, found that the typical apathetic could be characterized as follows:[7]

---

2. Bernard Berelson and associates, *Voting* (Chicago: University of Chicago Press, 1954), p. 241.

3. Herbert Goldhamer, "Public Opinion and Personality," *American Journal of Sociology,* 55 (1950), p. 350.

4. Herbert E. Krugman, "The Role of Hostility in the Appeal of Communism in the United States," *Psychiatry, 16* (1953), pp. 253-61; Gabriel Almond, *The Appeals of Communism* (Princeton: Princeton University Press, 1954); Morris Ernst and David Loth, *Report on the American Communist* (New York: Holt, 1952).

5. H. Goldhamer, *op. cit.,* p. 350.

6. Paul H. Mussen and Anne B. Wyszynski, "Personality and Political Participation," *Human Relations, 5* (1952), pp. 65-82.

7. *Ibid.,* p. 78.

Inability to recognize personal responsibility or to examine—or even accept—his own emotions and feelings; vague, incomprehensible feelings of worry, insecurity, and threat; complete, unchallenging acceptance of constituted authority (social codes, parents, religion) and conventional values . . . relative absence of responses emphasizing self-expression, ego-strivings and satisfactions or warm interpersonal relationships.

Thus political expression (on a college campus) which implies responsibility for what takes place, and which leads into areas where authority and conventionality are challenged (either by yourself or someone else) is not only alien but inadmissable to this group.

The politically active group, on the other hand, shows an over-all pattern of willingness to assume responsibility for one's own—and other's—destiny:[8]

There is an emphasis on strivings for ego-satisfaction, independence, maturity, and personal happiness. Instead of vague, unmanageable feelings of threat which form part of the passive pattern, active attempts to achieve self-understanding, (many responses in categories pertaining to self-examination, self-awareness, and consciousness of shortcomings) . . . sensitivity to other's feelings and emotions . . . . The final aspect of this coherent pattern, the active group's great social consciousness and emphasis on social contribution and love-giving, involves a positive, active relationship with society generally.

It should be stressed, however, that social consciousness is not the *cause* of political activity—rather a personality orientation which stresses the active self-aware role in life is the cause of a general behavior pattern which includes social consciousness and political activity.[9]

1. Greater candor and frankness, unpretentiousness.
2. Selfdisciplined, but tolerant of others.
3. Broader cultural and intellectual interests.
4. Sense of identification with and acceptance of the group.
5. Poise, assurance, and more effective social skills.
6. Greater optimism, drive, and "zest for life."

See Harrison Gough, "Predicting Social Participation," *Journal of Social Psychology, 35* (1952), pp. 227-33.

Yet, plausible as these findings are, and they are supported by a range of statistically significant relationships, they nevertheless reveal only one of the lines of behavior for the person with feelings of "worry, insecurity, and threat." Here, in a conformist middle-class college campus, he withdraws and he accepts. He devotes his energies to the "management" of his psychic life. But under other circumstances where channels are available for expressing his conflict, displacing his aggressive feelings, and finding release in joining some alienated group, a different resolution is possible, at least for some so-called

8. *Ibid.*, p. 79.
9. Although not on the specific subject of political participation, a study by Harrison Gough on extra-curricular "social participation" in high school offers some relevant findings. Gough found that the students who participated more in the extra-curricular life of the school could be characterized, on the basis of interviews and attitude tests, as follows:

apathetics.[10] The political resolution of psychic conflict then, is shaped by circumstances, and, partly for this reason, indeterminate.

If the intra-psychic tension does, in fact, find political expression, how does this come about? Two means are particularly relevant: first, the use of political participation as a means of blocking out the tension, distracting the individual from his personal troubles, and, second, the use of political participation as a means of expressing the troublesome impulse, or as a means of rationalizing the resolution of the conflict in socially acceptable terms. The first is illustrated by the case of the woman who, unable to adjust to her hostility toward her children (for whatever reason), assumed important responsibilities in the political life of her community. These took her out of the home and preoccupied her mind so that she did not have to "think" about her home problems. Or again, there is the incipient drug addict who, because of certain intra-psychic difficulties, could not face the problem and chose, instead, to keep busy with committee meetings or public affairs which removed him from temptation. Unable to accept the death of a person on whom he had grown dependent, a third person plunges into politics to keep from indulging his suicidal fantasies.[11]

More usual, however, since political expression is a product of total personality, is the case of the person who expresses his ego-alien impulses through political means. The political discharge of such intra-psychic tensions, on the whole, has two main themes, precisely the same themes which occur most frequently in clinical cases. These themes turn on the question of expression of hostile, aggressive feelings and the expression of sexual drives. It is for a very good reason that these are the core of the problem for they are the areas of expression which society most closely controls in adult life and most vigorously represses in childhood. An additional theme of frequent importance lies in the expression of dependency needs.

Aggression: The sources of aggression are, of course, multiple. According to one of the most commonly accepted views, it is the product of frustration: frustration is always followed by some form of aggression, aggression is always preceded by some form of frustration.[12] Since aggression may be impounded

---

10. On this point Mussen and Wyszynski take too narrow a view: "The dissatisfied and hostile apathetic individual . . . must devote his energies to repressing his hostile feelings and conforming to conventional standards; hence he cannot become generally concerned with others or with the general welfare," *op. cit.*, p. 81.

11. Andrew Bonar Law, the leader of the British Conservative Party for a number of years and Prime Minister of Great Britain suffered an enormous personal loss when his wife, upon whom he had been heavily dependent, died in 1909. He plunged into even more active participation in politics as a means of distracting himself from his anguish. His biographer notes that for him to abandon politics at the time of his wife's death would have been "folly," as it was the only thing which could occupy his mind and prevent him from becoming obsessed with his grief. The success of this expedient was so great that Bonar Law became the leader of his party within twenty four months. Robert Blake, *Unrepentant Tory: The Life and Times of Andrew Bonar Law* (London: St. Martin's Press, 1956), pp. 61, 62.

12. See John Dollard and associates, *Frustration and Aggression* (New Haven: Yale University Press, 1939).

and expressed later, or may be directed against some irrelevant target such as an innocent bystander or the self, the channels of this relationship are difficult to trace. Learning theorists would add that aggression is a learned form of expression, rewarded at some time in the past and extinguished only when it ceases to be rewarding—with a time lag which may be of considerable importance. Whatever the source, it is a significant factor in political life and, because of the cultural control of this type of behavior, is almost always associated with problems of self-control and inner conflict.

My own case studies have led me to believe that persons who have a capacity for externalized aggression are more likely to become politically oriented than those for whom such external expression is inhibited.[13] Being *against* somebody, some group, or some thing is more easily turned into political channels than being impartial, or being *for* something. Aggression can almost always find an appropriate political target, and so become rationalized in socially and personally more acceptable terms. This is particularly true in those situations where the actual impact of politics is small—as is the case on a college campus. In those life situations where a political decision may in fact create a severe frustration of desired goals, aggressive responses have a totally different meaning. The concept of the "appropriate" expression of emotion, however vague, is often a necessary ingredient in such a theory. For the bulk of the electorate, however, intense political interests are certainly facilitated by a capacity to externalize aggression.

The political expression of outwardly directed aggression may take place in the context of deviant radical parties, where, in the American and British scheme of things, aggressiveness is the rule.[14] In this context, a particular source of aggression, such as sibling rivalry of an intense nature, may produce a continuing and habitual aggressive state with completely opposite forms of political expression. Authoritarians of the right (Fascists) who feel they were victimized by their siblings, tend to deny this, idealize their actual siblings in a "phoney" way, and express their hostility toward others in their politics. The authoritarians of the left (Communists) who feel that they were victimized by their brothers and sisters, may admit their hostility toward their actual siblings, but then over-react by talking about the brotherhood of man, somewhat after the manner of Mr. A., portrayed by Harold Lasswell in his *Psychopathology and Politics*.[15]

Of course, the political expression of such aggression may also take place within the framework of more orthodox politics, as the "total" acrimony between certain McCarthy Republicans and selected liberal Democrats in the

13. These views are based on twenty cases of political self-analysis by college men between nineteen and twenty one years of age. It should be noted that these findings apply to persons who have personal stakes in political decisions of a more remote and less visible nature than is true of working adults.

14. Gabriel Almond, *op. cit.*

15. Edward A. Shils, "Authoritarianism: 'Right' and 'Left,' " in Richard Christie and Marie Johoda, *Studies in the Scope and Method of "The Authoritarian Personality"* (Glencoe, Ill.: Free Press, 1954), p. 39; Harold Lasswell, *Psychopathology and Politics,* reprinted in *The Political Writings of Harold Lasswell* (Glencoe, Ill.: Free Press, 1951), pp. 78-105.

early 1950's reveals. The rivalry between nations, as in a cold war, and to a lesser extent all of foreign policy, presents ideal opportunities for those with aggressive impulses searching for a socially approved target. This is even more true of movements, such as those sponsored by the less responsible veterans' organizations, which pick out some unpopular group for attack in their own communities.

Although less usual, if such aggression is turned inward, nurtured by a sense of guilt, politics offers opportunities for expression of these feelings, too. These may, for example, take the form of atonement, expiation for the sins weighing upon a person's mind. Not a few of the active members of the Society for the Prevention of Cruelty to Animals, World Federalists, and even the white members of the National Association for the Advancement of Colored People are motivated more by unendurable feelings of guilt than by the objective requirements of their cause. Society is lucky when personality tensions erupt in this way, rather than in scapegoatism or even suicide.

Thus a person may reveal his characteristic manner of handling aggressive feelings by withdrawal and apathy or by launching into some outburst against a political figure, or by acts of atonement and dedication to a political cause.

Sex: The relationship between sex and politics is less quickly perceived for several reasons. One of the more important of these is the tabu which society places upon the discussion of sexual matters and the internal reflection of this in the anxiety which such discussion causes in each individual. But another reason is that the manner in which repressed sexual feelings, normal or perverted, are expressed politically is much more devious and the mechanisms are somewhat less well understood. One way to strike through these difficulties is to oversimplify the situation and present hypothetical cases in which sexual conflict finds its way into intense political beliefs. Two such hypothetical cases are presented by Money-Kyrle in a book on *Psychoanalysis and Politics.*[16] These are not presented for their life verisimilitude, but as theoretical models.

First, consider the case of a single woman "with no great desire or aptitude for marriage." After a hard struggle she has become a teacher or a civil servant. She is a socialist with deep humanistic feelings for those who have been thwarted or deprived in life, and this contributes to her politicization, but she also has a very intense hatred of the well-to-do or the managerial classes in society, regardless of their personal attitudes or their role in the "exploitation" of the poor. This also adds fuel to her political interests and it is this hatred, quite irrespective of persons, which needs explaining. According to Money-Kyrle, if a psychoanalyst were to pursue this line with her "he might well find that as a child she had been one of those girls who had desperately wanted to be a boy, that she had never outgrown this grievance, and that it was the unconscious source of her hatred of the over-privileged." A confusion

---

16. R. E. Money-Kyrle, *Psychoanalysis and Politics. A Contribution to the Psychology of Politics and Morals* (New York: Norton, undated, c. 1950), pp. 150-72.

of sex role, then, combined with a sense of her own sexual deprivation is the explanation given for her intense hatred of "the owning classes."[17]

The hypothetical conservative, identifying with upper status groups, traveled a different route. For him, freedom is erected into the highest value and hence a bureaucratic state is a threat. Such an attitude would politicize a person, but his politics would be endowed with a special intensity because of his intense hatred and suspicion of all those on the other side, regardless of their motives and the success of their acts in actually increasing certain areas of liberty. Psychoanalysis, according to Money-Kyrle, might very well find that this intense hatred towards bureaucrats and laborites stems from early fears of deprivation as a child, fears which were generalized into habitual thinking in these terms. The practical and rational fear of economic deprivation by the conservative, then, as it is so often the case, is said to fuse with an earlier fear, and intense emotions expressed in the political sphere are a possible result.[18]

Of course, these two cases are grossly oversimplified, but they are intended to illustrate the way in which conflicts and drives with a sexual origin *may* give to political life an intensity of emotion (and an aura of pathology) which can become a significant source of overt political activity.[19]

If this is the model, what are the realities? On this topic we have available some material gathered from psychoanalysts treating Communists or former Communists.[20] What psychic services did membership in the Communist Party perform for these patients? In the answers to this question it was apparent, at least to the analysts, that the Party met their patients' needs, not only for legitimizing the expression of aggression, but also for accommodating deviant sex roles. Thus, in the Party, dependent and passive men (often with latent or overt homosexual tendencies) were able to profit from a situation where they were told what to do, what to think, and how to live their lives. Here they were permitted to slough off the masculine role of an independent and responsible group (family) leader. For women with sexual confusion, the

---

17. *Ibid.*, pp. 150-51.

18. *Ibid.*, pp. 152-53.

19. It must be noted at this point that these statements of the sexual basis of an inappropriately intense degree of political feeling leave something to be desired. They do not carry conviction to some people who have studied the mechanisms of the mind and the manner in which emotional life is expressed. They have no *prima facie* plausibility. But in their favor two considerations must be stated: a surprisingly large number of psychoanalysts, with very substantial amounts of empirical evidence to draw upon, have come to roughly the same conclusions. Of all people, they have probed most deeply into the sequence of causes which erupt into adult behavior. Secondly, there is as yet no better explanation for some of the emotional investment in politics which has been examined in certain instances. To the outsider this intensity of emotion is wholly inappropriate to the situation; sometimes it is directly contrary to a person's professed beliefs. There is no emotion without a cause. If sexual origins do not have anything to do with the situation, someone will come forward with a better explanation. In the meantime it is the part of prudence to lend a sympathetic ear to the sexual theories of social acts, but to maintain a polite reserve in the matter.

20. Herbert E. Krugman, *op. cit.*

Party offered masculine roles where aggression, dominance, and even masculine clothes and manners were appropriate.

But one need not go so far to discover the way in which sexual needs stimulate political activity. Earlier, we referred to political discussion which takes the form of scandal mongering or rumor. It has long been known that the passing on of rumors with sexual content (Senator blank is having an affair with so and so) serves the vicarious gratification of sexual needs. In another context, one need not imply anything sinister or indeed much beyond the ordinary in noting some generalized libidinal theme in the reply of one of Al Smith's backers who reported that he contributed to Smith's campaign for the "affection and love" he bore the man.[21] Lasswell speaks too broadly, but with insight, when he says "Political life seems to sublimate many homosexual trends. Politicians characteristically work together in little cliques and clubs, and many show marked difficulties in reaching stable heterosexual adjustment."[22] To the extent that this is true at all, it is more likely to be true of the unsuccessful politicians, and the pool house "corner boys" or ward heelers. On a more general level, the similarities between White House mail and "fan" letters with quasi-romantic themes may be noted for what they reveal of the sexual basis of political behavior. Behind the empty phrase, "I vote for the man, not the party," lies a prevalent libidinization of a leader. But perhaps more important than any of these, will be the channeling into politics of "blocked" sex drives: the unmarried middle-aged woman in the League of Women Voters, the homely girl who, for want of a date, sits in the party office at election time and stuffs envelopes, the young man who flees from the college dances into the "youth movement," and so forth. Escape from sex or the enforced sublimation of sex, rather than the direct expression of it, is a normal and perhaps even frequent source of political drive.

Dependency: A third kind of need which arises within the psyche to disturb the individual and whose satisfaction may lead along political paths may be said to be dependency needs. Like sex and aggression, the American society tends to repress these needs, to deny them, and to encourage tension where they are expressed in undisguised form.[23] This is because in America the male, at least (and also the female to a considerable extent), is expected to show independence, to "stand on his own two feet," to have a "strong character," and to assume responsibility for himself and his family no matter what happens. Since this is true, people will tend to repress their dependency needs and to disguise them in some more acceptable form, perhaps in the postures of conformity. Here, then, is another source of conflict, which, like other conflicts, may find expression in apathy or in sublimation and flight into politics.

---

21. Louise Overacker, *Money in Elections* (New York: Macmillan, 1932), pp. 169-93.

22. Harold D. Lasswell, "Psychopathology and Politics," reprinted in *The Political Writings of Harold Lasswell* (Glencoe, Ill.: Free Press, 1951), p. 178.

23. There is said to be a class difference in the repression of dependency feelings, the working class repressing these more than the middle class, while the middle class, on the other hand, represses aggressive feelings somewhat more. See Else Frenkel-Brunswik, "Interaction of Psychological and Sociological Factors in Political Behavior," *American Political Science Review, 46* (1952), pp. 44-65.

The nature of these needs in the political area comes most readily to light in analyzing the responses of the public to Eisenhower and Franklin D. Roosevelt. When asked about Eisenhower in 1952 more of the public mentioned his "leadership" and personality than any other feature of his candidacy.[24] Moreover, at an earlier point Eisenhower was most attractive to those members of both parties who were directionless or politically indifferent.[25] Although not all such leadership-oriented responses imply dependency needs, when they are unaccompanied by any idea of an appropriate direction for the leadership to go, when they are "blind followership," so to speak, they are assuredly an expression of a personality constellation including dependency needs and wishes.

This facet of political orientation was even more clearly brought out in the attitudes toward Roosevelt of a panel of about nine hundred Philadelphians.[26] For a large proportion of this public, particularly those in the working class and Negro groups, the major feature of their orientation to the New Deal-FDR complex was one of personal dependence and gratitude for what might be called "sustenance." This sustenance was not merely economic; it was also psychological in the sense that FDR seemed to give them reassurance that "everything would be all right" and so to relieve their anxieties. From such material as this it appears that very often the strongest motive in bringing people into the political arena is precisely this dependency motive— a need for a man in charge who will give to his constituency (one might almost say, his "flock") this sense of being taken care of by a person deemed appropriate for such a mission. For such people politics offers a dilemma: how to be *active* for a candidate who will serve one's need to be taken care of, that is, to be *passive*.

Following these themes, some of which we shall return to later in the discussion of displacement and generalization, we may tentatively set forth a few hypotheses as follows:

Political participation may offer assistance in the handling of intra-psychic conflicts through offering (a) a means of repressing the forbidden impulse or quieting the insistent conscience, or (b) offering "legitimate" channels for expressing the forbidden impulse, or (c) facilitating a life style embodying a particular compromise solution to the psychic conflict, but:

Political participation in non-deviant politics is generally inhibited by intra-psychic conflict since such conflict absorbs energy and impairs decision-making, interferes with successful inter personal relations, and weakens appropriate ego-strivings. Most commonly the sequence is: Threatening impulses and nagging consciences create anxiety, and anxiety impedes successful political participation.

Political participation (it follows) is related both to a (a) healthy self-expression by the person who accepts himself and his emotions, and (b) the neurotic

24. Angus Campbell and associates, *The Voter Decides* (Evansville, Ill.: Row Peterson, 1954), p. 59.

25. Herbert H. Hyman and Paul B. Sheatsley, "The Political Appeal of President Eisenhower," *Public Opinion Quarterly*, 17 (1954-5-), pp. 443-60.

26. Fillmore H. Sanford, "Public Orientation to Roosevelt," *Public Opinion Quarterly*, 15 (1951), pp. 189-216.

expression of the person with intra-psychic conflicts which are "engaged" with political phenomena.

Politics offers easy legitimation for aggressive drives since it is the area of controversy, electoral contests, scapegoating, and, particularly in foreign affairs, war and hatred.

Political participation is facilitated by a capacity for extra-punitiveness and externally expressed aggression; but, in a minority of cases, political participation may express intra-punitive needs for atonement.

Political participation may be the sublimation and rechanneling of blocked sex drives arising from the frustration of normal sex relations. It may be used to express broad sexual or libinal impulses in candidate orientation, "fan mail," and close interpersonal relations involved in work in a Common Cause.

Political participation offers means of expressing certain resolutions of Oedipal and other childhood situations involving fears of deprivation, mutilation, and restitution, and their symbolic continuation in the adult mind.

Dependency needs whose expression is discouraged by the culture create conflicts for the individual; these conflicts may be expressed in apathy or in political activity oriented toward "nurturant" political leaders.

THE PURSUIT OF POWER

In discussions of politics, the pursuit of power is often considered a primary motivating force. Thus Hobbes states:

So that in the first place, I put for a general inclination of all mankind, a perpetual and restless desire of Power after power, that ceaseth only in Death.[27]

This is, of course, Nietzsche's theme, and it is implied by those modern political theorists who think of politics as the study of power, although it should be noted that these later analyses evaluate the power drive differently.[28]

At the outset we must eliminate from consideration instrumental uses of power appropriate to achieving some other goal. We focus instead on the enjoyment of power as a satisfaction in itself. The discussion divides into two parts, one constituted by the view that there is a separate political type whose motives are unusually concentrated upon achieving power over others; the other, while not denying this, focuses upon the power drives as one of a number of forces accounting for the selection of interest and behavior of those active in politics.

The idea of a distinctive type of person, political man, is attractive in many ways: If there were such a type, it would do much to clarify the problems of leadership selection, circulation of elites, and so forth. Spranger's

---

27. Thomas Hobbes, *Leviathan*, reprint of 1st ed. (1651) (Cambridge, England: Cambridge University Press, 1904), p. 63.

28. See Friedrich Nietzsche, "The Will to Power," in *The Complete Works of Friedrich Nietzsche*, Oscar Levy, ed. (New York: Macmillan, 1924), Vols. 14, 15; Harold Lasswell, *Power and Personality* (New York, Norton, 1948); Charles E. Merriam, "Political Power" reprinted in Lasswell, Merriam and T. V. Smith, *A Study of Power* (Glencoe, Ill.: The Free Press, 1950).

work is illustrative of this approach, for he contends that in every personality there is a dominant value which makes its influence felt in wide areas of a person's life.[29] By the isolation and description of these dominant values, Spranger contended, some clarity could be given to the nature of men who might combine several values at once in real life. One of these values is power, and the type for which this is the supreme value is called the political type. Of this type, Spranger says:

The purely political type makes all value regions of life serve his will to power. Cognition is for him only a means for control . . . voir pour savoir, savoir pour prevoir, prevoir pour regler.[30]

He uses other men as means to his end; he is realistic, amoral, and ruthless; in short, Machiavellian.

A modification of this idea appears in Allport's attempt to define twenty-one significant variables in personality, one of which is labeled, "political interest."[31] But here again the main reference is to the power value (other factors are the aesthetic interest, the economic interest, and so forth), revealing the orientation of the life-striving of the individual.

Lasswell develops the power motif in a more modern style, although, still, with a heavy emphasis upon the concept of a particular type of person who can be called political man. Thus, he states, the political man

1. Accentuates power
2. demands power (and other values) for the self (the primary ego plus incorporated symbols of other egos)
3. accentuates expectations concerning power
4. acquires at least a minimum proficiency in the skills of power.[32]

This is, of course, a relative concept and, as Lasswell points out, the "accentuation" of power must start from a cultural base line to be meaningful.

In these terms, political man is a person who gives priority to power values and craves deference, employing power to achieve deference and whatever other subsidiary values he cherishes. "The conception of a political type is that some personalities are power seekers, searching out the power institutions of the society into which they are born and devoting themselves to the capture and use of government."[33] The origins of such an orientation may lie in a sense of deprivation of respect and affection at an earlier age and some success in employing coercive measures (as the child interprets them) to restore the deprivation. As a consequence all perspectives are colored by the power relationship. Adopting one attitude toward such power, the child (adult) succumbs and becomes a completely passive person—a political apathetic, perhaps. Adopting the other alternative, the child (adult) asserts himself in a

29. Eduard Spranger, *Types of Men*, translated from the fifth German edition by Paul J. W. Pigors (Halle: M. Niemeyer, 1928).

30. *Ibid.*, pp. 190-91.

31. Gordon W. Allport, *Personality, A Psychological Interpretation* (New York: Holt, 1937), pp. 229-30.

32. Harold Lasswell, *Power and Personality*, p. 57.

33. *Ibid.*, p. 20.

manner denying reciprocity (no power for the other person) and becomes rebellious and domineering.

These drives and attitudes do occur in persons in our culture with considerable frequency. In a sense they are like the needs for the expression of aggression, sex, and dependency which emerge in political form, that is, intrapsychic tensions which direct a person toward certain political goals. Like other such needs, the need for power is expressed in politics in sublimated or disguised form, rather than directly. The person who seeks power of the kind described cannot say so, but instead must rationalize this search in other terms. Analysis of the motives of some persons who wrote their Senators, on the conscription issue, brought to light their underlying satisfaction in an exercise of influence combined with a fear of genuine responsibility.[34] Extensive interviews with ward chairmen who ranked high in "authoritarianism" and pleasure in the exercise of power, as measured by certain projective questions, revealed that their own rationales of their jobs were limited to party support, issues, and images of the public welfare.[35] A need for power expressed in the area of public affairs may be concealed in a self-image of intellectual superiority and foresight based upon *knowing* names, dates, and places in the news.[36]

We have said that while it is true that power drives do find expression in politics, they do so only in a rationalized and sublimated manner. Now to what extent is it possible, even with this qualification, to accept the idea of political man as the man who has a higher than average power orientation. At the level of the electorate this is not a likely pattern. As indicated above in the reference to ward leaders, the power-oriented personality is close to the authoritarian personality in many ways. Yet in studies of authoritarianism, it appears that the latter do not vote more than others (nor do they vote less than others) and they tend to electioneer somewhat less than others and to have a lower level of political interest.[37] Furthermore, they are less likely than others to join quasi-political groups and to be selected as leaders of those they do join.[38] In the study of apathetic and active college students discussed above, it appears that the political activists on the campus have many more of the characteristics which go with a low power orientation than do the apathetics.[39] All of these findings tend to cast doubt upon the positive relationship of a

---

34. See Rowena Wyant and Herta Herzog, "Voting Via the Senate Mailbag—Part II," *Public Opinion Quarterly*, 5 (1941), pp. 616-24.

35. Louise Harned, *Participation in Party Politics*: *A Study of New Haven Committeemen*. Unpublished Ph.D. dissertation, Yale University Library, 1956.

36. This variation of "the neurotic need for power" is developed by Horney in her discussion of "the neurotic need to control self and others through reason and foresight . . . in people who are too inhibited to exert power directly and openly." See Karen Horney, *Self-Analysis* (New York: Norton, 1942), p. 57.

37. Robert E. Lane, "Political Personality and Electoral Choice," *American Political Science Review*, 49 (1955), p. 178; Arthur Kornhauser, Albert J. Mayer, and Harold L. Sheppard, *When Labor Votes* (New York: University Books, 1956), pp. 172-73.

38. F. H. Sanford, *op. cit.*, pp. 159-69.

39. Mussen and Wyszynski, *op. cit.*, pp. 72-82.

power value and political activity. Why should this initially plausible hypothesis not be true?

To be successful in politics a person must have sufficient interpersonal skills to relate himself effectively to other men and must not be so consumed with power drives that he loses touch with reality. A person with a raging desire for power who "attaches great importance to imposing himself on others" will constantly alienate his supporters, thereby making the achievement of power impossible for him. On the whole, persons with this value orientation are relegated to minor roles in a democracy, and the top positions go to people who value power as an implement to other life goals.[40]

The low interpersonal skills of the power-oriented person may represent one of the impediments to his ascendance in politics, but there are several others. One of the most common sources of the need for power over others is the deeper need for reassurance about the self—"I am not weak," "I am not insignificant," "I am not dependent." This need for reassurance is, of course, related to lack of self-confidence, feelings of unworthiness, or low self-esteem. Now, as we shall see in discussing political attitudes related to participation, a feeling of personal effectiveness is highly related to political participation. With this in mind, it is most logical to expect that persons who seek to achieve power over others, but who are fighting doubts about their own effectiveness, might resolve these conflicts in different ways; some of them seek reassurance more actively, others give way to their feelings of insignificance more often. Political man, defined in these power terms, then, is an unpredictable political unit.

Other reasons come to mind. A democracy is built upon mutual trust but the power-oriented person lives in an untrustworthy jungle world; his cynicism may flush away his desire for participation. Much of the political activity of a democracy carries little or no power and very little prestige. Authoritarians are less likely to say they will serve on civic committees, but more likely to say they will be willing to "head up a committee."[41] Democratic political activity may be unattractive to the power seeker for these reasons. And in any event, the power seeker may have his eyes on areas of life where power is less controlled and sometimes more effective than in the political arena.

On the basis of twenty student case studies of the etiology of political preferences in an Eastern university, we conclude that the search for power is just as likely to be expressed in non-political areas as in political areas. Indeed, among these students the power-oriented individual was somewhat more likely to seek expression for his needs on the student newspaper or in fraternity life, which were the real centers of power on the campus, rather than in student political groups. Similarly, in adult life the search for the jugular of power may very likely lead to the world of finance, journalism, or industry instead of politics.

---

40. Harold Lasswell, "The Selective Effect of Personality on Political Participation," in Richard Christie and Marie Jahoda, eds., *Studies in the Scope and Method of "The Authoritarian Personality"* (Glencoe, Ill.: Free Press, 1954), pp. 197-225.

41. F. H. Sanford, *op. cit.,* pp. 161-63.

Finally, it should be noted that there are anachronistic traces of two earlier approaches to politics in the search for a relationship between power values and politics. For one thing, the orientation strongly suggests the trait approach of earlier leadership studies, a search for universal traits which in all or most situations would set a leader apart from others. Today, the particular context, the substance of the task for which leadership is required, the qualities and needs of the followers are recognized as vitally important in defining leadership selection. And, in the second place, there is the suggestion that political life is an area where the need for exercising power over others is given greatest expression. This may have some roots in the still widely accepted view that the distinguishing mark of government is its "monopoly of force," a view which, to this author, has never proved to be a useful criterion for distinguishing government from other institutions.

For these and other reasons, one must phrase the relationship of the need to exercise power over others to political activity with great care. The hypotheses which emerge from this discussion, then, should be both negative and positive.

Among the leaders of a democracy there is little tendency for a higher-than-average concentration of persons with needs to exercise power over others. There is also little tendency of this sort among the active group in the electorate.

Among persons with needs to exercise power over others there is (in American democracy) little, if any, tendency to select activity in one of the major parties as a vehicle for exercising power. There is a tendency for power-oriented persons to find a vehicle for their needs in extremist or deviant political groups.

Among the qualities of those who are active in political life, a *moderate* desire to impose one's views and wishes on others, and skill in doing it, contribute to a person's willingness and capacity for political participation.

POLITICS AND THE NEED FOR SELF-ESTEEM

The need for self-esteem is best conceived as an ingredient in all need systems, permeating and modifying the needs for economic gain, understanding of the environment, social solidarity and the various unconscious needs. It is universal, although the fulfillment of this need takes many forms. Yet the need for self-esteem is not merely a generalized form of other needs; it is an independent need, the crucial feature of a person's self-image. Indeed, in one analysis of social motivation, the enhancement and maintenance of self-esteem (self-regard), together with the pursuit of meaning, comprise the total sum of motivating factors.[42] The self-aware person can validate the significance of the need for self-esteem through a moment's introspection.

It is a need of wide reference and great intensity: "The individual's desire for personal status is apparently insatiable. Whether we say that he longs for

---

42. Hadley Cantril, *The Psychology of Social Movements* (New York: Wiley, 1941), pp. 30-52.

prestige, for *self-respect, autonomy,* or *self-regard,* a dynamic factor of this order is apparently the strongest of his drives."[43] It serves as one of the more important of Horney's concepts, an ingredient in the normal personality which is easily distorted by the social pressures of today.[44] In Fenichel's concept of the need for "narcissistic supplies," the need for self-esteem is well supported.[45]

In a very important sense, life is devoted to the protection of the ego, the care and promotion of the self. Nor is the definition of what is ego or ego-involved confined to the body, or even to wholly personal attributes. On the contrary, it tends to be extended to people, symbols, ideas, and objects which in some way are associated with some aspect of the person. The selection of these ego-involved objects is the product both of social designation and idiosyncratic personal preference, the operation of the two factors making for individuality within a common framework. Self-esteem, then, inevitably rises and falls with the "fortunes" of the ego-involved objects. The socially determined sources of self-esteem have been termed "status," and the individually determined sources as "self-integrity." In reinforcing self-esteem from these sources, people fall back upon rationalizations as protective devices, as well as upon misperception, withdrawal, denigration of the opposition, and so forth.[46]

The need for self-esteem may be gratified by political participation in many ways. Merely having opinions or knowing bits and pieces of information tends to show a person off in a better light; he is "educated," *"au courant,"* "on the ball". On the other hand, to venture an opinion or even to entertain one privately, is to expose oneself to possible hurt and ridicule, for "An attack on a man's principles may often be seen as a blow to his self-esteem."[47] Thus a person may be torn between a desire to enhance his reputation for knowledgeability and a fear that his views will be attacked—both drives deriving from his need for self-esteem.

Self-esteem, of course, may be a prisoner of a moral sense or some other over-riding orientation. Where a person is dominated by a nagging super-ego, or in milder cases of moral orientation, his self-esteem will be enhanced by performing moral acts, or doing his duty. In this way, the sense of civic duty discussed below is tied to concepts of self-esteem. "Many people receive substantial superego gratification from political interest."[48]

Social motivation in general, then, and political motivation in particular, can be traced to an effort to maintain or enhance self-esteem. This effort lies

43. Gordon W. Allport, "The Psychology of Participation," *Psychological Review,* 52 (1945), p. 122.

44. See Karen Horney, *The Neurotic Personality of Our Time* (New York: Norton, 1937), especially pp. 178, 286.

45. See Otto Fenichel, *The Psychoanalytic Theory of Neurosis* (New York: Norton, 1945).

46. Hadley Cantril, *op. cit.,* pp. 37-52.

47. Morris Rosenberg, "Some Determinants of Political Apathy," *Public Opinion Quarterly, 18* (1954-55), p. 353.

48. Morris Rosenberg, "The Meaning of Politics in Mass Society," *Public Opinion Quarterly, 15* (1951), p. 7.

behind identification with ethnic groups, social classes, regions, and socia cliques which are ego-involved. Nothing reveals this more clearly than the pride in the achievements of the "old country" on the part of immigrant Americans. It is a prime force behind the emotional attachment to a party label of many political partisans here and abroad. We see it at work in the explanations of those who write letters to their congressmen, as in the case of the frail farmer's son who cannot do the chores about the farm and is fighting to achieve some life role which fulfills his need to think of himself as an "able" person. He says, in this connection, "an able person ought to take care of the opportunity to share in government. Many people are too lazy to think enough."[49] It is apparent in the reasons people give for serving as precinct chairmen,[50] and in the reasons for being merely "interested" in politics.[51]

Historically, social movements have been nurtured by the needs of men whose status was jeopardized by social developments. In the United States, the Progressive Movement of the Theodore Roosevelt era was heavily supported, not so much by the working class, as by the lawyers, ministers, teachers, and small businessmen whose status, relative to others, seemed threatened.[52] Abroad, the support by the lower middle class of the National Socialist movement was prompted, in large part, by their sense of status deprivation relative to the organized working class. Thus the undervaluing by the community of an individual or a group tends to lead such people into politics to redress their situation.

Not only may a discrepancy between the way a society esteems a person and his own sense of worth lead to active political involvement, it is also true that a discrepancy between a person's personal aspiration level and his achievement level has this effect.[53] It isn't the underprivileged who revolt, it is those whose privileges, status, and opportunities do not correspond to their expectations. The impetus behind the National Association for the Advancement of Colored People comes from the Northern Negro much more than from the less privileged Southern Negro.

In summary, then, the need for the maintenance of self-esteem is related to political participation in the following ways:

Political participation is encouraged by the need for self-esteem whenever politically linked objects (persons, ideas, groups, or symbols) become ego-involved, that is, whenever their fate is psychically linked to the fate of the self.

Political objects become ego-involved for an individual when (a) society invests them with a *status* attribute accepted by the individual, and (b) whenever the individual identifies with such objects in the pursuit of his private goals.

Political participation is increased by needs for self-esteem when political acts are socially valued. It is decreased by these needs when a political act exposes a person to charges of ignorance or socially disapproved deviance.

---

49. Wyant and H. Herzog, *op. cit.*, pp. 616-24.
50. See Hugh Bone, *Grass Roots Party Leadership: A Case Study of King County* (Washington: Univ. of Washington, 1952).
51. Unpublished material collected by Morris Rosenberg, 1956.
52. Richard Hofstadter, *The Age of Reform* (New York, Knopf, 1952), pp. 131-72.
53. H. Cantril, *op. cit.*, pp. 46-50.

The need for self-esteem may lead to political participation through satisfying the super-ego of the individual who sees participation as a duty.

Situations which tend to link political objects with the need for self-esteem include (a) discrepancies between social valuation of a person or his group and private or group self-valuation, and (b) differences between a person's aspiration level and his achievement level.

THE "OVERDETERMINATION" OF POLITICAL

PARTICIPATION

If any single lesson has been driven home by the investigations of the behavioral sciences in the past twenty years, it is the idea that all social acts are determined by multiple forces. In studying the genesis of neuroses Freud referred to a similar principle as "overdetermination", meaning that a symptom was the product of the culmination of influences; rarely, if ever, only one. Two things would follow from such a principle in the present context: (a) any one political movement will be attractive to persons whose needs differ from each other, and (b) any one person participates in politics in order to gratify a variety of personal needs. Something of this multiplicity of need fulfillment may be illustrated by reference to the Townsend movement in the thirties.[54]

The Townsend movement was nourished by the most severe depression in American history with attendant insecurity for all groups but especially for the young and the elderly. It was a movement which rapidly gained adherents, organized in Townsend Clubs, throughout the United States and developed an intensity of partisanship which approached the devotion of militant religious groups. Why did men and women join in such numbers and what functions did the movement serve for them?

In the first place, it immediately enhanced the self-esteem of people who had felt rejected and prematurely "shelved." It gave the elderly a voice and a "place in the scheme of things"—it gave the more active an opportunity for expression and a sense of usefulness. Thus it contributed immediately to the defense of a fragile ego for many persons whose egos had been cruelly injured.

The self-esteem motives became important in another sense. Many of the alternatives of the time—socialism, technocracy, native fascist movements— were identifiable as "foreign ideologies" or in some other way subversive. But the Townsendites, being elderly and conservative, could not identify with movements in this vein and retain their cherished image of themselves. By being Townsendites they could seek substantial reform, but in no way challenge private property, or the Constitution, or "the American way." In this way they could preserve their "self-respect."

Second, the movement offered future economic rewards for persons whose

54. Adapted from Cantril, *op. cit.*, pp. 169-209.

life status was almost always below the anticipations that they had built up during their lifetime. Their economic situations and their aspirations were at variance—hence discontent over economic values and vulnerability to the political appeals of the Townsend movement.

In the third place the Townsend Plan was so simple that it could be grasped by those who disliked and shrank from discussions of economic reform, monetary problems, world trade, and matters of that nature. It served to structure the world and offer meaning to those who sought it. Because it was simple it fitted easily into a naive frame of reference: tax commerce to pay pensions to the elderly; the money spent by the elderly will create prosperity. The politicization of discontent was thus given a broad clear channel of operation.

Fourth, the movement offered opportunities for renewed solidarity with others. The tragic isolation of the elderly in the American family was mitigated by the social interaction involved in the movement. As one community leader said, "We have meetings once a week and card parties once in a while. You have to have activities to hold people's interest in the Clubs."[55]

Fifth, some of the leaders, including Dr. Townsend himself, found expression for their needs to exercise power, to impose themselves on others. Perhaps the power drive of some of the leaders could be most clearly seen in the alliance of the leaders with Father Coughlin and Gerald L. K. Smith in the Union Party of 1936.

And finally, in the working out of intra-psychic difficulties many Townsendites found the movement a source of assistance and a vehicle for expression. Some of the dependency needs of the Townsendites are suggested by the terms used by the Townsend *Weekly*: "We believe Dr. Townsend's perception of such an idea is not an accident but rather an answer to the prayers of tens of millions of organized children of God lost in a wilderness of doubt."[56]

In this sense a political movement, like a political party, can, without hypocrisy, be all things to all men.

---

55. *Ibid.*, p. 199.
56. *Ibid.*, p. 186.

CHAPTER 10

How Emotion Is Expressed in Political Life

IF A MAN seeks to serve his needs through his political beliefs and behavior, politics becomes invested with emotion for him. In this chapter we will examine the focus of such emotion, its stability, and its expression in political behavior.

The central feature of political emotion is a sense of "concern" or caring about an election, a policy, or the fate of a beloved leader. This is captured in the phrases used to investigate such an emotional state: "do you personally care," "would it make a good deal of difference," "how important," "do you get worked up," "do you get indignant," and so forth.[1] A related attitude is one of "interest," which may be described as a sense that giving attention to some phenomenon is rewarding but does not necessarily imply a partisan atti-

1. Paul F. Lazarsfeld, Bernard Berelson, and Hazel Gaudet, *The People's Choice* 2nd ed. (New York: Columbia University Press, 1948); Bernard Berelson, Paul F. Lazarsfeld, and William N. McPhee, *Voting,* (Chicago: University of Chicago Press; 1954); Angus Campbell, Gerald Gurin, and Warren E. Miller, *The Voter Decides* (Evanston, Ill.: Row, Peterson, 1954); Hadley Cantril and John Harding, "The 1942 Elections: A Case Study in Political Psychology," *Public Opinion Quarterly,* 7 (1943), pp. 222-41; Gerhart H. Saenger, "Social Status and Political Behavior," *American Journal of Sociology, 51* (1945), pp. 103-13; David Riesman, *Faces in the Crowd* (New Haven: Yale University Press, 1952) p. 88; Elmo Roper, "New York Elects O'Dwyer," *Public Opinion Quarterly, 10* (1946), pp. 53-56. Variations on these questions have also been asked with good results. In the Survey Research Center study of attitudes toward foreign affairs, a comparison between one's own interest and others' interest was elicited by the question: "Do you feel that you are more or less interested in world affairs than most of the people you know?" (*Interest, Information, and Attitudes in the Field of World Affairs* [Ann Arbor, Mich.: Survey Research Center, 1949], p. 7.) Another type of comparative question, this time with the self at another point in time, was asked in the Elmira study: "Would you say you were *more* interested or *less* interested in this year's election than you were in the last Presidential election?" ("Why do you feel this way?").

tude. For certain purposes it is important to distinguish these two states of mind, but for the most part we combine them in the over-all concept of "involvement" and find justification in the observation that questions on "interest" and "concern" tend to select out the same populations and to be related to behavior in roughly the same way.

There are many reasons why people should be concerned about political events. Some of these may be said to be *direct,* in the sense that political decisions give and take away consciously pursued values.[2] Chapter 8, above, and the general literature emphasizing the role of interest groups in politics illuminates this aspect of electoral concern. Other discussions of political emotion emphasize the *displacement* of unconscious motives onto political objects.[8] These were analyzed in the previous chapter, and we pause here only to briefly explore why politics, rather than some other field of interest, should invite such displaced emotion.

Political objects and issues are everywhere available and familiar; they are ambiguous enough so that people can perceive in them whatever they need to perceive; politics is an area of legitimate conflict and therefore serves to legitimize aggressive feelings; it is "the arena of the irrational" or at least "politics is the process whereby the irrational bases of society are brought out into the open";[4] and politics offers leadership figures for the love or hate or submission or rebellion of those whose needs press them to express these emotions. Of course, there are opposing forces as well;[5] it would be a great mistake to think of politics as a great magnet, drawing to it the emotional commitments of the American public. For most people this is certainly not the case. But for some, at particular junctures of their lives, the magnetic field is irresistible.

---

2. Nixon and Marvick divide the politically involved into two groups: those with *social* concerns dealing with making friends, attracting clients, and other self-oriented advantages, and those with *political* concerns dealing with party growth, policy decisions, and candidate fortunes. The first group includes relatively more Republicans; the second, more Democrats. Charles R. Nixon and Dwaine Marvick, "Active Campaign Workers: A Study of Self-Recruited Elites," paper delivered at the American Political Science Convention, 1956.

3. See, in particular, Harold Lasswell, *Psychopathology and Politics* (1930), reprinted in *The Political Writings of Harold Lasswell* (Glencoe, Ill.: Free Press, 1950), p. 75. Riesman and Glazer argue that political emotion based upon the displacement of private sentiments is not *really* political, hence they consider such persons "apathetic." See David Riesman and Nathan Glazer, "Criteria for Political Apathy," in Alvin Gouldner, ed., *Studies in Leadership* (New York: Harper, 1950), pp. 540-47. A correction of the displacement theory is suggested in Stagner's work showing that it is precisely those who can and do express hostility to their parents who express radical ideas as young men. The correction, then, is that political emotion is more likely to be *generalized* from its original source than displaced onto politics from an area where its expression is blocked. See Ross Stagner, "Studies of Aggressive Social Attitudes," *Journal of Social Psychology,* 20 (1944), pp. 109-40.

4. H. Lasswell, *op. cit.,* pp. 183-87

5. See Ernst Kris and Nathan Leites, "Trends in Twentieth Century Propaganda," in Geza Roheim, ed., *Psychoanalysis and the Social Sciences* (New York: International Universities Press, 1947), pp. 400-404.

THE FOCUS OF POLITICAL INVOLVEMENT

We have said that political involvement is the investment of emotion in some area of the sphere of public affairs. But emotion can come to a focus in many different areas in that sphere, and it may be structured along several dimensions. Some suggestion of the various foci of concern over public issues is provided by a study of the five most frequent responses to survey questions asking people what they think are the most important problems facing the country.

TABLE 10.1.—Focus of National Interest and Concern, 1935-1954.

September 1935[a]		November 1939[b]		October 1945[c]	
Unemployment	27%	Neutrality, keeping		Jobs for all	42%
Balance the budget;		out of war	47%	Strikes and labor	
reduce nat'l debt	16	Unemployment	24	troubles	32
Neutrality; keeping		Depression; recovery	6	Reconversion	19
out of war	10	Labor problems; labor		Working out world	
Reduce taxes	6	vs. capital; strikes	3	peace	7
Axe Roosevelt,		Changes in fundamentals		Demobilization	5
New Deal	5	of our government	3		

June 1950[d]		April 1954[e]	
War; threat of war	40%	Threat of war, war in Asia, dealing with Russia	18%
Economic problems:		Communism in the United States	17
living costs,		Unemployment	16
inflation, taxes	15	High cost of living, taxes, economic problems	13
Unemployment	10	Working out world peace	9
Communism	8		
Atomic bomb control	6		

SOURCE: American Institute of Public Opinion, Princeton, New Jersey. The questions were:
(a) "What do you regard as the most vital issue before the American people today?"
(b) "What do you think is the most important problem before the American people today?"
(c) "What do you think will be the most important problem facing the country during the next year?"
(d) "What do you think is the most important problem facing the entire country today?"
(e) "What do you think is the most important problem facing this section of the country today?"

In the first place, patterns of agreement and disagreement on the salience of various problems may be seen to vary from time to time. The pattern is interesting because, as has long been noted by political scientists, threats from outside the country tend to increase consensus in two ways: The responses show greater agreement on what the problem is; and, secondly, the concentration on foreign threats diverts attention from the divisive domestic problems relating to unemployment, strikes, and the cost of living.

Even in peacetime, however, there is often agreement in these domestic areas, as in Elmira in 1948 when the public generally agreed that the cost of living was an important issue and government control of big business was not.[6] But, of course, the consensus on what is the "most important problem facing the country" does tend to break along the fault lines of the society. In terms of socio-economic class, something of this division is suggested by the data in Table 10.2.

TABLE 10.2.—Opinions on the Need for Institution Reform, 1938, by Occupation.

"Which of these—labor unions, public utilities, stock exchanges, the Supreme Court— is most in need of reform?" (U.S., Apr. 1938, Fortune)

	Labor Unions	Public Utilities	Stock Exchanges	Supreme Court	All of them	Don't Know
Executives	52.9%	13.9%	18.9%	3.3%	1.2%	9.8%
Factory labor	35.6	17.1	14.6	7.8	1.5	23.4

SOURCE: Hadley Cantrel, ed., "Public Opinion, 1935-1946" (Princeton: Princeton University Press, 1951), p. 680.

This apparently limited range of difference in focus of concern is also true of the partisans of the two parties. In analyzing what is said by candidates, it is often noted that they stress different topics, each talking about the issues which seem to favor his own candidacy and ignoring, rather than meeting, his opponent's arguments. But the electorate does not divide its focus of concern so sharply. For example, in the 1954 survey mentioned above, both Democrats and Republicans agreed in the selection of the five most important issues, but changed the order of priority within this group. In passing, it should be noted that agreement on the appropriate focus of concern does not imply agreement on the policy to be followed. Moreover, even if there is agreement on the correct policy, as there was in a number of areas in Elmira in 1948, there is still room for considerable disagreement on which party or candidate can best carry out that policy.[7]

The selection of an area of concern is, of course, multiply determined. A person's economic situation is reflected in worries about unemployment and cost of living; generalized anxiety may focus on the international situation and become rationalized into a fear of war—which may also have direct and rational determinants;[8] aggressive ethnocentric feelings come to the fore in the "communism in the U.S." responses.[9] But over and above that,

---

6. B. Berelson and associates, *op. cit.*, p. 186.

7. *Ibid.*, p. 198.

8. The Survey Research Center found that expectations of war were positively related to financial worry; and Farber found that desire for a showdown with Russia was related to general anxiety and unhappy life situations. See *Interest, Information and Attitudes in the Field of World Affairs*, p. 42; Maurice L. Farber, "The Armageddon Complex: Dynamics of Opinion," *Public Opinion Quarterly*, 15 (1951), pp. 217-24.

9. Samuel Stouffer, *Communism, Conformity and Civil Liberties* (New York: Doubleday, 1955), pp. 58-88.

the class and party divisions reveal another determinant—the selection of themes which favor one's own reference group and embarrass the opposition.

The division of the focus of concern in the above perceptions of the "most important problem" suggests a separation between those who concentrate on national and those who concentrate upon local issues. At least among the influential leaders of a moderate size town there is sometimes a "division of labor" of this kind. In a study of "Rovere" a group of "locals," largely born and bred in that town, were found to be oriented toward the town in such a way that they tended to appraise national events, including the war, in terms of their effect upon Rovere. Another group, "cosmopolitans," approximately as large, was more likely to be made up of professional men who had migrated to the town. These "cosmopolitans" were interested in national and international events, less for their effect on the town, than for their wider importance.[10] Further studies along these lines have modified the picture somewhat by showing that although local leaders may be interested in local affairs, they tend to agree that national affairs are more "serious"[11] and, furthermore, at the very top, the real elite among the "cosmopolitans" are also likely to be influential and interested in local affairs.[12] Under these circumstances the distinction between "locals" and "cosmopolitans" tends to blur, with a greater variety of patterns emerging.

But we are more concerned with the electorate than with the leadership and here the picture is generally clearer. The electorate is much more likely to be interested in national than in local affairs as shown both by the way they turn out for elections and by their explicit comments in surveys of public attitudes.[13] Of course this is not universally the case; it is not true at all in the South where, until recently, the one-party system tended to make local intra-party contests more interesting than national inter-party contests.[14] And, in general, it tends to be less true in rural areas, where local government has an intimate and usually personal connection with farm management.[15] But, such exceptions aside, the electorate in terms of "concern" or willingness to vote, or a feeling that the election "makes a difference," is nationalized. We are a nation of "cosmopolitans" not "locals."

As for the difference in focus of concern between national and international affairs, the evidence strongly suggests that on this level of affairs we are "locals," that is, nationally, not internationally, oriented. Surveys have

10. See Robert K. Merton, "Patterns of Influence: A Study of Interpersonal Influence and Communications Behavior in a Local Community," in Paul F. Lazarsfeld and Frank N. Stanton, eds., Communications Research, 1948-1949 (New York: Harper, 1949), pp. 180-219.

11. George Belknap and Ralph Smuckler, "Political Power Relations in a Mid-West City," Public Opinion Quarterly, 20 (1956), p. 80.

12. Kenneth P. Adler and Davis Bobrow, "Interest and Influence in Foreign Affairs," Public Opinion Quarterly, 20 (1956), pp. 89-101.

13. G. Belknap and R. Smuckler, op. cit., p. 80; G. Saenger, op. cit., p. 104; but compare Alfred de Grazia, The Western Public, 1952 and Beyond (Stanford: Stanford University Press, 1954), p. 172.

14. A. de Grazia, op. cit., p. 172.

15. Ibid., p. 124.

regularly shown that from 20 to 25 per cent of the population care only about immediate national issues and evince little interest even in the most important aspects of foreign affairs.[16] Who these people are we do not know, but in general an interest in foreign affairs (as contrasted to no interest in foreign affairs) is associated chiefly with level of education. Probably nationally, the "locals" (could one say the "domestics"?) are the less well educated and generally the lower status groups.

We have examined the way in which the area of concern and interest may be analyzed according to a division between public and private affairs, and according to a division among local, national, and international affairs. We now turn to a third division of interest, an interest in party matters and fortunes, an interest in issues and policy questions, and an interest in public personalities. Here again, as in the problem of local, national and international issues, there is a high degree of overlap; indeed if a person is interested in one, he is more likely to be interested in either or both of the others. But a somewhat different public is interested in each phase of elections:[17]

College educated people are especially interested in candidates and also in issues, but have only an average interest in party fortunes.

Union members and their families show somewhat greater than average interest in issues and only average interest in party fortunes and the candidates.

Women show more than average interest in candidates, but only average interest in party fortunes and less than average interest in issues. Furthermore, there is a difference in the behavioral consequences of these various interests. The person who is party-oriented is more likely to vote the straight ticket than the issue- or candidate-oriented person. He is also more likely to make up his mind early and is less likely to vacillate during the course of the campaign.[18]

Although such a concept is indeed hard on such theories as those embodied in the views of Ostrogorski and John Stuart Mill, it is clear that the main source of political emotion for most people in recent American history is not the issues *per se* but rather the political leaders (seen, it is true, against a background of issues) and the political parties.[19] These represent the principal foci of attention and the attractions which take people from their homes and put them in the streets ringing doorbells, or in the polling booths. But if the emotional stimuli narrow down to these, which is likely to be the more important?

In this connection, certain theoretical considerations are relevant. One

---

16. Herbert H. Hyman and Paul B. Sheatsley, "The Current Status of American Public Opinion," reprinted from *The National Council for Social Studies Yearbook, 1950,* in Daniel Katz and associates, eds., *Public Opinion and Propaganda* (New York: Dryden, 1954), p. 36.

17. Campbell and associates, *op. cit.,* pp. 152-56.

18. *Ibid.,* pp. 147-49.

19. See, for example, Alfred de Grazia, "The Limits of External Leadership over a Minority Electorate," *Public Opinion Quarterly, 20* (1956), p. 121; also Angus Campbell and Warren E. Miller "The Motivational Basis of Straight and Split-Ticket Voting," *American Political Science Review, 51* (1957), pp. 293-312.

of these is that displacement of emotion on persons is easier for most people than displacement upon groups or issues or even symbols, a phenomenon which, if true, would help to explain the personalization of politics both in the United States and abroad.[20] People feel that they can understand other people (are they sincere, upright, "a good Joe," etc?), and often are completely at sea with respect to generalized issues and their alternatives in the policy sphere. But it is easier to libidinize persons for another reason. The child first learns how to express his love and affection to a person—his mother or father or some surrogate for these persons. As he matures, and this libidinization finds ever broader objects and ideas on which to fasten, the original source still dominates the choice of cathected objects—a person or persons.[21] Thus Hitler, not the Nazi ideology, was the core of Nazi loyalties. And, if the analogy is not pressed, one might mention Farley's decision in 1936 to make Roosevelt the issue, not the New Deal.[22]

Of course, the emotional "pulling power" of men and parties varies from time to time, but when people in a metropolitan community are asked, "Why is this election important to you?" their thoughts turn overwhelmingly to the candidates rather than to any other facet of the election.[23] Time and again, however, it has been found that people who are for "the man rather than the party" discover that the best man is the candidate of the party they have consistently supported, so that such evidence must be taken with a little more than a grain of salt. In state elections, the process seems somewhat different, or at least one might alter the weights so that the emotional tug of party loyalty is considered greater and the appeal of the candidates somewhat less.[24] (In national elections the evidence is so ambiguous that no persistent pattern emerges.) Thus political emotion flows now to the man, now to the party—on the average, in local elections somewhat more to the man; in state elections, the party seems more important.

There is a curious absence of articulated self-interest in the way people think of what is important in elections. Many fewer people believe that they have anything personally at stake in an election than believe the nation has something at stake.[25] In one study only about a seventh of the people who were asked about the importance to them of a local election referred to any personal stake in the outcome.[26] Of course, the culture tends to deprecate this type of personal reference, reflecting a kind of Rousseauian concept of

20. See H. Goldhamer, "Public Opinion and Personality," *American Journal of Sociology*, 55 (1950), pp. 346-54.
21. John Bowlby, "Psychology and Democracy," *The Political Quarterly, 17* pp. 63-64.
22. See James A. Farley, *Behind the Ballots* (New York: Harcourt, Brace, 1938), p. 314.
23. A. de Grazia, "The Limits of External Leadership over a Minority Electorate," p. 121.
24. Robert M. Rosenzweig, *Participation in a State Election*, Ph. D. Dissertation, Yale University Library (unpublished), 1956.
25. G. Saenger, *op. cit.*, p. 104; E. Roper, *op. cit.*, pp. 54-55.
26. A. de Grazia, "The Limits of External Leadership over a Minority Electorate," p. 121.

the general will, but the implication that matters that affect the community or the nation are not seen as having much personal effect on the individual must be noted. Perhaps, in one sense, this is a confirmation of the view that politics is so opaque that the impact on the individual of a national or local policy is very often lost from sight. If this is true, the sources of involvement are evidently more often symbolic loyalties to groups and personal attachments to distant leaders than expectations of material or occupational gain or loss.

We have spoken as though the area of interest and concern were clearly defined for each individual but this is misleading. Riesman, for example, speaks of the "shapelessness of attention," twisted one way and then another by the variety of stimuli which happen to strike the individual's sensitivity at any moment. Attributing this in part to the nature of the "media," Riesman draws attention to the lack of continuity which is so characteristic —a sermon on television is followed by a commercial jingle; sex, crime, and politics serve indiscriminately as the main dishes on the journalistic bill of fare. Moreover these cacaphonic stimuli are received by a population said to be more sensitive than most to the modes and fashions and currents of the environment.[27]

If this be so, and there is some support in the theories and findings of Margaret Mead,[28] Karen Horney,[29] Alfred Jones,[30] and others, then we may find in this phenomenon supporting reasons for the shapelessness of attention of the American people.

In summary and extension of these ideas we may suggest the following hypotheses:

The greater the tension created by international affairs, the greater the concentration of focus of concern in this area and the less disagreement in domestic matters.

The smaller the degree of status-involvement, the smaller the degree of political involvement and the more limited the range of conflict.

Political involvement is, in large measure, a combined function of leadership appeal and group or party appeal. These vary in their proportions, with leadership appeal probably exercising greater influence at local (personal) and national (charismatic) levels than at intermediate state levels.

Involvement in local, as contrasted to national, affairs is encouraged by long residence and expectations of long residence in a community, group identifications with ethnic or other community groups, personal economic rewards for being active in the community. In spite of these localizing pressures, involvement in national politics is stronger and more prevalent than involvement in local affairs in most situations.

Under the influence of heterogeneous stimuli and "other-directed" personality

27. David Riesman, *The Lonely Crowd*, p. 213.

28. Margaret Mead, *And Keep Your Powder Dry* (New York: Morrow, 1942).

29. Karen Horney, *The Neurotic Personality of Our Time* (New York: Norton, 1937), pp. 102-34.

30. Alfred W. Jones, *Life, Liberty and Property* (Philadelphia: Lippincott, 1941), pp. 325-32.

tendencies, the focus of political concern in America tends to be shapeless and diffused.

STABILITY, TIMING, AND DIRECTION

For most of the public, involvement in the less immediate political problems appears to be rather "fragile" and ephemeral, incited by crises and sudden emergencies, but difficult to sustain. Men quickly come to the climax of their attention and then lose interest and seek to return to private affairs. At this point, "public opinion fatigues and presses toward closure . . . so far as the average man is concerned, it appears that democracy will have to be content with brief periods of participation.[31] This then might be called the *closure principle* and might be characterized as the rapid exhaustion of interest in public issues and the pressure toward terminating the tension of an unresolved problem. This principle has implications for foreign policy and for electoral campaigns. In foreign policy, some of the mood swings which are said to characterize the attitudes of the American public may reflect this search for closure and may explain the periodic revival of isolationist pressures. In this sense, these pressures would be interpreted as efforts to resolve the tension associated with our foreign policy by withdrawing from "foreign entanglements." Possibly, longer familiarity with the issues and a clearer orientation in foreign affairs will relieve these abortive and weakening strains in an isolationst direction.[32]

Although it is generally agreed that the political interests of the American public are intermittent, relatively high during campaigns and low at other times,[33] there is also a general belief that the public's interest during campaigns varies according to the phase of campaign developments and mounts with the approach of an election. On the whole, this latter proposition seems only partially true, and indeed, some evidence tends to reveal a strong counter trend, a growing fatigue over the campaign period. When people are asked about their interest in an election, the proportions of people claiming such an interest hardly change from June to October, although these constant proportions are made up of people shifting in both directions.[34] Moreover, the people who are interested in June are much more likely to do something about it—i.e., talk about politics with their friends.[35] Thus,

---

31. Gordon W. Allport and Janet M. Faden, "The Psychology of Newspapers: Five Tentative Laws," *Public Opinion Quarterly, 4* (1940), pp. 702-703.

32. See Gabriel Almond, *The American People and Foreign Policy* (New York: Harcourt, Brace, 1950), pp. 75-76.

33. This cyclical interest is, of course, true of every country with periodic elections, but Bryce, who called the American phenomenon "intermittent fever," thought the changes of interest greater in the United States. See James Bryce, *The American Commonwealth* (New York: Macmillan, 1910), Vol. II, pp. 334-35.

34. Berelson and associates, *op. cit.,* p. 29.

35. *Ibid.,* p. 30.

expressions of an interest in an early phase of the campaign is, in some sense, more convincing; it is more likely to indicate a salient emotion. Furthermore, in some elections, the proportion of people who indicate an intention to vote *decreases* with the development of the campaign.[36] No doubt this has many causes, including a more realistic appraisal of one's own probable acts as the time for acting approaches—and this decrease may not be true of most campaigns. But at least it appears that the fatigue principle may very well be at work in the course of the long American elections and does not at all support those who argue that a long campaign period is necessary for developing interest in elections, although long campaigns do have certain other important effects. After the election, moreover, there is a sudden shift of focus in the press, indicating a kind of reader fatigue,[37] or at least an editorial fatigue.

Direction: With respect to the direction of emotion, an examination of interview material tends to reinforce the idea that most of the emotion expressed on political issues is negatively oriented—indignant rather than enthusiastic.[38] This view is reinforced by the nature of the mail received by congressmen on the conscription and tariff issues—more letters are expressed in opposition to measures than in support of measures.[39] Yet such a conclusion must be confined to issues, not candidates, for, in expressing their attitudes toward Dewey and Truman, between a quarter and a third of the voters could think of no special alienating characteristic of either man, while far fewer could think of nothing good to say about them. In 1952 there were many more positive references to the two candidates than negative references.[40] Perhaps, then, on the questions of the timing and direction of emotion, one might generalize these findings in summary and extension as follows.

Political involvement in a given political problem passes through a period of tension increase (anabolic), climax, and tension-discharge (catabolic) which may be out of phase with the evolution of the problem. If the climax and resolution of the problem are delayed beyond the public readiness for tension-discharge, a pressure for closure will be experienced by the public and public officials alike. This "fatigue principle" is revealed in patterns of interest in election campaigns and in foreign affairs.

Stability of particular political concerns is increased for an individual or group

---

36. *Ibid.*, p. 31.

37. Sheldon Korchin, *Psychological Variables in the Behavior of Voters,* unpublished Ph. D. dissertation, Harvard University Library, 1946, p. 362.

38. See Charles E. Merriam and Harold F. Gosnell, *Non Voting* (Chicago: University of Chicago Press, 1924), Ch. VII; D. Riesman, *Faces in the Crowd,* passim; Morris Rosenberg, "Some Determinants of Political Apathy," *Public Opinion Quarterly, 18* (1954-55), pp. 349-66.

39. Rowena Wyant and (for Part II) Herta Herzog, "Voting Via the Senate Mailbag," *Public Opinion Quarterly, 5* (1941), pp. 359-82. 590-624; Lewis A. Dexter, "What Do Congressmen Hear: The Mail," *Public Opinion Quarterly, 20* (1956), pp. 19-20.

40. Angus Campbell and Robert L. Kahn, *The People Elect a President* (Ann Arbor, Mich.: Survey Research Center, 1952), pp. 43, 46; Campbell and associates, *op. cit.,* pp. 57, 61.

by (a) long-term familiarity with a problem, and (b) clearly established public orientation.

Involvement in some political elections changes during a campaign for approximately half of the population, with approximately equal numbers increasing and decreasing their interest. Hence, changing patterns of individual involvement may create a stable pattern of public involvement.

The stability of an individual's political involvement varies with the (a) psychological basis of support, (b) economic or career stakes involved, and (c) social sustenance received.

Political involvement with issues or with politics as a general area of social life is more likely to be expressed negatively, while involvement with candidates is more likely to be expressed positively. (It is easier to attach libidinal feelings to people than to abstractions.)

INVOLVEMENT AND ACTIVITY

The investment of emotional involvement in public affairs—that is, generally speaking, an interest in these affairs, and specifically "caring" about the outcome of an electoral or a policy decision—inevitably affects the pattern of other attitudes and behavior in political life. As one might expect, interest in an election is positively related to a number of areas of political behavior: voting, talking politics, knowledge, exposure to the media, number and breadth of political opinions, and promptness of electoral decisions.[41] It is the obverse of this relationship, however, which is more significant. More people vote than are interested in the campaign, or care about the outcome.[42] Disinterested people even talk politics—about an eighth of them in Elmira—no doubt much as people talk gardening who loathe the subject when they are confronted by it at social gatherings.[43] Interest, moreover, is more closely associated with talking politics than with voting, a fact which suggests that involvement is more likely to affect those activities about which there is less social pressure than those which the society prescribes, such as voting. There is, then, something to the view mentioned earlier that spontaneous and inwardly generated emotion is a greater moving force than emotion aroused in response to the fashions of the times.

The investment of emotion in an election may be thought to operate differently in different social groups—but the result of several studies suggests that the dividing lines are not always the expected ones. With reference to social class, it appears that the decision whether or not to vote is mediated

41. P. Lazarsfeld and associates, *op. cit.*, p. 12; Berelson and associates, *op. cit.*, p. 26. On the nature of the knowledge which comes with political involvement, certain distinctions are sometimes made. Kriesberg differentiates between "awareness" and "information"; only the involved are informed. "Dark Areas of Ignorance," in Lester Markel, ed., *Public Opinion and Foreign Policy* (New York: Harper, 1949), p. 51. Riesman distinguishes between knowledge of specific events and concrete issues as contrasted to general issues; for him only the former are associated with political involvement (*Faces in the Crowd*, p. 556).

42. A. Campbell and associates, *op. cit.*, p. 36.

43. B. Berelson and associates, *op. cit.*, p. 31.

through "interest" at each class level in approximately the same way. People with the same interest in politics are likely to vote in about the same numbers regardless of their education; or, looked at from the other side, if a well-educated person has no interest in politics none of the other role and situational pressures of his position will more strongly influence him to vote than they will the uneducated (and also disinterested) person.[44] To give this phenomenon a name we may call it the *law of mediating interest,* since it is the interest which mediates between the sociological pressure and the expressed behavior. The problem then is to explain why better educated, more prestigeful, and wealthier groups should be more interested. As we shall see, this problem is partly solved by differences in several crucial attitudes, as well as a number of situational differences.

But when the division is made, not on the basis of class lines, but rather on the basis of party lines, separating Democrats and Republicans, it appears that, even among those with equivalent education or income, Democrats are less likely than Republicans to be interested or concerned about the outcome of an election. Furthermore, interested and concerned Democrats are less likely to follow up their interests with appropriate participation than are interested Republicans: in 1952, while 28 per cent of the Stevenson supporters who cared a "great deal" failed to vote, only about 10 per cent of the Eisenhower supporters who felt this way failed to vote.[45]

Why are Democrats less involved politically than Republicans, and why do those who are involved fail to implement their emotional commitments with action?[46] In the first place, the Democratic party, at least in the thirties and forties, generally received a disproportional share of youth, losing some of them to the Republicans as they grew older. In the United States, youth is characterized by low political interest and low voting rates and hence contributes these characteristics to the Democrats. In addition, the Republicans have, because of their regular clientele, become associated in people's minds with "the rich, the prestigeful, and the successful." The upwardly mobile, therefore, who are Democrats by family tradition or for some other reason, experience a kind of cross pressure which may lead them to lose interest in politics, or fail to vote, in the transitional phase when they cling to the Democratic label but aspire to be identified with the Republicans. Furthermore, it appears that at every educational and income level, not only are the Democrats less interested and less concerned about the election, but they are less likely to feel effective in politics, or to believe that their vote makes a difference. This larger group of "politically inert" people in the Democratic party (even within the same educational brackets), may be partially accounted for in historical terms. An influx during the New Deal period of apolitical people mobilized by the depression and captured by the New Deal program of the Democratic party crystallized their party loyalty, but could not, of course,

---

44. Lazarsfeld and associates, *op. cit.,* p. 47.

45. A. Campbell and associates, *op. cit.,* p. 37.

46. The following discussion is based upon Angus Campbell, "The Case of the Missing Democrats," *New Republic, 135* (1956), pp. 12-15.

change their more basic attitudes toward politics. Furthermore examination of the post-New Deal Democrats may shed further light on these hypotheses.

The uninvolved members of the electorate is, as might be expected, the most likely to change his views. He is more likely to shift away from his sociologically "natural" position between elections, when the pressure is off, and to shift back again when campaign pressures mount and his political group alignments are again brought into focus. More than the involved voter, he is likely to vote with his economic or ethnic group and to adopt whatever views are communicated to him through these sources.[47] He is, so to speak, more at the mercy of social pressures because of the lack of inner convictions to give him a steady orientation in the face of conflicting influences.

A sense of concern—emotional investment in the election outcome—tends to reinforce a more general "strain towards consistency." The more concerned a person is about the outcome of an election, the more likely he is to bring in line all his attitudes toward the candidates and issues so that none of them push him toward a different voting decision.[48] Presumably, this is also true if one of the issues becomes invested with great emotion, in which case other emotions will then be brought into line so that the decision can be made with a minimum of conflict.

As for the social effects of various levels of involvement, a variety of views have been offered and will be discussed in more detail in Chapter 22. In the meantime we may note six positions which have some currency on this point. In the first place, there is the *traditional* position—a democracy is best supported by indefinitely enlarging the group of persons interested and concerned in public affairs, and, in fact, the greater the concern the better. This view is reflected by those who ask, in minatory fashion, "Who in this crisis will forget that democracy is government not only of and for the people but also *by* the people?"[49] A second view is the *radical position,* referring to the "damned wantlessness" of the poor, the inappropriate lack of involvement when there is so much reason for their ardent interest in political life. Third, one might isolate the *fever chart position,* a position which holds that the higher the political involvement of the society the sicker it is, with revolutionary possibilities at the extreme of intense feeling.[50] Fourth, there is the view that a chronic separation between activity and emotional commitment is pathological and leads to unhealthy outbursts of emotion in socially disadvantageous ways.[51] This view may be labelled *"ego-syntonic"* in that it requires a harmony between act and feeling. Fifth, one may distinguish

---

47. B. Berelson and associates, *op. cit.,* p. 69.

48. *Ibid.,* p. 285.

49. Gordon M. Connelly and Harry M. Field, "The Non-Voter—Who He Is, What He Thinks," *Public Opinion Quarterly,* 8 (1944), p. 18.

50. See Francis G. Wilson, "The Inactive Electorate and Social Revolution," *Southwestern Social Science Quarterly,* 16 (1936), pp. 73-84; Herbert Tingsten, *Political Behavior, Studies in Election Statistics* (London: King and Son, 1937), p. 225.

51. Gordon W. Allport, "The Psychology of Participation," *Psychological Review,* 52 (1945), p. 121.

the view that only those forms of emotion which are appropriate responses to the specifically political situation are socially desirable; emotional responses to politics arising from displaced or generalized feelings when a person is responding more to internal tensions than external reality are considered politically dangerous (*anti-displacement* position).[52] Finally, there is the *division of labor* position, holding that it is a useful thing in a society to have both the highly involved and the indifferent. The former do the work of politics, introducing, resisting, and executing new policies, while the latter provide the ballast and afford the possibility of compromise.[53]

Reviewing these data and interpretations, we may say:

The more politically involved a person or group, the more he or they are likely to engage in political acts, but more people engage in political acts than are psychologically involved in the policies, persons, or issues at stake in a given political situation.

Interest in a campaign is related to turnout in approximately the same fashion in the major social (but not political) groups, suggesting a law of mediating interest. Interest and involvement are more closely related to participation among Republicans than among Democrats in every status level, because of (a) the higher proportion of youth in the Democratic party, (b) conflicting identifications of the upwardly mobile Democrats, (c) the politically inert residue of the New Deal period in the Democratic party.

Involvement, in general, tends to be associated with (a) greater stability of political attitudes over time, (b) greater consistency in electoral preferences and the elimination of attitudinal conflicts, (c) greater internal resistance to conflicting social pressures.

The social effect of the distribution and extent of political involvement in a democratic society has been variously interpreted as follows: (1) The greater the number of people who are politically involved, the better off the democracy (traditional position). (2) The greater the increase in involvement among the underprivileged the more equitable is a society likely to be (radical position). (3) The higher the intensity of political feeling in a society, the greater the danger for a regime (fever-chart position). (4) The more people engage in conventional political acts without an appropriate sense of commitment, the more likely is a violent outburst of some kind (ego-syntonic position). (5) The more political emotion is a response to objective reality, and the less it is a response to internal psychic states, the healthier a society (the anti-displacement position). (6) The division of a society between the involved and the uninvolved is healthy for a democracy (division of labor position).

---

52. See David Riesman and Nathan Glazer, *op. cit.,* p. 540.
53. Berelson and associates, *op. cit.,* p. 314.

CHAPTER 11

"Strength," Happiness, and Morality in Politics

STRENGTH AND A SENSE OF EFFECTIVENESS

IT WILL BE RECALLED that in our discussion of the several kinds of political behavior the capacity to make decisions, to assert oneself against the environment or in conflict with the will of others, was a constant theme. Those qualities which facilitate such decisions and assertion represent an area of strength in the individual which is more likely to be present in the participant than the non-participant—(although the conventional voter is not *necessarily* "strong" in this sense).

Lying behind the capacity to assert oneself against the environment is the general concept of *ego strength,* a quality which is usually associated with the capacity to order one's life in a rational fashion, controlling at once the impulses which rise anarchically to the surface from within, and external events, in so far as they can be controlled.[1] In infancy, of course, all egos are weak; impulses come and are discharged without the capacity of the individual to order them so as to be able to fulfill his long-run needs. The maturation process may be characterized as a process of ego-strengthening, that is, increasing rationality, increasing the capacity to postpone immediate pleasure in the interest of long-term goals, increasing the power of autonomy in the face of external stimuli, and learning the means and rewards of mastering the environment. Since, however, people mature to different degrees, and even regress after they mature, society is made up of people of varying degrees of ego strength.

---

1. The following discussion is based upon Otto Fenichel, *The Psychoanalytic Theory of Neurosis* (New York: Norton, 1945), pp. 15-17, 463-70; see also Anna Freud, *"The Ego and the Mechanisms of Defense,* trans. by Cecil Baines (New York: International Universities Press, 1946).

But if these experiences of the growing child provide or prevent a sense of mastery over the environment, does a modern industrial environment encourage such a sense of mastery in the adult? And if not, is there a tendency to depress this sense of mastery progressively as we become increasingly urbanized and industrialized? It has been said, for example:

The great economic and power blocs, typified by giant corporations and unions, thrust the individual about with pressures too powerful to resist. As a consequence, the individual is likely to feel overwhelmed and powerless. Given this feeling, the idea that his puny strength can match the giants is absurd, and he feels that a lonely individual can do nothing to change the way society is run.[2]

Such a feeling would reinforce whatever fears of weakness or impotence a person may have developed as a child. The force of this argument is hard to appraise. But there is evidence contrary to the view that industrialization makes a person feel impotent in the finding that the *less* industrialized rural groups, or other individuals at some distance from the "great corporations and unions," feel *less* politically effective.[3] It is doubtful whether modern society does in general decrease feelings of mastery over the environment and a sense of control over one's own destiny. Rather, what it has done is to break open the bonds of tradition so that the environment is, in fact, more likely to be seen as susceptible to control.

Ego strength will show itself in many ways, some of them obvious, and others less apparent, perhaps because they are linked to the personality base by a more elaborate chain of attitudes and behavior patterns. A person with a weak ego, one that has been thwarted in its development by repressive measures or simply never encouraged to develop—"babified," so to speak —will tend to view the social scene as something over which he has no control. Events happen to him; he lives in the passive tense; his future is viewed as a product of "what fate has in store" for him. He is the antithesis of the hero of Henley's Invictus, "the master of his fate, the captain of his soul." Fatalism, in a non-fatalistic culture, might be said to be a reflection of ego weakness, at least in one area.

Where this has been tested it does, in fact, appear that people with weak egos, that is, with little confidence in their capacity to plan ahead or live the lives they would like to lead, have a pervasive feeling that the world is an unpredictable place in which their influence is minimal and their mastery of the situation small.[4] Furthermore, they tend to think of the world as somewhat unfriendly, oppressive in its demands, and unrewarding in its gratifications. Nor should it be surprising that persons with this attitude also tend to feel that political decisions are made out of reach and that politicians do not listen to "people like us."

---

2. Morris Rosenberg, "The Meaning of Politics in Mass Society," *Public Opinion Quarterly, 15* (1951), p. 8; see also C. Wright Mills, *White Collar: The American Middle Classes* (New York: Oxford University Press, 1951).

3. See pp. 265-7.

4. Elizabeth Douvan and Alan M. Walker, "The Sense of Effectiveness in Public Affairs," Ann Arbor, Mich., Survey Research Center, 1954 (processed).

We may, at this point, link such psychoanalytically oriented views to another line of thought about the nature of man. At least two efforts have been made to measure what is called "ascendance" or "dominance" in human relations.[5] "The dominant person tends to be 'stronger' in face-to-face personal situations . . . his own feelings in most face-to-face situations seem to be feelings of safety, security, personal rightness, and self-confidence."[6] Such feelings of dominance are considered to be "a particularly important dimension in relation to political participation."[7] And the twin dimension of ascendance is found to be characteristic of those recognized as leaders in organized groups, persons who make contributions to causes in which they are interested, and opinion leadership.[8] In this general area of ego strength, sense of personal competence, ascendance and dominance, then, we have a complex of elements which do, in fact, lead people to engage actively in community affairs and participate, more than others, in the political process.

The qualities of person and mind embodied in these concepts tend to produce a more specific series of attitudes dealing with the relation of the individual to the political process. Men who have feelings of mastery and are endowed with ego strength tend to generalize these sentiments and to feel that their votes are important, politicians respect them, and elections are, therefore, meaningful processes. This constellation of attitudes has been variously called "a sense of political efficacy," "political self-confidence," and, in reverse, "sense of political futility."[9] It has, of course, two components—the image of the self and the image of democratic government—and contains the tacit implication that an image of the self as effective is intimately related to the image of democratic government as responsive to the people.

The distribution of these attitudes of political effectiveness are, in the main, clear enough:

Men are more likely to feel effective than women.

Groups with more education are more likely to feel effective than those with less education.

The more income one has, the more likely he is to feel effective.

The higher the status of an individual's occupation, the more likely he is to feel effective.

Non-Southerners are more likely to feel effective than Southerners.

---

5. Gordon W. Allport, "A Test for Ascendance-Submission," *Journal of Abnormal and Social Psychology, 23* (1928-29), pp. 118-36; Gordon W. Allport and Floyd H. Allport, *The A-S Reaction Study* (Boston: Houghton Mifflin, 1928). Harrison G. Gough, Herbert McClosky, and Paul E. Meehl, "A Personality Scale for Dominance," *Journal of Abnormal and Social Psychology, 46* (1951), pp. 360-66.

6. H. Gough and associates, *op. cit.*, p. 374.

7. *Ibid.*, p. 363.

8. G. W. Allport and F. H. Allport, *op. cit.*

9. Angus Campbell, Gerald Gurin, and Warren E. Miller, *The Voter Decides* (Evansville, Ill., Row Peterson, 1954), pp. 187-94; Morris Janowitz and Dwaine Marvick, *Competitive Pressure and Democratic Consent* (Ann Arbor, Mich.: Bureau of Government, 1956), pp. 30-34; Arthur Kornhauser, Harold L. Sheppard and Albert J. Mayer, *When Labor Votes* (New York: University Books, 1956), pp. 155-66.

The more populous the community in which a person lives, the more likely he is to feel effective.[10]

It is common to extract from findings of this nature some clues as to the determinants of attitudes, and with propriety this may be done here. In the first place, it is clear that the dominant groups are more likely than subordinate groups to feel effective in civic affairs; they feel that public officials care more about what they think and say; they believe that they have a say in what the government does; they feel they understand politics better; and (with less reason) they are more likely to believe their vote is effective in determining policy. Now, although plausible enough, this finding is not inevitable. For example, it might be supposed that upper status groups would contrast their political influence unfavorably with their relatively greater influence in private life. They don't; they generalize their attitudes from their private onto there public lives. Or again, it might be possible for the upper status groups to attribute less effectiveness to themselves and greater power to the masses, in a "grass is greener on the other side of the fence" attitude.[11] There is no evidence of this among the middle and upper status groups but the lower feelings of effectiveness among the lower status groups may reflect such a comparative attitude. Indeed, it has been said that the reason for relatively lower feelings of effectiveness among the lower status groups is based less on their own "sense of incompetence than a fear of the overcompetence of the higher strata."[12] This might be supported by the frequent references lower status people make to a nameless "they" who rule society. On the whole, however, it seems likely that this use by the lower-status groups of the middle and upper classes as points of reference to depreciate their own sense of effectiveness merely reinforces feelings about themselves which arise for other reasons.

A second matter of interest is the fact that, although clearly socially subordinate, metropolitan Negroes feel fully as politically effective as do white citizens in a similar status and environment.[13] This is notable for several reasons. In the first place, nationally, Negroes as a group do not have this feeling of political control in any degree equal to the white population, but this is probably due to regional, income, and educational differences as much as anything else.[14] More important, in the face of the evidence on the effect of discrimination on the human psyche—the loss of self-esteem involved [15]

---

10. A. Campbell and associates, *op. cit.*, p. 191.

11. Lester W. Milbrath, "Personality and Political Participation," paper delivered at the annual meeting of the Southern Political Science Association, Gatlinburg, Tenn., November 9, 1956.

12. David Riesman and Nathan Glazer, "Criteria for Political Apathy," in Alvin W. Gouldner, ed., *Studies in Leadership* (New York: Harper, 1950), p. 514.

13. A. Kornhauser and associates, *op. cit.*, p. 157.

14. A. Campbell and associates, *op. cit.*, p. 191.

15. See Abram Kardiner and Lionel Ovesey, *The Mark of Oppression, a Social Psychological Study of the American Negro* (New York: Norton, 1951).

—it is hard to believe that this sense of political effectiveness arises spontaneously from inner feelings of power and a sense of mastery over the environment. On the contrary,, here this feeling of political effectiveness seems to be, unlike the middle class feeling of effectiveness, not generalized from private life, but rather arising from the contrast between the political area where the universal franchise grants to the Negro a degree of influence which he so clearly lacks in private life. And this attitude is supported by frequent public recognition of Negro power and ardent political solicitation of Negro votes.

Third, the data on the relation between age and sense of political efficacy reveal almost no change from the beginning of voting age (twenty-one) to the beginning of later life (fifty-four). From then on, however, the sense of political efficacy drops dramatically.[16] It appears that the standard of influence, then, is established relatively early—and is not the product of occupational experience so much as of the family and strata where one is reared, plus the personality support which such an attitude implies. The attitudes associated with "change of life" in women and approaching retirement for men, however, may interfere with a strong sense of political efficacy. One is tempted to go further and, perhaps fooled by the several meanings of the word "potency," relate the decline in sense of political efficacy to the decline in sexual and physical effectiveness. Or, perhaps, it is related to the relative isolation of the older person (fewer group memberships) in working class, but not middle class, districts.

Fourth, the changing capacities of government to respond to shifts in public opinion has a clear relation to the "political efficacy" of the private citizen. There is some evidence that the public is aware of this. For example, a very large number of people who believed, prior to 1941, that the United States would enter the war also believed that this should not happen. Apparently, in time of crises the actions of government seem remote and less subject to control by the average man. Possibly, then, to some extent the sense of political efficacy relates less to deeper personality qualities than to the actual responsiveness of the governmental authorities.[17]

Finally, one might inquire whether the attitude tends to reflect the simplicity and complexity of life as these are said to exist in small towns and metropolitan areas. One might expect, theoretically, that the more heterogeneous the stimuli, the more remote the governmental officers, the smaller the proportionate voting influence of one person in the community, the lower would be the sense of political efficacy. In point of fact, the relationships are reversed, and those living in metropolitan centers have, in general, a higher sense of political efficacy than those in rural or small town areas. Perhaps because of the greater politicization of the urbanites, their exposure to more political news and comment, their more salient class and

---

16. A. Campbell and associates, *op. cit.,* p. 191.

17. Hadley Cantril, "America Faces the War: A Study in Public Opinion," *Public Opinion Quarterly, 4* (1940), pp. 387-407.

ethnic cleavages, and their higher educational level, they are led to make politics a more significant part of their lives.

Of course, people endowed with a feeling of political effectiveness of this kind are more likely to engage in politics: they are more concerned about the outcome of elections, they learn more about the political situation, and are more consistent in their support of their party's stands on various issues.[18] They know how to get things done in political life, and they are more likely to demand a greater role in governmental affairs.[19] All of this holds true, moreover, among people of similar education and background. These, then, are the "effectives;" the people who are ready, able, and willing to make the democratic process work at the grass roots level. They are willing, that is, if they perceive politics as a means for satisfying some one of their many needs; if their needs are politically *engaged*.

These feelings of effectiveness, of course, may not be general but may instead refer to some specific phase of political participation, such as discussing issues or writing letters. With respect to political discussion, in an interview, one person said, "Since I don't understand too much about politics, I just keep my mouth closed . . . People should know what they are talking about and this takes an education which goes beyond the high school level."[20] And the reverse of this is seen in a study of letter writing to Congress, where some of the participants seemed to enjoy writing letters because it was a social skill which they felt they had and others did not.[21] Writing letters is, in fact, generally related to a sense of effectiveness but much depends upon the nature of the subjects, who the letter writer is, and what he seeks to gain from his correspondence. In one specific area it appears that a relatively high sense of effectiveness prevails. When businessmen were asked whether they thought a Congressman who differed with business constituents on the tariff would follow his own views or go along with the position taken by the businessmen of his district, less than a quarter thought he would follow his own views. It may be noted, moreover, that small businessmen had a greater sense of effectiveness in this area than big businessmen.[22] Such a point of view stimulates letter writing as well as personally contacting legislators; but it should be noted that our own interviews with businessmen suggest that on other issues, and when less congenial administrations are in office,

---

18. This information is derived from some work done by LeRoy Ferguson on the relationship of the sense of political efficacy to other factors measured by the Survey Research Center's 1952 election study. Although most studies using this concept find that it is related to non-voting, Kornhauser and associates, *op. cit.*, p. 158, find no such relation.

19. Elizabeth Douvan, "The Sense of Effectiveness and Response to Public Issues," Ann Arbor, Mich., Survey Research Center, 1954 (processed), Table 7.

20. Riesman and Glazer, *op. cit.*, pp. 353-54.

21. See Rowena Wyant and Herta Herzog, "Voting via the Senate Mailbag—Part II," *Public Opinion Quarterly*, 5 (1941), pp. 590-624.

22. Frank Bonilla, "When is Petition 'Pressure'?" *Public Opinion Quarterly*, 20 (1956), p. 47.

businessmen are far less sanguine about their influence on governmental policy.[23]

But if a sense of effectiveness tends to increase political participation, might it not be true also that political participation tends to increase a sense of political effectiveness. That is, exercise of the franchise, writing to public officials, or engaging in political discussion will tend to make people feel that they are influential and increase their sense of efficacy.[24] Like role-playing, voting and talking politics may alter a person's attitudes toward the activities he engages in.[25] On the other hand, would it be true that political activity might spoil the illusion of efficacy, on the grounds that "familiarity breeds contempt"? Evidently both processes are at work. Those who give money to parties tend to think that the influence of money in politics is smaller than those who do not give money.[26] Those who electioneer have about the same sense of political efficacy as those who do not.[27] And while men who serve as ward chairman tend to feel that they can influence policy; chair-ladies do not share this view about their influence.[28] Evidently the effect of activity upon a sense of influence in politics is multiple and varied.

As for the relation between styles of thought and the sense of political efficacy, the data are clear about the greater awareness, information, and partisanship of the "effectives."[29] But what is the person with a low sense of effectiveness to do about the problems that face him? They do not disappear because he does not feel he can control them. On the contrary, they remain to bother him and to create a sense of tension. He solves this problem, in part, by being less aware of the problems, or by undifferentiated and obscurantist modes of thought, particularly when dealing with distant and complex problems such as those related to foreign policy or atomic warfare. But when the discussion deals with the rising cost of living, he cannot completely shut it out; rather he turns to it as a personal problem, not a social problem, and focuses entirely upon how it affects him.[30] The world of the person with a low sense of political effectiveness is a personal world, not a social or political world, and it is filled to overflowing with his own immediate and personal problems.

---

23. Robert E. Lane, *The Regulation of Businessmen* (New Haven: Yale University Press, 1954).

24. Some support for this view may be found in Diamond's argument that membership in the Communist Party served positive therapeutic purposes in a number of cases. Activity in such cases tended to strengthen the ego (or so it is said). See Solomon Diamond, "A Study of the Influence of Political Radicalism on Personality Development," *Archives of Psychology*, 29 (1936), No. 203.

25. See Irving L. Janis and B. T. King, "The Influence of Role Playing on Opinion Change," *Journal of Abnormal and Social Psychology*, 49 (1954), pp. 211-18.

26. L. Milbrath, *op. cit.*,

27. E. Douvan, *op. cit.*, Table 7.

28. Louise Harned, "*Participation in Party Politics: A Study of New Haven Committeemen*," unpublished Ph. D. dissertation, Yale University Library, 1956.

29. L. Ferguson, *op. cit.*

30. E. Douvan and A. Walker, *op. cit.*

In relation to the discussion of this feeling of ineffectiveness, the accusations of the radical fringe of participants to the effect that government is controlled by Wall Street, big business, or other members of some elite from which they feel excluded take on new meaning. Is this, in effect, a variety of low sense of political effectiveness, a variation of the theme that the average citizen, or "people like me" have no influence upon policy makers? In stating that both parties are the same and therefore that elections in a capitalist system are futile, are they rationalizing their low sense of personal effectiveness and cloaking it in a less personally disturbing costume? Although for some, there are doubtless other reasons for adopting these particular radical views, reasons having to do with the expression of hostilities, or the frustration of ego-involved schemes of reform, for a few, at least, this may be a radical's version of feelings of low effectiveness.

We have been talking about a person's attitude toward his own influence upon government. When he felt powerless we said he had a low sense of political efficacy. But it is a common enough phenomenon for a person to project upon others—including, perhaps, such an "other" as the government itself—one's own attitude and feelings. It would not be surprising, therefore, if those who felt powerless themselves also felt that the government was powerless and could do nothing to solve a special problem or relieve distress. Now this was once a common view among businessmen and some economists, especially those affected by the thinking of Herbert Spencer, and it still has its devotees. Of course, this philosophy of government is chiefly held by those who have something to gain from "laissez-faire," but not all such people hold that view and many who have little to gain therefrom also believe it. Might it not be possible, therefore, that some advocates of extreme laissez-faire doctrines are projecting upon government their own sense of powerlessness, their own sense of low efficiency?

In summary, then, we may hypothesize:

Feelings of mastery and control over oneself and the environment, nurtured in childhood and reinforced (or inhibited) by society, tend to be generalized into a sense of political effectiveness.

A sense of political effectiveness leads people to become more alert to their political environment, more informed and partisan in their views, and more active in the political process. The person with a low sense of political efficacy is likely to live in a closed world filled with private problems.

Upper-status groups generally tend to have greater feelings of political effectiveness, generalizing from their experiences of control in private life as well as realistically appraising their greater influence. Lower-status groups tend to contrast their own power to those with upper status, thus reinforcing their feelings of social inferiority.

Negroes in Northern metropolitan areas, but not elsewhere, contrast their political power to their lesser power in other areas of life, and so achieve a relatively high sense of political efficacy.

Declining strength and vigor, and lack of occupational or family effectiveness tend to be associated with a declining sense of political effectiveness.

A sense of political effectiveness is likely to be increased by association with industry, unions, and the complexity of urban living; it is negatively related to rural life and its less dense constituencies and greater face-to-face contact with politicians.

A sense of political effectiveness is not always closely related to conventional participation such as voting, but it is closely related to interest and concern with politics and to letter writing to officials.

A low sense of political efficacy may partly explain the radical view that government is operated by a remote all-powerful "Wall Street" elite.

The projection of a low sense of effectiveness upon the government may partly explain the conservative view that the government is incapable of effective action.

SATISFACTION AND THE PURSUIT OF HAPPINESS

It has been said that American politics is the "politics of happiness."[31] But it is also said that politics is the area where a citizen is most likely to express his discontent.[32] Here we turn to the problem of the happiness and unhappiness, the satisfaction and dissatisfaction, of the political participant at the grass roots level.

Of course the immediate response to such an apparent conflict of views is to ask: Happy about what? Satisfied with what? One answer, the most general, is "satisfied with one's life and with oneself." In this sense, happiness or satisfaction assumes the aspect, not of a specific attitude in a specfic situation, but of a general personality dimension. Just as we found that the basic quality of ego strength, is at the root of the feeling of political effectiveness, so there is a basic personality quality underlying the specific areas of political satisfaction and dissatisfaction. There is no name for this, although "euphoria" comes close, but it is basicly a lack of psychic tension, a personality free of anxiety, a state of mind where the dominant needs and attitudes may be said to be ego-sytonic. In this sense, it emerges from healthy socialization processes and warm affectionate relations in childhood which are not undone by traumatic experiences in adolescent and early adult life.

There have been two attempts to measure these basic feelings of happiness or life-satisfaction and to relate them to political participation. In one, at Cornell College, the index of these feelings was a pair of highly interrelated questions: "How would you say you feel most of the time—in good spirits or in low spirits?" and "What kind of a time are you having at college?" the "cheerful," compared to the "despondent," were much more willing to trust public officials and to believe that writing to them was effective. At the same time, they were more likely to believe that democratic electoral processes were valid and useful means of determining public policy.[33]

---

31. Heinz Eulau, "The Politics of Happiness," *Antioch Review, 16* (1956), pp. 259-64.

32. Harold Lasswell, *Psychopathology and Politics,* reprinted in *The Political Writings of Harold Lasswell* (Glencoe, Ill.: Free Press, 1951).

33. Morris Rosenberg, unpublished material.

The second of these tests of the basic personality dimension underlying a person's general state of happiness dealt more specifically with his attitudes toward his life and his opportunities to enjoy life, his state of worry, and his feelings about the future: the basic theme was "satisfaction with life."[34] Now, as might be expected, social groups differed in their state of satisfaction: Negroes and lower income groups of both races generally felt less satisfied with their lives. Yet, it was not those in the lowest income groups (in this sample of working people) who were most likely to feel dissatisfied, but those with middle status, people who might have expected more out of life, and who were caught between their achievements and their aspirations. Level of education, surprisingly, made little difference.

Now the dissatisfied vote neither more nor less than others, but they are less interested in politics: they care less, do less, and know less about a political campaign. They feel that public officials are less responsive to their wishes and needs,[35] and they tend to be authoritarian in their orientation toward people and politics. The apathy and lack of political involvement of those who are most unhappy in their life situation has been observed before, but this finding tends to reinforce our earlier analysis of the relation between psychic tension and withdrawal. In the absence of an alienated political movement which would have resonance with their underlying sense of dissatisfaction with life, withdrawal is the most congenial alternative. Here, then, lies a reserve army for the charismatic candidate on a misanthropic mission.

But it is by no means true that the euphoric personality does not have areas of dissatisfaction. Like others, he may become annoyed at tax policy, or a change in zoning regulations, or a foreign policy he regards as mischievous. But his dissatisfactions are specific and more likely to be related to objective conditions than to express a general embitterment toward politics. Moreover, among both the euphoric and dysphoric, life situation tends to structure the areas of specific interest and concern. For example, the upper class is said to be more likely to be concerned with its opportunities to enjoy life, the middle class more with the opportunities available for its children, and the lower class more with its jobs and conditions of work.[36] In each of these areas, public policy will arouse different degrees (and kinds) of dissatisfactions calculated to produce a more or less active political response.

Yet, even in this more specific political range of satisfaction, is it true that "people are more inclined to cast their ballot when they are disgusted or tired of something than when they are generally satisfied"?[37] The evidence which supports this view relies upon findings that more non-voters than voters were satisfied with office-holders, thought that office-holders were

34. A. Kornhauser and associates, *op. cit.*, pp. 182-189.

35. This finding is supported by the Douvan and Walker study, cited above, as well as by A. Kornhauser and associates.

36. Arthur M. Kornhauser, "Attitudes of Economic Groups," *Public Opinion Quarterly*, 2 (1938), p. 267.

37. Gordon M. Connelly and Harry M. Field, "The Non-Voter—Who He is, What He Thinks," *Public Opinion Quarterly*, 8 (1944), p. 181.

honest, and would be willing to see their sons go into politics. But the evidence is weak because of the failure to hold educational differences constant and does not correspond to the findings of a more carefully controlled study, to the effect that those satisfied with "governmental and community services" were more likely to vote than were the dissatisfied.[38] Moreover, history does not support this view. The greatest turnouts are not necessarily in depression years, nor in rural areas when farm prices are low, nor in post-war years when adjustment problems are maximal. Turnout, in fact, responds very little to the situations which might be expected to maximize dissatisfaction; on the contrary, it seems to be related to other things.

In summary, then, we conclude:

Lack of tension and anxiety, generalized into a basic satisfaction with oneself and one's life (euphoria), tends to increase a person's interest and participation in the non-deviant areas of American politics.

Euphoria tends to produce a greater trust in politicians, and greater interest and awareness of the political world.

American politics tends to express the needs and wishes of the more contented and satisfied citizens at every level in society, rather than the discontent and alienation of the dissatisfied.

MORALITY IN CIVIC LIFE

As was noted in the introductory comments on the changing status of the franchise during the struggles in the late eighteenth century, both in Europe and the United States, participation in electoral decision-making was considered as a "right" which had to be won. In the United States this right was not established in the Constitution, except for certain amendments which limit the reasons for which a person may be denied his franchise. It was, instead, turned over to the states where, for the most part, it is still in the category of "privilege," conferred by law and withdrawn by law. The idea that the exercise of this privilege was also a duty, however, won early acceptance because of the nature of the forces behind it. Every group and faction in the society quickly saw that only through mobilizing all of their potential strength would they be able to maximize their influence: these groups, endowing their efforts with moral sanction, converted the privilege into duty. The duty, moreover, was clothed not in the language of duty to the group, but in larger terms of duty to society and implementation of

---

38. William Buchanan, "An Inquiry into Purposive Voting," *Journal of Politics, 18* (1956), pp. 281-96.

democratic theory. Today, citizen groups are unanimous in the tribute they pay to this democratic duty.[39]

The meaning of the attitude "citizen duty" requires interpretation. Broadly speaking, there are two possible sources of those feelings we call sense of duty: guilt and shame. The first of these, guilt, describes the emotion that is induced by the super-ego, or conscience, when a person has violated one of his own moral canons of behavior or thought. Duty sentiments in such instances are acts of service to the super-ego and may be conformist or non-conformist, modal or deviant. They are the products of a socialization which implants in the individual a stern or relaxed, "reasonable" or compulsive, conscience. Including civic acts within the realm of duty may be produced either by early indoctrination where parents have brought up a child to be "civic-minded" or by a social pressure to include "civic-mindedness" within the scope of what may be called a free floating conscientiousness. Here, too, as with ego strength and euphoria, we find a basic element of personality which sustains and supports the more topical attitudes. This element is a conscience or super ego which makes a person receptive to the moral claims made for civic participation.

A sense of social responsibility is a feature of conscientious attitudes which has been shown to be related to social participation in community or school activities.[40] Where this has been tested, "the responsible person" is defined as "one who shows a ready willingness to accept the consequences of his own behavior, dependability, trustworthiness, and a sense of obligation to the group."[41] Students who are described by their associates in this way tend to be more careful and more honest, less despondent, and less neurotic than others. They show greater concern for social and moral issues, disapprove of privilege, are self-disciplined, and tend to be somewhat conventional in their attitudes. To the extent that a sense of civic duty is congruent with a sense of social responsibility, then, these qualities will characterize the dutiful citizen. They are reflected, for example, in the comments of a college professor who explained in the following terms why he wrote to his senator: "It gives me a sense of maybe having been of assistance, in a small way, to prevent harmful things." He is said by his interviewers to fear exhibitionism and power, but to be driven by a sense of responsibility regarding his citizen duties.[42]

Duty arising from the forces of shame, however, is a somewhat different thing, for it is partly the product of the conformity needs of the moment and related to the problems of immediate social adjustment. It is, by definition,

---

39. In some versions not only was there a duty to vote, but also a duty to vote for the public interest, raising the question of overburdening the moral sense of the electorate. Thus John Stuart Mill stated: "In any political election . . . the voter is under an absolute moral obligation to consider the interest of the public, not his private advantage," quoted in Bernard Berelson, "Democratic Theory and Public Opinion," *Public Opinion Quarterly, 16* (1952), p. 328.

40. Harrison G. Gough, Herbert McClosky, and Paul E. Meehl, "A Personality Scale for Social Responsibility," *Journal of Abnormal and Social Psychology, 47* (1952), pp. 73-80.

41. *Ibid.,* p. 74.

42. R. Wyant and H. Herzog, *op. cit.,* p. 621.

always modal, at least with reference to the group norms that are salient for an individual at any given time. The aspects of behavior and thought which are included in the concept of duty are defined by the group, their importance is defined by the group, and the particular mode of expression is outlined by the group. Politically, one might expect the person who is dutiful from a sense of shame would not only participate in the same extent and manner as the group but would vote in the same direction and entertain the same opinions as the group. Moreover, if Riesman is right, a sense of duty of this character is replacing the inwardly directed guilt-sanctioned sense of duty—a trend from conscience to conformity.[43]

The social support which a sense of citizen duty based upon conformity may receive in a community is of two kinds: *active* and *verbal*. Active support means that the community does more than pay lip service to an attitude or behavior; it positively encourages such behavior. "Attitudes of political awareness and participation by voting enjoy both active and verbal sanction; people vote and encourage others to vote also."[44] But this is not true of other kinds of behavior even though they may be approved in theory, such as acts of racial tolerance in the North. Such participation in community affairs as working with a political party, or joining a labor union, or, in some communities, tolerance for the opposition party, usually comes under this limited verbal sanction.

However different shame and guilt may be in theory, they tend to come together in practice. In the first place, the conscience is likely to define as moral whatever the society, or at least the individual's salient reference group says is moral. This is what is meant by the internationalization of social norms. Each individual during his life cycle seems to experience this process, with an individual trend countering what Riesman has said is a social trend, a trend from conformity to conscience. As a youth a man experiences a distinct feeling of conflict between desire and duty, but as he grows older these seem to fuse until finally in later middle age he is likely to report that his pleasure is to do his duty.[45] Thus in a manner of speaking, Rousseau is wrong; over time the "might" of the pressure to conform is transformed into "right."

In our culture, a citizen's duty is defined in part as the duty to participate in the life of the community, to vote, to write letters to his congressman, to be informed on political matters. To some extent, at least, the sense of citizen duty may be measured by the circumstances under which a person feels obliged to vote: if the election is a foregone conclusion? if the election is unimportant? if the individual doesn't care about the outcome? if he does not believe his vote will contribute much to the results?[46] So defined and measured, it appears that a sense of citizen duty is, like the other attributes

---

43. David Riesman, *The Lonely Crowd* (New Haven: Yale University Press, 1950).

44. Joseph T. Klapper, "Mass Media and Persuasion," in Wilbur Schramm, ed., *The Process and Effects of Mass Communications* (Urbana, Ill.: University of Illinois Press, 1954), p. 319.

45. See J. C. Flugel, *Man, Morals, and Society* (New York: International Universities Press, 1947), pp. 17*ff*.

A. Campbell and associates, *op. cit.*, pp. 194-99.

we have examined, higher in the upper status groups. One explanation for this is the general rule that subordinate groups tend to think of such social norms as somehow belonging more to the higher status groups and therefore not really relevant to their own group in the same intimate way. Another factor may be the weaker force of any concept of "social duty" in a stratum where personal considerations may be pre-emptive.[47] Put differently, one might agree with Riesman that "conscience," the internalized norm, is more a property of the middle class than of the working class.[48] A third reason may be the lower capacity of the working class to visualize and be moved by abstract and moralized rewards. Or again, cross pressures between class interest and the messages of the favorite media may create confusion and a weakened sense of duty. These, and other attitudes, may be more significant than the failure of a lower status group to embrace a norm associated with a higher status group. For whatever reason, it is a curious phenomenon in the United States, but not in all democracies, that those who are in greatest need of government assistance, because their position in the market is relatively weakest, feel the duty to vote in the lowest degree.

As for other group differences in the sense of citizen duty, it is of interest to note that as a person grows older he is unlikely to increase his appreciation of the moral imperative to vote.[49] Since, in spite of this similarity among age groups, youth votes to a lesser extent than its elders, one can read into this discrepancy between ought and act, the state of tension mentioned earlier; it is not yet their pleasure to do their duty. Like age, sex bears little relation to differences in the sense of citizen duty, although it is true that there are somewhat more women who lack this entirely (12 per cent) than there are men (7 per cent). The fact that almost as many women as men have a strong sense of duty in this area is in line with the tendency for women today to vote almost as frequently as men do. It is via this moral route that they come to the polls, not because of their interest in elections,[50] nor because of their ambition to see certain policies put into effect.[51] As the moral custodians of the family and the community, women now find that they must include citizenship among their other duties.

It is appropriate to ask, in this connection, "duty toward whom?" There are, of course, occasions when performance of duty is, so to speak, categoric, that is, is considered a moral good in itself. But usually, even in such cases, a rationale grows up around the duty so that it becomes invested with ideas of the benefits to be attained by dutiful or moral behavior. It is this way with the duty to vote. In unpublished interview material gathered by Morris Rosenberg, some of the beneficiaries and symbols toward which duty is oriented emerge clearly. Among others, one seems to be a sense of duty toward "our forbears" who fought for a democratic system. Non-voting is,

47. See discussion of economic motivations in lower income groups, pp. 220-34.

48. D. Riesman, *The Lonely Crowd*, p. 44.

49. A. Campbell and associates, *op. cit.*, p. 197.

50. See Alice S. Kitt and David B. Gleicher, "Determinants of Voting Behavior," *Public Opinion Quarterly, 14* (1950), pp. 393-412.

51. See p. 213.

in this sense, an act of irreverence or at least an act which makes their efforts appear to have been in vain. At the other end of the family line, children and posterity are conceived to be the beneficiaries of the vote; one votes to maintain a world which will receive them properly. For others, the duty to vote is seen as a duty to those for whom one is, or thinks he is, a leader— those for whom one sets a pattern of moral conduct. Still others generalize this even further and conceive the duty to be to all those who do take the trouble to vote. If one doesn't vote one is shirking something which others have not shirked.

Notable by their absence, however, are two other kinds of reference: duty to one's class, ethnic group, or party, and duty to God. Although the moralization of the electoral franchise is aided by the nature of the appeals made by group leaders mobilizing their strength at the polling booth, it is not in the American culture to express the duty in these group-loyalty terms. And, although *vox populi* may be *vox dei,* the duty is not expressed in religious terms.

As a review of these interpretations of morality and conscience in political participation, we may note the following hypotheses:

An active conscience is likely to be receptive to the general claims of social responsibility and to the specific claims of citizen duty. These moral appeals are, in turn, strong forces prompting people to vote.

Social norms endowing political participation with moral value reinforce a sense of citizen duty, either through a person's desire to conform, or through his internalization of social norms. Sense of citizen duty reinforced through such exterior pressure—a type of morality said to be increasingly prevalent—focuses upon the conventional and relatively less effective types of participation.

Young people tend to experience a sense of duty that has not been integrated into their personality system and hence are less likely to respond to their feelings of duty than are older people who have integrated desire and duty.

Persons of lower status tend to develop weaker feelings of citizen duty (a) because they do not identify with what is considered to be middle-class or upper-class morality, (b) because of cross pressures between the injunctions of the media and the perceived loyalties of their own groups, and (c) because of preoccupation with urgent needs which exclude certain aspects of "morality."

Women's relatively high sense of citizen duty suggests that their increasing participation is prompted more by their role as moral leaders than by their concern with parties or issues.

Political participation is seen by the electorate as duty to sacrificing forbears, posterity, followers, and other voters, but not to economic or ethnic groups, and not to divine authority.

CONCLUDING NOTE

Not by design, but by the cumulative force of the evidence, this discussion has created a pattern of three specifically political attitudes with clear psychodynamic roots. We have said that ego strength supports a sense of political effectiveness, that euphoria or lack of anxiety supports the sense of life satisfaction which leads to political participation, and that a sense of citizen duty may often be related to a receptive social conscience or super ego. At the base of political man active in American model politics there lies a political personality—the strong, happy, and moral democratic citizen.

CHAPTER 12

Political Man and His Social Attitudes

INTERPERSONAL RELATIONS

A‌T THE HEART of a man's relation to his society is his relation to other people. He may accept the beliefs of the society, and may have mastered the skills necessary to earn a living, but unless he relates well to the people he meets daily, he is unlikely either to be a happy individual or to be effective, at least in urban living. In the very concept of citizen, indeed, there is implied the notion of a man among men, a social human being. The prospects for a democracy in which men do not get along well with one another, do not trust one another, and do not associate with one another is unpromising. Such a society would be one where "the life of a man is solitary, poore, nasty, brutish, and short."

What can be said, then, of men's relations to one another in a society where all are expected to take part in governmental processes? It seems clear, in the first place, that those who are inclined to participate have, in fact, a faith in their fellow men. Those who believe that others can be trusted, are cooperative, will help a person when he needs help, and care about each other are more likely to believe in the democratic process in several ways. Studies at Cornell show that students with "faith in people" of this kind also believe that the public is generally qualified to vote, implying thereby a conviction that democratic procedures are a sensible way of arriving at governmental decisions.[1] They tend to think that officials are genuinely "inter-

---

1. Morris Rosenberg, "Misanthropy and Political Ideology," *American Sociological Review, 21* (1956), p. 691.

ested in the problems of the average man." And they tend to reject the notion that political candidates are "run by political machines." Thus those with a relatively greater faith in people are psychologically prepared to accept the democratic process and to believe that they, and others like them, may be effective in elections. Indeed, certain similarities in the measuring instruments suggest that faith in people supports the attitude we have previously discussed as a sense of political effectiveness.

Now there are good reasons why this should be so. If one cannot trust other people generally, one can certainly not trust those under the temptations of and with the powers which come with public office. Trust in elected officials is seen to be only a more specific instance of trust in mankind. And in the long run, this is probably a projection of attitudes toward the self—self-approval.

But if it is true that a faith in other people creates the frame of mind conducive to acceptance of democratic procedures, it is not necessarily true that people have the skill to go along with the faith. They may not relate easily to people, or have those small gifts of grace and familiarity which make friendly relationships easy to come by. Since political participation is, in many of its forms, composed of social acts which bring men into association with one another, it would not be surprising to learn that persons who had social gifts were, in fact, more likely to participate in politics than those who did not. The report of a study in North Carolina is interesting in this connection.[2]

From a battery of questions dealing in general with interpersonal relations, four were found to bear a special relationship to political participation. These dealt, in general, with ability to find topics of conversation with new acquaintances, acceptance of responsibility for other people, and, specifically, the willingness to take responsibility for introducing friends to each other when they meet for the first time. In general they reflected a "feeling of ease, graciousness, and confidence in social situations" (and formed an acceptable Guttman scale). These attitudes and skills—"sociability"—were found to be significantly related to an over-all tendency to participate in politics in the ways we have discussed in Part II of this book. The same relationship, moreover, is apparent separately among both those with greater income and those with less income, although the relationship between these skills and attitudes and participation is much weaker at the low income level.

But not all political participation requires the same amount of sociability, for some ways of engaging in political activity do not immerse individuals in close interpersonal relations to a very great extent. Thus, the study mentioned shows that in each of the two major income classes contributing funds to a party does not depend upon sociability, but soliciting contributions does. Merely attending party meetings shows no relationship to sociability, but campaigning and electioneering does. In such a fashion as this, the nature

---

2. Lester W. Milbrath, "Personality and Political Participation," paper delivered at the annual meeting of the Southern Political Science Association, Gatlinburg, Tenn., November 9, 1956.

of one's skills and attitudes tends to direct the type of activity which a person may engage in, once he has faith in the democratic process and has his interest in politics aroused. In one sense we might compare the fund of skills a person has to the amount of money he has: he makes his contribution to his party and candidate according to his resources.

But if it is true that those with faith in people and those with social skills tend to relate more effectively to the democratic process, is it also true that those who are in fact in frequent and active contact with others are more likely to become participants in the democratic process? Much evidence supports the view that they are. Not only is it clear (as noted above) that in general, those who belong to more organizations of any kind tend to vote more, and to be more likely to become opinion leaders, it is also true that if they have more friends, they are more likely to be high participants. A combination of these two indicators of an active social life (number of group organizations and number of friends) into a "gregariousness scale" has been shown to be intimately related to discussion of political affairs and opinion leadership.[3] And this is true whether or not a person is well informed and regardless of social status. The person who seeks out his fellow man, even if he is not well informed, is more likely to assume positions of grass roots leadership in the political life of his community.

A person's attitudes to his community, however, are something different from his attitudes to his circle of friends and his associations. A man can certainly enjoy his associates but remain disaffected with his community and critical of it as a place to live. Such a disaffected person might, moreover, be active in politics, either expressing his disaffection in some alienated manner, perhaps writing crank letters to the paper, or in more constructive ways embodying reform principles. In point of fact, however, it is the person who finds his community "a good place to live in" who is more likely to be active in public affairs—and this is not only true for those with higher status, it is also true for the prosperous and the less prosperous alike.[4] Moreover, if this attitude is broadened to include a more active sense of "belongingness" to the community the same relationship holds true. Thus a belief that a person has a "say in what goes on here in this community" and never considers "going somewhere else to live," and wants to have his children "settle and raise their families" in his own community, all tend to be associated with active political participation in political affairs.[5] And here again this is true for the rich and the poor, the upper-status and the lower-status citizens of a community. And since these studies have investigated communities in the North and in the South, the relationship must be a national one.

Taking these several findings together, then, we find that the person who has faith in people, the sociable man with many social contacts, and the

3. Elihu Katz and Paul F. Lazarsfeld, *Personal Influence* (Glencoe, Ill.: Free Press, 1955), pp. 287-89.

4. Alice S. Kitt and David B. Gleicher, "Determinants of Voting Behavior," *Public Opinion Quarterly, 14* (1950), pp. 408-409.

5. William Buchanan, "An Inquiry into Purposive Voting," *Journal of Politics, 18* (1956), p. 290.

man who likes his community is the effective citizen in our democracy. His relationships with his social environment are good; he is in rapport with others; he works for political ends not in a spirit of antagonism but in a spirit of cooperation. Or at least this is the more prevalent pattern.

Now these findings shed some light upon other facets of political behavior: the importance of friends and work groups in shaping the individual's political decisions. There can no longer be any doubt that a person's attitude toward politics is intimately affected by the interests and preferences of his associates. Nor is this merely because of the information and opinions which they provide to help a person in his political orientation. It is a product also of the identification and sense of "closeness" which the citizen has with others; for if he has faith in people and is sociable he will positively value his friends' estimates of him as a man.

It may be thought that "other-directedness" and pressures for conformity are, so to speak, the negative side of the faith-in-people, sociability, gregariousness complex. But, at least with respect to faith in people, this conclusion would be wrong, for it is precisely those who are high in this respect who are also more tolerant of deviants.[6] Good and trusting relations with others do not breed demands for conformity, they breed tolerance of the other fellow's differences. Thus, we may say:

The more people believe that others are trustworthy, cooperative, and care about each other ("faith in people"), the more likely they are to believe that government officials have these qualities and hence the more likely they are to participate in democratic processes.

People who have social skills and get along well with others ("sociable") are more likely than others to be active in politics, but this is true only for those activities which require close interpersonal contact.

People who have many friends and belong to many organizations ("gregarious") are more likely to be active in politics and to be opinion leaders, regardless of their social status or information.

People who are satisfied with their communities and feel integrated in the community life are more active in politics than those who do not; integration, not alienation, forms the basis of most political motivation in modal non-crisis American politics.

ANOMIE

Ever since Durkheim described the effect of social disintegration and lack of internal and external regulation upon an individual, and gave it the term *anomie*,[7] both idea and term have captured the imagination of social scientists.

---

6. See Footnote 1, above.

7. See Emile Durkheim, *Suicide. A Study in Sociology,* John A. Spaulding and George Simpson, translators (Glencoe, Ill.: Free Press, 1951), pp. 246-54.

On the basis of his investigation of the mind of the American working man, Mayo states that "Durkheim's findings in 19th century France would seem to apply to 20th century America," and suggests that this "social disintegration" operating upon a man's values accounts for much of the political phenomena of our time.[8] It may, indeed, be true that the phenomena Durkheim observed have heightened relevance for contemporary society, for the present concentration of all attention and social evaluation upon economic success tends to denigrate other values and leave the intensely competing individual stripped of his culture.[9] Among the elements of culture which are abandoned in this way are political ideals and interests; exclusive focus upon economic success leaves no psychic energy for them.

This is not without its danger, for anomic individuals, however many there are, may attempt to reintegrate with the society, ideologically and socially, through some totalitarian movement.[10] Apparently this was true in Germany in the 1930's, and it has been said that the reason why immigrant groups in the United States have been more susceptible to Communism than the native groups, is that the culture has been transmitted to the immigrant in a weak and diluted fashion. Some respond with apathy, others with the total politics of the alienated.[11]

Leo Srole has attempted to define in measurable form the cluster of feelings of alienation, lack of relatedness to society, and value loss associated with the term anomie.[12] The concept and the questions used to measure this attitudinal dimension may best be put forward in Srole's own words.

1. The individual's sense of the unresponsiveness to his lot and to his needs shown by community leadership: "Most public officials (people in public office) are not really interested in the problems of the average man. In general do you agree or disagree?"

---

8. Elton Mayo, *The Human Problems of an Industrial Civilization* (New York: Macmillan, 1933), pp. 131, 132.

9. Robert Merton, "Social Structure and Anomie," in Merton, *Social Theory and Social Structure* (Glencoe, Ill.: Free Press, 1949), pp. 125-49.

10. Erich Fromm, *The Sane Society* (New York: Rinehart, 1955), pp. 120-208.

11. Philip Selznick, *The Organizational Weapon. A Study of Bolshevik Strategy and Tactics* (New York: McGraw-Hill, 1952). It may also be noted that David Riesman employs the concept of anomie, although in a slightly different sense: "My concept of anomic covers a wider range than Durkheim's metaphor; it is virtually synonomous with 'maladjusted,' a term I refrain from using because of its negative connotations." Riesman finds the anomic individual, so defined, is likely to be apathetic or overconformist in his political interests, waiting for some call which will transport him into politics and away from his disagreeable self. See *The Lonely Crowd* (New Haven: Yale University Press, 1950), p. 287.

12. Leo Srole, "Social Dysfunction, Personality, and Social Distance Attitudes," paper read before American Sociological Society National Meeting, Chicago, 1951 (mimeographed). The five questions formed an acceptable Guttman Scale. See also Srole, "Social integration and certain corollaries," *American Sociological Review, 21* (1956), pp. 709-16. A critique of the anomie scale is available in Alan H. Roberts and Milton Rokeach, "Anomie, Authoritarianism, and Prejudice," Ms. loaned by Rokeach, Dec. 1955.

2. The individual's perception of the social order as essentially fickle, unpredictable and orderless, giving rise to the feeling that he could do little to direct his life with any degree of time perspective or planning ahead: "Nowadays a person has to live pretty much for today and let tomorrow take care of itself."
3. Loss of faith in the doctrine of progress as applied to the self: "In spite of what some people say, the lot (situation, condition) of the average man is getting worse, not better."
4. Deflation or loss of meaning of internalized group norms, values, and goals, resulting in extreme form in the individual's sense of the meaningless and futility of life itself: "It's hardly fair to bring children into the world with the way things look for the future."
5. The individual's sense that the framework of immediate personal relationships, the very rock of his social existence, was no longer predictive or supportive: "These days a person doesn't really know whom he can count on."

Now when a working class sample of a large metropolitan city was asked these questions, certain properties of the anomie complex in America came to light.[13] In the first place, surprisingly enough, the Negro workers who might be expected to experience a sense of value-loss, were no different from the white workers in this respect. On the whole it was only age and education that seemed to affect people's sense of anomie: the older and the less well educated were, so to speak, "the lost generation."

Now how would one expect people who had lost their bearings, or for whom life had been stripped of meaning, to behave politically? One would expect them to vote less than others and to be interested in politics less than others. As Merton has suggested, political ideals would have no more meaning than any other kind of ideals for these people[14] and the point of voting would be lost from view. This is the case. The anomics were markedly less interested in the 1952 campaign and voted less than others. One of the reasons for this was their sense of political ineffectiveness, the feeling that government officials are not interested in them and do not care what happens to the average man.

The belief that governmental authorities are not interested in what happens to the individual members of their constituencies is probably part of a larger constellation of attitudes and beliefs dealing with all authority figures. It tends to be generalized in many areas of life, as may be seen in Table 12.1., based upon a study of student attitudes at Cornell.

The student who believes that government officials are not interested in the average man, i.e., oneself, also tends to believe that instructors are not interested in their students. And lying behind this general attitude, there lurks the childhood experience of parents who were not interested in their children, the experience of emotional abandonment. These expriences are likely to produce separation anxiety in the child, and, if this anxiety turns to hopelessness, it is a state of mind which leads away from political participation,

---

13. Arthur Kornhauser, Albert J. Mayer, and Harold L. Sheppard, *When Labor Votes, A Study of Auto Workers* (New York: University Books, 1956), pp. 189-95.
14. R. Merton, *op. cit.*, pp. 125-49.

TABLE 12.1.—Instructors' Interest in Students and Officials' Interest in Average Man.

"How many of your instructors do you think take a personal interest in their students?"

"There's little use writing . . . officials because . . . not interested in problems of average man"	All or most	About half	Few	None
Agree	16%	21%	28%	48%
Disagree	66	65	51	32
Don't know	17	15	21	20
N =	(406)	(398)	(700)	(44)

SOURCE: Unpublished material supplied by Morris Rosenberg.

not back into politics. Here, as so often in the analysis of politics, the original theories of government as an extension of the family, both historically and functionally, turn out to have psychological validity.

The second major relation between anomie and electoral participation is the tendency of the anomic to be deviant. In the metropolitan study mentioned, the anomic, although immersed in the pro-Democratic pressures of union, metropolis, and working class membership, tended, more than non-anomics similarly situated, to be a Republican in 1952.[15] This was not because he was alienated from the union or the union ideology but for some other reason. In all probability this deviance reflected in this case, not a principled stand in favor of another range of policies, but both confusion and disorientation, on the one hand, and a strong attraction to Eisenhower on the other. Eisenhower caught up the anomic's feeling of lack of direction and, because he appeared strong and purposeful, whereas Stevenson permitted himself to show indecision in public, drew the anomic toward him with powerful psychic bonds.

Summarizing this discussion on interpersonal relations and politics we may say:

"Anomie," a sense of value loss and lack of direction, inhibits political participation in several ways: (a) it implies feelings of ineffectiveness; (b) a general feeling that authority figures do not care about "you" is associated with anomic feelings; (c) activity loses its urgency when goals are devalued. In addition to being apathetic, the anomic individual is more likely than others to be politically deviant for his group.

PURSUIT OF POLICY

The early advocates and the later spokesmen for democracy believed that in a representative system members of the electorate would focus their atten-

---

15. A. Kornhauser and associates, *op. cit.*, p. 193.

tion upon the issues debated during elections and would make up their minds accordingly. In some versions, these policy decisions of the electorate were conceived to be guided by a desire for the public interest, in others by reference to group or factional interests, and in other and more cynical versions, by self-interest pure and simple. If this is the case today, we must believe that men participate in politics in order to achieve some public policy, either for themselves or for others. Let us examine this belief.

Policy orientation of this kind relies upon certain underlying attitudes, beliefs, and goals. In the first place it implies that men have needs which can be served by government and politics. And so they do. In the second place it suggests that these needs are translated into policy terms, that is, statements of what the government should do to fulfill these needs. From the evidence that most men do, in fact, have some policy preferences (though by no means on every issue) we may conclude that this translation is widely made.[16] Generally speaking it is made in three ways, as suggested by the references to the rationale of democracy mentioned above. Some policies are desired because they provide some material or career gain to the individual (change in zoning, change in taxes); some policies are desired because they offer one's group some particular gain (party advantage, religious support); and there are policies which are desired because they serve ideological or projective needs (support of the United Nations, repression of "subversives").

These policies which relate immediately to one's own life situation (so-called "self-interest") might be thought to be the core of policy orientation, but such is not the case in national elections. This is partly because, as 73 per cent of an urban working sample claimed, "Politics and government are so complicated that the average person can't really understand what's going on."[17] As a consequence, the individual citizen rarely sees a relationship between electoral outcome and his own life situation.[18] Thus policy orientation in national politics is, in a very large measure, mediated by group loyalties and symbolic or ideological references.

A need which can be satisfied by governmental action, *and* the translation of this need into policy terms, then, comprises the first condition of effective policy orientation. This in itself would not be sufficient to promote active participation; a participant must also believe that democratic processes are meaningful. Here we come back to the sense of political effectiveness, focusing not upon the person's image of himself as effective, but rather upon the responsiveness of democratic officials. Most Americans do, in fact, see the democratic process in this way. About three-quarters of an urban working-class sample agreed that "The way people vote is the main thing that decides how things are run in this country."[19] The image of the functioning of the American democracy is, on the whole, a sanguine one.

---

16. See Angus Campbell, Gerald Gurin, and Warren E. Miller, *The Voter Decides* (Evanston, Ill.: Row, Peterson, 1954), pp. 118-19.

17. A. Kornhauser and associates, *op. cit.*, p. 155.

18. See, for example, Gerhart H. Saenger, "Social Status and Political Behavior," *American Journal of Sociology*, 51 (1945), pp. 103-13.

19. A. Kornhauser and associates, *op. cit.*, p. 155.

In passing we may note that over the last thirty years this sanguinity seems to have grown. The interview material of the twenties featured "disgust with politics" and seemed in many ways to echo the "shame of the cities" motifs carried over from an earlier era. With the decline of the bosses, the shift from the old style (mercenary) lobbying to new style (electoral threat) lobbying, and the expansion of middle-class mentality and morality downward in the social structure, these "disgust with politics" motifs have become less apposite and, impressionistically speaking, seem to be less frequent in interview material.[20] Of course, it is possible to go too far in the other direction; and indeed there is a touch of naivete in the response that the elections are "the main thing that decides how things are run in this country." There is a kind of parallel between the split between over-idealized versions of democracy and the cynical corrupt versions on the one hand, and the classification of women as pure (mother) and impure (sex-object) often found in psychoanalytic material, on the other, Politically, neither the pure version, with its unrealtistic and uninstrumental account of the means of participation (and the added risk of disillusionment and reaction against politics), nor the cynical version, with its unwholesome and degrading picture of the political process, offer an adequate basis for participation..

In addition to the translation of needs into policy, and the appreciation of the democratic process as meaningful, there is a third attitude which sets the stage for policy-oriented participation. This is the belief that political rather than private channels are the most suitable means of achieving the policy. Community improvement goals, for example, may be pursued through extra-political church or civic groups, rather than through change in governmental policy. Here some evidence from a study of politics in a small Southern community is relevant.[21] A sample of 278 adults in this community were asked to name the community's "two biggest problems" and then requested to state "what are you yourself doing to improve this situation?" and "whether you had a part in anything recently" to make the community "a better place to live in." In this way it was possible to ascertain the relative preference for political activity and the kind of political activity seen as instrumental in attacking community problems. The responses are given in Table 12.2.

Although there is a certain ambiguity in the evidence (and no doubt in the minds of the respondents as well) regarding the roles of the churches and civic groups, it seems clear that voting in elections has a low priority. This is the first point. The second derives from further analysis of those who mentioned voting in this connection or in another part of the study. This analysis shows that persons who seek change through direct political activity, also seek change through other means. It will be recalled that this

---

20. Compare Charles E. Merriam and Harold F. Gosnell, *Non-Voting* (Chicago: University of Chicago Press, 1924); with Morris Rosenberg, "Some Determinants of Political Apathy," *Public Opinion Quarterly, 18* (1954-55), pp. 349-66.

21. W. Buchanan, *op. cit.*, pp. 281-96.

TABLE 12.2.—Personal Actions to Help Meet the Community's "Biggest Problem" or to Make it a "Better Place to Live in."

Type of Action	Per cent of Total Responses
Work through civic clubs	22
Work through churches	20
Talk or complain about it	19
Vote for candidate or bond issue	14
Work through business, profession	12
Pay taxes	4
Other actions	10
All actions mentioned (275)	100

SOURCE: William Buchanan, "An Inquiry into Purposive Voting," "Journal of Politics, 20" (1956), p. 293.

is not true of all voters (only a fraction of the voters join organizations, petition Congress, etc., although those who do these things are almost certain to vote), but the purposive policy-oriented voter is a special, more generally active type of citizen. And, in the third place, voters of this policy-oriented nature may be characterized as follows:[22]

They are not people dissatisfied with their government, they are rather a tolerant, educated, experienced, active minority in community affairs. One might even call them "leaders" of the community. These people who see their vote as a tool for shaping their environment do not prefer the political to the social techniques; in fact, they are more likely to use the latter. Though more sanguine than others, even these purposive voters are not particularly optimistic about the results they can achieve through the franchise.

Finally, the policy-oriented participant not only has a policy and seeks to implement it politically, but he does not permit other phases of politics to exercise superior attraction. Thus, the 1952 voters who switched from a Democratic vote in 1948 to a Republican vote in 1952, in spite of their agreement with the Democratic stand on the 1952 issues, were insufficiently policy-oriented to withstand the attraction of Eisenhower's appeal.[23] Some hint of this "sublimation of policy" is suggested in a study of voting patterns in a Midwest metropolis.[24] In response to the question, "Why was this election important to you," the following pattern emerged (evaluation of total response to the interview):

Because of a man I wanted	100%
Because of issues, conditions (no mention of a man)	17
Because of Party	10
Because of Myself (e.g., my first election, meant my job)	14
Other	5

22. *Ibid*, p. 295.

23. See Angus Campbell, Gerald Gurin, and Warren E. Miller, "Political Issues and the Vote: November, 1952," *American Political Science Review, 47* (1953), p. 367.

24. Alfred de Grazia, "The Limits of External Leadership over a Minority Electorate," *Public Opinion Quarterly, 20* (1956), p. 121.

As we have said earlier, issues by themselves are of low saliency; issues embodied in a candidate may be very important.

These four conditions then are necessary for the pursuit of policy goals to become a strong motive for political participation: translation of need into policy, respect for democratic processes as a means of change, acceptance of political channels as appropriate means to achieve the goals, and an issue orientation which is not over-ridden by other aspects of the political scene.

There is substantial evidence that people who take stands on the issues of the day are more active in politics, those who are aware of party differences on these issues are more active in politics, and those who are more partisan in their policy orientation are more active in politics.[25] Moreover, this was true in the 1952 election, characterized by a strong candidate appeal, and it is even true separately for those with different degrees of education. It is certainly plausible on the face of it.

Yet it does not answer the question of the degree to which people are motivated to enter the political arena because of their policy preferences. At this point, in addition to the relatively low priority given to issues in the Midwest metropolis mentioned above, and the general feeling that the outcome of elections will make little difference to the individual, we find evidence in history for low priority of policy preferences. If it were true that voting is primarily a response to the perceived needs for policy changes, we would expect that electoral turnout would increase in times of depression and slacken off in good times, on the theory that depression would create many new demands for policy changes. In point of fact, as we shall see in Chapter 21, there is no increase in turnout in depression times; the phases of that business cycle and political participation are unrelated.

In the second place, if people were primarily motivated in their political activity by their concern for achieving policy changes, electoral turnout would be related to the closeness of the contest, on the theory that the less close contests would make people whose main goal was a policy change consider the exercise of their franchise to be either futile or superfluous. Again, as we shall see later on, it appears that the relationships between turnout and closeness of election is extremely tenuous. On both counts, then, we are forced to the conclusion that an instrumental approach to political change is a minimal feature of electoral activity. It is there, but subdued.

With respect to other forms of participation, the evidence again casts doubt upon the importance of policy orientation as a motive. Among the Republican precinctmen questioned in Seattle in 1952, "the majority of the respondents gave little evidence of carefully thought out reasons for assuming the precinct leadership"; most of what they said was in the form of cliches: "promoting Americanism," "to save the two-party system," "a

---

25. A. Campbell and associates, *The Voter Decides*, pp. 120-34.

sense of civic duty."[26] Other attitudes were relevant: (1) many felt that they were forced by circumstances or pressure of friends into the work, or, as one said, "I was trapped;" (2) family traditions of politics were important; (3) some, particularly women, sought to broaden their acquaintance with the neighborhood and possibly to "improve" it socially as well; (4) some did it for the "love of the game;" and (5) some from a sense of civic or party duty. Very few could be said to be policy-oriented.

Moreover, of those who wrote letters to their Senators on the issue of conscription, a substantial number were not at all interested in the policies they wrote about, but wrote rather for other reasons, such as the wish to gratify a friend or a sense of duty.[27] There were, of course, many letters which did reflect the immediate policy concerns of the correspondents; some were specific, as in the case of a man afraid of losing his job; others were general, as with the man who said "Democracy is slipping and it is necessary to keep it up." On other issues, moreover, the concern with policy is greater, as is usually the case with mail on the tariff.[28] But in writing letters to legislators, where the substance of the act is an expression of policy preference, it is clear that the policy itself is only part of the general focus of concern. And even with respect to financial contributions it is more often the case that the donor seeks the personal rewards of gratitude from the solicitor than the more distant rewards of policy fulfillment.[29]

Glancing back over this discussion, we find evidence for the following hypotheses:

The pursuit of policy changes in government through political action requires: (a) translation of needs into policy terms, (b) belief in democratic political action as, first, effective and, second, suitable in a given instance, and (c) a policy orientation strong enough to withstand competing claims for political allegiance and activity.

The translation of personal needs into policy preferences is impeded by the obscurity of the relationship of policy to a person's own life situation; hence this translation is largely mediated by group alignment and ideological or symbolic references.

Political participation as a means of effecting policy changes in government is increased by acceptance of the traditional rationale of democracy (an increasingly prevalent attitude) and is inhibited by a view of democratic processes as "fraudulent;" but a realistic appraisal of the place of popular action in policy formation serves as the best long-run basis for policy-oriented participation.

---

26. Hugh Bone, *Grass Roots Party Leadership: A Study of King County, Washington* (Seattle: University of Washington, 1952, mimeographed), pp. 26, 29-31. In the analysis of party workers in the Elmira study, a few "young actives," were found who were policy oriented. See Bernard R. Berelson, Paul F. Lazarsfeld, and William E. McPhee, *Voting* (Chicago: University of Chicago Press, 1954), p. 165.

27. Rowena Wyant, "Voting Via The Senate Mailbag, Part I," and, with Herta Hertzog, "Part II," *Public Opinion Quarterly, 5* (1941), pp. 359-82, 590-624.

28. Lewis A. Dexter, "What Do Congressmen Hear: The Mail," *Public Opinion Quarterly, 20* (1956), pp. 16-27.

29. Herbert Alexander, unpublished material from a study of contributions to campaign chests in New York City.

Citizens interested in community policy changes place voting relatively low in the priority of instruments of change; those who think of voting in this way also employ other instruments of change and are generally active in the community. Policy-oriented voters tend to be the "natural" grass roots community leaders.

Those who see policy differences between the parties and take stands on current policy issues are more active than others in politics (at every educational level); but analysis of precinctmen, letter writers, and even campaign donors, and historical analysis suggests that a desire to affect governmental policy plays a relatively minor part in eliciting political participation.

PARTISANSHIP

The attitudes and behaviors which are, at various times, called "partisanship" are multiple and diverse. A "partisan" person may do any number of things to show his partisanship and the things may all be radically different. Yet throughout all of the various meanings of the word, one theme is apparent: identification with one side in a controversy. Broadly speaking, this involves three questions about a single attitude: (1) Has a person taken sides, or is he independent? (2) How strongly does he feel about his preference? (3) Is this a preference which admits a balanced perspective of both sides, or is it a blind one? In everyday conversation we use the term "partisan" in all three senses, but here it is useful to distinguish among them.

Now, the person who identifies with a political party is a partisan in the first sense, as the terms "non-partisan election" and "bi-partisan foreign policy" suggest. Partisans of this kind will clearly be more likely than are independents to electioneer and contribute to party campaign chests. But what of letter writing, petitioning, and voting? Do independents or party adherents vote more frequently? In 1948 and 1954 those who did not have any party attachments or leanings in one direction voted less than those with party attachments, but in 1952 there was no discernible difference between this group and others.[30] Tentatively, at least, these findings suggest that party identification is more closely related to turnout when other factors such as strong feelings on candidates are absent. Furthermore, it seems to be the case that it is his party identification which sustains a person's interest in politics and determines his vote decision when his party is in the clear minority, rather than his views on issues or candidates.[31] Only party loyalty remains to make a person persist in his locally deviant political behavior.

---

30. Samuel J. Eldersveld, "The Independent Vote: Measurement, Characteristics, and Implications for Party Strategy," *American Political Science Review,* 46 (1952), p. 747; A. Campbell and associates, *The Voter Decides,* p. 108; Angus Campbell and Homer C. Cooper, *Group Differences in Attitudes and Votes, A Study of the 1954 Congressional Election,* Ann Arbor, Survey Research Center, 1956, p. 39.

31. Warren E. Miller, "One-Party Politics and the Voter," *American Political Science Review,* 50 (1956), pp. 707-25.

Our culture, with its emphasis on "independence," does not make partisanship in this sense of party-identification an easy choice. Beyond this, however, a person's personal situation may also make such a choice difficult. Consider the case of a pleasant young man who has sought to demonstrate to the world that he was not the inferior person which sickness, physical weakness, and timidity during childhood made him appear to be. One method of demonstrating this, particularly to his father, was always to make the right decision; "be ye perfect in all things," he tells himself. In autobiographical material, he reports his feelings about the political parties as follows:

I am somewhat attracted to the Republican Party as I feel that a professed alignment with that group may act as a compensatory measure (to inferiority feelings), allowing me to identify with successful men. . . . There are other factors, though. One of these is my attachment to my father which draws me to the Democratic party and vests yearnings in the other direction with fears and apprehensions.

He does not seek political information because if he knew more he might have to decide for one or the other party—and he might make a mistake, a terrible thing in his own eyes. Hence, with respect to politics,

This lack of information is a welcome thing and I actually avoid extending my knowledge since the lack of it serves as a protective measure to avoid making a decision and as a rationalization to myself and to others for this avoidance.

For such a person partisanship comes hard.

When identification with a party is made and a clear party loyalty emerges, that is, when a person is partisan in this sense, this partisanship could easily be interpreted as the product of a policy preference. Party loyalty could be the pursuit of policy in disguise. And for many people this is undoubtedly the case, as the general correspondence between party identification and issue-orientation suggests.[32] But for many others party identification is clearly not based upon policy preferences, but rather on something else. Only 53 per cent of a sample of union urban working-class adults in Detroit thought there were any important differences between the parties in 1952—and this in spite of the fact that union members are more policy-oriented than average.[33] For the rank and file individual, at least, party partisanship is more likely to be a product of group loyalty than of policy interests, however the group leader may arrive at their position.

A party partisanship, however, may vary in intensity, as well as being based on different kinds of attraction. Among those who admit to a party identification it is clearly true that the more intense the identification ("strong" contrasted to "not very strong") the more likely a person is to vote and participate more generally in the electoral process. And this is true for partisan attitudes on party-linked issues as well.[34]

What is a "strong" identification with a party? How salient is it? Such

---

32. A. Campbell and associates, *The Voter Decides*, p. 131.
33. A. Kornhauser and associates, *op. cit.*, p. 163.
34. A. Campbell and H. Cooper, *op. cit.*, p. 39; A. Campbell and associates, *The Voter Decides*, pp. 130-35.

questions are hard to answer, although answers to general questions on "why you care personally" about the outcome of an election give important clues. Unfortunately, the evidence provided by these questions is inconclusive. Only 10 per cent of a city-wide sample of metropolitan voters, interviewed in the context of a municipal election, referred to a party victory as a reason for considering the outcome of the election important, although about double that number of Negroes gave party reasons for caring about the election outcome.[35] On the other hand, 40 per cent of a working-class union sample cared "very much" about the 1952 national election for party reasons.[36] Evidently, party is more salient for lower income and ethnic status citizens; this is the group then which is more likely to be moved to vote for reasons of party identification.

Now political partisanship implies not only an identification with one side in a controversy, but also a relative disidentification with the other side. The nature of the two attitudes, the pro and the con, are significant for a number of reasons, one of which is the growing view among psychologists that what you believe is often less important than the grounds for your belief.[37] The intolerant person who stereotypes "good guys" and "bad guys" is a partisan of a different character from one who sees good and bad on both sides. Differences of this kind are revealed by asking people to select from a list of adjectives those that they think apply to the candidates running at the time. When this was done in 1948 it was discovered that those who associate *only* favorable words or *only* unfavorable words with the (then) President Truman, (and who were more partisan in this sense) were rather less likely to participate in politics than the more balanced person who could see Truman as part good and part bad.[38] Not all studies, however, show this same relationship. The same kind of evidence based on a free answer test in 1952 shows that "For people who indicate some reaction to the candidates in personal terms, the lack of a clear choice between the candidates *does not appear greatly to inhibit* their political participation." [39] This is in contrast to the policy area where bipartisanship or non-partisanship dampens political ardor in a clearly demonstrable manner. The effective American citizenry "has a good word for everybody"—but not every policy.

Another aspect of this same question of tolerance in partisanship is revealed in a study of union members' attitudes toward unions and business in politics. Most union members believe that both unions and business

---

35. A. de Grazia, *op. cit.*, p. 121.

36. A. Kornhauser and associates, *op. cit.*, pp. 132-33.

37. On this point see the work of Milton Rokeach, particularly; "The Nature and Meaning of Dogmatism," *Psychological Review, 61* (1954), pp. 194-204; "Political and Religious Dogmatism: An Alternative to the Authoritarian Personality," *Psychological Monograph, 70,* No. 18; and with Benjamin Fruchter, "A Factorial Study of Dogmatism and Related Concepts," *Journal of Abnormal and Social Psychology, 53* (1956), pp. 356-59.

38. Julian L. Woodward and Elmo Roper, "Political Activity of American Citizens," *American Political Science Review, 44* (1950), p. 883.

39. A. Campbell and associates, *op. cit.*, p. 141. My italics.

groups should be allowed to work for their candidates, but a few thought it was all right for one but not the other.[40] What were the characteristics of these partisans who would allow "their" side to enjoy privileges denied to the other side? They were, on the whole, somewhat more likely to be authoritarian and anomic in the sense described above. This is in line with theory about "authoritarians" and "anomics": they tend to be intolerant of ambiguity and to classify people into rigid groups of good and bad. They also tend to be less well educated than average.

But notice that this group is made up of those who are intolerantly partisan *for* their own group, i.e., pro-labor and pro-Stevenson, and those who are intolerantly partisan *against* their own group. This turns out to be important for our inquiry inasmuch as those who are intolerantly partisan for their own group are much less interested in politics and much less likely to vote than the average man. Not so with the group that is intolerantly partisan against the views and interests of their union-associates. This is a group with more than average political interest and high rates of voting. Here, then, are those whose partisan interests erect barriers between them and their general environment (we do not know about their primary groups) but who defy the environment and carry out their convictions with more than average vigor. For them the usual solution of the cross-pressured individual, the withdrawal of affect, offers no solace. For whatever reason, they retain their partisanship, are intolerant of their opponents' rights and practices, and go to the polls in proportionately great numbers. The lesson to be learned from these data is that the effect of intolerant partisanship reinforced by one's larger environment is in the direction of apathy; the effect of intolerant partisanship in opposition to one's larger environment is political action.

Elections and campaigns tend to arouse partisanship, in part, at least, because campaign appeals reinforce class, ethnic, and regional group loyalties. They "activate" the predispositions which lie latent in the public, pushing the marginally-interested and wavering voter back into his "natural" group. Having done this, campaign stimuli encourage the "consistency effect," that is, encourage an organization of attitudes about candidate, issues, and party which add up to a partisan attitude. They elicit emotional investment in the outcome, at least to some extent. But then, when the campaign is over and one group of voters has lost, the intensity of emotion on the part of the losers tend to evaporate and they salve their wounds with various psychologically soothing devices. The losers find that they didn't care so much, or see aspects of the situation they did not see before.[41] Just after the 1952 election, for example, 17 per cent of the Stevenson voters in an urban union sample said they were "glad" Eisenhower won, and another 37 per cent reported that while they were not glad, neither were they sorry.[42] Those who were glad developed a new faith in Eisenhower, and those who were neutral

---

40. A. Kornhauser and associates, *op. cit.*, pp. 101-102.

41. Sheldon J. Korchin, *Psychological Variables in the Behavior of Voters*, unpublished Ph.D. dissertation, Harvard University Library, 1946, pp. 342-46.

42. A. Kornhauser and associates, *op. cit.*, pp. 134, 342-43.

felt that the people's will should be respected or merely hoped for the best in an obscure situation.

Whether this withdrawal of affect is as complete as it appears on the surface, is, of course, open to question. At least it is true that belonging to the "out" party produces a latent dissatisfaction even when overt statements indicate relative agreement at the moment with current policies. For example, one study found that although net change in dissatisfaction with government policy over a short period following the 1940 elections was small, the change to dissatisfaction was twice as high among the 1940 Wilkie voters as among the 1940 Roosevelt voters.[43] Thus the losers who say that the decision of the electorate was for the best and that they are reconciled, are probably more ready than others to be disappointed in the way the administration handles its problems.

However temporary, this withdrawal of affect and rationalization on the part of the losers, termed the *fait accompli* effect, reflects the low involvement in politics of the American voters and is said to have the socially useful function of facilitating adjustment to changes in administrations.

Partisanship has other effects upon the political behavior of the individual. The selection by partisans of commentators on television reflects their partisan feelings, as do the degree of trust they place in the newspapers, and their preferences for (but not their exposure to) one medium as contrasted to another.[44] But, in view of the experiments on learning and forgetting of controversial material,[45] and the known preference for exposure to one's own point of view, it is the similarity in knowledge and exposure which should attract our attention, not the differences. Partisans of different sides tend to know the same items and to listen to the same political speakers (as contrasted to commentators).[46] Of course, they may interpret what the speakers say in different fashion, as did the Republican Elmira voters who twisted Dewey's stand on price control to fit their own preferences on this issue,[47] but the exposure patterns and patterns of information are remarkably homogeneous. Here, too, we find the effect of relatively low political involvement operating to reduce the pain of exposure to the arguments of "the other side." But we also find one of the reasons for low involvement: similarity of exposure, following from the nature of the media in America, tends to reinforce the low level of tension characteristic of American politics.

---

43. Paul F. Lazarsfeld and Ruth Durant, "National Morale, Social Cleavage, and Political Allegiance," *Journalism Quarterly, 19* (1942), pp. 150-58.

44. A. Kornhauser and associates, *op. cit.,* pp. 78-84; Paul F. Lazarsfeld, Bernard R. Berelson, and Hazel Gaudet, *The People's Choice* (New York: Columbia University Press, 1948), p. 130.

45. Jerome M. Levine and Gardner Murphy, "The Learning and Forgetting of Controversial Material," *Journal of Abnormal and Social Psychology, 38* (1943), pp. 507-17.

46. B. R. Berelson and associates, *op. cit.,* p. 245n; A. Kornhauser and associates, *op. cit.,* p. 82. Note that while exposure is roughly the same among the partisans of both parties, the degree of trust in each medium tends to reflect the diverse partisan attitudes.

47. B. Berelson and associates, *op. cit.,* pp. 213-33.

On partisanship, then, we may say:

Party partisanship, as contrasted to independence, tends to be associated with political participation, except when some other strong motive, such as attraction to a "charismatic candidate," is operative. Because the policy differences between the parties are obscure to many people, party-partisanship is more often the result of ethnic, class, or other group identification than of policy preferences.

The more strongly a person feels about his partisan identifications with a party or with party-linked issues, the more likely he is to vote; the salience of party identification is higher among lower status people and contributes more to their motives for participation than to the motives of others.

Intolerant partisanship in the sense of a black and white categorization of the sides in a controversy is related to participation as follows: intolerant partisanship with respect to candidates is either unrelated or negatively related to participation; intolerant partisanship on policy matters is positively related to participation. The relation of participation to acceptance of the political rights of ones "own" group while denying political rights for the opposition group depends upon the context: intolerant partisans of this kind who are in agreement with their larger environment tend to be apathetic while those who are in opposition to their larger environment tend to be politically active.

Election campaigns tend to increase partisanship by reinforcing group loyalties and forcing individuals to achieve consistently partisan positions; the effect of losing an election is to weaken partisan feelings among the losers, but this withdrawal leaves a latent disposition toward partisan criticism at a later stage.

Although partisanship tends (a) marginally to affect patterns of exposure to political material in the media, and (b) marginally to affect patterns of information and perception, there is a remarkably similar pattern of exposure and information among partisans of the two major parties in the United States. This is partially a *product* of the low political involvement of the American public and partly a *cause* of this low involvement.

EXPECTATIONS

What a person expects from future events has a bearing on what he is willing to do today. This central truth forms the basis of Lasswell's concern with expectations as the basis for attitudes and acts.[48] As a feature of the attitudinal pattern which evokes political action, expectations play many parts. Let us consider three of them.

One inclusive expectational pattern is captured in the term "fatalism," the belief that future events are predetermined in some way beyond human, or at least one's own, control. This view of the future is associated with low political participation although we cannot agree with the view that the frequent frustration of expectations of success in the American culture have led

---

48. Harold D. Lasswell and Abraham Kaplan, *Power and Society, A Framework for Political Inquiry* (New Haven: Yale University Press, 1950), p. 21.

to widespread feelings of fatalism.[49] It is a feature of the anomie complex and is present in the apolitical tradition-directed mentality delineated by Riesman. Fatalism, whether or not clothed in religious doctrine, is a frame of mind easily associated with general political (and social) apathy.

A second manner in which expectations enter into participant motivation turns on the particular interpretation of the probable course of history. For example, a person will not be psychologically involved in the question of government policy on atomic civil defense if he does not expect another war: he will not be involved in issues of unemployment relief if he does not anticipate another depression. Similarly, and quite logically, people will be less likely to be concerned about or participate in civil defense activities if they do not believe there will be an atomic attack on their country.[50] And with respect to elections, if a person believes no important decisions affecting him personally will be altered by the outcome of the election, he will be less likely to vote. Projections of history into the future and the expected relation of future events to the individual enter into participant and non-participant motivations.

Finally, expectations regarding the probable winner in an election enter into calculations in two ways. The first has to do with the feeling of futility in expending energy for a victory which will take place in any event or to prevent a defeat which is inevitable. On the whole, these feelings seem to be minimally operative in American elections. The second has to do with bandwagon sentiments, the need to be on the winning side. There is some evidence of the force of bandwagon sentiment, disentangling it from the projection phenomena,[51] and it is probable, though not proven, that this is related to the overt acts of participation, as well as the psychological feelings of involvement and partisanship which it elicits.

To summarize these three areas we may say:

Political participation may be inhibited by fatalistic attitudes or by specific expectations of the course of history (war, depression, electoral outcome) making the proposed participant acts seem useless or irrelevant for the society or the individual; *but* bandwagon appeal may make participation in a sure victory an inducement to engage in politics, and group loyalties, sense of duty, support of a well-loved candidate, and so forth, may make expectations of future events irrelevant to the act of participation.

49. See M. Rosenberg, "The Meaning of Politics in Mass Society," *Public Opinion Quarterly*, 15 (1951), p. 9.

50. William A. Scott, "Attitudes Toward Participation in Civil Defense: An Analysis via Psychological Constructs," *Public Opinion Quarterly*, 17 (1953), p. 377. Incidentally, Berelson and associates found no important difference between Democrats and Republicans with respect to their expectations of war and depression; see Bernard Berelson and associates, *op. cit.*, p. 187.

51. Paul F. Lazarsfeld and associates, *The People's Choice* (New York: Columbia University Press, 1948), pp. 107-109.

Part IV

The Influence of Group Life
on Political Man

CHAPTER 13

How Social Structure Affects Political Life

SOCIAL STRUCTURE affects political behavior in two ways: it influences motivation (and the attitudes, goals, and needs which are associated with it) and it influences the availability of means to pursue political ends. In the first sense it makes political action of a given sort more or less desirable to the individual; in the second sense, it makes such action more or less easy. In the latter sense we speak of the *facilitative* effect of social structure; in the former sense, the *motivational* effect.[1]

Some of the utility of such a mode of analysis (Figure 13.1) is suggested by a modification of Tinbergen's "arrow scheme" which has been commonly used in explaining voting behavior.[2]

The construction of the boxes is intended to illustrate that every event has two aspects (the inner motivational experience and the outer facilitative events), and that while some events would be significant primarily because they affected the situation of the individual, his environment, others would be significant because they affected his attitudes directly. Thus, joining a union may mean (a) a person must pay dues, be out of the house the second Thursday of every month, and receive the union journal, and also (b) an increased indentification with fellows in the shop, a new sense of class consciousness, and smoldering ambitions to be shop-steward. Paying dues may provide a small increment in party funds, but may be more import-

---

1. This is, in some ways, similar to Merton's analysis of the effect of social structure upon economic behavior where the acceptance and rejection of "cultural goals" and the availability of "institutional means" form the variables in a "typology of modes of individual adaptation." See Robert K. Merton, *Social Theory and Social Structure* (Glencoe, Ill.: The Free Press, 1949), p. 133.

2. See Bernard R. Berelson, Paul F. Lazarsfeld, and William N. McPhee, *Voting* (Chicago: University of Chicago Press, 1954), p. 281; Seymour M. Lipset and associates, "The Psychology of Voting: An Analysis of Political Behavior," in Gardner Lindzey, ed., *Handbook of Social Psychology*, Vol. 2 (Cambridge: Addison-Wesley, 1954), pp. 1, 151.

FIGURE 13.1.—A Psycho-Social Model for S—O—R Sequences Over Time.

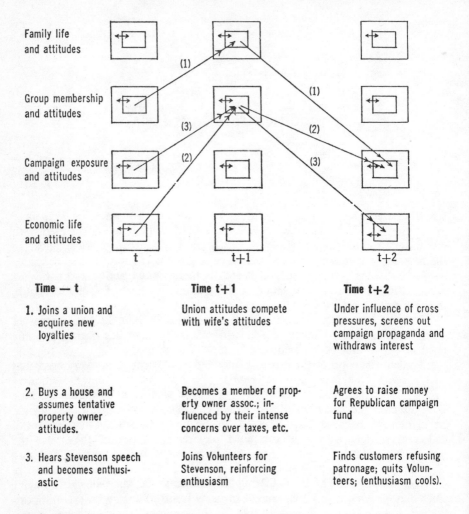

Time — t	Time t+1	Time t+2
1. Joins a union and acquires new loyalties	Union attitudes compete with wife's attitudes	Under influence of cross pressures, screens out campaign propaganda and withdraws interest
2. Buys a house and assumes tentative property owner attitudes.	Becomes a member of property owner assoc.; influenced by their intense concerns over taxes, etc.	Agrees to raise money for Republican campaign fund
3. Hears Stevenson speech and becomes enthusiastic	Joins Volunteers for Stevenson, reinforcing enthusiasm	Finds customers refusing patronage; quits Volunteers; (enthusiasm cools).

ant in the psychological indentification of the union man with the local Democratic party.

In this section, we shall examine how social institutions encourage members of the public to find political solutions to their problems and facilitate political expression, or, on the other hand, how they impede political expressions. First we examine the influence of group memberships, including voluntary associations, family, class, and ethnic groups. We then discuss the effect of community organization upon politics. Finally, we analyze the way in which the media, government, and economic institutions modify grass roots political life.

CHAPTER 14

Group Influences on Political Participation

W HAT IS THE NATURE of group influence on political activity? How do groups make a political being out of a private citizen? Which groups perform this service or disservice for society? Which members of a group are likely to experience group forces more keenly? What happens when group loyalties conflict? In this chapter we turn to these general considerations; in the following chapters we consider specific groups: the family, social class, ethnic groups, political parties, and the community.

Political attitudes and behavior are learned from associates, friends, co-workers, and the fellow members of organizations to which a person belongs. Referring to electoral behavior, Campbell and associates find that "nonvoting, as well as the direction of voting, tends to be shared behavior . . . 90 per cent of the people whose friends did not vote were themselves non-voters."[1] When parents are apolitical, children tend to be apolitical.[2] On the other hand, when a progressive school or a progressive college develops intense interests, the non-political neophyte tends to absorb these interests.[3] The more politically conscious are a person's friends and associates and fellow group members, the more likely he is to be politically conscious and active.

There is another force at work which is quite independent of the political consciousness of friends and the organizations to which a person belongs. Isolation tends to make a person politically apathetic; group memberships in themselves increase his political interests and activity. This is true in the general sense that the more friends and organizational memberships a person has, the more likely he is to be asked his views on politics, regardless of the

---

1. Angus Campbell, Gerald Gurin, and Warren E. Miller, *The Voter Decides* (Evanston, Ill.: Row, Peterson, 1954), p. 202.
2. See Chapter 15.
3. David Riesman, *Faces in the Crowd* (New Haven: Yale University Press, 1952), pp. 552-63; Theodore M. Newcomb, *Personality and Social Change* (New York: Dryden, 1943).

amount of information he has.[4] He is more likely to vote if he has more organizational memberships, no matter where he is in the social system.[5] And this is true of relatively non-political recreational groups as well as unions and business organizations.[6] The range and scope of the kinds of behavior related to group memberships is indicated in Table 14.1.

TABLE 14.1.—Group Memberships and Political Activity.

Per cent who:	Group Members	Non Members
Say they voted in last Presidential election	72%	63%
Discussed labor problems in last week	63	36
Discussed the atomic bomb in last week	43	24
Discussed relations with Russia in last week	53	31
Expressed opinions on atomic energy policy	78	59
Expressed opinions on China policy	91	85

SOURCE: Herbert Hyman and Paul B. Sheatsley, "The Authoritarian Personality—A Methodological Critique," in Richard Christie and Marie Jahoda, eds., "Studies in the Scope and Method of 'The Authoritarian Personality' " (Glencoe, Ill.: Free Press, 1954), p. 62 (data from unpublished NORC study).

There is a third general relationship between political participation and relations to social groups. A person may identify with a group whether or not he is recognized by others as a group member. A manual laborer, for example, may see himself as a member of the middle classes and try to think and behave like them, even though in terms of education, income, or occupation he does not belong. A group with which a person identifies, whether or not he is a member of the group, is a positive *reference group*.[7] A group which is important in his thinking but with which the individual does not want to be identified is a negative reference group.

Political opinions and activity are almost always affected by reference groups whether or not a person is, in fact, a member of these groups. Indeed

---

4. Elihu Katz and Paul F. Lazarsfeld, *Personal Influence* (Glencoe, Ill.: Free Press, 1955), pp. 287-89.

5. This general relationship between number of group memberships and political activity is supported by unpublished material of the Survey Research Center showing that in 1952 in each of eight demographic categories those with more group memberships were more likely to participate in politics. Special community studies in Pittsfield, Mass., and a southern town also support the relationship: See Philip K. Hastings, "The Non-Voter in 1952: a Study of Pittsfield, Massachusetts," *Journal of Psychology, 38* (1954) pp. 301-12; and William Buchanan, "An Inquiry into Purposive Voting," *Journal of Politics, 18* (1956), pp. 281-96. In view of this fact, the limitations on the relationship between group memberships and voting found in Frederick H. Harris, "A Study of Political Participation in Two North Carolina Counties," *Research Previews,* Vol. 3, No. 1 (1955), p. 7, published by the Institute for Research in Social Science, Chapel Hill, N. C., must be interpreted as reflecting a special situation in the counties studied.

6. P. H. Hastings, *op. cit.,* p. 303.

7. For a discussion of the differences between membership groups and reference groups, see Theodore M. Newcomb, *Social Psychology,* (New York: Dryden, 1950), p. 225.

it has been said that having no opinion on a public issue means (a) that the individual has no reference group with a position on the issue, or (b) the individual cannot "shift psychologically to the appropriate reference group," or (c) he is confused as to what the reference group identification implies for this issue.[8]

Thus:

Political participation for an individual increases with (a) the political consciousness and participation of his associates, (b) the frequency and harmony of his interpersonal contacts and group memberships, and (c) the salience and unambiguity of his group references.

HOW GROUPS AFFECT POLITICAL BEHAVIOR

Although there are an infinite number of ways of classifying various kinds of groups (including classifications based on size, type of organization, purpose, nature of membership, activities, leader-follower relations, and social functions),[9] let us simply divide groups into two kinds: those whose members meet together, both formal associations and informal friendship groups, and those whose members do not meet together as a group, such as class, race, or region. These latter we shall term categoric groups.[10]

Groups who meet together can have a powerful effect on the attitudes and behavior of their members. Clearly this effect takes place through what the members of the group say to each other and through the use of the printed word in specialized newspapers, magazines, or bulletins. But, more specifically, the mechanisms whereby groups affect their members involve an understanding of what takes place in this group communication. In the first place, a person gets his standard of judgment of right and wrong from a group. Here, then, he learns the nature and content of civic duty. In the same way, he acquires beliefs about his social environment.[11] There is considerable justification for anchoring social opinions in group opinion. A person cannot

---

8. Eugene L. Hartley, "The Social Psychology of Opinion Formation," *Public Opinion Quarterly, 14* (1950-51), p. 673.

9. For a review of the various classifications of groups in social science literature, see Roger W. Brown, "Mass Phenomena," in Gardner Lindzey, ed., *Handbook of Social Psychology* (Cambridge, Mass.: Addison-Wesley, 1954), Vol. 2, p. 837ff. For other classificatory schemes, see Dorwin Cartwright and Alvin Zander, eds., *Group Dynamics* (Evanston, Ill.: Row Peterson, 1953); *American Sociological Review* (special issue on small group research), *19* (1954), pp. 651-781; Paul Hare, Edgar F. Borgatta, and Robert F. Bales, eds., *Small Groups* (New York: Knopf, 1955).

10. This term is borrowed from David Truman, *The Governmental Process* (New York: Knopf, 1951), p. 23.

11. The way in which beliefs and perceptions are structured by group opinion has been illuminated by the early work of Muzafer Sherif in his *The Psychology of Social Norms* (New York: Harper, 1936). See also Solomon Asch, "Effects of Group Pressure upon the Modification and Distortion of Judgment," in D. Cartwright and A. Zander, eds., *op. cit.*, pp. 151-62.

test most of the relevant propositions for himself; by drawing on a pool of beliefs and experience he is more likely to be right than by relying on his own private evidence.[12] He learns about himself from the group. This is true in two ways. As George Herbert Mead has pointed out, a person derives his self image from the images which others have of him: he "discovers" that he is a leader, a friendly person, a "responsible citizen."[13] But also, in another sense, he learns about himself by finding his identity partially defined by his group memberships.[14] He comes to think of himself as a "member of the country-club set" or a "shantytowner" or simply a "Rotarian." He develops new life-goals through group contacts, such as changes of career or value changes. Thus, from the group he learns what to think about the political world and what to think about himself as a political individual. And, in most groups, he learns how to act out his beliefs and is encouraged to do so.

Other learning takes place of a more specifically political nature. For example, joining a group redefines what is public and what is private. Goals become shared goals, attitudes shared attitudes, and proposed solutions come into relation with other people's solutions. Rather than attempt to solve an economic problem by changing jobs, a person together with others can attempt what he could not do before: bargain (collectively) with new leverage. Rather than attempt to solve a housing problem by house-hunting, he may attempt to secure public housing for himself and others.

Joining a group provides new grounds for partisanship—own group versus others. And partisanship, as we know, is closely related to political activity. There emerges a new recognition of an individual's position with respect to collective gain when he joins a group. His circumstances depend upon the circumstances of the group and he discovers that whatever aids them aids him (although, of course, some gains may be achieved by being an exception, turncoat, or whatever). The group provides new information on the stakes of the individual in social processes and decisions. Visibility of these stakes may be enhanced by group membership. When the group has a political program, the group member who identifies with his group will usually also identify with the program and make it part of his own. For example, those who show marked attachment toward a union are more likely to adopt the union's political orientation than those who do not.[15]

These represent considerations on *how* the group politicizes the individ-

---

12. See Kurt Lewin and Paul Grabbe, eds., "Problems of Re-education," *Journal of Social Issues*, Vol. 1, No. 3.

13. George Herbert Mead, *Mind, Self and Society* (Chicago: University of Chicago Press), 1934.

14. For a discussion of the way American soldiers developed images of themselves from their group memberships, see Robert K. Merton and Alice S. Kitt, "Contributions to the Theory of Reference Group Behavior," in Merton and Paul F. Lazarsfeld, eds., *The American Soldier, Continuities in Social Research* (Glencoe, Ill.: Free Press, 1950), pp. 40-105.

15. Arthur Kornhauser, Harold L. Sheppard, Albert J. Mayer, *When Labor Votes* (New York: University Books, 1956), p. 150.

ual. But why is the individual so vulnerable to these effects? The truth of the matter is that he has much at stake in the conditions of his group life. He has joined the group to satisfy certain needs. If it is a need for social adjustment, he has valued friendships at stake and he will adjust his interests and behavior so that he alienates as few fellow members as possible. If he seeks power within the group, he will accommodate his political views so that he can gratify these power drives. If the group offers economic rewards he will extract these better from the group if he retains his membership in good standing. In short, as Lewin has pointed out, the group is a "life-space" in which a person can achieve some part of his life goals.[16] He will not lightly sacrifice these goals.

Now, assuming that a group develops a political interest—say a veterans' organization becomes concerned about veterans' preference in the civil service—under what circumstances will this group be able to enlist its members in political activity to advance its veterans' preference goals? The first consideration, will be the *valence* of the group for the individuals. How important is it for them, how urgent are the needs the group satisfies and what alternatives are available? Persons for whom the group satisfies urgent needs (the Legionnaire who values his drinking parties with the boys, the individual who seeks to run for sheriff with Legion support) are more active in advancing the organization's program. Furthermore, the man without alternative ways of satisfying his needs, for example, the man whose only club is the Legion Post, is also more likely to support the organization program.[17] If the Legion Post or other group is small, it will have more effect upon its members than if it is large.[18] Members of voluntary associations with fewer members were found in Washington State to rely more upon the political advice of their organizations than members of larger organizations.[19] If the members have a hand in selecting the political program, rather than having it handed down to them by the leaders, they will be more active in advancing it through letter writing or voting behavior.[20] If the group morale is high, the political program will benefit thereby, with more members working for its advancement. If members identify with and "libidinize" the group leader, these sentiments will be generalized to the group's political program.

---

16. Kurt Lewin, *Resolving Social Conflicts* (New York: Harper, 1948), pp. 85-86.

17. See Leon Festinger, Stanley Schacter, and Kurt Back, *Social Pressure in Informal Groups* (New York: Harper, 1950).

18. Frederick F. Stephan and Elliot G. Mishler, "The Distribution of Participation in Small Groups: An Exponential Approximation," *American Sociological Review, 17* (1952), pp. 598-608.

19. Howard E. Freeman and Morris Showel, "Differential Political Influence of Voluntary Associations," *Public Opinion Quarterly, 15* (1951-52), pp. 703-14.

20. Kurt Lewin, "Studies in Group Decision," in Cartwright and Zander, *op. cit.,* pp. 287-301. Harold H. Kelley and John W. Thibaut put it this way, ". . . group decision studies suggest that member acceptance of group goals is heightened by a goal-setting procedure involving discussion and participation in selecting the goals." See their "Experimental Studies of Group Problem Solving and Process," in Gardner Lindzey, *op. cit.,* p. 757.

An important consideration is the relevance of the political program to the general aims of the group and the specific reasons members have for joining the group. Where politics is relevant to the general *raison d'etre* of the group, that is, *group relevant,* members are more easily influenced to go along with the group.[21] Members of a union who see the relationship of the political activity of the union to its bread-and-butter functions are more likely than others to become politically active.[22] The American Medical Association is more successful in mobilizing its members on political issues dealing with the practice of medicine than on such matters as balancing the budget or foreign policy. And when the members of an organization fail to see the group-relevance of the political aims of the group, they are less likely to be moved by group appeals. Apparently this was the case with the Legion's attempt to interest its members in a drive to defeat Congressmen who voted against the veterans' bonus in the 1920's and 1930's; these pressures were ineffective.[23] There is a specificity about the nature of the "reference"—the degree to which a person is guided by his group-identification. Some identified-with groups have no political reference at all. But it should be added, that if there is a group political reference, it is unlikely to be negative for its members. Even when the leadership is exposed as corrupt or "subversive," members still tend to cling to their group identification and follow the political guidance of the group leaders. For example, disclosure of the corruptions of Democratic politicians in New York did not seem to affect the political loyalties or "references" of New York Democrats. The disclosures did not jeopardize the benefits they derived from party membership.[24]

Socially homogeneous groups have a greater political influence upon their members than do heterogeneous groups. This is true because political loyalties tend to follow income, occupational, residential, and ethnic lines. Where group memberships cross these lines, it is more difficult to achieve agreement upon a political program. As a consequence, the political program of a heterogeneous group is likely to be less extensive as well as less effective.

Groups that facilitate their members' political expression are more effective in inducing such expression than those that do not. Political parties provide transportation to the polls; unions give their members postcards to sign and send to their congressmen; Chambers of Commerce organize deputations to visit the governor; the Knights of Columbus invite local political leaders to speak to them. But the face-to-face groups which, like church groups, are often constrained in their political activity; and the large categoric reference groups with no facilities or organization do not mobilize their "members."

---

21. See Leon Festinger, "Informal Social Communication," *Psychological Review,* 57 (1950), pp. 271-82.
22. Harold L. Wilensky, "The Labor Vote: A Local Union's Impact on the Political Conduct of its Members," *Social Forces,* 35 (1956), pp. 111-20.
23. See V. O. Key, *Politics, Parties, and Pressure Groups,* 3rd ed. (New York: Crowell, 1952, pp. 127-29.
24. See G. D. Wiebe, "Responses to the Televised Kefauver Hearings: Some Social Psychological Implications," *Public Opinion Quarterly,* 16 (1952), pp. 179-200.

Political appeals to "be active" without affording means for being active are likely to be ineffective.

Finally, certain kinds of groups have influence only upon their members; others influence both members and non-members alike. Those groups with the widest influence among non-members are the business, political, and veterans associations. Those with influence almost exclusively among their own members are the church and labor organizations.[25] Undoubtedly, as mentioned above, this is related to the way in which the major fault lines of politics lie along class and ethnic boundaries, as well as to the culturally endowed respect for business.

What are the important political reference groups, that is, which groups are more likely to be effective in influencing political views and behavior? Among the categoric groups the following are effective: the socio-economic class strata; the residential groups identified with rural-urban status, community, and region; and the ethnic complex, including race, religion, nationality, and immigrant status. Their effectiveness depends on the nature of culturally-induced identification, not on anything the groups do or do not do. Among those that meet together, the most effective groups include family, friendship cliques, work groups, and various civic and other voluntary associations. Most of these groups are analyzed elsewhere, as are the political parties; here we turn to the voluntary associations. Which of these most frequently serve as political reference groups; which are most influential with members and non-members?

A study in the State of Washington of the associations which people would, and would not, turn to for advice on elections sheds some light on this problem.[26] The results of this inquiry are given in Table 13.2. In large part, of course, the frequency of mention is related to the size of the organization; the large church, labor organization, and business groups are mentioned more often than the smaller ones. But, allowing for the factor of size, we also see that there are important differences in the political effects of the various groups. These differences may be considered in terms of (a) the number of favorable references, (b) the total number of references, and (c) the number of the favorable references minus the unfavorable ones, divided by the total number of references. This latter measure gives an index of net positive influence. These data for the five most important organizations are presented in Table 14.3. On the whole it appears that in a national election the groups whose concerns are most likely to include issues salient in political discussion (with the exception of the Protestant Church and the Grange) are most likely to be turned to for advice and are most important in people's minds at election times. On the other hand, associations which are not generally embroiled in political controversy are more likely to have a

25. H. E. Freeman and M. Showell, op. cit., p. 707.
26. Ibid.

TABLE 14.2.—Positive and Negative Political Influence of Selected Social Organizations.

Organization (those mentioned 50 or more times)	Number of Members	Number positively influenced	Number negatively influenced	Total times mentioned
Protestant Church	152	74	29	103
American Federation of Labor	134	67	68	135
Parent-Teacher Association	54	47	12	59
Congress of Industrial Organizations	46	14	59	73
American Legion	34	54	7	61
Grange	29	60	10	70
Democratic Party	28	77	54	131
Republican Party	27	50	68	118
Catholic Church	27	11	57	68
Veterans of Foreign Wars	21	53	6	59
Chamber of Commerce	11	59	28	87
Better Business Bureau	4	54	10	64
Pension Union	3	12	49	61

TABLE 14.3.—Five Most Influential Organizations Indicated by Three Different Measures of Influence.

Advice most likely to take		Most frequently referred to (positive + negative)		positive minus negative refs ÷ total references	
Democratic Party	(77)*	Am. Fed. of Labor	(135)	Vet. of Foreign Wars	(77)
Protestant Church	(74)	Democratic Party	(131)	American Legion	(77)
Am. Fed. of Labor	(67)	Republican Party	(118)	Grange	(71)
Grange	(60)	Protestant Church	(103)	Better Bus. Bureau	(68)
Chamber of Commerce	(59)	Chamber of Commerce	(87)	Parent Teacher Assn.	(59)

* Numbers in parentheses are either number of references or indices, as noted.

SOURCE: Howard E. Freeman and Morris Showel, "Differential Political Influence of Voluntary Associations," "Public Opinion Quarterly, 15" (1951-52), p. 707.

net influence in the sense that more people accept their advice than reject it.[27] In this sense, the general theory of the influence of group relevance in politics must be modified. In a partisan situation, many people may be guided by groups for which politics is non-group relevant. Groups seen as somehow

---

27. Taking the advice of an organization and going to an individual for advice are two different kinds of phenomena. This is suggested by the findings in the Elmira study: "when panel members were asked whom they would go to if they 'had some question in connection with the presidential campaign and wanted to discuss it with someone,' only 15 per cent of those mentioning someone named a party leader or a party committeeman." Bernard Berelson, Paul F. Lazarsfeld and William M. McPhee, *Voting* (Chicago: Univ. of Chicago Press, 1954), p. 168. Compare this however to a study in Philadelphia where a relatively high number of people in the lower economic groups named persons in a "political role" as "the individuals who have been accepted as leaders by the people around here." Ira DeA. Reid and Emily L. Ehle, "Leadership Selection in Urban Locality Areas," *Public Opinion Quarterly*, 14 (1950), pp. 262-84.

"above the battle," with less at stake in the partisan contest, may become the salient reference group for many people. Aside from this, however, the theory of reference groups in politics outlined in the above discussion is generally sustained by the Washington State study.

In summary then:

Groups influence the political activity of their members generally by (a) defining the content of morality and duty, (b) structuring their beliefs about their social environment, (c) influencing their opinions about themselves (self-images), (d) affecting their life-goals, and (e) suggesting means for instrumenting these goals.

Groups orient a person in a political direction specifically by (a) redefining what is public and private in their lives, (b) providing new grounds for partisanship, (c) providing new insight into the individual's stake in the status of his group, (d) revealing the relevance of specific policy matters to the individual's personal situation, and (e) stimulating group loyalties which are generalized to include group political goals.

Individuals are "vulnerable" to group appeals for political action in proportion to the *valence* of the group for the individual, that is, the urgency of the needs satisfied by the group and the alternative means available for satisfying these needs.

The effectiveness of group appeals for membership political action is influenced by (a) size of the group, (b) democracy in program determination, (c) group morale, (d) membership identification with the group leadership, (e) the group-relevance of the political goals, (f) social homogeneity of the group, and (g) group facilitation of political expression.

Groups with low political content are more likely to be positive political reference groups for non-members than are groups with high political content.

HOW A PERSON'S POSITION IN A GROUP AFFECTS
HIS POLITICAL INTERESTS

Again let us assume that an organized group seeks to enlist membership support for a political program. Who will be most likely to be affected by organizational pressure? The relations of individuals to their groups are various and often fluid: some persons are leaders and others are members of the rank and file; some are popular and others are isolated; some are orthodox and others are heretic: Using the term broadly, we refer to these different kinds of situations with respect to other group members as "positions," and identify four such positions: (1) spatial position (accessibility), (2) sociometric or affectional position,[28] (3) hierarchical position, and (4) substantive position (orthodoxy).

---

28. For those unfamiliar with sociometric methods, see J. L. Moreno, *Who Shall Survive?* (Washington, D. C.: Nervous and Mental Disease Publishing Co., 1934). For a political science application of this technique, see Floyd Hunter, *Community Power Structure, A Study of Decision Makers* (Chapel Hill, N. C.: University of North Carolina Press, 1953).

With respect to the spatial position of the individual, the more centrally located a person is and the more accessible he is to others, the more likely he is to be informed on group-relevant issues, the more discussion he takes part in, the more interested he is in these issues. In a housing project in Massachusetts, for example, those whose apartments were strategically situated at a cross path or at the bottom of the stairs were more likely to be involved in the controversy over self-government for the project.[29] In a community, those who are more accessible to others in the sense that they belong to more organizations are more likely to be opinion leaders, whether or not they are interested in politics or better informed than average.[30]

Centrality of location is also related to the number of friends a person has. The analysis of these friendship choices naturally, then, shows that the "overchosen" individuals are also those who are more likely to have a higher interest in the political questions at issue. If one looks at a person's interpersonal relations in a group more in terms of tension with others than in terms of number of times chosen, somewhat the same picture emerges. Thus, in a highly political progressive school, it was found that those who showed less tension with others in their free discussion of the school situation were more likely to have adopted the school norm of high politicization.[31]

A further analysis of the less politically involved in Riesman's study, as in the Bennington study, showed, that they were more likely to be oriented around the home where political interests were generally less important. Others among the non-political were isolated from both home and school and showed the symptoms we have referred to as anomie in the discussion above.[32]

A third type of position has to do with a hierarchical classification and formal office of leadership. Generally, the politically active member of a social group has slightly higher occupational status and is somewhat better educated than average.[33] In a study of 207 persons in several veteran, fraternal, and women's groups in the Middle West, McWilliams found that those who were most active (attended most meetings, etc.) and those who had leadership positions in these groups were more likely to vote and engage in electoral activity than the rank and file members.[34] In unions, too, the people who are active in union affairs are likely also to be more than normally active in political activities.[35] Leadership and activity in these groups is not a substitute for political interest but a correlate of such interest. This is true for several reasons. First, selectivity in the choice of leaderships such that "civic minded" persons who share the community norms are likely to

---

29. L. Festinger, Schacter, and Back, *op. cit.*

30. Bernard B. Berelson, Paul F. Lazarsfeld, and William N. McPhee, *Voting* (Chicago: University of Chicago Press, 1954), p. 110.

31. D. Riesman, *op. cit.*, p. 559.

32. See above, pp. 166-69.

33. B. Berelson and associates, *op. cit.*, p. 113.

34. Robert O. McWilliams, *A Study of the Relationship of Political Behavior to Social Group Membership*, unpublished Ph.D. dissertation, University of Michigan, 1953.

35. H. Wilensky, *op. cit.*, pp. 119-20.

be chosen. The reverse of this is also important: those who are chosen must conform to the norms of the group. Also, the leader or activist is more likely to know political leaders and to be exposed to their influence; indeed he may cultivate their acquaintance to advance group interests.[36] The "activist" generalizes activity in many directions partly because of greater energy, partly because as a mode of adjustment to life, a life style, activity and "responsibility" become habitual and are easily assumed in new areas of life. Group leaders develop "transferable skills," useful in political activity. Finally, the more intense emotional involvement in the group is generalized to the group's political program which is thus also invested with emotion.[37]

The fourth position in the group has to do with the substance of a man's opinion in relation to others' opinions in the group. Generally speaking, the politically active leaders are those who know and approve of the main political orientation of the group. They are the group orthodox, partly because they help shape what is orthodoxy.[38] But the deviant may also be poltically active, particularly if his deviance or apostasy is rooted in rival group memberships. As Goldhamer points out, "cutting off retreat by the apostasy in deserting the in-group and the guilt and sacrifice involved in apostasy . . . requires more intense devotion to the new loyalties."[39] Hence deviance of this kind is likely to be associated with greater activity because of what must go into crossing the threshold of deviation. More moderate kinds of deviance, the Republican in a Democratic group, for example, do not show this pattern of increased participation. The relationship between opinion deviance and political activity in a group are curvilinear: the least and the most deviant are most active.

Briefly, then, we may suggest the following hypotheses:

Political participation in a group (primary, secondary, and categoric) is positively related to (a) spatial or geographic centrality and accessibility, (b) high sociometric and affectional choice by other group members, (c) leadership positions in a group.

Moderate substantive deviance tends to decrease political activity; extreme substantive deviance tends to increase political activity.

CROSS PRESSURES AND CONFLICTING
IDENTIFICATIONS

It is usual for a person to identify with a number of groups, perhaps several associational groups and several categoric groups and at least one or two primary groups, his family and friends. These reference groups usu-

36. *Ibid.;* B. Berelson and associates, *op. cit.,* p. 112.
37. H. Wilensky, *op. cit.,* p. 119.
38. B. Berelson and associates, *op. cit.,* p. 113.
39. Herbert Goldhamer, "Public Opinion and Personality," *American Journal of Sociology,* 55 (1950), p. 354.

ally exert pressure in predominantly the same political direction, at least in part because the group structure of society follows class and ethnic lines. Where this is the case the several groups exercise reinforcing pressures on the individual, easy to assimilate and easy to act upon. But where this is not true, where the system of group identifications embodies conflicting pressures (liberal vs. conservative, Democratic vs. Republican, isolationist vs. internationalist) a problem of choice arises for the individual. Such choices involve not only the solution of a political problem, but also the accompanying loss of solidarity within a given group, the giving up of something usually prized. Such choices may therefore be painful to the individual.

By no means all conflicts identified as "cross pressures," are, in the first instance, conflicts between reference groups. The distinctions between reference group conflicts and more strictly ideological conflicts may be observed by reviewing a list of certain cross pressures present in the 1940 election situation in Erie County, Ohio.[40]

1. Affiliation with a religious group predominantly associated with one party in conflict with membership in an economic status predominantly associated with another party.

2. Objective membership in one social status group versus subjective identification with another social status group.

3. Vote decision in the preceding election in conflict with an intention to vote for the opposing party in a current election.

4. Membership in a politically divided primary group, family.

5. Membership in a primary group (friends) predominantly in favor of the candidate the individual currently opposes.

6. Identification with one party in conflict with preference for the kind of experience and background of the opposing party's candidate.

While all of these conflict situations imply some kind of group reference, for the third and sixth conflicts, the group reference is secondary, and for the fifth instance the conflict is apparently between a private attitude (however reinforced) and a group identification. In the following discussion we are concerned only with conflict where the group reference is salient.

Theoretically, one can discriminate among three major conflict situations on the basis of the *direction* of the identifications.[41] These be composed of two (or more) positive attractions, as when a person is torn between a desire to "go along with" his ethnic group and a desire to stay in solid with his "non-ethnic" friends who have a different preference. The conflict may be between two disidentifications, as when a person opposes the ethnic group of "his" candidate but also dislikes the party of the opposition. Or, as is often the case, the conflict may be between two alternatives each of which is partially attractive and partially repellent, as when a person is rebellious against, but dependent upon, his family with one political preference and is

---

40. Paul F. Lazarsfeld, Bernard B. Berelson, and Hazel Gaudet, *The People's Choice* (New York: Columbia University Press, 1948), pp. 56-64.

41. This conception follows along lines similar to those of Kurt Lewin. See his *Field Theory in Social Science* (New York: Harper, 1951), pp. 248-97.

in roughly the same situation with his friendship group who share another preference. With respect to the conflict between attractive alternatives, the total pressures tend to keep the voter in the field of action and his rate of participation should therefore be higher than the voter who dislikes both alternatives and may very well conclude with "a plague on both your houses" kind of response. The third alternative (attractive and repellent features on both sides) is, of course, more ambiguous in this respect.

There is some controversy on the effect on political behavior of conflicting identifications with different categoric groups. Lazarsfeld and his associates found that cross pressures in general (of the types mentioned above) tended to delay the voting decisions, and, where interest was lacking, contributed to a withdrawal from the voting decisions entirely, that is, non-voting.[42] Implicit in this view is the idea that memberships in conflicting categoric groups (socio-economic, religious, rural-urban residence) contribute to non-voting. A study of conflicts of this kind on a national basis in 1948 offers some small support for this theory, although the support applies only to non-voting, not to time of decision, and even for non-voting the relationship is a tenuous one.[43] In addition to this lukewarm to negative support based upon research findings, even more trenchant theoretical criticism can be made of the cross pressure withdrawal hypothesis as it applies to such demographic groups. One cannot assume that every individual who has some "Democratic" categoric memberships and some "Republican" categoric memberships actually experiences any cross pressures. After all, according to the Erie County study, these groups include lower-middle-class rural Protestants, middle and lower-middle-class urban Protestants, well-to-do and middle-class rural Catholics, and well-to-do urban Catholics, many of whom may live in environments where the Democraticness of Catholicism, or the Republicaness of rural life may be obscured for them. "Both society and the individual are more than capable of establishing means of negating a conflict of interests: a 'Catholics for Wilkie' organization handles the matter at the social level; an identification with the business community can handle the 'cross pressure' at the psychological level."[44] What the demographic cross pressure does is to locate individuals who are likely to have other and more intimate group cross pressures, or in certain instances, to be conflicted in their political beliefs.

The evidence of the effect of conflict between primary groups, for example, the conflict experienced by the person whose friends or co-workers

42. P. Lazarsfeld and associates, op. cit., p. 64.

43. Morris Janowitz and Warren E. Miller, "The Index of Political Predisposition in the 1948 Election," Journal of Politics, 14 (1952), pp. 710-27. Two problems relating to the findings of this study should be noted: (1) There is no control for the influences of social class, hence the social factors making for low voting in the most Democratic groups may conceal the effect of the lack of conflict in these groups. (2) Demographic groups are aligned with different parties in different sections of the country, hence what is a cross-pressured situation in one section may not be in another.

44. Brewster M. Smith, Jerome S. Bruner and Robert W. White, Opinions and Personality (New York: Wiley, 1956), p. 13.

think one way and those whose family thinks another, is nowhere clearly stated, although one explanation of the relatively lower political interests of the younger voting group relies upon the more frequent cross pressures of this kind in the youthful voting bracket.[45] One study on such a conflict between peer group and family on a non-political matter, religious observances, shows the greater influence of peer-group references in such a situation.[46]

Another kind of conflict situation dealing with reference groups is posed when the group itself is divided so that identification with either faction in the group threatens loss of the support of the other faction. Some evidence for the withdrawal effect of such a situation is provided by a study of the "political activity" of 400 Yale undergraduates. Of those whose parents agreed in their political preferences, 20 per cent claimed to be "very active," while of those whose parents disagreed only 2 per cent made this claim. A minority position in a group, whether or not one has associates in this minority situation (thus making a split reference group), tends to make for non-voting.[47]

Yet here, as is often the case, the nature of the group and the relevance of politics for the group affect the resolution of the conflict. A study of the politics of young urban adults twenty-one to twenty-four years of age shows the effect of intra-group conflict on the extent of political discussion in the group.[48] In the family group, if husband and wife disagreed on politics, there was likely to be *more* political discussion. Among friends, disagreement was not related to the amount of political discussion in the group. Among co-workers, if the group disagreed on politics there was likely to be *less* discussion. The greater cohesiveness of the family and the greater group relevance of politics in the family, as contrasted to the group of co-workers, tend to increase conscious efforts to resolve the political conflict through discussion. High salience for politics was the result.

As for categoric groups, those with divided loyalties tend to exercise a weaker politicizing influence than those whose members are not in conflict. For example, in cities where a given ethnic group divides its vote more or less evenly between the parties, ethnic loyalties can not easily be enlisted to induce ethnic voting.

Still another kind of reference group conflict occurs when the conflict

---

45. B. Berelson and associates, *op. cit.*, pp. 89-93.

46. Bernard C. Rosen, "Conflicting Group Pressures: A Study of Parent-Peer Group Cross Pressures," *American Sociological Review,* 20 (1955), pp. 155-61.

47. B. Berelson and associates, *op. cit.*, pp. 121-22. However, in a study of division and cohesion in primary groups in 1952, Campbell and associates say: "Being in a group of divided political loyalty does not appear to produce any inhibitory effect on the individual's political participation." The evidence shows that those in split groups have non-voting rates lower than solidly Republican groups and higher than solidly Democratic groups, suggesting that demographic factors are concealing the influence of group division upon non-voting. A. Campbell and associates, *op. cit.*, p. 203.

48. Eleanor E. Mccoby and others, "Youth and Political Change," *Public Opinion Quarterly,* 18 (1954), pp. 32-33.

arises between identification with a group of which a person is objectively a member and a group of which he is not a member, but with which he nevertheless identifies. This is most obvious in the case of the working-class person who identifies with the middle class, or the middle-class person who identifies with (and speaks of himself as) working class. The Erie County study showed that people in this group did tend to delay their voting decision, but there seems no reason to believe that they tend to vote less than others.[49] Probably the participation norms of the group with which they identify are the governing factors in such situations. For example, in the auto worker's union, those members who identified with business more than labor were just as likely to vote as the others.[50] If they did experience a conflict which made a voting decision difficult, the business identification over-rode the withdrawal tendencies associated with conflict.

With reference to the attitudes which we know to be associated with political participation, cross pressures do not have any clear effect on sense of citizen duty or sense of political efficacy, but might well exaggerate anomic feelings and weaken attachment to community. The principal politically relevant psychic mechanism at work in conflict situations, however, is the weakening of partisanship. Cross pressures tend to diminish partisanship because the individual loses valued group identifications through any whole-hearted commitment to one side. Cross pressures may also tend to decrease concern or a feeling that much is at stake, since the situation of the cross-pressured person brings to his attention the arguments on both sides, the benefits as well as the disadvantages of a given choice. Where such a bipartisan or multi-partisan set of arguments is heard, a common conclusion would be "there is much to be said on both sides" and hence a weakening of concern.

In short, the theory of the withdrawal effect of the conflict between an individual's reference groups has some support, but requires specification of the nature of the identification (intensity, objective-subjective), the nature of the group (type and homogeneity), and the nature of the issue (group relevance, individual salience), before accurate prediction can be attempted.

The alternative response patterns to such conflict, however, are much broader than activity versus withdrawal. A brief glance at several of the studies made of individuals caught in such reference group conflict will illustrate the possibilities.

In Newcomb's study of the political and social behavior of Bennington college girls caught between identifications with predominantly conservative homes and a liberal college community, he found that those who identified with the home were more conservative as they went through college and this conservation often had the effect of blocking their bid for college leadership. But also those who made a bid for leadership and failed, tended to

49. Lazarsfeld, Berelson, and Gaudet, op. cit., pp. 58-59; see Heinz Eulau, "Perceptions of Class and Party in Voting Behavior: 1952," American Political Science Review, 49 (1955), pp. 364-84.

50. A. Kornhauser and associates, op. cit., pp. 110-14.

identify with the home rather than with the college, showing a kind of reciprocal relationship between identification with one of the reference groups and social and political activity.[51]

Kriesberg's study of the conflicting reference groups for Catholics in a Communist-dominated union shows several patterns. In the first place many of the persons so situated tended to screen out the cross pressures (which were relevant chiefly on attitudes toward the Soviet Union) and to be unaware of them. In the second place, they tended to minimize the importance of attitudes toward the Soviet Union in their vote decision and possibly to reduce their interest in election issues altogether. This psychological device is common for the cross-pressured individual in national elections, that is, he takes refuge in the view: "both parties are the same."[52] In the third place, although there tended to be a moderation of outlook—"something to be said on both sides"—this moderation was often an inconsistent and confused acceptance of the points made on either side.[53]

A third study, suggestive of many other similar situations, is offered by Child's investigation of the Italian-American, a person marginal between two cultures. Child notes that he may identify with the parental group and retain his ethnic identification; he may seek identification with the native group in the search for assimilation; and, in the third place, he may respond with a kind of generalized apathy, seeking to avoid commitment wherever this is possible—as it is possible in politics.[54]

On the problem of conflict between reference groups with different views on some subject of political relevance, the following hypotheses are suggested:

Reference group conflict (to be distinguished from other conflicts where the group reference is only indirect) may involve (a) incompatible identifications, (b) incompatible disidentifications, and (c) conflicts between reference groups each of which has attractive and repellent features. Incompatible disidentifications are more likely to reduce participation than incompatible identification.

Conflicts between identifications with categoric groups have been shown to be tenuously related to decreased political participation in a single community, but the relevant groups and the direction and intensity of the identification vary from community to community.

Conflicts between primary group references (college and home, family and peer group) may increase withdrawal tendencies but are more likely to be resolved in favor of the preferred group with the acceptance of its political norms.

Conflicts on political issues within reference groups (categoric, secondary, and primary) tend to decrease political participation, partly through decreasing partisanship, and causing a withdrawal of involvement. A minority position in a group tends to decrease political participation.

Where reference group conflict tends to decrease participation it does so

---

51. Theodore M. Newcomb, *Personality and Social Change, op. cit.*

52. Gerhart H. Saenger, "Social Status and Political Behavior," *American Journal of Sociology, 51* (1945), pp. 105-06.

53. Martin Kriesberg, "Cross Pressures and Attitudes," *Public Opinion Quarterly, 13* (1949), pp. 5-16.

54. Irvin L. Child, *Italian or American? The Second Generation Conflict,* (New Haven: Yale University Press, 1943).

through reducing partisanship and involvement, altering the means of social adjustment, encouraging anomic feelings and weakening community ties, not through any effect on sense of political effectiveness, or sense of citizen duty.

In specifying the effect of reference group conflict, the nature of the group, the nature of the identification, and the relation of the group to the issue in conflict must also be specified.

Withdrawal from a decision involving conflicting reference groups is only one of several means of solving the conflict problem; others include (a) identification with one of the conflicting reference groups (sometimes because of frustration in the other), (b) moderation in viewpoint, a moderation which may be either confused and eclectic or synthesized, (c) minimization of the issue, (d) failure to "see" the conflict, (e) generalized apathy (where the conflicting groups embrace large areas of life).

CHAPTER 15

Family, Sex, and Age in Political Life

FAMILY

THE FAMILY incubates political man.[1] It endows him with the qualities necessary to operate a democratic system and infuses him with the appropriate attitudes and beliefs—or it fails in these respects. How is it done?

More specifically, *does the American family make the child feel that his voice counts and that people will listen to him;* that is, does he acquire a junior version of a sense of political efficacy? By and large, he does. Although the decline of child labor on the farm as well as in industry has probably served to reduce the economic base for this sense of importance, and in spite of certain culturally approved means of depreciating the importance of the child, such as the "kidding" in Plainsville analyzed by Kardiner,[2] the American family takes the child's demands seriously. As Erikson and Riesman have pointed out, the family in the United States proceeds by consensus, that is, every member of the family has a kind of

---

1. The relationship of family practices and styles of life to effective citizenship training in a democracy has not been investigated by political scientists and only tangentially by psychologists. A bibliography of 400 items on the family compiled by Oliver E. Byrd, *Family Life Source Book* (Stanford: Stanford University Press, 1956) provides almost no help with this problem. In many ways, psychoanalytic studies of national character, such as Abram Kardiner, *The Psychological Frontiers of Society* (New York: Columbia University Press, 1945), and sociological community studies, such as Robert and Helen Lynd, *Middletown* (New York, Harcourt, Brace, 1929), prove to be more useful. Here, of course, we can do no more than touch upon two or three central topics.

2. See A. Kardiner, *op. cit.,* pp. 326-27. Some idea of the congruence between child training methods and political systems may be seen by contrasting the "reward for effort" or "conditional love" in the American scheme with the systematic frustration of the child in other cultures with different political systems. See Margaret Mead, "Public Opinion Mechanisms among Primitive Peoples," *Public Opinion Quarterly, 1* (1937), pp. 5-16.

[204]

liberum veto on the family plans.[3] Inevitably this gives each a feeling of importance and effectiveness. Moreover, the very confusion of parents on the proper canons of child rearing, the fact that "a prevalent mood among Middletown parents is bewilderment, a feeling that their difficulties outrun their best efforts to cope with them"[4] enhances the feeling of the young that their opinions are as good as anyone else's. Open inter-generational differences on such matters as dating practices, clothes, church attendance, and pocket money, imply that parents are fallible, open to persuasion, and, not on an inaccessible pedestal but rather on a gradient which all may climb. Psychodynamically this parental image is related to activity and participation in later life and its reverse is associated with apathy.

The [political] apathetic's glorification of his parents, together with his basic hostility toward people and his view of the world as hostile and threatening, suggests that the parents may have been rigid and severely punitive, discouraging independence of thought or action and encouraging passive acceptance of authority from early childhood.[5]

Thus the mutuality of the "conversation across the generations," while it may lead to braggadocio in the child because he is, in fact, speaking from weakness instead of strength, does tend to give the individual a sense of importance, competence, and efficacy in influencing affairs.[6]

But, there are also standard child-rearing practices which deprive children of the feeling that they can influence decisions. The practice in the first third of this century was to feed the infant by the clock—no amount of crying would do any good. Such practices produce fatalistic attitudes of enduring significance. Thus the advent of "demand feeding," the swing from Holt to Spock, has laid important foundations for the American democracy. But the work is unfinished. The early and severely sanctioned demand that the infant eliminate only when he is placed on the toilet, is experienced as an important deprivation of the right to decide. Erikson says, on this very point, "Much political apathy may have its origin in a general feeling that, after all, matters of apparent choice have probably been fixed in advance— a state of affairs which becomes fact, indeed, if influential parts of the electorate acquiesce in it because they have learned to view the world as a

---

3. See Erik H. Erikson, *Childhood and Society* (New York: Norton, 1950), pp. 275-76; David Riesman, *The Lonely Crowd* (New Haven: Yale University Press, 1950), p. 69.

4. R. and H. Lynd, *op. cit.*, p. 151.

5. Paul H. Mussen and Anne B. Wyssinski, "Personality and Political Participation," *Human Relations*, 5 (1952), p. 78.

6. Margaret Mead makes the point that Americans learn braggard habits because they are encouraged to assert themselves at the breakfast table, thus speaking from a position situationally weak in contrast to their parents' strength. The British learn understatement because of the habit of the family to listen to father, who speaks from a position of strength. Compare this with the German habits of paternal dictation at the table; David Levy found that those families allowing the children to speak at the table were less likely to produce active Nazis than those where this was not true. See his "Anti-Nazis: Criteria of Differentiation," in Alfred H. Stanton and Stewart E. Perry, eds., *Personality and Political Crisis* (Glencoe, Ill.: Free Press, 1951), p. 215.

place where grown-ups talk of choice, but 'fix' things so as to avoid overt friction."[7] It is not that children must be permitted to "have their own way;" rather the point is that consideration of the child's needs and desires and tentative attitudes at every age level, however trite this may seem, underpins the citizenly attitude "authorities care about me; authorities listen to me."

People vote and write letters to their congressmen because of a sense of civic duty. *How does the American family orient a child to social duty?* At an earlier stage in our history it would have seemed appropriate to rely upon the cultural persistence of Puritan themes as conveyed through family and church indoctrination. More recently, the Victorian emphasis upon repression of the frivolous and enjoyable might have seemed to reinforce the importance of concepts of duty. But today both the means of learning about duty and the nature of the duties learned are different. Neither the internalization of a religious code, nor the indoctrination of stern parents operate to provide a strong sense of civic duty in the "old-fashioned" sense.

The essence of duty is doing what one *ought* to do as contrasted to what one *wants* to do, although as people mature these tend to fuse.[8] But today in infancy and early childhood, the authorities suggest that a child ought to do what he wants to do, a cultural theme which Martha Wolfenstein calls the "fun morality."[9] When he goes to school, it will be argued that without motivation a child will not learn, thus he must be brought to enjoy his studies. And in adulthood, he must learn the arts of leisure and have hobbies, partly, perhaps, because it has been found that those with hobbies are more likely to stay in their jobs for a longer time. He is encouraged to enjoy himself. The route to politics through sense of duty sanctioned by punitive guilt feelings is not the vehicle which the modern American family is most likely to employ.

But there is a sense in which social duty is encouraged by the prevalent child-rearing practices. The general pattern of child-development encourages adjusting to the will of others, performing social roles as the society prescribes them. This is illustrated in Riesman's analysis of "Tootle," the engine that kicked up its heels and went wandering in the meadow instead of staying on the track and developing into an orthodox locomotive.[10] The people of the town, in good-natured but conscientious fashion, wave red flags in the field, employing Tootle's conditioned aversion to red flags to get him back on the track. Tolerant but inexorable social pressure makes a good "conforming" citizen of the errant Tootle. And, as the President of New York University pointed out upon taking office in 1957, the schools and colleges are in danger of reinforcing these conformist themes learned in the family

---

7. E. H. Erikson, *op. cit.,* pp. 269-70.

8. John C. Flugel, *Man, Morals and Society, a Psycho-analytic Study* (New York, International Universities Press, 1945), pp. 10-14.

9. Martha Wolfenstein, "Fun Morality: An Analysis of Recent American Child-Training Literature," *Journal of Social Issues, 7,* No. 4 (1951), pp. 15-25.

10. David Riesman, *op. cit.,* pp. 107-11.

culture.[11] Family and school together create adults sensitive to the prescribed views of their culture, including views on the content of citizen duty.

This tolerant adjustment motif is reinforced by the lack of systematic patterned rebellion against the father, such as is said to be typical of the adolescent in Germany. The American boy, according to Erikson, does not go through this stage and is therefore deprived of a strong motive which often turns young men to politics.[12] A tolerant and easy-going Dad does not build up in the son the head of steam which creates the political rebel (a rebellion which is said to be only a passing phase in the life of each German youth). Even where this rebellion does happen in our culture, the more likely avenue of expression is, in typically individualistic non-ideological American fashion, delinquency.[13]

The specific content of the attitudes toward politics encouraged by the family vary enormously. Among adults, at least, if one member of the family is interested in world affairs or an election, the other members are also more likely to be interested; "the whole level of interest is likely to be contagious from one family member to another."[14] But *does the American family focus attention on politics and create intense political loyalties?* Generally speaking, the level of interest is low, partly because of what is said to be an "over emphasis" upon career, work-life,[15] and "success" and partly because of the growing cult of having a good time, the adult version of Wolfenstein's "fun morality." Moreover, children are rarely encouraged to enter political careers. In answering the question "If you had a son twenty-one years old (or starting out in life) what business or profession would you like to see him go into," in 1939 and again in 1945 almost no one mentioned a political career.[16] And when at various times people are asked specifically about political careers, only a fifth to a quarter approve of this as a career for their sons. Furthermore, the reasons of those who do approve have to do rather more with the need for good and honest men in government than with the advantages of such a career for the boy himself, hardly an endorsement of the

11. "The American educational system, as presently constituted, gives recognition to conformity and uniformity more than it encourages the intellectual growth of students as individuals." Carroll V. Newsom, *New York Times*, April 13, 1957, p. 21.

12. E. Erikson, *op. cit.*, p. 277.

13. See Ben Karpman, "Psychodynamics of Child Delinquency: Further Contributions," *American Journal of Orthopsychiatry*, 25 (1955), pp. 238-82.

14. Paul F. Lazarsfeld, Bernard B. Berelson, and Hazel Gaudet, *The People's Choice*, 2nd ed. (New York: Columbia University Press, 1948), p. 142.

15. See Florence R. Kluckhohn, "The American Family and the Feminine Role," in Hugh Cabot and Joseph A. Kahl, eds., *Human Relations, Concepts and Cases in Concrete Social Science* (Cambridge, Mass.: Harvard University Press, 1953), Vol. 1, pp. 240-81.

16. Hadley Cantril, ed., *Public Opinion 1935-1946* (Princeton: Princeton University Press, 1951), pp. 529, 534. It is interesting to note, in connection with the above discussion, that more non-voters than voters want their sons to go into politics, although this is probably due to the influence of intervening class variables. See Gordon M. Connelly and Harry M. Field, "The Non-Voter—Who He is, What He Thinks," *Public Opinion Quarterly*, 8 (1944), p. 183.

field of politics. The low intensity of partisanship of the parents, combined with relative tolerance for filial apostasy, does not make for intense political emotion in the adolescent or young adult. And even where political loyalties are strong among the parents, the second generation's repudiation of immigrant parents and middle-class children's repudiation of working-class parents makes the transmission of these loyalties more tenuous in America than in many other countries.

INTRA-FAMILY AGREEMENT AND CONFLICT

In spite of ethnic and class discontinuities the intimacy of the family does produce common interests and some political loyalties. In one study only one married couple in twenty-two, and only one parent child relationship in twelve, disagreed on vote decision, with the incidence of disagreement increasing as the family relationship became more distant.[17] Another study shows that nationally in 1952, only one married couple out of eleven disagreed.[18] Such agreement eases the friction of family living; but what happens if there is conflict in the family?

What evidence we have shows that conflict between husband and wife, when it occurs, produces a greater degree of discussion than political conflict in other groups,[19] followed usually by the wife's being "persuaded" on the point. The wife is "'persuaded" rather than the husband partly, at least, because her role is culturally prescribed as less political; she loses less by yielding. An alternative reaction is for the wife to retain her views but not to vote because she does not want to "cancel her husband's vote."[20] As for the children of such a politically conflicted union, they are likely to become somewhat less political when their parents take conflicting views, except where they identify clearly with one or the other parent in the general family constellation.[21]

In review then, we may say:

The more the family treats a child's needs and demands with a seriousness appropriate to his age, the more is he, as an adult, likely to believe that his political

---

17. P. Lazarsfeld and associates, *op. cit.*, p. 141.

18. Angus Campbell, Gerald Gurin, and Warren E. Miller, *The Voter Decides* (Evanston, Ill.: Row, Peterson, 1954), p. 203.

19. Eleanor E. Maccoby, Richard E. Matthews, and Anton S. Morton, "Youth and Political Change," *Public Opinion Quarterly,* 18 (1954), pp. 23-39.

20. See Charles E. Merriam and Harold F. Gosnell, *Non-Voting* (Chicago: University of Chicago Press, 1924), p. 114.

21. Unpublished study of political attitudes of 400 Yale students in introductory course in political science, 1950. There is some contrary evidence in Campbell and associates (*op. cit.*, p. 203) which shows that conflict in family views does not tend to produce lower turnout among unmarried grown children, but lack of control on age and socioeconomic status may obscure the relationship. It may be, for example, that female independence in politics is predominantly a middle-class phenomenon.

efforts will be rewarded. American socialization practices generally reinforce the view: "authorities listen to me."

American family practices fail to engender strong duty-morality in children, but by encouraging conformity, adjustment, and modal role performance, the family imbues children with a low tension sense of civic duty.

In the modal American family political attitudes of parents offer neither targets for rebellious youth, nor objects of strong partisan familial identification; parental political views generally prevail with the children because of broad social reinforcement rather than familial indoctrination; where there are inter-generational barriers of class, region, and immigrant status, political views and emotions are transmitted only weakly.

Although the great majority of husband-wife pairs agrees on political matters, occasional conflict in views produces the following results: (a) argument becomes more intense than in other small groups, (b) the wife usually yields to the husband's view, or, at least, fails to vote for her candidate, (c) the children withdraw their political interests, unless they clearly identify with one parent and reject the other.

MALE AND FEMALE

"At every social level women vote less than men." This is true in national elections and in local elections in Europe and in the United States.[22] The data in Table 15.1 reveal the general nature of the sexual differentiation in voting participation, although the evidence suggests that the differential is getting smaller in presidential elections. But the difference is still there, not only in voting but also in letter-writing, which might be thought of as more "feminine" since the women often handle the social correspondence for the family.[23]

That women should vote less than men has become a fact so familiar now that it has been taken for granted. Yet in many ways it is a remarkable phenomenon. Women have special reasons to be interested in problems of price control, housing, zoning, education, playgrounds, prevention of war, and so forth—all of which may be issues in national and local campaigns. Women receive almost the same amount of education as men; and in women's colleges the political science courses are as popular as they are in men's colleges. If men read the paper with more care than women, women listen to the radio more than men and look at television with the same fre-

22. Herbert Tingsten, *Political Behavior, Studies in Election Statistics* (London: P. S. King & Sons, 1937), p. 29; Maurice Duverger, *The Political Role of Women* (Paris: UNESCO, 1955). Only in one instance, so far as we know, have women voted proportionately more than men: Ann Arbor, Mich., 1928. Here a middle-class and heavily Republican community may have experienced alarm about the moral and cultural values of the Democratic candidate, Al Smith, who openly expressed his opposition to prohibition. See James K. Pollock, *Voting Behavior: A Case Study* (Ann Arbor: University of Michigan Press, 1939).

23. Rowena Wyant, "Voting Via the Senate Mailbag, Part I," *Public Opinion Quarterly*, 5 (1941), p. 365.

**TABLE 15.1.—Per cent of Men and Women Voting in the Nation
and in Delaware, Ohio, in Five Elections.**

	United States				Delaware, Ohio	
	1944	1948	1952	1954*	1924	1948
Men	75	69	79	53	72.9	63.1
Women	61	59	69	41	57.1	61.5

* Non-presidential election.

SOURCE and NOTES:
(national)
1944: Gordon M. Connelly and Harry Field, "The Non-Voter—Who He Is, What He Thinks," "Public Opinion Quarterly, 8" (1944), pp. 175-87.
1948 and 1952: Angus Campbell, Gerald Gurin, and Warren Miller, "The Voter Decides" (Evanston, Ill.: Row, Peterson, 1954), p. 70.
1954: Survey Research Center, "Group Differences in Attitudes and Votes" (Ann Arbor, Mich.: 1955, preliminary).
(Delaware, Ohio)
1924 and 1948: Ben A. Arneson and William H. Eells, "Voting Behavior in a Typical Ohio Community," "American Political Science Review, 44" (1950), pp. 432-34.

quency. Why, then, should the same available stimuli receive a differential attention and exert differential effect on people with similar social backgrounds and roughly similar degrees of education?

First, we should dispose of certain uniquely feminine reasons for not going to the polls, reasons which were more persuasive twenty years ago than now. Women with small children may find it hard to get away— although many political parties provide baby sitters for such cases. In the 1924 Chicago study, however, of all female non-voters, only 2.8 per cent gave care of children (or the presence of an invalid in the house) as the reason why they did not vote.[24] Illness is another possible explanation of a higher rate of female stay-at-homes on election day—and in the Merriam and Gosnell study this was an excuse claimed by 13.8 per cent of the female non-voters (as compared to 8.3 per cent of the men).

Clearly the home duties and the physiology of women do not offer much explanatory power in dealing with a male-female differential in voting. But the Chicago study gives other clues: 11.4 per cent of the women interviewed said that they did not believe in women voting, and another 1.5 per cent said their husbands did not believe in it. It appears that a large percentage of the women in the 1920's, and a somewhat smaller per cent now, do not include "voting" in their concept of the things women do, that is, in their image of the female role.

This is brought out most clearly in an examination of some of the responses of women who held this view a third of a century ago, and also more recently, in 1940:[25]

An elderly woman of German extraction said, "Woman is a flower for men to look after," and should not vote on this account. (1924)

24. The following data are from C. Merriam and H. Gosnell, *op. cit.*, p. 47.
25. *Ibid.*, 109-22; P. Lazarsfeld and associates, *op. cit.*, p. 49.

An elderly woman of Irish extraction said, "Women have no business voting. They would be better off staying home and minding their own affairs." (1924)

A moderately well-off white woman said that voting is a man's business, adding that if she were a widow or had property in her own name, she would vote. (1924)

Several women thought that women's voting jeopardized the relationship between the sexes, particularly in that it kills off such few remaining gallantries as giving up seats in buses and streetcars. (1924)

A well-to-do native white woman of Southern extraction said, "I'm a lady and do not want to be anything else but a lady. I was raised in Virginia and promised mother not to break any of my promises. Mama always thought politics was men's business." (1924)

In 1940, women in Erie County, Ohio, said:

"I don't care to vote. Voting is for the men."

"I think men should do the voting and the women should stay at home and take care of their work."

"I have never voted. I never will. . . . A woman's place is in the home. . . . Leave politics to the men."

No doubt many of the persons who refer to their non-voting in these terms are screening their real motives. But there is also little doubt that the interpretation of the female role in this fashion is a genuine one. Evidence for this is seen in the fact that women are, for one thing, rather more willing to admit that they are not interested in politics, and more importantly, follow out their interest or lack of interest in logical fashion. If they say they are not interested, they are likely not to vote, while men who admit that they are uninterested are more likely to vote anyway.[26] Social pressures experienced by men are not experienced by women in this regard and hence they are, to some extent, correct in interpreting political role expectation as different for women.

This view of the female role, however, can hardly be considered widespread. As we have seen, the difference in turnout runs only around 10 per cent nationally, and in some communities, such as Waukegan, Ill. (1950), there is no difference at all.[27] But there is more direct evidence on role interpretation in the responses of women and men to questions about their duty to vote. These questions, summarized in the citizen duty scale mentioned in Chapter 11, show the following pattern:[28] The figures suggest that women do not experience the social pressure to vote are limited to a small group in the population. Since, as mentioned earlier, the difference in turnout is around 10 per cent, the fact that there is a difference as large as 5 per cent between the men and the women who fail to see a duty to vote under many circumstances is significant. This is particularly true since the citizen duty scale is a very good predictor of turnout.

The reasons for this role interpretation exist partly in the unique history

26. P. Lazarsfeld and associates, *op. cit.*, p. 48; Alice S. Kitt and David B. Gleicher, "Determinants of Voting Behavior," *Public Opinion Quarterly*, 14 (1950), pp. 406-07.

27. Mungo Miller, "The Waukegan Study of Voter Turnout Prediction," *Public Opinion Quarterly*, 16 (1952), p. 394.

28. A. Campbell and associates, *op. cit.*, p. 197.

TABLE 15.2.—Sense of Citizen Duty, by Sex, 1952.

	High	Medium	Low	Not Ascertained	Total
Male	44%	48%	7%	1%	100
Female	42	44	12	2	100

of feminine voting, partly in the way women see themselves reflected in the media, and partly in the contents of the female stereotype itself. The culture, of course, draws upon the past for its definition of every role and the past which excluded women from public affairs is still too close at hand for them to be entirely free of this history. That this is a diminishing force, however, is suggested by the trend of female voting and the interpretation of citizen duty given above.

The media, and also the literary heritage reread by every generation, tend to create images of women in domestic, or, perhaps, artistic and literary or dramatic or even career roles—but not in political roles. Nor is television, radio soap opera, and other entertainment any better in this respect. For example, in forty-three radio serials audited for two weeks in 1941, public affairs accounted for only 10 per cent of the problems treated, less than courtship, marriage, and "economic and professional," i.e., career, and about the same as crime or illness.[29] There is little reinforcement for the image of "political woman" in this area.

But the problem of the impact of the radio, screen, and printed page in maintaining woman's apathetic regard for politics is much broader and deeper and subtler than that. Consider the image of the female vote as a "reform" vote, that is, impersonal and detached from personal gain, qualitatively different from the male vote which is imbued with matters of self-interest (protection from the law, a job, a contract, etc.)—a kind of bloodless love of the good. We know that the reform vote is a cyclical phenomenon which has to be kicked off periodically in municipal elections by revelations of new and greater corruption. If it is the matrix of "idealism" which is supposed to bind women to politics—at least as the public sees it—there is little wonder that the binding loosens in many areas.

The roots of this moralistic orientation of women in the American culture are relevant. For one thing, a primary concern and responsibility for the young tends to focus attention upon engendering in them a suitable morality.[30] In addition, there is some suggestion that the custody of moral values is often acquired as a consolation prize for exclusion from these activities which have the highest value in the society.[31] This is consonant with the frequent preference of those who fail to achieve a given level of success

---

29. Rudolf Arnheim, The World of the Daytime Serial," in P. F. Lazarsfeld and F. N. Stanton, eds., *Radio Research 1942-43* (New York: Duell, Sloan and Pearce, 1944), pp. 43-81.

30. David Riesman, "Orbits of Tolerance, Interviews, and Elites," *Public Opinion Quarterly*, 20 (1956), pp. 49-73.

31. Seymour M. Lipset, "The Sources of the 'Radical Right,'" in Daniel Bell, ed., *The New American Right* (New York: Harper, 1955), pp. 224-25.

to talk about the moral attributes of those who do. And in the third place, the more limited orbits of women, their more restricted contacts in society and narrower range of experience may tend to reinforce the view that the values they are familiar with are the only values—a lack of cultural relativism.[32] The evidence of the somewhat greater intolerance of women seems to support this view.[33]

The net effect of this moralistic orientation has been not only to provide an ineffective and relatively "ego-distant" tie with political matters but also, as Riesman has remarked, to limit attention to the superficial and irrelevant aspects of politics.[34] Furthermore, such an orientation gives an illusion of comprehension because it is relatively easy to compare political acts and statements with moral symbols to assay moral worth, while it is difficult, indeed, to ascertain causes and estimate results. Finally, such moralism may account for the relatively greater candidate orientation of women,[35] since persons—as contrasted to issues—are even more clearly perceived as "good" or "bad." Hence, women, more than others, contribute to the personification of politics both in the United States and abroad.

The public image of the woman's role in politics has other facets. A major feature of our culture's typing of the two sexes is the assignment of the ascendant, power-possessing role to the man and the dependent, receptive role to the woman. This has some basis in physiology, of course, although the degree of such male super-ordination and female subordination may be considered less intense in the United States in the middle of the twentieth century than has been usual in most cultures at most times. But since the sentiment is still present in a persistently strong degree, it is certain to affect the cultural perspectives in any area closely associated with gaining and wielding power. Politics is precisely such an area of power, and a woman enters politics only at the risk of tarnishing, to some extent, her femininity. Although voting and talking politics are only at the threshold of this power-saturated area of life, the woman who seems too active in these areas seems, to some people, to have moved from the properly dependent role of her sex and to seek the masterful and dominant role of men.[36]

Some further evidence for this may be found in the low sense of political efficacy which characterizes women. As noted in Chapter 11, the Survey Research Center political efficacy scale measures, among other things, the feeling that "I am important enough to have officials pay attention to me." We would not expect women to rate high, and the scores show this.[37]

The dominant-efficacy theme is intertwined with another—that of competence. A number of women interviewed by Merriam and Gosnell indicated that they thought women were incompetent in politics, guiding their decisions

32. D. Riesman, "Orbits of Tolerance, Interviews, and Elites," p. 57.

33. Samuel Stouffer, *Communism, Conformity, and Civil Liberties* (Garden City, New York: Doubleday, 1955), pp. 131-55.

34. D. Riesman, "Orbits of Tolerance, Interviews, and Elites," p. 58.

35. A. Campbell and associates, *op. cit.*, pp. 152-56.

36. The relation of "ascendance" and "dominance" to political participation is analyzed on p. 149.

37. A. Campbell and associates, *op. cit.*, p. 191.

TABLE 15.3.—Sense of Political Efficacy, by Sex, 1952.

	High	Medium	Low	Not Ascertained	Total
Male	35%	47%	17%	1%	100
Female	20	55	23	2	100

by wrong criteria or eccentric judgments. Thus, those against prohibition tended to blame prohibition on women, and others registered the broader claim that "women have no experience or knowledge in the field of voting." Other women approved women's non-voting because "the men understand more about it."[38]

The incidence of this sex-differentiation of political roles varies according to the situation and group memberships of the women. Women, of course, share in the influence of class, religion, race, and nationality. It might be asked, therefore, whether the influences of these factors on political role interpretation are significant. In order to answer this question we may state the evidence as follows:

1. Middle-class women vote more frequently than the working-class members of their sex—to a greater degree than is true of men. This has resulted in making woman suffrage a benefit to the middle classes in American politics—in particular, since the thirties, a benefit to the Republican party. As the unequal participation of the sexes declines, this advantage of the middle classes in a sexually disproportionate electorate will also decline.

2. Although the evidence is uncertain, it appears that there is an unclear relationship between the voting record of a given nationality and the voting record of the women of that nationality group. Thus, in Chicago the Irish participated in elections more than did most other groups, but Irish women participated proportionately less. This was also true of the Scandinavians, but there were other groups, like the Italians, where both men and women were on the low side of the scale. As an average of all nationality groups, however, it may be said that for women, membership in such ethnic groups tended to depress the record of participation below the level of native white women. This was not the case at all for men.[39]

3. There is some tendency for Negro women to vote less than men to an extent not paralleled by the sex difference within the white community.[40]

---

38. Merriam and Gosnell, *op. cit.*, p. 113.

39. *Ibid.*, pp. 119-231.

40. This is true in spite of the fact that in Tuscaloosa, Alabama, where 2.7 per cent of the Negro population voted in 1940, the "sex distribution of the few Negro registrants did not differ greatly from that of white registrants." Charles W. Smith, *The Electorate in an Alabama Community* (University, Ala.: Bureau of Public Administration, University of Alabama, 1942), p. 29. Contrast this, however, with the situation in Austin, Texas, where the proportions of male to female voters was: white, 1.7 to 1; Negro, 3.7 to 1; Mexican, 5.0 to 1. (Computed from data in Roscoe C. Martin, "The Municipal Electorate: A Case Study," *Southwestern Social Science Quarterly, 14* (1933), p. 231.) Notice that in these ethnic data income levels may serve as mediating and distorting third factors.

Generally, for women, the effect of low income status, foreign birth, low educational attainment, or membership in the Negro race is to depress the rate of electoral participation.

Why these relationships should hold for women more than for men is partly explained by several factors. Although the lower rate of interaction ethnic women have with members of the majority group in the community is a moderately politicizing influence, since this reinforces partisan opinions and reduces the cross pressures on them, this insulation reduces contacts with class groups possessing norms of high participation.[41] More important are the more patriarchal family norms of ethnic groups; the exaggerated sense of deficiency in political or social efficacy which the subordinate partner in a subordinated family will have; the preoccupation with home and children necessary in predominantly lower income groups—exaggerated by the large families which are sometimes associated with ethnic groups; the lower educational attainments of women in these groups—thus reducing the visibility of their stakes in any election. Confronted with such a situation, a woman is surely tempted to say, with short-run truth pre-eminently on her side, "I've got troubles enough; don't bother me with politics."

In addition to the differential degrees of political interest and participation in various social groups, there is a difference in the nature of those interests which the two sexes exhibit. In a study of political discussion (foreign policy, labor relations, local affairs) between middle-class husbands and wives, it was found that a kind of specialization occurred such that the husband assumed leadership in the areas of labor relations, and, to a lesser extent, in foreign policy.[42] Male leadership, however, was markedly smaller in the area of local policy where the wife often took the lead in the discussion and assumed a more dominant role. Furthermore, in a ranking of topics "most appropriate for discussion within the League of Women Voters," there was a marked agreement between husbands and wives.[43]

Women's political role is not only experienced differently in different social groups, but is experienced as properly concerned with substantively different problems within the same social groups.

In summary, therefore, we may advance the following propositions:

The culture emphasizes moral, dependent, and politically less competent images of women which reduce their partisanship and sense of political effectiveness and define a less active political role for them.

41. Speaking of the differences in voting patterns of Jewish men and women, Fuchs says: "Most of the women rarely leave the [Jewish] ward. Their contacts are almost exclusively neighborhood and family contacts, nearly all of which are Jewish. . . . On the other hand, the men from Ward 14 often work outside the area, and are thereby exposed in Lazarsfeld's phrase, to 'cross pressures' in mixed work and friendship groups." Depending on the nature of these cross pressures (see Chapter 12) they might reduce the kind of partisanship which leads to higher participation. See Lawrence H. Fuchs, "American Jews and the Presidential Vote," *American Political Science Review, 49* (1955), pp. 393-94.

42. James G. March, "Husband-Wife Interaction over Political Issues," *Public Opinion Quarterly, 17* (1953-54), pp. 461-70.

43. *Ibid.*, p. 468.

**TABLE 15.4.—Ranking of "Most Appropriate" Areas of Discussion
by the League of Women Voters, by Sex.**

Policy Area	Rank by husbands	Rank by wives
Local government	1	1
Education policy	2	2
Civil rights	3.5	3
Foreign policy	3.5	4
Administrative reform	5	6
Social welfare policy	6	4
Tax policy	7	7
Labor policy	8	8

Women are slightly less likely to include voting among their social duties and have slight, but declining, cultural reinforcement for this interpretation.

A moralized political orientation characteristic of women, arising from maternal responsibilities, exclusion from more socially valued areas of activity, and narrower orbits, tends to focus female political attention upon persons and peripheral "reform" issues.

The common association of politics with power and ascendance tends to exclude women from many political roles in Western culture.

Within the political sphere, a sexually differentiated role system makes appropriate a female interest and responsibility for local affairs, particularly as they relate to education, reserving labor and foreign relations more particularly for men.

For women, as contrasted to men, class subordination (with its sociological and psychological correlates) and membership in an ethnic group (with its different cultural roles) is relatively more politically inhibiting.

AGE LEVELS AND POLITICAL PARTICIPATION

Whether or not there are exactly seven parts, as Shakespeare says, it is true that each man in his time plays many roles. Each such role may demand a differentiated political stand, or at least produce a change in political attitudes to go with the changed situation. Certainly over the life span changing physiology, economic conditions, occupational roles, domestic responsibilities and community status, all affect the "public man."[44]

In dealing with the family we have pointed out that parents affect political interests by their attitudes toward their children's decisions, by influencing the nature and content of a sense of duty, and by their specific attitudes toward politics. Nor are these qualities molded only by the home; they are, of course, constantly influenced by schools, peer groups, and membership in ethnic

---

44. See Seymour M. Lipset, Paul F. Lazarsfeld, Allen H. Barton, and Juan Linz, "The Psychology of Voting: An Analysis of Political Behavior," in Gardner Lindzey, ed., *Handbook of Social Psychology* (Cambridge, Mass.: Addison-Wesley, 1954), Vol. 2, pp. 1124-75. See also Herbert Hyman, *Political Socialization* (Glencoe, Ill.: Free Press, 1958).

and status groups. The influence of the school on the political interests of youth, as Riesman and Newcomb have shown, can be crucial.[45] Sex is important, in this respect too, for the future political role of the man influences the boy to become more politically alert than the girl of the same age.

Whether or not adolescence is the most significant period of political crystallization, as has been alleged, there can be no doubt that this phase of life has significant influence upon political behavior patterns. This is not only because it is at this point that important career decisions are made (whether to go to college, for example), and the silver cord is broken, but also because this is a time when abstract thinking is possible, and to some extent encouraged, and Utopian visions of the world are said to be prevalent. On this latter point, at least, it may be possible that this interpretation is a product of a specific adolescent generation observed in one culture;[46] in many ways the youth of the twenties, and also the fifties, in the United States were prone to discount in advance all Utopian proposals for a better world. The maladjustments of adolescence, however, do raise the psychic value of Utopian politics so that although the group is small, a disproportionate number of communist recruits come from this age bracket.[47] In a different resolution of their psychic tension, young authoritarions of the right may respond to their insecure status between childhood and maturity by seeking authoritarian nativist movements which offer channels of escape from the feared father—and a substitute for him at the same time.

The marginal youth, the assimilationist immigrant, the Negro in an integrated high school, the adolescent child of the upwardly mobile former junk dealer, all are specifically sensitized to their environment. Depending upon the resolution of these pressures, adolescents at such time may become hyper-political—witness the high ethnic composition of the so-called "youth movement" of the thirties.

But generally for normal, non-marginal adolescents, with egos not yet hardened and defenses still not quite developed, a reality testing apparatus still inexperienced, a career to make, a husband still to catch, and a "self" to discover, conformity and low involvement offers the greatest rewards. Youth goes with the political trends of the era—and so helps to confirm them. In a poll related to the question of lowering the voting age to eighteen, the American Institute of Public Opinion found only minor distinguishing characteristics of the eighteen-to-twenty-year-old group contrasted to the rest of the adult population.[48] On the whole they are somewhat better informed than adults with respect to "basic political information" (electoral college,

45. See p. 196ff; for a somewhat different interpretation of the data in the Riesman analysis see, Rose Laub Coser, "Political Involvement and Interpersonal Relations," *Psychiatry, 14* (1951), pp. 213-22.

46. A statement of this position may be found in Edward Spranger, *Psychologie des Jugendalters* (Leipzig: Quelle und Meyer, 1925).

47. For case material see Gabriel Almond, *The Appeals of Communism* (Princeton: Princeton University Press, 1954), pp. 258-92; Morris L. Ernst and David Loth, *Report on the American Communist* (New York: Holt, 1952).

48. American Institute of Public Opinion releases, 3/5/54, 3/6/54.

three branches of government, first ten amendments to Constitution, etc.). They are also, in a moderate way, more liberal, that is, they are slightly more likely to favor teaching the facts of Communism, Fascism, and Socialism in schools; they are more likely to favor increased trade with Russia; about half as many (9 per cent to 21 per cent) favor higher tariffs, and about half as many (7 per cent to 15 per cent) might properly be called isolationists. As for their political preferences, they corresponded, in 1954, to adult party preferences, that is, they are about evenly divided. On the basis of this evidence, it appears that the late adolescent or pre-adult is oriented much like his parents, but is somewhat more likely to embrace views which can only be described as very moderately liberal.

The young adult, psychically more secure and with a personality which has, so to speak, "jelled," but situationally probably less secure, has only ambiguous social support from shifting peer groups, and uncertain vocational stakes. For these reasons he is low in participation, even though he is aware of his citizen duties and accepts them intellectually as much as any other group and has a considerable belief in the effectiveness of political action in a democracy.[49] As far as direction of support is concerned, he is rather more likely than those who have achieved a more stable position in life to adopt his parents' political views.[50]

In maturity certain things occur in the normal lifetime which tend to increase the motivation and the pressure to take part in the political life of the community. A person acquires property, hence one of the most important forces politicizing the local citizen comes to bear upon him—the question of the assessment and tax on his house. Then too, the family includes children who need playgrounds and schools and therefore the mother finds new stakes in politics. Because of the children, and the importance of their view of the parents, the parents become conscious of themselves as civic models for their growing children. They are geographically less mobile. For such reasons as these the married of both sexes vote more than the unmarried.[51] Dreams of solving status and income problems through rapid personal mobility may suffer erosion, and a more solid alignment with class and ethnic groups emerge. Vocational interests become more salient. The increased economic security associated with middle age provides freedom of attention and psychic energy for political matters often not available at an earlier stage in life. Thus in 1952 most of the Republican precinct leaders in King County, Washington were over fifty.[52]

As for the elderly, apparently several things happen at these later stages in life. Persons over fifty-five lose their sense of political effectiveness to some extent,[53] and perhaps, with retirement, lose their feeling of vital economic stake in political decisions of many kinds. The well-to-do remain integrated in the community, with large numbers of group memberships; but the less

---

49. See A. Campbell and associates, *op. cit.,* pp. 191, 197.

50. B. Berelson and associates, *op. cit.,* p. 89.

51. H. Tingsten, *op. cit.,* p. 95.

52. Hugh A. Bone, *Grass Roots Party Leadership: A Case Study of King County, Washington* (Seattle: University of Washington, 1952, mimeographed).

53. A. Campbell and associates, *op. cit.,* p. 197.

prosperous have fewer group memberships as they grow older.[54] Perhaps something like this is at work in feelings of citizen duty; apparently as people grow older there is a slight tendency to move from a moderate sense of civic duty toward either a feeling of greater duty or a feeling of almost no sense of civic duty at all.[55] For the successful and the unsuccessful, aging may have substantially different effects.

During this process of growth and development over the life cycle, great historical events will have a differential effect on the different generations. Thus, for those who achieved early maturity in the "emancipated" days "following the First World War, the term "flaming youth" seemed to capture something of their abandoned style; those who came to maturity in the depression of the thirties, and who sought jobs in a bankrupt job-market sometimes called themselves the "unwanted generation." If late adolescence and early maturity are periods of political crystallization, whole generations have been "fixed" by the events which caught them at this age level. It is in this sense that Mannheim, Heberle, and Lipset, et al. speak of "political generations"—generations who have endured similar experiences at roughly the same stage in life and so had their thinking similarly, and perhaps permanently, affected by these experiences.[56]

In this brief overview of the possible influences associated with different age periods, the following hypotheses emerge:

The socialization of the child includes a political sector which focuses interest, inculcates attitudes, develops relevant personality characteristics, and molds feelings of duty. Sex typing in terms of political roles is apparent at an early age.

Late adolescence and early maturity may be a critical period for establishing political attitudes. At this age level psychic tensions created by the burdens of social adjustment tend to lead a small but disproportionate number of youth into alienated political movements. However, most youth solve their "age-political" problems by conformity and low emotional involvement in the face of feelings of political effectiveness and acceptance of prevailing codes of citizen duty.

Marginal youth, because of their greater sensitivity to the social environment, become more quickly oriented to political phenomena than others.

Life conditions associated with middle age, including property ownership, family responsibilities, acceptance of group status, and more homogeneous social environment, tend to promote greater political interests and participation.

Later life for the successful tends to bring closer community integration and higher sense of duty; for the less successful and less prosperous later life tends to isolate the individual and lower his sense of citizen duty. Feelings of political effectiveness tend to decline in these years.

Because of the similar impact of major historical events upon an age group facing similar problems, generations may differ in their political attitudes and behavior. Stratified in this way, the population may include several distinctive political generations.

---

54. Wendell Bell and Maryanne T. Force, "Urban Neighborhood Types and Participation in Formal Associations," *American Sociological Review, 21* (1956), pp. 25-34.

55. A. Campbell and associates, *op. cit.,* pp. 191, 197.

56. Karl Mannheim, "The Sociological Problem of Generations," in *Essays on the Sociology of Knowledge* (New York: Oxford University Press, 1952), pp. 276-322; Rudolf Heberle, *Social Movements, An Introduction to Political Sociology* (New York: Appleton, 1951); S. Lipset and associates, *op. cit.,* pp. 1147-48.

CHAPTER 16

Why Lower-Status People Participate Less

than Upper-Status People

CLASS STATUS is indicated by objective criteria (such as income, occupation, and education), plus a network of social relations, plus a person's conception of his own place in society.[1] It both defines and serves as the instrument of a man's aspirations and ambitions. Where one lives, what church one belongs to, one's style of life are usually functions of social class. The position of a person's class in the total class structure determines the benefits he receives from his class membership. A social class is a life space with various ranks and restrictions and pressures of its own; its non-mobile members, therefore, come to grips with life largely within the terms of their own class.[2] Yet, like other groups, it has a reference function both for members and for those who are not, by objective criteria, members. Thus people in working-class occupations who think of themselves as middle-class may pattern their behavior after middle-class norms.[3]

Social classes develop characteristic attitudes, belief, and goals, indicating a kind of class differentiation of sub-national culture patterns.[4] For example,

1. For a bibliography of social stratification see *Current Sociology*, Vol. II, Number 1, 1953-54 (a UNESCO publication). For an excellent review of current theory, see Kurt Mayer, "The Theory of Social Classes," *Harvard Education Review*, 23 (1953), pp. 149-57. See also, Rienhard Bendix and Seymour M. Lipset, eds., *Class Status and Power* (Glencoe, Ill.: Free Press, 1953).

2. G. W. Hartman makes the point that competition for status occurs largely within classes, rather than between them. See "The Prestige of Occupations," *Personnel Journal*, 13 (1934).

3. On the general subject of subjective class status, see Richard Centers, *The Psychology of Social Classes* (Princeton: Princeton University Press, 1949); also Heinz Eulau, "Perceptions of class and Party in Voting Behavior, 1952," *American Political Science Review*, 49 (1955), pp. 364-84.

4. See Arthur W. Kornhauser, "Public Opinion and Social Class," *American Journal of Sociology*, 55 (1950), pp. 333-45.

WHY LOWER-STATUS PEOPLE PARTICIPATE LESS

people in different social classes read different magazines. The Yankee City study shows that while 83 per cent of the *New Yorker* subscribers in that community were members of the upper class (and 17 per cent upper-middle), 54 per cent of the *True Story* subscribers were members of the lower class (and 46 per cent middle class).[5] Television appears to be a great equalizer in this respect, but if television is like the radio, where there are marked class differences in listening habits the appearance of uniformity is deceptive.[6]

It has long been known that political participation in the United States increases with increasing status. This is illustrated in Woodward and Roper's findings on the socio-economic groups who rate high on a composite index of political participation:[7]

"A" Economic Level
Executives
Professional people
Stockholders
College educated
Those who scored lowest were:
Laboring people
Housewives
People with only grade school education
Negroes
"D" economic level

The "A" economic level had twelve times as great a proportion of very active participants (top 10 per cent on index) as did the "D" economic level. Why are social status and political participation so closely linked in the United States?

The gains from governmental policy for lower income groups must be collective gains, gains granted to classes or groups of people, which may or may not accrue to any one individual. In contrast to this, a large category of middle-income persons, businessmen, are in a position to gain some specific individual advantage from government such as a fast tax write-off, a paving contract, or a real estate deal. As a consequence, the relationship between political effort and personal gain is usually closer for businessmen than for working-class people.

Beyond this, however, the means available for participation are different in the different status groups. The poor man can contribute no significant sums of money, nor is his individual social and occupational position likely to give him, as an individual, much influence over governmental actions. Poor people can exert influence only by collective action; really, only through

5. See W. Lloyd Warner's Yankee City series, especially Warner and Lunt, *The Social Life of a Modern Community* (New Haven: Yale University Press, 1941), pp. 390-93.

6. Paul F. Lazarsfeld and Patricia L. Kendall, *Radio Listening in America* (New York: Prentice-Hall, 1948); see also, Genevieve Knupfer, "Portrait of the Underdog," *Public Opinion Quarterly, 11* (1947), pp. 108-09.

7. Julian L. Woodward and Elmo Roper, "Political Activity of American Citizens," *American Political Science Review, 44* (1950), p. 877.

organizations designed for this purpose. The more prosperous individual, however, can make larger financial contributions and can use his personal and professional influence to some effect. The working-class person must speak through an agent; the business or professional person may delegate his politics in the same way, but he may also exercise personal influence.

Among the objective criteria which we have said are indices of socio-economic status, is it education, income, or occupation which makes the greatest difference? Connelly and Field, with reference only to voting, find that when a cross-analysis of income and education is made, the differences between the income levels for each educational classification are greater than the differences among the educational level for each income classification.[8] Foskett, on the other hand, finds that indices of more general community participation reveals greater differences among educational groups when income is held constant than among income groups when education is held constant.[9] Perhaps for a simple conventional act such as voting, income is more important, while more complex forms of participation are more dependent upon qualities associated with education. Occupation is hard to grade along a similar, single dimensional continuum, but from inspection of the 1952 Survey Research Center data, it is apparent (for what it is worth) that differences among standard occupational classifications are smaller than differences among the educational or income classifications.[10]

Education affects attitudes toward political participation in several directions at once. A preliminary study of 400 students at Ohio Wesleyan University and others in the local community showed that college students (particularly those who had political science courses) were significantly more willing than high school students to work for a political party, but among the college students those who were most willing to work for a political party were the Freshman and those generally least willing to do so were the college Seniors.[11] Furthermore, these attitudes of willingness or unwillingness were supported in the various college class groups by "appropriate" differences in attitudes toward the political system: more cynical among Seniors and more hopeful and conscientious among Freshmen. Thus, the micro-processes whereby the gross experiences of education are converted into a higher sense of duty and willingness to participate remain still to be made clear.

Returning to the more molar level of explanation, however, the substan-

8. Gordon M. Connelly and Harry M. Field, "The Non-Voter—Who He is, What He Thinks," *Public Opinion Quarterly, 8* (1944), p. 179.

9. John M. Foskett, "Social Structure and Social Participation," *American Sociological Review, 20* (1955), p. 434.

10. Angus Campbell, Gerald Gurin, and Warren E. Muler, *The Voter Decides* (Evanston, Ill.: Row, Peterson, 1954), p. 72.

11. *The Development of Attitude Scales in Practical Politics* (Delaware, Ohio: The Evaluation Service, Ohio Wesleyan University, 1955, mimeographed), pp. 21, 26. See also a subsequent report by the Ohio Wesleyan Evaluation Service, *Changes in the Political Attitudes of Students at Ohio Wesleyan University During Their First Two Years* (1957). Apparently two additional years of college increases willingness to participate in politics.

tial social class differences in political activity require a general social analysis. Why should persons in higher socio-economic status positions in the United States engage more actively in the political process than those with lower status positions? A number of answers have been brought forward and of these, eleven deserve examination.

In the first place, there is sometimes offered a simple answer in terms of time and energy available for matters not immediately related to the daily problems of living. Saenger points out, for example, that political activity is not merely a matter of awareness of what is going on, but is also affected by the "amount of time and energy specific activities require."[12] It takes an amount of leisure above the minimum to ring doorbells, write letters, read magazine articles, go to forums, and serve on committees, and a differential in leisure may account for some of the differential in activity. Bryce attributes many of the differences between British and American politics to the lack of a leisure class in the United States.[13] Lipset and associates consider that leisure time differences help explain the discrepancies in voting rates in different income groups.[14]

At least for men, the leisure theory fails to explain class differences in participation in the United States at this time, however useful it may have been in other cultures at other times. Leisure has a wide variety of contexts and meanings among which are isolation from working companions; retirement, and hence a more tenuous relation to economic strivings; unemployment and the depression and apathy which this often entails; travel with its loosening of community bonds; and so forth. If, all other things remaining equal, the hours of work are varied, probably there is an inverted "u-shaped" curve relating leisure and political participation.

Also, there is no clear relation between working hours and income. For example, in Connecticut (February, 1956, and also generally throughout the year), workers in the apparel industry worked an average of thirty-six hours a week and received the lowest hourly wage rate and the lowest weekly earnings of all manufacturing production workers, while those in primary metal industries worked an average of forty-seven hours a week, and had among the highest hourly rates. The most prosperous workers had the least leisure.[15] Although the data are not available, it is equally uncertain that the executive or professional man today works less hours than the factory worker. And perhaps he carries his occupational burdens with him rather more than the manual or clerical worker—he is more preoccupied.

Furthermore, those with the most leisure, the retired, seem to be less

---

12. Gerhart H. Saenger, "Social Status and Political Behavior," *American Journal of Sociology, 51* (1945), p. 105.

13. James Bryce, *The American Commonwealth* (New York: Macmillan, 1910), pp. 62, 67.

14. Seymour M. Lipset, Paul F. Lazarsfeld, Allen H. Barton, and Juan Linz, "The Psychology of Voting: An Analysis of Political Behavior," in Gardner Lindzey, ed., *Handbook of Social Psychology* (Cambridge, Mass.: Addison-Wesley, 1954), pp. 1124-75.

15. *Connecticut Labor Department Monthly Bulletin, 21* (April, 1956), p. 6.

politically active than others of their age bracket. Arneson and Eells, for example, found that out of seventy categories of people analyzed, the "retired" group had the lowest voting rate in 1948, far lower than those classified as "over 70 years of age."[16] Furthermore, in Erie County in 1940, of those who reported that they had attempted to convince someone of their political ideas or had been asked for political advice, the unemployed, next to the housewives, revealed the lowest rate of participation of this kind.[17]

For reasons of this nature the availability of time and leisure does not seem to account for the variation in class participation among men, although allowance should be made for the inconvenience to working men of the opening and closing times of the polls.[18] But among women, the situation may be different. Katz and Lazarsfeld found not only that upper-status women are more likely to be political opinion leaders than lower status women, but that women with small families are also more likely than women with large families to be opinion leaders of this kind.[19] These authors suggest that greater leisure to increase social contacts outside the home is an important factor in accounting for these differences. Thus, for women, if not for men, class differences in participation may, indeed, reflect differences in amount of leisure.

If time and leisure seem to be ambiguously related to different rates of political participation in different socio-economic classes, what of economic security? Here the basis for a reliable class difference seems somewhat better supported. In Albany, New York (1949), upper income persons were found to be substantially less worried about the possibility of a depression and about their own personal finances than persons of lower income.[20] But worry of this kind seems to have various results. On the one hand, it does not seem to absorb attention and time so that an interest in foreign affairs is made less likely.[21] On the other hand, another study shows that people who "feel quite secure financially" are likely also to feel that they are politically effective and have an effective voice in the affairs of the republic.[22] These attitudes, as we know, form a solid basis for political activ-

---

16. Ben A. Arneson and William H. Eells, "Voting Behavior in 1948 as Compared with 1924 in a Typical Ohio Community," *American Political Science Review, 44* (1950), p. 434.

17. Paul F. Lazarsfeld, Bernard Berelson, and Hazel Gaudet, *The People's Choice,* 2nd ed. (New York: Columbia University Press, 1948), p. 50. But, note that, for some reason, the retired, as distinct from the unemployed, were among the highest participants in this study.

18. See Charles E. Merriam and Harold F. Gosnell, *Non-Voting* (Chicago: University of Chicago Press, 1924), pp. 78-108.

19. Elihu Katz and Paul F. Lazarsfeld, *Personal Influence* (Glencoe, Ill.: Free Press, 1955), pp. 273, 291.

20. Survey Research Center, *Interest, Information, and Attitudes in the Field of World Affairs* (Ann Arbor, Mich., 1949, mimeographed), p. 100.

21. *Ibid.,* p. 38.

22. Elizabeth Douvan and Alan M. Walker, "The Sense of Effectiveness in Public Affairs," Ann Arbor, Mich., Survey Research Center, c. 1954, (mimeographed), p. 17. The question was: "Some people feel quite secure financially: others have many worries about how they will get along. How is it in your case?"

ity. On the whole, it seems justifiable to say that the lack of financial worry which is generally associated with a better income provides one cause for substantial socio-economic class differences in political activity.

Turning now to a third argument which seeks to explain why members of upper-status groups participate more than do members of lower-status groups, one comes to an essentially economic concept. This argument, following the familiar lines of the Federalist papers,[23] states that those with property (or larger incomes?) have a greater stake in the society and therefore not only do but should have greater influence on governmental policy-making. Leaving out of account the moral phase of the argument, there is a theory, which we believe false, that men do naturally participate in politics somewhat in proportion to their stake in society and further, that the more prosperous have a greater stake in society.

Since the idea of "stake in society" is a chimerical argument leading into premiseless debate, let us consider the proposition to mean stake in governmental policy. With the rise of the welfare state, the proportion of policy designed to be of immediate assistance to the working class has clearly increased. Just as the bearing of public policy upon fair employment practices brought the Northern Negro increasingly to the polls, so the increase of welfare legislation helped to increase the rate of participation of the urban worker. If there ever was a time when ownership of property or greater income necessarily gave a man greater status in governmental decisions than lack of such property or income, that time is fast disappearing.

Nevertheless, there are differences in the way in which the government impinges on individuals in different income groups. It is psychologically more painful to be threatened with deprivation of something you have than it is psychologically rewarding to be offered something you want but have never experienced. On such grounds as these, perhaps, more emotion is invested in a 10 per cent increase in taxation than in a 10 per cent increase in standard of living due to federal subsidy of housing. This difference between social classes in the nature of the rewards and punishments of government policy may help to explain differential turnout among these social classes.

Perhaps even more important than the extent and nature of the relevant policies and the means available to affect them is the degree to which they are visible to the affected groups. We have argued that the society distributes education and access to sources of information unequally to the several

---

23. "Government is instituted no less for protection of the property, than of the persons, of individuals. The one as well as the other therefore, may be considered as represented by those who are charged with the government. Upon this principle it is that in several of the States, and particularly in the State of New York, one branch of government is intended more especially to be the guardian of property, and is accordingly elected by that part of the society which is most interested in this object of government." Moreover, "If the law allows an opulent citizen but a single vote in the choice of his representative, the respect and consequence which he derives from his fortunate situation very frequently guide the votes of others to the objects of his choice; and through this imperceptible channel the rights of property are conveyed into the public representation." Federalist Paper No. 54 (Hamilton or Madison), see E. M. Meade, ed., *The Federalist* (New York: Random House, c. 1937), p. 357.

social classes, and that the media make visible the relevance of governmental policy to upper status groups when they do not do so to the same degree for the lower status groups. This argument is borne out by the fact that education is positively related to a perception of "whether the outcome of an election would make any difference or not," but it must be confessed that the relationship is not so great as one would expect (67 per cent grammar school to 77 per cent high school and college).[24] In any event, if domestic politics are related to a distribution of rewards and punishments on a socio-economic status basis and the parties favor different status-groups, as most observers believe, the fact that the proportion of the working class voting Republican is larger than the proportion of the middle class who vote Democratic suggests (but does not prove) a lower visibility of objective group interests in the working class.

A fourth approach to class differentials lies through a complex of attitudes of self-confidence and effectiveness and the correlates of these views. Genevieve Knupfer puts this position clearly in focus: "the economic and educational limitations accompanying low status produce a lack of interest in and lack of self-confidence in dealing with certain important areas of our culture; as a result, there is reduced participation—a withdrawal from participation in these areas."[25] This lack of self-confidence in the lower-status groups is, in fact, reflected in the lower sense of political effectiveness which already has been noted; and interest in politics follows the same class pattern. It is seen in the higher percentage of "don't knows" among the lower-status groups in the survey responses. Lack of self-confidence is, moreover, associated with fewer group memberships, inasmuch as a refusal to join parent-teacher organizations or even fraternal groups where persons of different status mingle, often is the product of fear of how one will appear to others of somewhat higher status.[26]

When the democratic illusion—all men are powerful; all men are informed—comes into conflict with the realities of the politically powerless lower-status situation, the working man or woman is caught and made to feel uncomfortable. It is this situation that Riesman and Glazer confront when they speak of the dangers of divorcing opinions from influence. Contending that this is a relatively recent condition, they point to the unrealistic nature of opinion lodged in the minds of those who have no experience with the relevant situations and have no reason to expect that their views will ever be tested.[27] These are, by and large, lower-status persons, and the discrepancy helps to explain qualitative differences in participation— the marginal character of the views expressed, the ineffective measures employed, and the fringe movements which draw their clientele from the lower socio-economic classes.

---

24. G. H. Saenger, *op. cit.*, p. 104.

25. G. Knupfer, *op. cit.*, pp. 104-105.

26. *Ibid.*, p. 105.

27. David Riesman and Nathan Glazer, "The Meaning of Opinion," *Public Opinion Quarterly, 12* (1948), pp. 631-48; see below, p. 000.

There are those, like C. W. Mills, who dispute that the working class is actually the group with these deficiencies of influence. For them, it is the white collar middle class:[28]

The white-collar people slipped quietly into modern society. Whatever history they have had is a history without events; whatever common interests they have do not lead to unity; whatever future they have will not be of their own making. . . . Internally, they are split, fragmented; externally, they are dependent on larger forces. Even if they gained the will to act, their acts, being unorganized, would be less a movement than a tangle of unconnected contests. . . . The white collar man is the hero as victim, the small creature who is acted upon but who does not act, who works along unnoticed in somebody's office or store, never talking aloud, never talking back, never taking a stand.

But in many ways the evidence tends to run against this view. The middle classes belong to more organizations, are better informed, have greater facility with the verbal means of influence, and participate in elections more than do the working classes. Indeed, in 1948, the white collar group had the highest voting record of any group in the nation, including the professorial and managerial group.

A fifth line of argument seeks to explain class differentials in political participation in terms of class differences in child-rearing practices. Middle-class child-training, say Davis and Havighurst, is characterized by the insistence of parents on certain typically restrictive values, such as cleanliness, punctuality, responsibility, and so forth. The effort to instill these values in the growing child creates a sense of anxiety and desire to conform, a stricter regulation of impulses, and an over-developed conscience.[29] These qualities, so the argument goes, are carried over from private life to public life where they appear as a civic conscience, and are reflected in attendance at forums, a dutiful reading of the "duller" section of the paper dealing with distant policy questions and electoral participation. The lower-class child, according to Davis and Havighurst, is brought up with less restrictions on his bodily functions, fewer inhibitory commands, and hence a different attitude toward indulgence of impulses and an unwillingness to impose a sense of duty over a sense of what would be more fun. Therefore, given the choice, they read these newspapers which give play to their instinctual life, prefer television comedy to the forum, and consider that it is too much trouble to go and vote.

There are two difficulties with this argument. The first deals with the presumption that strict training encourages those attitudes which we have lumped together as "civic conscience." There is no evidence to support this view and as discussed earlier, on theoretical grounds one might more plausibly argue that a controlled permissiveness, and a relaxed attitude toward weaning and elimination would lead to a set of civic attitudes which

---

28. C. Wright Mills, *White Collar: The American Middle Classes* (New York: Oxford University Press, 1951), pp. ix, xii.

29. W. Allison Davis and Robert J. Havighurst, *Father of the Man* (Boston: Houghton Mifflin, 1947), pp. 186-87, 217.

might more appropriately be termed "conscientious," and to greater civic participation. Erikson, for example, argues that strict toilet training encourages the child to believe that he has no "say" in the important decisions which affect him.[30] The second difficulty with this argument, deals with the evidence of class differences in washing and toilet training procedures. On the whole these seem to be minimal and not generally in the direction suggested by Davis and Havighurst in their original Chicago study.[31]

But there are other suggestions in the data on child-rearing which may account for higher middle-class political and social participation. In both Boston and Chicago, "middle class children (are) allowed more freedom of movement away from home during the day."[32] Middle-class parents, more than working-class parents, seem to understand and permit a kind of controlled aggression among their children. The techniques of imposing discipline suggest greater reliance on building up the super-ego regulating devices. Parents expect greater educational attainments for their children. In general, the middle-class child seems to receive at the same time, greater encouragement to explore and be ambitious, and greater capacity for internal regulation and purposive action.

A further (sixth) difference between the various socio-economic class groups lies in the political roles which persons in each group are expected to play. Is there such a difference? On the whole, it seems clear that there is. Descriptively, we find in Elmtown that a five class system reveals:

Class II focuses its attention upon the aggressive manipulation of economic and political processes; consequently, its members are hyperactive in the power wielding associations, such as Chamber of Commerce, Rotary, Masons, country club, and the major political parties. The women are as active as the men within their own sphere. . . .

Although political activity [in class III] is more widespread than in any other stratum, and from two-thirds to three-fourths of the several county offices are staffed by persons either elected or appointed from this class, these facts do not lead to the conclusions that Class III is politically powerful. On the contrary it looks to Classes I and II for its leadership.[33]

The sociologist's profile does not include political activity for Classes IV and V; here politics is sporadic and not a part of the cultural roles as they appeared in a Middle Western town of about 6,000.

The Elmira study of Berelson and his associates, tends to confirm this picture of the location of political participation roles in the class just under the small closed elite at the top: "Class I" for Hollingshead, "upper-upper"

---

30. Erik H. Erikson, *Childhood and Society* (New York: Norton, 1950), pp. 269-70.

31. See Robert J. Havighurst and Allison Davis, "A Comparison of the Chicago and Harvard Studies of Social Class Differences in Child Rearing," *American Sociological Review*, 20 (1955), pp. 438-42.

32. *Ibid.*, p. 441.

33. August B. Hollingshead, "Selected Characterization of a Middle Western Community," *American Sociological Review*, 12 (1947), pp. 385-95.

in Warner's terminology.[34] This study finds that active political roles are
rarely assumed by Class I individuals, but instead such persons delegate this
function to those at an intermediate level of society who serve their interests
in return for various psychic (and sometimes economic) rewards. Financial
participation, on the other hand, is more appropriate for Class I persons,
whose per capita rate of giving was the highest in Elmira. On the other hand,
the lower economic groups tend to delegate their political responsibilities
to those who have somewhat more education and somewhat more income
than they themselves possess. Thus, there is a principle of social proximity
for political activities in that each of the major parties and allied classes dele-
gates toward the middle. To some extent, perhaps, this may explain the
pragmatic similarity of the major parties. In any event, it is clear that the
working and upper classes define political roles somewhat differently; there
is a tendency to push these obligations toward middle-class groups, and the
net result is that the expectations of active participation in each group
differ in such a way as to encourage middle-class more than working-class
participation.

There are exceptions to the proposition that upper status people
avoid overt political leadership, as some of the great names in politics
indicate: Roosevelt, Harriman, Lodge, Stevenson, Byrd. In analyzing the
upper-class complexion of the Progressive movement leadership, Hofstadter
throws some light on the motivation of political leaders from this social
group.[35] The Progressive movement somehow enlisted the active support of a
number of men, whose economic interests, narrowly interpreted, seemed
not to lie in the direction of this movement. Among the selecting factors
which Hofstadter finds important for the wealthy Progressive leaders are
their Protestant faiths and, to a large extent, their New England origins
with their emphasis upon conscience and duty; the fact that they represented "old" wealth as contrasted to the new plutocracy whose politics
reflected their economic mode of life; and, less altruistically, their fear that
if they did not capture the reform movement, radicals might do so to their
(and society's) lasting detriment. In some ways this was an extension of the
stewardship doctrine which Carnegie expressed in the economic sphere:
success showed that they had been called by Divine powers to govern the
economy—why not also the same mission with respect to the political life
of the nation. But also, as Almond has shown, behind the division between
plutocracy and progressive reform, were personality factors attributable to
the differences in the nature of their earliest training.[36]

Nor is this elite sense of responsibility for the state of the nation (a

---

Bernard R. Berelson, Paul F. Lazarsfeld, and William N. McPhee, *Voting* (Chicago:
University of Chicago Press, 1954), pp. 156-60.

35. Richard Hofstadter, *The Age of Reform, from Bryan to F.D.R.* (New York:
Knopf, 1955), pp. 132-212, also Hofstadter, *The American Political Tradition* (New
York: Knopf, 1948), pp. 204-222. I am indebted to Raymond Wolfinger for bringing
this theme to my attention.

36. Gabriel Almond, "The Political Attitudes of Wealth," *Journal of Politics, 7*
(1945), pp. 213-55.

seventh factor) limited to the very wealthy or to the early years of this century. In that sophisticated panegyric of the American Way produced by the Editors of *Fortune* and Russell M. Davenport,[37] there is evidence that among the grass roots elite, the business leaders of small communities, something of the same attitude prevails. Looking into the "busy, busy" lives of such men, these authors find them constantly active in civic and political groups of all kinds, partly from self-interest, but partly also from a sense of responsibility for their communities and a desire to pour non-material meaning into their lives. They are quoted as saying: "It seems to me that none of us can look forward with hope over the years unless all of us can find solutions to problems bigger than our immediate interests," "I was brought up to serve the community," and, referring to participation in civic affairs, "paying our civic rent."[38] The authors, uniquely qualified as spokesmen for business interests, report their conclusion that "The basis of American economic development has been private initiative in economic matters; the basis for American social development must be private initiative in social matters."[39]

As an eighth consideration, we may look at the cross pressures which tend to reduce partisanship and emotional commitment to politics. If it could be established that there are class differences in the incidence of such conflicts, a further reason for differences in political participation in different social classes would follow. There is some evidence for believing that working-class groups are in the midst of such cross pressures in four respects. First, much of the politics of metropolitan areas with large ethnic populations presents a picture of conflicting ethnic and class identifications. In New Haven, for example, the large Italian population tends to vote Republican in local elections when their ethnic loyalties are aroused, but their class status tends to confirm them in their indentification with the national (New Deal, Fair Deal) democratic programs. Such conflicts may operate to reduce their wholehearted commitment to either party and hence weakens their inducement to participate in electoral matters.

A second kind of cross pressure with a heavier incidence in the working class lies in the conflict between the stimuli which reaches them in the union press, or in the addresses directed to them by liberal political leaders, and the more conservative (Republican) stimuli of the daily press, television, and radio. As noted above, the media raise to visibility the attractions of Republican identification and voting more than the attractions of Democratic identification, hence working-class persons are in the stream of conflicting propaganda. The middle-class voter, due to his, one is tempted to say "natural," selection of reading matter, does not experience this conflict.

Third, as MacRae points out, there is a tendency in non-working class districts for lower status people to identify more with the community and

---

37. *U.S.A., The Permanent Revolution* (New York: Prentice-Hall, 1951).
38. *Ibid.*, pp. 128, 137, 145.
39. *Ibid.*, p. 200.

the community leaders than with their own class-linked spokesmen.[40] These leaders are, by and large, upper-or middle-class persons, and the possible conflict of identifications in such instances might further be said to depress political participation.

Finally, there is more of a tendency for members of the working class, objectively defined, to think of themselves as middle class (36 per cent) than for the middle-class members (objectively defined) to think of themselves as working class (24 per cent).[41] Such a conflict between objective class position and subjective identification would lead to a cross-pressured situation, and hence, like other cross pressures, could lead to a failure of partisanship and weakening of political interest. The different incidence of such a conflict, then, would help to account for lower working-class participation.[42]

A ninth reason for class differentials in political participation turns upon the previously discussed factor of group memberships. Nationally, and perhaps in every local community to some degree among some groups, number of group memberships tends to be associated with greater political participation. Since middle-class and upper-class people tend to belong to more groups than working-class people, greater mutual contact makes for greater awareness of political problems, and greater reinforcement of class values and partisanship among upper-strata groups than lower-strata groups.

In this connection, an extremely important modification of the prevailing lower-class pattern should be pointed out—the rise of labor unions, which have the effect of increasing the political activity of their members.[43] In Pennsylvania, for example, the widespread indifference to politics among workers was substantially modified by the great organizing drives of the thirties.[44]

For any social class, joining homogeneous groups tends to reinforce political beliefs and stimulate political interests. But joining heterogeneous class groups has different effects upon lower-status members than it does upon higher-status members.

For lower-status persons, inter-strata contact establishes a cross pressure which the upper-strata person does not feel, since he does not experience the divergent views of the lower-stratum person (when expressed) as a "pressure."[45]

Not only is it true that lower-status people have fewer group member ships, it is also true that they have fewer friends and informal social contacts. Evidently the "warmth" and solidarity of the working class is a product

---

40. Duncan MacRae, Jr., "Occupations and the Congressional Vote, 1940-1950," *American Sociological Review*, 20 (1955), pp. 332-44.

41. Heinz Eulau, "Identification with Class and Political Perspective," *Journal of Politics*, 18 (1956), p. 242.

42. But on the influence of such cross pressures, see pp. 197-203.

43. Angus Campbell and associates, *op. cit.*, p. 73.

44. Harold F. Gosnell, *Grass Root Politics* (Washington, D. C.: American Council on Public Affairs, 1942), pp. 21-37.

45. Lazarsfeld and associates, *op. cit.*, pp. 146-47.

of the romantic notions of the middle-class observer, projective in origin and filled with pathos for what it implies about the observers. In Middletown, for example, while one-eighth of the "business class" women said they had no intimate friends, one-third of the working class made this statement.[46] Other studies on other communities tend to support this relationship. Without such informal clique group reinforcement, political partisanship tends to wither and political discussion which feeds interest is made impossible.

A tenth consideration, which has some prima facie value, deals with the skills required for participation and their distribution among the social classes. Here certain discriminations must be made between those qualities whose distribution has a linear relation to class status and those which do not. Education falls in the first category and has a clear effect upon capacity to understand and deal with the kinds of issues which are present in national politics—particularly foreign policy issues.[47] But there are other qualities which seem present in the middle ranges of the working class, although not in the lowest group. Among these are, apparently, capacity to serve as opinion leaders in informal discussion. Skilled workers in Erie County had among their group almost as many opinion leaders as did the professional and clerical groups.[48] Furthermore, although in general the evidence shows that lower-status people are less aware of the features of their environment which affect them intimately, such as price control during the war, one suspects that this ignorance is largely concentrated in the lower ranges of the working class.[49] The skill differential and the allied information and "alertness" differentials among classes may help to explain the lower rates of participation among the lower-status groups, but some relevant skills are apparently absent only in what Warner would call the "lower-lower" class.

Finally (eleventh), we come to the question of identification with society or its absence, sometimes termed alienation. Is this class-linked? Alienation, in the sense of personal dissatisfaction with one's job and life prospects, is indeed more prevalent in low-status groups.[50] Also, those in the upper-status groups are generally more satisfied with their community, or better integrated in it, than those on lower-status levels.[51] Since both satisfaction with one's own life prospects and one's community (with status held constant) tend to increase participation, the distribution of these attitudes helps to explain lower turnout in lower-status groups. Yet the possibility of mobilizing these dissatisfactions in the service of extremist political movements is always present.

The eleven reasons for class differentials in political participation given

---

46. See Robert and Helen Lynd, *Middletown* (New York: Harcourt, Brace, 1929), p. 272.

47. Survey Research Center, *op. cit.*, p. 34.

48. Lazarsfeld and associates, *op. cit.*, p. 50.

49. G. Knupfer, *op. cit.*, p. 111.

50. See Donald Super, "Occupational Level and Job Satisfaction," *Journal of Applied Psychology*, 23 (1939), p. 550.

51. Alice S. Kitt and David B. Gleicher, "Determinants of Voting Behavior," *Public Opinion Quarterly*, 14 (1950), pp. 393-412.

above operate through some of the attitudes originally shown to be related to political participation. In most instances they tend to depress for one status and elevate for another stratum the sense of political effectiveness, the sense of citizen duty, partisanship, perception of and concern for group stakes in an election, satisfaction with the society in which they live and work, interest in political affairs, or partisan identification with some politically connected group. Furthermore, some of the class differentials tend to facilitate political expression, while others inhibit or erect barriers to such expression. In the American society wherever status is marked, therefore, some or all of these variables will be in operation—although, of course, in European societies where group memberships and cross pressures and attitudes are differently distributed status may operate in a quite different fashion.

Of course, class status is not a fixed assignment in the United States, and is decreasingly so in Europe.[53] Consequently the forces operating upon the person who moves from one status level to another may assume significant proportions. Among these forces is the weakening of group and community attachments. Vertical mobility may very well require a change of residence, from tenement to suburban development or from exclusive suburb to middle-class apartment. Furthermore, changes in social status often imply changes from union membership to Rotary Club membership, or from fraternal order to street corner society, depending upon whether the movement is up or down. These kinds of changes tend to weaken the forces making for active political life.

On the other hand, the norms of the group to which a person moves or from which he moves will have other effects, possibly complementary but possibly also conflicting. In general the upwardly mobile person seeks to adopt the norms of the group toward which he is moving; the downwardly mobile person retains, so far as possible, the norms of his former associates.[53] Both of these tendencies tend to increase participation—increasing class differentials for the upwardly mobile, decreasing them for the downwardly mobile.

In summary, then we may set forward the following hypotheses on the influence of socio-economic status upon political activity.

A socio-economic status group (social class) is: (1) a significant reference group for many persons because of the many ties which link them with their class, and (2) a sub-national culture because of the common experiences, attitudes, interests, and values which are significantly different for the different socio-economic classes.

Identifying socio-economic status groups by income, education, and occupation, we can discover in each of these factors contributions to differential political behavior.

The lesser degree of political participation and interest in lower status groups is partly accountable by the following factors: (1) Lower-strata women (but not

53. See Seymour M. Lipset and Natalie Rogoff, "Class and Opportunity in Europe and the U.S.," *Commentary*, 18 (1954), pp. 562-68.

53. See Eleanor E. Maccoby, Richard E. Matthews, and Anton S. Morton, "Youth and Political Change," *Public Opinion Quarterly*, 18 (1954), pp. 34-36.

men) have less leisure available for political activity. (2) Lower status persons have less economic security, and, partly for that reason, feel less of a sense of control over their (political) environment. (3) The threat of deprivation to upper-strata groups present in the politics of the welfare state provides greater motivation than the promise of reward to the lower-status groups.

The relation of public policy to the group stakes at issue in that policy is made more visible to upper-status groups than to lower-status groups.

Lower-status individuals can influence and benefit from governmental action only socially, by group activity and membership, while upper-class persons can influence and benefit from such action individually. Therefore, upper-class persons have a higher incentive to participate.

Lower-status people, feeling at a disadvantage compared to upper-status people, tend to avoid social contact in mixed groups, withdraw interest, defer to others in "difficult" matters, and generally reveal a lack of self-confidence. Actually, lack of experience and influence combined with pressures to be "opinionated" leads to unrealistic participation in some instances.

Child-rearing practices in the lower-status groups tend to provide a less adequate personality basis for appropriately self-assertive social participation.

The social norms and roles in the lower-status group tend to emphasize political participation less than do the norms and roles of the upper-status groups. There is a tendency for these political roles to be concentrated in middle-class rather than upper-class or working-class groups.

High status sometimes implants attitudes of social and civic responsibility in persons who enjoy this status, depending upon moral, religious, and cultural reinforcement for such attitudes, i.e., "with privilege goes responsibility."

Lower-status persons experience greater cross pressures with respect to (a) ethnic versus class identifications, (b) divergent political appeals of the media to which they are exposed, and conflict between media and status identification, (c) community leadership and own-group leadership, and (d) subjective versus objective class identification.

Lower-status persons belong to fewer formal organizations and have fewer intimate personal friends. However, union membership tends to modify this pattern.

Lower-status persons have less capacity to deal with abstract issues and less awareness of their larger social environment.

Lower-status persons are less satisfied with their lives and communities, leading, in a minimally class conscious society, to withdrawal from civic activities, or, alternatively, to participation in deviant politics.

Inter-class mobility tends to weaken the forces for political participation, a tendency modified by identification with upper-status (participant) norms by both upwardly mobile and downwardly mobile groups.

CHAPTER 17

The Way of the Ethnic in Politics

How do race, religion, immigrant status, and origins in other than Anglo-Saxon countries, a complex of factors which we refer to as "ethnic," affect political participation? Unlike subordinate class status, subordinate ethnic status is, in general, unlikely to depress political interests.[1] The most visible ethnic minority, the American Negro, is, it is true, systematically deprived of the right to participate in civic affairs in the South, but in the North he votes as frequently as the average—indeed, perhaps a little more frequently than is common among those of similar economic position. This is true in relatively small towns, such as Delaware, Ohio, and in the large cities of Detroit and Chicago, and "across the board" in the North.[2] And, like color, recency of immigration is not a systematic factor affecting rates of turnout.[3] Once the minimum legal period has been achieved and citizen-

1. See also Chapters 4 and 5. The general conclusions on ethnic voting are supported by evidence in the following: Charles E. Merriam and Harold F. Gosnell, *Non-Voting* (Chicago: University of Chicago Press, 1924); Harold F. Gosnell, *Getting Out the Vote* (Chicago: University of Chicago Press, 1927); Angus Campbell, Gerald Gurin and Warren E. Miller, *The Voter Decides* (Evanston, Ill.: Row, Peterson, 1954); Ben A. Arneson and William H. Eells, "Voting Behavior in 1948 as Compared With 1924 in a Typical Ohio Community," *American Political Science Review, 44* (1950), pp. 432-34; Louis Harris, *Is There a Republican Majority?* (New York: Harper, 1954); Edward H. Litchfield, *Voting Behavior in a Metropolitan Area* (Ann Arbor, Mich.: University of Michigan Press, 1941); Gerhart H. Saenger, "Social Status and Political Behavior," *American Journal of Sociology, 51* (1945), pp. 103-13; Alfred de Grazia, "The Limits of External Leadership over a Minority Electorate," *Public Opinion Quarterly, 20* (1956), pp. 113-28.

2. On Negro voting, see also, Gunnar Myrdal, *An American Dilemma* (New York, Harper, 1944), Vol. I, pp. 474-504; V. O. Key, *Southern Politics in State and Nation* (New York: Knopf, 1949), pp. 517-22; Donald S. Strong, "The Rise of Negro Voting in Texas," *American Political Science Review, 42* (1948), pp. 500-09; Paul Lewison, *Race, Class, and Party* (New York: Oxford, 1932); Harold Gosnell, *Negro Politicians* (Chicago: University of Chicago Press, 1935).

3. H. F. Gosnell, *Getting Out the Vote*, p. 87.

ship won, the immigrant votes now, as he did thirty years ago, fully as frequently as the non-immigrant. Nor does generation time in this country affect frequency of participation—at least not in any systematic way.[4]

On the whole, as might be expected, those nationality groups that settled in the cities (Irish, Italian, Polish) have somewhat higher rates of participation than those who have substantial proportions in rural areas (German, Scandinavian), and, it may be noted, each group has slightly higher rates than the natives in circumstances similar to its own. This is a change in the proportions which prevailed in the twenties, when nationality groups other than natives of "Yankee" origin tended to participate in politics much less than the average.[5]

As for religious differences in rates of participation, the rising standards of living and assimilation of Catholics and Jews, has now brought their rates of participation equal to or above the rates of similarly situated Protestants. Today, of all ethnic and religious groups, the Jews are the most frequent participants.[6] Among the various ethnic groups, however, different patterns of participation sometimes emerge; Jews write more letters to their congressmen; Catholics are more likely to be membrs of political clubs; Negroes have a higher than average rate of formal group membership (perhaps chiefly focused upon church membership).[7]

ETHNIC STAKES IN POLITICS

Persons of ethnic background are interested in politics for the same reasons as the rest of the population: they have occupational interests which may be affected by tariffs or regulation, they are subject to local and national taxation, they have personal preferences among candidates and parties. But there are additional reasons for ethnics to be concerned about political decisions. The first of these has to do with the ethnic rivalry or conflict which takes a variety of forms throughout the country. In "Eastern City" in the 1920's the dominant Irish group in certain wards heightened their activity to keep control from the invading Italians. But the Italians, partly through the use of "repeaters," gained control of a number of wards.[8] In New Haven, the Italian challengers, unable to win concessions from the Irish Democrats, organized their strength in the Republican party and the tensions between the

---

4. A. Campbell and associates, *op. cit.,* p. 78.
5. B. A. Arneson and W. H. Eells, *op. cit.,* p. 433; E. H. Litchfield, *op. cit.,* p. 12; see also Hugo V. Mailey, *The Italian Vote in Philadelphia Between 1928 and 1946* (Philadelphia, Hugo V. Mailey, 1950).
6. B. A. Arneson and W. H. Eells, *op. cit.,* p. 434; E. H. Litchfield, *op. cit.,* p. 18; A. Campbell and associates, *op. cit.,* p. 70. See also Lawrence H. Fuchs, *The Political Behavior of American Jews* (Glencoe, Ill.; Free Press, 1956).
7. G. H. Saenger, *op. cit.,* pp. 105-06.
8. William F. Whyte, *Street Corner Society* (Chicago: Chicago University Press, 1955), pp. 194-96.

two groups became politicized. Similarly, in the first decade of this century the Jews in Boston went to work for the Republicans because "wherever . . . they moved they found the Democratic organization tightly controlled by Irishmen."[9] In the same way the native white Protestant group may respond to ethnic challenge by political organization. In Jonesville, at the turn of the century, the native Protestants organized a branch of the anti-Catholic American Protective Association to stop the growing power of the Democratic Irish Catholic group originally brought in to work on a nearby canal.[10] In New York and Massachusetts the Yankees sought allies in the same basic struggle with the Irish: The "Republicans attempted to woo the Italians and Jews to break the hold of the Irish Democrats on the city vote."[11]

There are many areas of domestic policy which are of special concern to one ethnic group or another.[12] National policy dealing with immigration was a matter of considerable concern for Italian groups in the 1920's. The National Origins Act, limiting Italian immigration to 5,802, not only "made the Italians (in America) fully aware of their nationality," but was defended in terms which wounded their dignity and aroused a great wave of protest.[13] In 1948 the Citizens Committee on Displaced Persons had the largest single number of lobbyists of any group in Washington, a fact which reflects the Jewish demand for a more generous admission policy toward Nazi victims.[14] Efforts to pass the child labor amendment in New York produced a flood of postcards from Catholic communicants who were told by the Church leaders that this represented "youth control" contrary to Church policy.[15] It has been said that the Democratic bosses of certain Massachusetts cities, on occasion, have eagerly sought to have birth control referendum on the ballot in state elections because this enlisted the efforts of the Church in getting out the Catholic—and Democratic—vote. The March on Washington Committee of the mid-forties, organized by A. Phillip Randolph of the Brotherhood of Sleeping Car Porters, revealed the intensity of political feeling among a group of Northern Negroes once an ethnic issue of relevance to them had been developed.[16] The prohibition issue for Protestant Church members and for such immigrant groups as the Philadelphia Italians, the desegregation issue, the alien registration acts of the two world wars, grants in aid for education excluding private, i.e. parochial, schools, all reveal the

9. L. H. Fuchs, *op. cit.*, p. 56.
10. W. Lloyd Warner, *Democracy in Jonesville* (New York: Harper, 1949), p. 215.
11. Oscar Handlin, *The Uprooted* (Boston: Little, Brown, 1951), p. 216.
12. For a discussion of the history of American suffrage for aliens and naturalized citizens see above pp. 13-14.
13. H. V. Mailey, *op. cit.*, p. 82.
14. Robert E. Lane, "Notes on the Theory of the Lobby," *Western Political Quarterly*, 2 (1949), p. 157.
15. Tom Ireland, *Child Labor as a Relic of the Dark Ages* (New York: Putnam, 1937), pp. 207-39.
16. See Louis C. Kesselman, *The Social Politics of FEPC* (Chapel Hill, N. C.: University of North Carolina Press, 1948).

fact that in large measure the national domestic issues which have excited the public are often not class issues but ethnic issues.

The interest which members of various ethnic groups take in foreign policy also leads these groups into the political arena. In explaing the relatively high rate of voting of Jews and Catholics in New York in the 1940's, Saenger says, "Jews and Catholics in New York City are first-, second-, or third-generation Americans. As such, they are more closely identified with the population of their home countries and may be more aware of the effect of recent political events abroad and at home."[17] In Albany (1948) more first- and second-generation citizens said that they are interested in foreign affairs than did third and fourth generation citizens.[18] The specific relation of religious, as contrasted to immigrant-based interest in foreign affairs, is revealed in the greater number of Catholics than Protestants who were aware of and excited about the imprisonment of Cardinal Mindszenty in Hungary.[19] Similarly, Jews, regardless of country of origin, have displayed concern about the status of co-religionists abroad.

It is only natural that such an interest in foreign affairs should create pressure for changes in American foreign policy. Gradually "In the party platforms appeared planks that espoused the immigrant causes: Irish independence, Italian nationalism, Zionism."[20] The American commercial treaty with Russia in 1907, which permitted the Imperial Government to exclude American Jews from entry into Russia, aroused a wave of protest causing both parties to promise a revision in their 1908 platforms.[21] During the Italo-Ethiopian war, the American Italian Red Cross held a "monster rally" in Madison Square garden which, according to the *Progresso Italiano-Americano,* was "to show that 5,000,000 Italian Americans who live in the United States are ready to immolate themselves on the altar of the great motherland."[22] Republicans were quick to remind the Italians that the man responsible for sanctions against Italy was Franklin D. Roosevelt and to enlist their support on these grounds. In the Second World War (following Roosevelt's "stab in the back" speech when Italy invaded France, a speech which set off a great protest from the American Italians), the Democrats wooed the Italians by having Italy declared a co-belligerent against Germany and by publicizing the economic aid going to Italy.[23] After World War II the Polish-Americans came to believe that "the Democrats had sold their homeland down the river at Yalta and in the years that followed."[24] As a consequence, a solidly Democratic group moved dramatically toward the Republican camp in 1952. In these many ways ethnic groups with special interests in events abroad, identification with co-religionists or fellow-

---

17. G. H. Saenger, *op. cit.,* p. 104.
18. Survey Research Center, *Interest, Information, and Attitudes in the Field of Foreign Affairs,* Ann Arbor, Mich., 1949, (mimeographed), p. 44.
19. *Ibid.,* p. 10.
20. Oscar Handlin, *op. cit.,* p. 208.
21. L. Fuchs, *op. cit.,* p. 53.
22. H. Mailey, *op. cit.,* p. 95.
23. *Ibid.,* p. 97.
24. Louis Harris, *op. cit.,* pp. 100, 102.

countrymen, and special stakes in American foreign policy, are politically activated by foreign policy issues.

But in a real sense, the seat of ethnic politics is the local community, not the national capitol. This is evidenced by the fact that although ethnic groups often vote no more frequently than native white Protestants in national elections (with the Jews excepted) and sometimes less frequently, they usually vote more frequently in local elections.[25] This means, among other things, that the difference in turnout between local and national elections is almost always substantial for non-ethnics, but is usually much smaller for ethnic groups.

There are many reasons for this greater interest in local politics. One of them, as Myrdal has pointed out, is the failure of American cities to develop an impartial non-political bureaucracy and local magistracy, attributable in part to a traditional fear of bureaucracy going back to revolutionary days.[26]

... this means a mutually greater dependence of public officials on the voters and of the voters upon public officials. In this system it has become customary to distribute jobs, protection, and public service in some relation to the voting strength of the various regional, national and religious groups in the community.

This relationship between political strength and distribution of rewards becomes even more important if, as is usually the case, the ethnic groups live in physically segregated areas, for then street-paving, sewage disposal, street-lighting, school facilities and other municipal services become ethnically related matters.

A few instances of how local issues become ethnic issues will illustrate this aspect of the problem. In the twenties, in the Russian Jewish wards of New York still under the control of the Irish, peddlers without a license were often badly treated by the police, and, "in some places school children often received bad grades for being absent on Jewish holidays."[27] In an Italian district of Eastern City, political contacts could expedite a WPA job for "deserving" voter in the thirties.[28] And "in Memphis, where Negro votes are an important support of the Crump machine, there are relatively few Negroes killed by the police."[29]

Some of the rewards and services of government, particularly local government, are termed patronage; ethnic politics breeds a kind of group patronage in which awarding jobs, contracts, or privileges to a member of the group, rather than to the individual, becomes important. Part of the Negro support for Huey Long in Louisiana in the thirties was based on the fact that "he put Negro nurses in the hospitals, Negro servants in the state Capitol."[30] When they came into power in 1953 the Democrats in New

---

25. E. H. Litchfield, op. cit., pp. 10, 24-25; H. Mailey, op. cit., p. 33.

26. G. Mydral, op. cit., p. 435.

27. L. Fuchs, op. cit., p. 62.

28. W. F. Whyte, op. cit., p. 196-97

29. G. Myrdal, op. cit., p. 499.

30. Idem.

Haven sought to win back the Italian vote by retaining the very large number of Italians in the Department of Public Works placed there by the previous Italian Republican mayor.

Although at the lower levels of patronage economic motives are generally salient, when the positions at stake achieve visibility, prestige, and power a different range of motives comes into play. These include having a "friend at court," that is, a co-member of the ethnic group who can intercede on one's behalf, and, more importantly, symbolic recognition of the group with implied estimation of its worth and dignity. Lubell labels the desire of the Rhode Island Italians to achieve political recognition of this kind a "passion," gratified when Salvatore Pastore was elected governor in 1946.[31] The *Jewish Day* held that the appointment of Jews to high office by Roosevelt and Wilson was "a high compliment unmatched by anything the Republicans had done."[32] Negro representation on a ballot has an even greater effect:[33]

With the election of a Negro judge every colored person in the country felt that he was benefited in some way, however slight. Likewise, a Negro congressman, who sits in the national capitol and who is the sole representative of an entire racial group in the federal legislative process [in 1957 there were two Negroes in Congress], is in a position of great respect in the eyes of his racial kinsmen. . . . It is all part of the process of the emancipated group struggling for freedom in a larger field.

In 1956 the Republicans prepared for circulation in Negro districts and colleges some brochures listing the Negro appointments to important posts in the National government. Most of the row offices in both state and municipal elections represent a careful balance of the several important ethnic groups (although Negro representation in these administrative posts is rare).[34] One index of the strength of ethnic identification is the fact that voters tend to vote for candidates of the "opposite" party more often than they vote for candidates of a religion different from their own.[35]

In this connection, it may be noted that the short ballot tends to weaken ethnic involvement in political contests. This is also true of city-wide elections for city council, where the ethnic candidates stand less of a chance of getting on the ballot as ethnic group representatives. On the other hand, proportional representation gives ethnic voting an important means of expression.[36]

---

31. Samuel Lubell, *The Future of American Politics* (New York: Harper, 1951), p. 67.

32. L. Fuchs, *op. cit.*, p. 65.

33. H. Gosnell, *Negro Politicians*, p. 92.

34. *Ibid.*, p. 91.

35. Madge M. McKinney, "Religion and Elections," *Public Opinion Quarterly, 8* (1944), pp. 110-14.

36. The change to city-wide elections in Chattanooga in 1920 reduced Negro representation on the board of aldermen. On the effect of proportional representation on ethnic voting, see Belle Zeller and Hugh A. Bone, "The Repeal of P.R. in New York City—Ten Years in Retrospect," *American Political Science Review, 42* (1948), pp. 1127-48.

The ethnic, like others, is often drawn into the political arena because of his identification with a political leader. In Oscar Handlin's account of the way in which immigrants in mid-nineteenth century became politicized, he stresses the role of the ethnic "Boss Laborer" (shortened later to Boss) in mobilizing his ethnic following in politics.[37] Partly, this represented an exchange of votes for jobs, but partly it represented ethnic solidarity behind a leader of their own. This kind of identification is today apparent in ethnic responses to criticism of a leader drawn from their own ranks: Regardless of the nature of the criticism it is interpreted as a criticism of the ethnic group itself. In a mayoralty election in "Metropolis" a reform group found that "the exposé of criminal-political ties led directly to the Negro boss and other Negro politicians, among others; any attack on Negro leaders would be considered by many Negroes and white liberals as an attack upon the Negro people."[38] The bond between ethnic rank and file and leader is more than a functional relationship, it is a bond of common identity. This does not always prevail, of course. Gosnell found that in the 1920's and early 1930's many of the Negro rank and file lacked confidence in their own leaders and trusted white leaders more.[39] But the closeness of the tie, particularly when the leader is challenged—as he is in politics—is usually stronger among ethnics than among non-ethnics.

At least in the past, members of most urban ethnic groups have had persistent trouble with the law, partly because they come from social strata where lawlessness is more common, partly because of the strains of assimilation and identification, partly because the laws have represented cultural norms which they do not share, and partly, according to Kardiner, because of the psychology of low self-esteem.[40] Politics, then, in many ethnic wards becomes affected by the necessity to secure protection from the police. The Italian politicians of "Eastern City" admit in private that they are dependent upon the racketeers for funds and organizational support.[41] The gambler must develop political strength to achieve police protection, but he does not find this difficult. Mailey explains it this way:[42]

The gambler is worth at least five votes within his immediate family because of the proximity of relatives. Added to this number are the people who "play"

---

37. O. Handlin, *op. cit.*, p. 210.

38. A. de Grazia, *op. cit.*, p. 126.

39. H. Gosnell, *Negro Politicians*, p. 358.

40. Crime statistics are notoriously difficult to interpret, but the evidence seems to show that Negroes have a higher than average rate of crime while the foreign born have a lower than average rate. Criminality among foreign nationality groups, then, is likely to be a second-generation problem more than an immigrant problem. See U.S. Department of Justice, Federal Bureau of Investigation, *Uniform Crime Reports*, Washington, D. C., issued quarterly.

41. "Let's not kid ourselves, Bill; when we want to win, we go to the racketeers—all of us," says an Eastern City politician to William F. Whyte. See his *Streetcorner Society*, p. 205.

42. H. Mailey, *op. cit.*, p. 105.

with the [policy] writer. His plea to them is "if you don't help, you won't be able to play."

He quotes one Democratic legislator as saying:

Why number writers mean more votes than jobs on election day. My ward is infested with them. They control my people.

And,

There is a good deal of truth in the assertion that the main return for the Negro vote in the machine dominated cities is protection for the Negro underworld and minor administrative jobs for the petty Negro politicians who marshal the Negro vote.[43]

One reason for this is that in the Negro community, and also in other relatively impoverished ethnic groups,

Of all the contestants, the gambling kings, the vice lords, and the liquor magnates were most likely to have political funds of their own which they could invest in politics.[44]

A party which achieves a reputation for friendship for one or another ethnic group on such grounds as those mentioned above survives for a time upon such traditional support. The party name itself becomes part of the ethnic "ethnocentric" pattern of identification. The authors of the Elmira study found that none of the old issues which tied the Catholics to the Democratic party were salient in 1948, yet Catholic party loyalty persisted. "'Here . . . we find a condition not anticipated nor endorsed by classical political theorists: a non-political, associative factor with strong influence upon the electoral decision."[45] Is party loyalty stronger, or less strong, among ethnic groups? In 1903 it was said that "The Jews (of Boston) are not wedded to any party or faction, and the handling of their vote is a strain on the sagacity of even an Irish politician."[46] But in 1948 and 1952, Jews of all classes showed a party loyalty to the Democrats which resisted the tide of growing Republicanism.[47] The Italian loyalties, which had been predominantly Democratic in the thirties, switched to Republican because of the war, when other groups continued to be Democratic, but swung back again in 1948 and 1952.[48] Negroes switched from the Republican to the Democratic party in 1934 and 1936, stayed in the Democratic camp when other groups went Republican in 1952, and in 1956 tended to drift back to Republicanism—although they gave the Democrats a majority. It can only be concluded that ethnic political loyalties are no more stable than the political loyalties of other groups although, because of a more total

---

43. G. Myrdal, *op. cit.*, p. 499.
44. H. Gosnell, *Negro Politicians*, p. 361.
45. Bernard R. Berelson, Paul F. Lazarsfeld, and William N. McPhee, *Voting* (Chicago: University of Chicago Press, 1954), p. 66.
46. L. Fuchs, *op. cit.*, p. 121.
47. *Ibid.*, p. 81.
48. H. Mailey, *op. cit.*, pp. 48-57.

and emotional involvement in politics, with some element of ethnic pride at stake in many elections, they may be more intense. Party loyalty for the ethnic is often a derived loyalty, receiving its emotional charge from the primary ethnic loyalty and dependent upon an ethnic-party identification for its direction.

In summary, then, we may generalize as follows:

The greater the ethnic conflict in a community (where all may vote) the greater the rates of participation of the conflicting groups.

Ethnic participation is increased by the ethnically (group) relevant nature of a wide range of national domestic issues as well as foreign policy. In the United States the more usual class-based issues are frequently subordinated to such ethnically-relevant national issues.

The less impartial and "bureaucratized" the administration of justice and services, the more ethnic (and other socially identifiable groups) will be drawn into politics. The conduct of American municipal administration is unusually sensitive to the relative voting strength of ethnic groups.

The more residentially segregated a group, the more municipal administration becomes politicized for that group.

The more self-conscious and status-conscious an ethnic group, the more the members of that group will be sensitive to the politics of "recognition," i.e., appointment to office and political candidacy of fellow ethnics. Sensitivity of this kind limits opposition criticism on ethnically irrelevant grounds.

Ethnic groups establish special needs for the protection of illegal activities (sometimes conducted with wide ethnic popular support); these activities create strong politicizing motives and the organizations to make them effective.

Ethnics usually participate more in local politics than non-ethnics (for the above reasons).

Party loyalty for ethnic groups is partially based upon an identification of the party with ethnic goals; this loyalty derives its emotional charge from ethnic feeling and, because it is derived, is often unstable.

ETHNIC BELIEFS AND SOCIAL PATTERNS

The immigrant and the emancipated Negro enter the political scene with a heritage of belief and culture which influences their political activity in a variety of ways, not just for the first generation, but, in dwindling force, for subsequent generations, as well. A majority of immigrants were, in their old world status, peasants. Of the Polish peasant's attitude toward government in the old country, Thomas and Znaniecki say:[49]

The political order appears to a certain extent as an impersonal and a moral power, absolutely mysterious, whose manifestations can possibly be foreseen, but whose nature and laws cannot be changed by human interference. But this order has also another side, more comprehensible but more unforeseen, with some moral character, that is, capable of being just or unjust and of being influenced; in this

---

49. William I. Thomas and Florian Znaniecki, *The Polish Peasant in Europe and America* (Boston: Richard G. Badger, 1918), Vol. 1, p. 141.

respect it is the exact parallel of the divine world. . . . This whole system, this combination of impersonal power and half-religious hierarchy, evidently permits a certain explanation of everything, but excludes absolutely any idea of political activity.

Handlin agrees that for the immigrant generally, "In the business of ruling, he did not act, was only acted upon."[50] Nor was it different for the rural Negro emigrating North for many decades following the Civil War.[51] Such, then, was the political frame of mind which encountered the institutions and demands of American democracy.

By 1924 the immigrants, in Chicago at least, and presumably elsewhere, were participating in political life as frequently as the native white, and the urban Negroes followed close behind.[52] What occasioned this change in political mentality? And what forces deterred it? For the most part, the immigrant came to America, not for political liberty, but for the economic opportunities said to exist here and because he was said to be welcome. Yet when he came, he entered a slum and found the living precarious and the welcome less than cordial. He was uprooted, and sought to protect himself by reinstituting the institutions and practices of the old country. He banded together in colonies of fellow-ethnics, sought to re-establish the Church as he knew it back home, and organized associations of fellow nationals who held the same loyalties and faced the same problems. He was pitifully conservative, seeking amidst so much change to maintain some traces of what he had known. Above all, he was religious.[53] What then, was the role that this religious revival played in his political transformation?

In the first instance, it retarded political development. Because there was no established church in the United States, there was no occasion for the ethnic churches to create strong political connections and no need to protest against governmental favoritism or official discrimination against church schools. The question of government aid to religious schools was to come later. Moreover to some extent, the focus upon religion served, as Marx said it would, as an "opiate" for the immigrant; his attention was diverted from the real world and what might be done about his troubles. God and Caesar were kept separate. Friction between nationality groups tended to fractionate the broader denominations, so that congregations, parishes, and synagogues tended to be organized on a nationality basis, reinforcing the inward-looking features of immigrant status. For some groups, like the Norwegian-Lutherans in the Middle West, the puritanical code of the religious group tended to prevent members from joining or mixing in the

---

50. O. Handlin, *op. cit.*, p. 202.

51. See G. Myrdal, *op. cit.*, p. 758. Even today in parts of Harlem, David Riesman finds the same basic "tradition-directed" orientation toward politics. See his *Faces in the Crowd* (New Haven: Yale University Press, 1952), pp. 73-151.

52. H. Gosnell, *Getting Out the Vote*, p. 87. Apparently the Negro rate of voting in Chicago increased markedly from 1924 to 1930. Compare Merriam and Gosnell, *op. cit.*, p. 40 and Gosnell, *Negro Politicians*, p. 17.

53. O. Handlin, *op. cit.*, p. 110, 117.

social events of other groups.[54] In the first instance, then, religious influences led away from politics. And this was true of the Negro church, as well.

But today, the more highly organized religious groups, the Jews and Catholics, participate more than Protestants and the Protestants participate more than those with no acknowledged religion.[55] A number of complicated factors are at work. In the first place the mere fact of organized relationships tends to increase a sense of mutual interest and raise the salience of group membership. This influence is increased by the organized social life centering in the Church. In one study of twenty-three urban Southern Catholic parishes, it was found that each parish had an average of 13.2 church-associated societies for lay people designed to serve a variety of non-religious social needs.[56] The Protestant churches in Jonesville (rather more than the Catholic Church) also surround themselves with many allied societies. Yet the proportion of communicants who participate in their activities is not large: 3.6 per cent in the case of the Southern parishes. And the extra-curricular life of the church is divided by educational barriers and ethnic rivalries just as in the large society.[57] Church-related organizational life is important, then, but limited.

This interaction, where it exists, tends to reinforce the dominant interests of the group. As Myrdal says "the Negro church fundamentally is an expression of the Negro community itself."[58] And among Italians, "the priests did not lead the people to accept Roosevelt. They merely followed direction of the parish itself."[59] When, for other reasons, the community becomes interested in politics, the church tends to reflect and, to some extent reinforce this interest. This may not be the intention of the church leaders, who have other things on their mind, but the communal gathering of people with common interests will usually achieve this effect. The Negro church becomes politicized even though the leaders may drag their feet. While "the protest has been rising in the Negro community, the church has, on the whole, remained conservative and accommodating."[60]

But church leaders are not free of political pressures either. "The bosses of political machines frequently like to do 'favors for Father,' with more or less subtle expectations that Catholic votes will be thereby influenced."[61] And Negro ministers are often wooed by political leaders with the same expectations. If it is clear that one party is more sympathic to the group than another, the priests, ministers, and rabbis will not remain indifferent.

54. See W. L. Warner, op. cit., pp. 174-75.

55. G. Saenger, op. cit., p. 104. But care should be taken in interpreting figures on "agnostics" or people with "no religion." This group seems to be made up of a small well-educated participant group and a group of poorly educated disoriented individuals.

56. Joseph H. Fichter, S. J., Social Relations in the Urban Parish (Chicago: University of Chicago Press, 1954), p. 157.

57. Ibid., pp. 49-50.

58. G. Myrdal, op. cit., p. 877.

59. H. Mailey, op. cit., p. 124.

60. G. Myrdal, op. cit., p. 876.

61. J. Fichter, op. cit., p. 132.

Religion leads into politics through other channels. As we have noted many issues have religious or church relationships: Quakers and disarmament, Catholics and the struggle against "atheistic communism," Jews and Zionism. Thus a church may organize a political campaign for or against a policy. In New York State, when nine constitutional amendments of interests to unions, parties, and the Catholic Church were presented to the voters, analysis of the voting pattern revealed that the influence of religious leaders on the vote was greater than that of either party leaders or union leaders.[62] And at every class level, religious identification still influences the vote decision.

There is even some evidence that the Church can influence the vote without greatly affecting the political convictions of the communicants. In 1944 there was a disproportionate increase in the Catholic vote in New York at the same time that Catholics reported that they did not believe that the outcome of the election would make much difference to themselves or to the nation. It is certainly possible to believe with Saenger that this reflects the concern not of the "flock" but of the Church leaders about the rise in Communism in the world.[63] Pressure without much persuasion seems to be at work here.

There are indications that this force is waning. In younger age groups the religious differences in vote decision is less than in older groups. Moreover, the forces which are said to be generally weakening the hold of religion on the public also weaken the force of religious identification and church pressure on political participation. As one Italian priest said, "How could we influence their (parishioners') selection of candidates when we couldn't get them to come to church?"[64] But with the rise of church attendance, perhaps this too will change.

The role of the church in politics is, in the United States, a matter on which parishioners do not agree. In a study of the attitudes of members of a large Protestant sect toward the proper role of the minister in politics and of the injection of the church in social and international issues, persons who wanted to keep church and politics separate were generally (a) those with less education, (b) those least informed and presumably, therefore, least interested in public issues, and (c) those whose organizational life was built more around church-centered organizations (and who also attended church more regularly). In interpreting these findings the authors of this study suggest that the more traditionalistic group, those who seek to

---

62. Madge M. McKinney, "Constitutional Amendment in New York State," *Public Opinion Quarterly, 3* (1939), pp. 635-45. In this study, McKinney reports: "Repeatedly evidence was discovered which indicated that this endorsement of certain amendments by the Roman Catholic clergy had effect upon Catholic laymen. In contrast to this, no evidence was produced that the leaders of organized labor or that the leading gubernatorial candidates exerted great influence upon their followers in regard to the amendments," p. 636.

63. G. Saenger, *op. cit.,* p. 104.

64. H. Mailey, *op. cit.,* p. 124. But Mailey says of the increased church attendance by Italian Catholics: "They will gradually be taught to listen to the dictates of the priest and exhibit the meekness that American prelates expect to find in other American Catholics" (p. 124).

return to a closer tie between church and family, resist and resent the intrusion of the secular political world in this relationship.[65] Yet it is precisely this group that is most influenced by the political orientation of the clergy.[66] Vulnerable, they wish to avoid exposure.

The specific content of the religion, the religious teachings, seem to bear little relationship to the development of political interest. The alleged emphasis upon duty in the Protestant religion may be focused upon avoidance of liquor and the value of hard work just as much as upon civic duty. The focus upon this world and enjoyment thereof of the Jewish religion failed to bring the Jews into the political arena in the early years of their migration when religious influences were strongest.[67] Only a few of the Catholics who become interested in politics have ever heard of the Papal Bulls of Leo XIII.[68] The relationship between politics and religion is based on organizational pressure, group interaction and identity, and group interest, not theology.

The nationalist component of the rise of ethnic interests in politics came later than the initial turning to religion. It flowered into a mass of organizations such as the Sons of Italy or the Polish National Alliance. Like the churches, these organizations brought people together, but in these instances the focus of interest was political, though foreign. For the most part, the initial orientation was to "look homeward" to the old country, not toward the local issues of jobs, street-paving, and protection from the police. "The task of the Polish National Alliance, as conceived by its initiators, was thus to turn the Polish immigrants in this country into a strong and coherent part of the Polish nation."[69] Only the Negro "nationalist" organizations were primarily focused on the home scene, with the National Association of Colored People and the Urban League as the two principle enduring groups.

These organizations for nationality groups and Negro groups alike, served important political functions. They served as vehicles for political action, including lobbying. They were important means of communicating political messages. They increased the group's sense of power and importance. But perhaps even more important they provided first-hand experience in the ways of democracy. People with no intimate personal experience with democratic forms and usages cannot be expected to participate in democratic affairs on a national or even community scale.

---

65. Benjamin J. Ringer and Charles Y. Glock, "The Political Role of the Church as Defined by its Parishioners," *Public Opinion Quarterly*, 18 (1954-55), pp. 337-47. There are broader forces involved in this question of church and politics: "To many, for the church to lobby for political measures weakens its spiritual position, for such actions violate the American tradition of separatism of church and state." W. Lloyd Warner and associates, *Democracy in Jonesville*, p. 149.

66. B. Berelson and associates, *op. cit.*, pp. 67-69.

67. See L. Fuchs, *op. cit.*, pp. 189-90. Fuchs takes the view that elements of the Jewish culture have a direct and important bearing on their "political style." This is probably true, but those elements of the culture which are found in the theology of Judaism probably have the most tenuous relationship to politics.

68. O. Handlin, *op. cit.*, p. 224.

69. W. I. Thomas and F. Znaniecki, *op. cit.*, Vol. 5, p. 113.

It cannot be said, generally, that broad ideologies, such as socialism, anarchism, fascism, or communism, played much part in politicizing ethnic groups. Although there were some leaders, like Carl Schurz, who fled Europe for political reasons, and carried their convictions to America, these were in the minority. By and large the immigrants were conservative, turning for solace to religion rather than radicalism. And the radical's antipathy to religion served to alienate him from his fellow immigrants.[70]

Among the Poles, before the First World War, for example, the Alliance of Polish Socialists sought to ensure that Poland should be a socialist nation when it achieved nationhood. But the membership of this group was infinitesimal compared to the Polish National Alliance. And, in any event, even this small socialist group inevitably became fractionated and those interested in American socialism joined the Polish section of the American Socialist Party.[71] Nor was the Negro drawn into politics through ideological or "radical" doorways. The efforts of the Communists to enlist Negroes ran into the frame of mind expressed in the statement: "It is bad enough being black, without being black and red."[72]

Only the Jews, with their European traditions of socialism, assumed an ideological posture. As one settlement worker in a Jewish district put it, "the real university of the East Side was Marx's *Capital.* . . . What the East Side was excited about was Socialism."[73] In part this was because of the internationalist character of socialism, and the Jews, because of their history, had long been internationalists. In part it might be said that it stemmed from elements of Jewish culture focused upon the concepts of *Torah* (learning) and *Zedekah* (charity).[74] But the important causes for this liberal-socialist ideal seem more likely to come from the fact that the Jews were an urban group with a long history of persecution which had prepared them for the general ethnic discrimination in America. They were ready when persecution came, so to speak, while others were not.[75]

Certain changes in perspectives on themselves also brought the ethnics into politics. At first the concepts of equality were as alien as they were in fact unreal. This doctrine of equality "did not square with their own deep-rooted ideas of status, with their own acceptance of differences of rank. . . . These people could find nothing in their life in the Old World or the New that would confirm the democratic hypothesis that they themselves could participate meaningfully in the exercise of power."[76] But their children

---

70. O. Handlin, *op. cit.,* p. 192.

71. W. I. Thomas and F. Znanieicki, *op. cit.,* p. 127.

72. G. Myrdal, *op. cit.,* p. 509.

73. L. Fuchs, *op. cit.,* p. 124.

74. *Ibid.,* pp. 184-203.

75. While ideological politics seems to have had a minimal appeal to the immigrant and Negro group (Jews excepted), reform politics up until the New Deal was no more attractive. The issues of the time: tariff, trust-busting, civil service, municipal corruption and reorganization did not strike home to this group, absorbed as they were in the immediate problems of earning a living and keeping out of trouble. See O. Handlin, *op. cit.,* pp. 218-23.

76. O. Handlin, *op. cit.,* p. 206.

learned in school that everyone was equal and that democracy was built on the principle "one man, one vote." At this point, the doctrine of equality became a powerful politicizing influence; not only were they equal in their electoral rights, but they might use this weapon to achieve status and equality in other areas of life. Moreover, they could feel, as the working classes never could, that their lack of status was due to discrimination. The American culture said that only an individual was to blame for economic failure. For the ethnic failure to achieve status, one could blame a discriminatory society. In large part this explains why the ethnic underdog developed an active political life aimed at increasing status while the economic underdog ("proletariat") did not.

But the most important politicizing force for the ethnic was the political machine. This dealt with affairs of immediate and practical interest: jobs, protection, services. In politics the ethnic leader was able to convert his ethnicity into a positive advantage, whereas in other areas of life it served him ill. The ethnics had a marketable commodity: votes. They understood from the Old Country the utility of petitioning for favors and now they found that they could petition with sanctions behind them. As a consequence, in Chicago, Elmira, Philadelphia, "Eastern City," and wherever ethnic politics has been studied, the rapport between ward leaders and constituencies has been a crucial force in mobilizing ethnic groups for political action. If a ward changed ethnic complexion and the old leader of a different ethnic group remained in office, the ward tended to become depoliticized.[77] And in Elmira it was found that the more self-contained and isolated the group, the more important is this ethnic political tie with the machine.[78] The assimilation into American life of the ethnic group is, indeed, one of the main reasons for the decline of the great political machine.

Ethnics are mobilized for political action by certain intermediary leaders, of whom the ward captains represent only one group. To some extent, these leadership patterns will be molded by the occupational choices and social organization of the group. For these reasons, Negro leadership comes on the one hand, from the Church, and to a lesser extent from fraternal organizations, rather than from lawyers and business men. On the other hand, many Negro politicians come from the leaders of the demi-monde, the gambling, vice, and racketeering elements.[79] The Jews, because of their concentration in the professions, have been fortunate in the availability of many lawyers, for whom politics is a congenial profession, and a large merchant class. Among the Italian group, the concentration of Italian leadership in building and construction, with its close political ties, has led to politics through this door, just as gambling and the connection with liquor established in Prohibition days opened a back door to Italian politicians. For the Italians (and for the Negroes also) the undertaker is often an important political person in the community, with leisure for politics and the incentives provided in operating

77. C. Merriam and H. Gosnell, *op. cit.*, pp. 210, 228.
78. B. Berelson and associates, *op. cit.*, p. 165.
79. G. Myrdal, *op. cit.*, pp. 730-33.

a regulated trade.[80] Thus each ethnic group may have a specialized approach to politics reinforced by its occupational and leadership patterns.

The union in a trade where one ethnic group has a solid majority is a prime vehicle for ethnic political action. "To the immigrant Jews in New York, the two most important sources of political opinion were the trade unions and the Yiddish newspapers."[81] The intense political activity of both the International Ladies Garment Workers Union and the Amalgamated Clothing Workers Union is traceable, in large part, to their origins at predominantly Jewish unions. The leadership of the Brotherhood of Sleeping Car Porters formed the nucleus of the March on Washington Movement of the World War II years, continuing after the war as the Committee for a Permanent Fair Employment Practices Commission.[82] The Irish in the building trades unions, and the Italians in certain locals of the teamsters union, also tended to mix ethnic politics with union politics. And the close relations between the unions and the political machines tended to make complementary appeals for ethnic votes, although occasional trouble developed (as in Jersey City) when the machine leaders became jealous over union intrusion on their political power.

As indicated above, the foreign language or nationality press, or the Negro press, and, more recently, the nationality radio stations have given political indoctrination to the ethnic public. "The influence of a foreign language paper in the past has been so great crafty politicians conspired to buy the foreign vote through the newspaper."[83] The owners of such papers became important political magnates through such means. But today most of them have converted to the English language and are losing their clientele. The power of the Italian press and perhaps other nationality papers was temporarily sustained by the rise of ethno-nationalism during the war, but, at least in Philadelphia, both Democratic and Republic leaders agree that these papers today have very little influence.[84] This is not true of the Negro press which, in 1942, included 210 weekly papers and 129 magazines of various kinds. Myrdal says: "The importance of the Negro press for the formation of Negro opinion, for the functioning of all other Negro institutions, for Negro leadership and concerted action generally, is enormous."[85] Although a relatively small percentage of the content of this press has to do directly with politics, by indirection—by the reporting of police treatment of Negroes, appointment of Negroes to office, and so forth—the political impact is substantial. Since this press "defines the Negro group to

---

80. Myrdal speaks of "burial societies" rather than professional undertakers. Whyte says "If he has an established funeral business, the undertaker will be well known and well supplied with personal contacts before he enters politics. He counts on his own kind as a nucleus for political support. . . . A political campaign advertises his funeral business, and the funeral business widens political contacts," *op. cit.*, p. 202.

81. L. Fuchs, *op. cit.*, p. 125.

82. See Louis Kesselman, *op. cit.*, pp. 13, 25-46.

83. H. Mailey, *op. cit.*, p. 116.

84. *Ibid.*, p. 118.

85. G. Myrdal, *op. cit.*, p. 923.

the Negroes themselves," the image in the press of the Negroes as politically active serves to politicize an entire group.

In review then, the following hypotheses may be set forth.

Political apathy is a function of peasant (or rural Southern) origin with its associated views of government as part of a natural order beyond control.

The early religious orientation of immigrant and Negro groups tended to reduce political interests because (a) the separation of church and state reduced the opportunity for political conflict, (b) religion offered an otherworldly solace for temporal ills, (c) church groups became fractionated and narrowly in-group oriented, (d) the reinforcement of some religious norms imposed barriers to broader social participation by communicants.

Religious interests and organization (at a later stage) increased political activity of communicants through (a) increasing the social interaction of communicants and increasing their perception of group stakes in political matters, (b) direct political pressures on clergymen, (c) development of church-related political issues, (d) providing an organ of political expression. Those who resist the intrusion of the church in politics are those most vulnerable to church influences. The theological content of the religion is only marginally important for politics.

Immigrant nationalism and nationalist groups served as a means of politicizing ethnics, but the program of nationalist groups failed to relate to the most urgent needs of the ethnic groups. (In this respect Negro organizations were an exception.) Nevertheless, they served as important politicizing agents, particularly as they trained groups and their leaders in the use of democratic processes.

Ethnic groups (with the exception of the Jews) failed to become politicized by broad ideological programs because of the interposition of other-worldly religious orientations, fear of further rejection by society, rural backgrounds and low education, and lack of preparation for their alienation in the New World.

The political machine with its ethnic ward connections was the chief instrument politicizing the ethnic group. Through this means the ethnic leader converted his ethnic membership from a liability to an advantage and the group could achieve group rewards through its local party connections.

Labor unions in trades where ethnics were concentrated politicized their members because of mutually reinforcing ethnic, occupational, and class interests. The nationality press and radio politicized ethnic groups, but due to waning language barriers and broadening ethnic interests the nationality media have lost much of their influence. In contrast, the Negro press has grown in political and social influence.

ETHNIC STATUS AND POLITICAL ATTITUDES

Membership in an ethnic group produces attitudes and, indeed, qualities of personality, which have a bearing on the social and political participation of the individual. Among these is the sense of subordinate status, the feeling that society undervalues the individual and his group, or at least the feeling that they are constantly on trial. Let us consider some of the implications of this attitude.

In the first place, as Kardiner and Ovesey points out in an analysis of the psychological effects of being a Negro, social evaluation may be accepted, or partially accepted, by the individual, and he comes to think of himself as a person of low worth and little consequence.[86] This, by itself, leads to apathy, hedonism, living for the moment, expectations of other worldly rewards, and low political participation. The Southern Negro and many Northern Negroes are said to embody this pattern. This is the basic, first-order response, one which explains in part why the most oppressed groups rarely revolt, or even take advantage of their democratic rights. Contrary to some statements on the subject, not low self-esteem but doubts about how to esteem oneself serve as the basis of many political drives.[87]

But the ascription of low status to a group may produce other attitudes of political consequence. It may produce a withdrawal from contact with outside society and the Ghetto psychology which Lewin says produces a kind of personal security for the individual, counteracting the abrasive force of social undervaluation. Thus, until the 1930's, the Jews created politically withdrawn, but culturally rich and psychologically secure, ethnic communities which were isolated from the larger society.[88]

As contact with the larger society increases for groups losing their language and custom differences, the ethnic group looks outward and becomes an embattled social group, enormously sensitive to reflections on group status and eager to advance group interests by all available means. Under these circumstances, undervaluation by society produces, not acceptance of low esteem but doubts and anxiety about the self and the group, which may be resolved by individual or group achievement. It is said that this accounts for the restlessness of the Jews as the Ghettos disappear.[89] It produces the ethnic's "passion for respectability" to be won by political recognition. But, it also produces fear of personal participation in groups of higher status, for fear of slight or humiliation.[90]

This is the point at which many of the American ethnic groups have now arrived. Although they live in ethnic colonies, the borders are often vague, and outside culture contacts are, at least for the men, relatively frequent. Their ethnicity is important to them and leads to high participation in the more ethnically relevant local politics. To some extent their politics also reflects their alienation: for the Negro and the Italian social undervaluation and self-doubts combined with hostility lead to crime, rackets, and the

---

86. Abram Kardiner and Lionel Ovesey, *The Mark of Oppression: A Psychosocial Study of the American Negro* (New York: Norton, 1951).

87. Harold Lasswell is ambiguous on this theme, but in general he agrees. Thus: "The accentuation of power is to be understood as a compensatory reaction against low estimates of the self (*especially when coexisting with high self estimates*)." *Power and Personality* (New York: Norton, 1948), p. 53 (emphasis supplied).

88. See Kurt Lewin's discussion of "Psycho-Sociological Problems of a Minority Group," in his *Resolving Social Conflicts* (New York: Harper, 1948). See also Louis Wirth, *The Ghetto* (Chicago: University of Chicago Press, 1928), p. 279.

89. K. Lewin, *loc. cit.*

90. See Genevieve Knupfer's account of the way the underdog feels in PTA, or civic group meetings in the presence of persons of higher status; "Portrait of the Underdog," *Public Opinion Quarterly, 11* (1947), pp. 103-14.

political connections these imply; for the Jews, the alienation leads to radicalism and support of socially disapproved third parties.

The recent history of each group dictates a somewhat different political solution. The Negro in the North is emerging from acceptance of social undervaluation and low self-esteem and is becoming a politically embattled solidary ethnic group. From research data we can see the psychological change underlying this change in political status. In a national sample, including the South, Negroes indicated a very low sense of political effectiveness (I cannot influence authorities; they will not listen to me); but in a sample of Detroit union members, Negroes had a higher sense of political efficacy than did the whites.[91] Moreover, in the South, in addition to a low sense of political efficacy, the Negro must often overcome a "psychopathological form of apathy" brought about by the fear techniques of the ruling class.[92] For the Negro the time has not yet come for assimilationist politics. On the contrary, it is still true that the "Negro will be able to extract the maximum advantage by acting as a political unit."[93] In his situation ethnic salience must, for practical reasons, remain high.

The Jews, Italians, Poles, Greeks, Mexicans, and other ethnic groups, however, are in a somewhat different position. Both Jews and Italians are emerging from a period of reinforced ethnic solidarity occasioned by, in the one case, the rise of Naziism and the Zionist movement, and in the other, by the Second World War which pitted America against the Italian motherland. As a partial consequence, the Jews have moved from a relatively nonpolitical group to "the most politicized group in the United States." The Italians generally have not been so politically aroused and have been much more divided in their political loyalties. After the war their relative rates of participation tended in some places to decline.[94]

What will assimilation do to the political participation of these ethnic groups? Mailey puts it this way:[95]

Italian political recognition blossomed with Roosevelt and by the end of World War II Italians in Philadelphia were turning a deaf ear to ethnic solidarity. As one intelligent political leader put it, 'It lost its punch with the war.' Many Italians feel that the Italians would suffer in the long run if they continue to assert their background too long. . . . [In Philadelphia they] feel that this [ethnic] appeal can only be afforded by Italians who are a large part of the electorate as in New York. Otherwise, the Italians wish to assimilate quickly and make their demands for political rewards on another basis.

Politically speaking, assimilation means new motives for old. This means a shift in the psychological bases of participation but not necessarily an increase or a decrease in political salience. The more assimilable immigrant

91. A. Campbell and associates, op. cit., p. 191; Arthur Kornhauser, Albert J. Mayer, and Harold L. Sheppard, When Labor Votes (New York: University Books, 1956), p. 157.
92. G. Myrdal, op. cit., p. 490.
93. Ibid., pp. 505-06.
94. L. Fuchs, op. cit., p. 202; H. Mailey, op. cit., p. 42.
95. H. Mailey, op. cit., p. 91.

groups, such as the Canadians or English, in Ann Arbor in the thirties, sometimes voted more and sometimes less than those with greater religious, language, or cultural barriers to overcome.[96] In depriving ethnic voters of one motive for an interest in politics, assimilation may make room for others. Loss of ethnic group identification may create personal restlessness and drives for *personal* achievement which find political expression. In this context it is probably true that moderate anxiety over group status represents one of the main drives for entering politics. Or assimilating ethnics may accept the dominant citizen duty norms of middle-class society and participate for these conventional reasons. Or they may develop stronger socio-economic class interests and place their political loyalties on this footing. Litchfield finds that "insofar as participation is concerned, there is greater solidarity among economic than ethnic and race groups," but a close examination of his figures shows that while this is true of native whites, it is only tenuously true for nationality groups.[97] The ambiguity of these data reflect the fact that the unassimilated ethnics are clinging to ethnic reference group criteria whereas the assimilating ethnics are free of the necessity to vote as an ethnic bloc and are developing other criteria for political preference.

But the assimilating ethnic with rising status runs certain risks. The ethnic politician who assimilates may lose his clientele. The rank and file ethnic may find himself caught between two worlds and withdraw into apathy, as Child says the second-generation Italian has often done.[98] Perhaps it is for this reason that in Philadelphia, although there was no consistent relationship between income and turnout in presidential elections, in local elections there was a tendency for lower income and presumably less assimilated Italians to participate to a greater extent than Italians with higher incomes.[99] One reason for this is that once homogeneous parish groups become divided along class lines they lose their cohesiveness.[100] Another reason is suggested by Frazier's view of middle-class Negroes. Negroes who rise above their former working-class status and become members of the "bourgeoisie," says Frazier, suffer from "nothingness" and their lives generally lose both content and significance. In a state of "nothingness" politics can have little meaning.[101] In this connection it is worth noting that one study of Negro voting in Philadelphia finds that prosperous Negroes have lower rates of voting than the less prosperous Negroes.[102] Or these groups may take the view of the upper-class Jews who, caught between their class pressures

---

96. See James K. Pollock, *Voting Behavior: A Case Study* (Ann Arbor, Mich.: University of Michigan Press, 1939), p. 28.

97. E. H. Litchfield, *op. cit.*, pp. 25-26. On the intensity of ethnic identification and ethnic voting norms see B. Berelson and associates, *op. cit.*, p. 72; also see L. Fuchs, *op. cit.*, pp. 88-90.

98. Irvin L. Child, *Italian or American? The Second Generation in Conflict* (New Haven: Yale University Press, 1943).

99. H. Mailey, *op. cit.*, pp. 39-41.

100. J. H. Fichter, *op. cit.*, p. 49.

101. See. E. Franklin Frazier, *Black Bourgeoisie* (Glencoe, Ill.: Free Press, 1957).

102. J. Errol Miller, "Atypical Voting Behavior in Philadelphia," *Public Opinion Quarterly*, 12 (1948), pp. 489-90.

and their ethnic identifications, express the opinion that "both parties are the same."[103] If they do not withdraw from the polling booth, they withdraw their affect from politics. This may account for the later vote decisions of those in both Erie County and Elmira who were caught between religious and class identifications of this kind.[104] In the kind of assimilation represented by the rise from working-class to middle-class status, the risks of depoliticization are substantial.

In reviewing these problems of ethnic status and approaches to politics, we may say:

Ethnic groups (based on nationality, religions, recency of immigration, and race) are generally accorded lower than average status in the American society. Low political participation is a function of the acceptance and internalization of this social image of low status and worth by the members of an ethnic group.

Social estimates of low status and worth of a group may turn a group inward so that they withdraw from social and political participation whether or not they accept these estimates.

Social contact with the majority in the American (equalitarian) society weakens the acceptance of low status and worth and replaces it with doubts which encourage efforts to repudiate the "low worth" doctrine through political participation. Some of these efforts find outlet in alienated or anti-social politics but most remain in the main political stream.

Progress in assimilation means a change in political motivation for members of ethnic groups. To the extent that citizen norms, economic interests, and pressure for individual (as contrasted to group) achievement can serve as substitutes, ethnic political participation will not suffer a relative decline.

But assimilation tends to depoliticize groups when it breaks up the homogeneity of ethnic associational life, leads to lack of direction and "anomie," or creates cross pressures which weaken partisan political attachments.

---

103. G. Saenger, *op. cit.*, p. 104-05.

104. See Paul F. Lazarsfeld, Bernard B. Berelson, and Hazel Gaudet, *The People's Choice* (New York: Columbia University Press, 1948) pp. 58-59; B. Berelson and associates, *op. cit.*, p. 131.

CHAPTER 18

The Political Community

SOME communities develop among their members a relatively high degree of civic and electoral participation, and at election time may be counted among those with the highest turnout. Other communities, superficially the same in most respects, reveal apathy and indifference. Why should there be these differences among the communities of a state or nation?

One cause for these differences lies in the different proportions of the population with those attributes associated with high participation: education, income, status. Thus Jonesville, with, it appears, a relatively higher rate of participation than Yankee City, had only 14 per cent of its members in the demoralized lower-lower class, while Yankee City had 25 per cent.[1] These differences in class distribution were, in turn, related to a greater emphasis on commercial activities, the smaller proportion of ethnics (who tend to be lower-lower), and the relative youth of Jonesville.[2] Similarly, state capitals generally show higher rates of participation than similar cities with less politically-relevant occupational emphases.

But even communities which have roughly similar demographic characteristics often differ considerably in political life. Something about the community itself may be important.

CONCENTRATION OF POWER

Most of the community studies, such as those of Middletown, Yankee City, and Regional City, draw attention to the concentration of power in

---

1. W. Lloyd Warner and associates, *Democracy in Jonesville* (New York: Harper, 1949), p. 24; W. Lloyd Warner and Paul S. Lunt, *The Social Life of a Modern Community* (New Haven: Yale University Press, 1941), p. 88.

2. W. L. Warner, *Democracy in Jonesville*, pp. 24-25.

the hands of relatively few people, generally those of high status and great wealth.[3] In Middletown it is the "X family," in Regional City it is a group of economic leaders who, for the most part, remain behind the scenes. Generally, these leaders use others of somewhat lower status as their political "front men," men who then may develop some autonomous power of their own like the Bailey family of Jonesville, but only of a limited sort.[4] In a two party community, like Middletown during the depression, the leaders of the central power elite may seek to dominate both parties, as when a member of the Middletown X family joined the Democrats so that they would not then get out of hand.

The techniques whereby these dominant families control the political life of the community are intricate and varied.[5] By their leverage over the economic institutions of the community, they can exercise sanctions over many of the civic leaders and professional people in town; they can intimidate workers through the control over their jobs; they control the credit institutions of the community and can influence such matters as admission to a hospital or a mortgage on a house; they generally control the local press and radio; they subsidize the party (or parties) of their choice and hence influence their selection of candidates. In Regional City

The political organizations are so completely dominated by the power interests [i.e., business elite] . . . that there is little hope of adequate expression being fostered by them at this time.[6]

They control admission to the prestige associations and clubs; they set the patterns of approved behavior and opinion. At least from the available evidence they can do these things in relatively small communities (like Jonesville) wherever situated, in most Southern communities, and in some medium-sized Northern communities (Middletown).

Where such predominance of control is exercised, the terms of conflict are so unequal that motivation for political or civic participation by the lower-income groups suffers. In a Southern community it was found that voting, and particularly voting with some specific purpose in mind, was related to a feeling that the two or three most influential industrial and landholding families did not "completely control things."[7] On this point the Lynds speak of the "alternating exasperation and apathy" of the Middle-

---

3. The following discussion is based upon the two books by Warner and associates cited above; Robert and Helen Lynd, *Middletown* (New York: Harcourt, Brace, 1929) and *Middletown in Transition* (New York: Harcourt, Brace, 1937); Floyd Hunter, *Community Power Structure* (Chapel Hill: University of North Carolina Press, 1953); Alfred W. Jones, *Life, Liberty, and Property* (Philadelphia: Lippincott, 1941); William Buchanan, "An Inquiry into Purposive Voting," *Journal of Politics,* 18 (1956), pp. 281-96 (a study of politics in a small southern community), and Elihu Katz and Paul F. Lazarsfeld, *Personal Influence* (Glencoe, Ill.: Free Press, 1955).

4. W. L. Warner, *Democracy in Jonesville*, pp. 215-16.

5. These techniques are most adequately described by Hunter in his study of Regional City, *op. cit.,* Chapters 4, 7, and 8.

6. *Ibid.,* p. 236.

7. W. Buchanan, *op. cit.,* p. 294.

town voters;[8] Hunter speaks of the great "silence found in the mass of the citizenry of Regional City,"[9] and Hoffer finds that interest in political affairs in a Michigan community ranked eighth in a list of twelve community interests.[10] Although often only dimly aware of their stakes in community politics, the man of lower status is discouraged from participating because of overwhelming power of the elite arrayed against him.

These implicit class relationships have many facets. On the one hand it appears that the participation by members of the high-status community power elite in civic affairs and political life is inadequate. In Middletown "the best citizens are no longer to be found among Middletown's public officials," unlike a period in the nineties when the mayors, judges, and councilmen came from the leading families in town. The leading families now are more likely to locate their sons in business positions, positions which have higher standing than public offices and which can be used as places of leverage to control political life at a distance. In this respect, there was little change between the 1920's and 1930's, for even during the troubled depression years the business and professional men "shied away from participation in politics" even though they were then more active in "civic" affairs.[11]

A more careful examination of the class status of persons in designated governmental positions in Yankee City indicates that if politics is broadly interpreted, the highest status groups may, in a numerical sense, be "over-represented."[12] There, the upper classes, with 3 per cent of the voters, had one member on the sixteen-man city council, two members on the nine-man school board, and three members on the eleven-man library board, with others on the welfare and other boards and commissions. Yet even when such participation is taken into consideration, it is clear that the highest status members of the community although proportionately over-represented in the "high control" positions of government (Warner does not go beyond the superficial aspects of "control" in defining this group), are not participating in politics or government in a degree commensurate with their status or unofficial influence. Certainly in party affairs, members of the upper-class groups stay behind the scenes. In Jonesville, of the six Republican precinct committeemen, five are upper lower-class, and one, in a "silk stocking district," is upper-class.[13] Elite influence over the party takes other forms.

It cannot be said that the elite exercise their influence to enlarge the participation of others. In Regional City, the power elite consciously used techniques of exclusion, employing "public relations" to gain the consent of others after a decision had been made. In Middletown and Jonesville,

---

8. R. and H. Lynd, *Middletown in Transition*, p. 321.

9. F. Hunter, *op. cit.*, p. 228.

10. C. R. Hoffer, "The Interests of Rural People as Portrayed in Weekly Newspapers," Mich. Agricultural Experiment Station *Special Bulletin*, 298, Feb. 1939, p. 12.

11. R. and H. Lynd, *Middletown*, p. 421, and *Middletown in Transition*, p. 320.

12. W. L. Warner, and P. S. Lunt, *The Social Life of a Modern Community*, pp. 37-43.

13. W. L. Warner and associates, *Democracy in Jonesville*, p. 223.

pressure may be put upon workers to vote for the candidate approved by the employing interests, but all of the devices of persuasion and control are used to prevent the working class from making their own "free selection." In both Regional City and Middletown the upper-status groups supported state laws making it harder for the more liberal third parties to get on the ballot. And in Jonesville, Middletown, and Regional City, as elsewhere, the power elites have fought the formation of trade unions whose leadership would be independent of their control. None of this should occasion surprise; it would be naive to expect it to be otherwise. But it should be pointed out that where a few families or a narrowly defined "power elite" control the civic and political life of the community, there are strong active forces working to limit political and social participation.

These oligarchical tendencies in local life shed light on two political phenomena with broad distribution. One of these is the almost universal tendency of the electorate to turn out for national elections in larger numbers than for local elections. If there is a national power elite controlling events behind the scenes, as C. Wright Mills says there is,[14] the electorate is not aware of it; and in point of fact, there is no such national oligarchical structure. The other phenomenon is the tendency of people in large cities, and particularly in metropolitan areas, to vote more frequently than those in smaller cities or villages. At least in part, this may be due to the greater likelihood that larger communities afford a pluralistic power structure, one which permits several power hierarchies to exist in competition with each other. In such communities political participation of individuals, even though they each represent a smaller fraction of the total, may be seen as making a real and visible difference.

Plural hierarchies of power imply the organization of working-and middle-class people in associations of their own with a leadership independent of the "power elite," or the "leading families," or the "vested interests." One suggestion, advocated by Saul Alinsky and the sponsors of the Cincinnati "social unit plan," is the organization of the working class on a neighborhood basis,[15] but in general these plans have been short lived. There is no tradition of leadership endemic in these groups,[16] and in any event they are not functionally related to the major preoccupations of life. A second possibility is the organization of trade unions and, in fact, the union man is more likely to vote and participate in civic activities than his non-union counterpart. It is, in large part, the presence of the United Rubber Workers Union in Akron that makes Jones' community study read so differently from that of Middletown, Jonesville, and others. Here, an alternate to the authority of the industrial elite won power through violence and organization in the

14. See Charles Wright Mills, *The Power Elite* (New York: Oxford University Press, 1956).

15. Saul D. Alinsky, *Reveille for Radicals* (Chicago: University of Chicago Press, 1946); Harvey W. Zorbaugh, *The Gold Coast and the Slum* (Chicago: University of Chicago Press, 1929).

16. H. W. Zorbaugh, *op. cit.*, pp. 265-66.

thirties.[17] A third possibility lies in the two party system. In both Jonesville and Middletown the political parties are revealed as somewhat more autonomous of the industrial or landed elite than in Regional City, in spite of the fact that Regional City is much bigger; and the reason is that in the two northern cities the Democratic (lower-status) party can sometimes win local elections in spite of the opposition of the controlling groups. In other northern cities, with more vigorous Democratic parties, the type of business elite control over politics revealed in Regional City is impossible. This is not because the Democratic party, with its machine organization, is democratically controlled; it is because the political machine offers an independent power hierarchy in these communities. Finally, as we have noted in the previous chapter, ethnic associations may offer alternative means of participation not dominated by the business interests, although the assimilation of immigrant and foreign-nationality groups leaves the Negro associations to perform this task.

The associational life of a group may lead its members into politics or it may distract them from political issues. In Jonesville the strictly upper-class associations were devoted to social (in the sense of "society page"), recreational and cultural affairs, and chiefly populated by women. The upper middle-class associations, such as Rotary (which included some upper-class men), the Woman's Club, the P.T.A., the Red Cross, "grapple with the problems which face all segments of the community every day." Here civic mindedness has a flowering. While upper-middle and upper classes participate in many of the same kind of associations, "in general there is a sharp break between the upper middle and the lower middle classes with respect to the kind and amount of participation in associations." These lower-middle class associations, chiefly lodges, women's auxiliaries, and small informal social groups, are largely devoted to "having a good time" and have little political or civic content to their programs. For the upper-lower classes, with fewer associational memberships, the lodges, including the American Legion and its auxiliaries and particularly the church organizations, offer scope for associational activities, though again with little political content and a general "failure to relate their members to the community."[18] For the lower-lower class there is very little associational life of any kind, revealing again the general demoralization of this group. The absence of effective unions in this situation is critical. As may be seen, it is the middle classes, and particularly the upper-middle class, which show concern for the state of the community and conduct activities designed to do something about it.

---

17. "There are very few places in this country where the tension [between classes] has been as high and the industrial struggle as intense as in Akron." A. W. Jones, *op. cit.*, p. 137. Yet too much reliance should not be placed on the political capacity of unions, at least so long as the collective bargaining "bread and butter" aspects of unionism retain their overwhelming primacy. See Joel Seidman, Jack London, and Bernard Karsh, "Political Consciousness in Local Unions," *Public Opinion Quarterly*, 15 (1951-52), pp. 692-702.

18. Analysis of social class and associational life is based on W. L. Warner and associates, *Democracy in Jonesville*, pp. 137-43.

In passing, it may be noted that a separate and relatively isolated organizational structure for a group does not necessarily draw it away from community affairs or political participation. In Elmira the Negroes and the Jews tended to have their own associations paralleling the other community associations but this did not decrease their political interests or activity.[19] On the other hand, the separation of the Norwegians in Jonesville does seem to have reduced the political and civic interests of the group. In general the separately organized groups must rely upon "gatekeeper" leaders who serve as the means of effecting group influence in the community at large.[20] Obviously much depends upon the quality and interests of these strategically placed leaders.

In review, then, we may set forth the following hypotheses on political participation in American communities.

Political participation increases with (a) the proportion of commercial, as contrasted to industrial, occupations in the community, (b) the proportion of occupations, such as civil service positions, with high political relevance, (c) the smallness of the proportion of lower-lower class members in the community.

Political participation decreases with the concentration of power in an elite group because (a) the elite itself fails to participate openly in political life, and (b) the elite discourages effective participation by members of the working class, lower-status ethnics, and residents of slum and low-status political districts.

Concentration of power in a local community tends to exaggerate the discrepancies between national and local turnout. Because power is more concentrated in smaller communities than larger communities, larger communities tend to have higher participation rates among those of lower status than do smaller communities.

The better organized a social stratum (class, ethnic group, residential area) is under its own leadership, the more politically effective it will be. Possible types of organization include (a) the generally short lived neighborhood associations, (b) trade unions, (c) political parties and machines, and (d) ethnic associations. Metropolitan areas offer greater opportunities for pluralistic patterns of organization than smaller communities.

Among "non-political" associations, upper middle-class associations are more likely to focus attention on civic and political affairs than those of any other class (at least this is true where unions are weak).

Associational structures, organized separately from the main body of community associations, may lead to high political interest and activity, but politically oriented "gatekeeper" leaders must serve as links between the community and the separated association members.

ECOLOGY AND POLITICS

Patterns of residence of various social groups in a community tend to

---

19. Bernard R. Berelson, Paul F. Lazarsfeld, and William N. McPhee, *Voting* (Chicago: University of Chicago Press, 1954), p. 63.

20. This term and concept, "gatekeeper," is developed by Kurt Lewin in his "Group Decision and Social Change," in Guy E. Swanson, Theodore Newcomb, and Eugene L. Hartley, eds., *Readings in Social Psychology* (New York: Henry Holt, 1952).

mark out neighborhoods where the members of the various social classes and ethnic groups are concentrated. Jonesville has its "Towpath" area where the lower-lower class is concentrated, its "Frogtown" where the Polish population lives, and its "Top Circle" where the upper-status groups live. Political divisions such as precincts or wards often follow these ecological boundaries or at least differ markedly in their class and ethnic compositions. Here we inquire about the effect on civic and political participation of such ecological patterns.

For the working class, and possibly for other classes as well, the higher their proportion in a voting district, the more likely their members are to vote. The most convincing statement on this point comes from Herbert Tinsten's analysis of voting statistics of Basel-Stadt.[21]

In those districts where the workers make up more than 40 per cent of the electors, their average voting frequency is 69.3 per cent, in districts where they make up 30-40 per cent their voting frequency is 63.5 per cent, in districts where they are less than 20 per cent of the electors, their voting frequency is 53.7 per cent.

To this phenomenon Tingsten gave the name, "law of the social centre of gravity," and it serves very well as a general principle, even though, in particular instances, other forces may over-ride this "law."

This pattern also seems to hold true for ethnic groups, if the following evidence from Bridgeport, Conn. is typical. In two comparable wards, one predominantly Italian, the other ethnically heterogeneous, it was found that in the predominantly Italian ward the Italians were likely to know the name of their (Italian) councilman, to be familiar with the problems of the ward and to rank high in an index of "civic interest."[22] Their social structure reinforced this. In the ethnically heterogeneous ward, the social intercourse was lower, people were unfamiliar with the ward problems and tended generally to be low in civic interest.

Two influences are at work here: the *proportion effect,* and the *concentration effect.* The proportion effect, referring to the numerical proportions of a group in a district, follows from the increasing chances of electoral success associated with increased proportions in the population. This, in turn, increases the group-members' sense of political effectiveness, the sense that authorities will listen when you talk. It increases the stakes in participation by opening up the possibilities of gaining command over governmental resources, increases the "recognition" for an ethnic group, and, for these reasons, attracts money and leadership talent. On the other hand, for a group to comprise only a small proportion of the population of a district, encourages a sense of hopelessness and, because the chances of winning are small, makes the attraction of money and leadership difficult. Possibly it is for reasons of this kind that in Ann Arbor in the thirties the Polish nationality group with

21. Herbert Tingsten, *Political Behavior, Studies in Election Statistics* (London: P. S. King, 1937), pp. 126-27.

22. Harry Elstein, "The McLevy Complex," New Haven, Yale University, 1956 (unpublished paper).

the fewest members of any ethnic group ranked last in order of electoral turn-out, whereas in Detroit, where it was the largest of the ethnic groups, it ranked first.[23]

The concentration effect dealing with the physical concentration and dispersion of group members, follows from the greater group interaction where the group is concentrated, and the consequent reinforcement of group solidarity, sentiments, and knowledge of their community. With ethnic groups, this concentration tends to make of the restaurants and taverns meeting places for the exchange of gossip, some of which is political.

A third effect increasing participation (which may or may not be present in the above Basel-Stadt and Bridgeport cases) follows from the group's sense of differentiation from the surrounding population. This we may term, the *enclave* effect. Although we have no community data on this principle, it is applicable to larger voting units, including congressional districts and even states, where the religion, national origin, or party loyalty of the inhabitants tends to set them apart from the surrounding areas. Two such distinguishing characteristics are illustrated by the Mormon enclave of Utah, and the Republican enclave in Tennessee. On the whole it appears that, like proportionality and concentration, the enclave effect increases participation. Table 17.1 reveals the consistently high voting frequency of Utah.[24]

TABLE 18.1.—Per cent Voting of Potential Voters in the Three States with Largest Turnout, 1950, 1952, 1954.

1950 (House)		1952 (President)		1954 (House)	
Utah	67.7%	Utah	79.6%	Idaho	64.2
Conn.	62.2	Del.	79.1	Utah	63.5
Ind.	62.1	Idaho	78.5	Conn.	63.0

And in Tennessee, while 16 per cent of the total population of the First (Republican) District voted in the 1950 congressional election, only 7 per cent voted in all the other districts in Tennessee in which there were contests for the House of Representatives.[25] Moreover, neither urban influence nor "two-partyness" can account for this relatively greater turnout.

The hypotheses which emerge from this discussion may be stated as follows.

In areas where elections are close, the larger the proportion of a politically cohesive group to the population of a voting district, the greater the participation of group members in politics (proportion effect).

---

23. Compare James K. Pollock, *Voting Behavior: A Case Study* (Ann Arbor, Michigan: University of Michigan Press, 1939), p. 28, and Edward H. Litchfield, *Voting Behavior in a Metropolitan Area* (Ann Arbor, Michigan: University of Michigan Press, 1941), p. 12.

24. Computed from data in *Congressional Quarterly Weekly Report, 14* (1956), p. 420.

25. Based upon data in Richard M. Scammon, *America Votes: A Handbook of Contemporary American Election Statistics* (New York: Macmillan, 1956).

The more concentrated are the members of a politically cohesive group in a voting district, the greater the participation of group members in politics (concentration effect).

The greater the sense of differences between group members of a voting district and surrounding populations, the greater the participation of group members in politics (enclave effect).

PARTY ALIGNMENT OF GROUPS

We have been assuming a certain political solidarity in the ethnic or class group; otherwise those factors of proportionality and concentration which increase group consciousness and expectations of rewards would have somewhat different effects. Indeed, concentration of members of a group, say, Italian-Americans, with conflicting political loyalties might reduce participation rather than increase it. Thus, some group political solidarity has been implicit in the above discussion.

But inclusion of *all* the members of a class or ethnic group in one party is a rare phenomenon and, indeed, this rarity has been made the basis of a social law. Schattschneider terms this principle the "law of the imperfect political mobilization of interests,"[26] and persuasively points to the multiplicity and conflicting nature of individual interests as a guarantee that every group will have a minority of persons in the "other" political camp. Berelson and associates also deal with this aspect of group division in the political process, relating it to the dangers of over-developed political interests. For any group characteristic (x) such as ethnicity, working-class status etc., they postulate three possible divisions of party support.[27] Thinking of Condition A as a system of deep social cleavages, politically expressed, these authors say:[28]

FIGURE 18.1.—Three Patterns of Party Alignment for Groups with Attribute X.

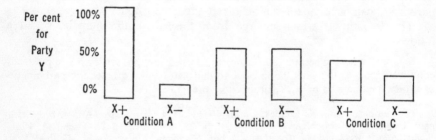

---

26. E. E. Schattschneider, *Party Government* (New York: Rinehart, 1942), p. 33.
27. B. R. Berelson and associates, *op. cit.,* p. 319.
28. *Loc. cit.*

The issues of politics would cut so deeply, be so keenly felt, and, especially, be so fully reinforced by other social identifications of the electorate as to threaten the basic consensus itself. This might be called "total politics"—a conception of politics, incidentally, advanced by such leading theorists of National Socialism and communism as Carl Schmitt and Lenin.

Thus a rise beyond some given point of the percentage of Negro or working class or Catholic votes going to one party would alarm these authors because it would intensify political partisanship to the danger point. Under these circumstances there would be too much participation, too intensely felt. On the other hand, Condition B fails to relate political choice to the most meaningful social divisions in the community and hence makes politics too insipid and unattractive. Only Condition C, which is the one the authors found to be characteristic of socio-economic and ethnic status in Elmira, offers both enough meaning to make elections significant and enough consensus to prevent dangerously intense political action. Although in local communities, and particularly in smaller voting districts, divisions like those pictured in Condition A occur, nationally in 1948 and 1952 (but not in 1956) the only group which seemed to approach this distribution was the Negro group.[29]

In summary, then, the following hypotheses may bear some weight.

The more nearly congruent are group boundaries and party boundaries, the higher the intensity of political feeling and the greater the level of participation in the group. The accomplishment of this congruence is inhibited by the "law of the imperfect political mobilization of interests." The result of such congruence may be dangerous cleavages in the community.

URBANISM AND POLITICAL LIFE

What is it about community life that makes residents of larger cities participate in elections more than those in smaller cities and residents of smaller cities (in the North, at least) more likely to vote than residents of rural areas? Some of the evidence is available in data already collected, other elements of evidence, however, must be inferred from what we know of the psychology and sociology of urbanism.

In the first place, two of the major group tensions which find political expression in our time are hightened in urban communities: tensions between social classes and tensions between ethnic groups. Many years ago, Holcombe noted that the urbanization of America tended to shift the basis of national politics from sectional alignments to class alignments.[30] One of the reasons

---

29. Angus Campbell, Gerald Gurin, and Warren E. Miller, *The Voter Decides* (Evanston, Ill., Row, Peterson, 1954), pp. 70-73.

30. Arthur N. Holcombe, *The New Party Politics* (New York: Norton, 1933); and *The Middle Classes in American Politics* (Cambridge, Mass.: Harvard University Press, 1940).

for tensions between working and managerial or owning groups in the city is that there the working classes sometimes have an opportunity of developing their own leadership and their own organizations, whereas in the rural areas they are more likely to accept the established upper-status leadership.[31] In part, at least, this is because working conditions in the city bring members of the working class in intimate contact with each other but not with the employing group. In the rural areas, however, work exchange during harvest (and other) times, tends to bring members of several status groups together and "this system of cooperation in farm labor is one factor which has in the past tended to integrate the rural community across class and ethnic lines."[32] Rural women, who are less likely to be brought into this cross-status relationship, are more status conscious than rural men.

The other major tension found in greater abundance in urban than in rural communities is inter-ethnic tension.[33] There are, of course, ethnic tensions in rural areas; indeed, in rural Jonesville, it is said that "there are two classes in this community—Yankees and Norwegians,"[34] but the cleavages are less sharp, there are few rural ghettos, the inter-ethnic interaction is greater, the political machines based on the political solidarity of ethnic groups are weaker, and above all, the rural population is ethnically more homogeneous.

There are other reasons for the lower rate of turnout in less densely populated areas. Sense of citizen duty increases with the population density of the voting area, evidently reflecting a higher rate of assimilation of civic norms by lower-status people in such areas. It is also true that sense of political efficacy is higher in metropolitan areas than in other areas (although there is no difference between rural and urban non-metropolitan areas in this respect).[35] Residents of cities (regardless of size) belong to more organizations than do rural residents, increasing their contact with like-minded people and making politics more salient for them. Contact with the media is, to some extent at least, greater in urban than in rural areas, and probably greater in metropolitan areas, with their competing press, radio, and television stations, than in smaller cities. Levels of education, and therefore of understanding of the issues and visibility of personal and group stakes in electoral decisions, are higher in urban communities. Also the physical difficulty of voting is less in urban communities where distances are smaller and polling places more numerous. On the other hand, we know that both home-ownership and feelings of permanence in the community are associated with a more active local political life and higher voting in a national election. Neither of these is encouraged so much by metropolitan living as by small town living.[36] Hence, as with all

---

31. See Dundan MacRae, Jr., "Occupations and the Congressional Vote, 1940-1950," *American Sociological Review, 20* (1955), pp. 332-44.

32. W. L. Warner and associates, *Democracy in Jonesville*, p. 261.

33. See, for example, Samuel Lubell, *The Future of American Politics* (New York: Harper, 1951), p. 28-99.

34. W. L. Warner and associates, *Democracy in Jonesville*, p. 239.

35. A. Campbell and associates, *op. cit.,* pp. 191, 197.

36. Survey Research Center, mimeographed material on "social integration," 1953, p. 23.

social phenomena, multiple identifications and minor pressures each contributes its small force, leading, on some occasions, to an overwhelming climax, as when the men of Lilliput immobilized Gulliver.

In terms of generalizations, little can be added to the above statements of fact and inference, but the following hypotheses seem to apply:

Political activity increases with the density of population of an area because factors making for higher participation (analyzed throughout this book) have a higher incidence and prevail over counter-forces in this area.

MIGRATION, COMMUNITY GROWTH, AND
POLITICAL ACTIVITY

"Even when demographic and socioeconomic differences are taken into account, *the longer the length of residence in the community, the greater the likelihood of voting.*"[37] With a few exceptions, this seems to be true of communities of 6,000[38] and 20,000,[39] and Detroit[40] and Chicago[41] clearly show. Nor are the reasons for this relationship hard to find. People who first come into a community are likely to have fewer associational ties, less information on community affairs, fewer political contacts, fewer emotional and material stakes in the group tensions that express themselves in politics.

The force of these impediments to electoral participation are apparent in the rates of turnout in rapidly growing communities. In Colorado, for example, the growing communities had a lower rate of participation than those of similar size where the population remained stable or declined.[42] And in 1952, the West, as a region, with by far the largest increase in population of any area in the United States, showed a rate of 23 per cent of a national sample not voting, compared to 16 per cent for the Northeast and 15 per cent for the Mid-

---

37. Harry Sharp, "Migration and Voting Behavior in a Metropolitan Community," *Public Opinion Quarterly, 19* (1955), p. 209. (Sharp's italics). But note that among union members in Detroit in 1952 those who had lived in that city all their lives were less likely to vote than those who migrated there more than seven years prior to the study. See Arthur Kornhauser, Harold J. Sheppard, and Albert J. Mayer, *When Labor Votes* (New York: University Books, 1956), p. 49.

38. Ben A. Arneson and William H. Eells, "Voting Behavior in 1948 as Compared with 1924 in a Typical Ohio Community," *American Political Science Review, 44* (1950), pp. 432-34.

39. Basil G. Zimmer, "Participation of Migrants in Urban Structures," *American Sociological Review, 20* (1955), pp. 218-24.

40. H. Sharp, *op. cit.,* pp. 206-209.

41. Charles E. Merriam and Harold F. Gosnell, *Non-Voting* (Chicago, University of Chicago Press, 1924), pp. 29-32. It should be noted that in all of these studies except that of Arneson and Eells, the differences are of a magnitude such that legal residence requirements could not account for the results. In the study by Zimmer a specific allowance was made for residence requirements.

42. Richard F. Whalen, "An Exploratory Study Based on Aggregate Statistics of the Relation of Voting Turnout to Population Change," Yale University, 1956.

West.[43] Alfred de Grazia, after a careful analysis of the Western data, says, "A very large proportion of the non-voters in California comes from those who have moved into that state since 1932."[44]

Newcomers into a community differ in their rates of electoral assimilation (achieving a rate of turnout similar to that of matched groups of longer residence in the community), but these differences are not, as might be expected, according to age, (urban) occupation, or education.[45] Rather they are according to where the newcomers came from. Southerners moving North tend to have rates of participation lower than matched Northern groups—and this is not because of race. Conversely, although the evidence is tenuous, it appears to be true that Northerners moving South approximate or exceed the voting rates of Southerners almost immediately. Foreigners (and foreign countries have higher voting rates than the United States) also take quick advantage of their electoral rights. Moreover, those coming from rural backgrounds, wherever these may be, tend to take longer to acquire the voting habits of the city than those moving from urban areas. All of this suggests that the most important single factor affecting the rate of electoral assimilation is the voting norms of the community from which a person comes.

Like the nature of the participants, the nature of the community makes a difference. In terms of size, the evidence suggests that people moving into a medium-sized city (one of 20,000) approximate the voting norms of their social groups more quickly than those moving into a metropolis the size of Detroit.[46] Apparently the anonymity and looser organization of the metropolis serve as obstacles to the enforcement of community voting norms.

As for other forms of participation, such as joining civic and other associations, the same kind of relationships prevail with the exception that class status makes a greater difference.[47] Not only do farmers show a slower than average rate of assimilation to their appropriate norms for participation in associations, but manual workers do too. This may suggest that middle-class associations are more open to outsiders, or, because they are more numerous, are easier to locate, or, possibly, because they are more likely (unions excepted) to serve civic or economic functions have more objective criteria for membership. Also, as Zimmer points out, it may be that "there is a standardized urban culture shared by white collar workers which transcends the limiting influence of migration"[48]—a culture learned by the middle classes but not by the working

---

43. A. Campbell and associates, *op. cit.*, p. 76.

44. Alfred de Grazia, *The Western Public: 1952 and Beyond* (Stanford: Stanford University Press, 1954), p. 152.

45. Rates of electoral assimilation are generally based on the analyses of H. Sharp and B. G. Zimmer, cited above. Inferences on electoral assimilation of Northerners moving South are based on R. F. Whalen's study also cited above.

46. Compare B. G. Zimmer and H. Sharp, *opera cit.*

47. B. G. Zimmer, *op. cit.*

48. *Ibid.*, p. 220.

classes or by the farmers. On the basis of these kinds of evidence we may say:[49]

The longer a person lives in a community, the more likely he is to vote. Therefore: the more rapidly a community grows, the lower the turnout in that community is likely to be.

Rates of electoral assimilation (achieving a rate of turnout similar to that of matched established groups) vary more with the participation norms of the migrants' place of origin than with the education, sex, or (urban) occupation of the migrants. Therefore: the lower the participation norms of the migrants' place of origin, the lower the rate of electoral assimilation.

The rate of electoral assimilation of newcomers in a community decreases with the size of the community to which they move.

The rate of assimilation in the associational life of the community increases with the social class of the newcomers and with the size of the community of origin.

POLITICS AND COMMUNITY IDEALS

The central theme of politics is group conflict. Where groups are organized under leaders of their own selection, political life will flourish—at least in the sense of broadened interest and participation. But it does not serve the interest of the dominant groups of a community to encourage the organization of the working class or ethnic groups, or wards and precincts other than those in which they live. Neither the press, nor radio and television stations will cooperate in such an enterprise. Unions are discouraged and when they get a foothold in a community they encounter legal and moral resistances to their political efforts. If they attempt to organize in political parties they meet official opposition:

---

49. Further study of the characteristics of migrants, the intra-national migratory flow, and the effect of transience on wide areas of social life would reveal much of importance to the political scientist. Some hints as to migratory patterns are offered by an analysis of 347 communities in California neighborhoods showing that the people who move into a community are so similar to established community residents that after a 90 per cent turnover in ten years the communities remain constant demographically, socially, economically, and politically. (Robert C. Tryon, *Biosocial Constancy of Urban Social Areas,* paper delivered before the American Psychological Association, September, 1955). In Chicago, Merriam and Gosnell found that in 1923-24 recent migration was related to low participation partly because of the high proportion of Southern Negroes in the group. In 1936, evidently migration patterns into Chicago had changed such that for selected urban areas there was a positive correlation (+ .68) between migrant status and education and (+ .62) between migrant status and median rental. Merriam and Gosnell, *op. cit.,* p. 80; Harold F. Gosnell, *Machine Politics, Chicago Model* (Chicago, University of Chicago Press, 1937), p. 109. In Austin, Texas, Roscoe Martin found that place of birth was a significant variable: among the Austin electorate those born in Texas voted more than those born in any other state. Roscoe C. Martin, "The Municipal Electorate: A Case Study," *Southwestern Social Science Quarterly, 14* (1933), p. 227. Demographers and political scientists may here join in fruitful union.

Business-class Middletown fears any tendency on the part of labor to enter politics, either by massing its vote behind a single one of the older parties or by putting forward a new party. During the summer and fall of 1936, the labor majority in Middletown's population was constantly encouraged to split itself up among *all* the parties, with no central political philosophy as a class.[50]

When political parties establish strong ward and precinct organizations, they are termed "machines" and "decent people" are encouraged in the press to oppose them. Ethnic associations organizing an ethnic vote are said to be violating the American assimilationist creed. Thus there are inherent contradictions in the middle- and upper-class ideals: universal political participation versus middle-and upper-class dominance.

This does not mean that the business leaders of the community have it their own way. While "the business class have . . . little respect for local politics and politicians, viewing them as a necessary evil which business supports only enough to ensure cooperation in certain necessary matters, . . squabbles between the city hall and The Chamber of Commerce arise from time to time."[51] The machine develops an autonomy from business domination, not representing the working classes, the ethnic groups, or the depressed areas, but instead rather using them for the machine's own purposes. This does not precisely serve the interests of the power elites of the community, but it is better than handing over political power to an active, well-organized working class or to ethnic groups—groups, which are, in any event, difficult to organize.

In this situation, the municipal reform ideal of non-partisan, efficient, apolitical politics is certain to seem attractive to white, native, Protestant, middle-class citizens. By abolishing party labels, the lower-status groups are disoriented and become the unwitting clients of the upper-status press. By doing away with "peanut politics" (which apparently got its name from a political row over an Italian peanut vendor's stand), abolishing the small constituencies, and making the election of councilmen city-wide, ethnic solidarity is weakened. "Negro apathy in Detroit seems to be due to the city-wide type of election, the nonpartisan character of the election with a concomitant weak party organization and lack of organization and leadership among Negroes."[52] More than the better educated, the less well educated require the colorful personality of a political leader to draw them into the political fray. The council-manager plan does away with the office which is a "natural" for such characters. Municipal reforms of this nature: non-partisanship, smaller city councils, the replacement of mayors by city-managers, may serve admirable technical purposes and in the long run be in the best interests of most groups in the community—but they weaken the political ties of the disorganized and depressed groups in the community. And, in doing this, they serve a strong, but usually repressed, interest of the community "power elite," whose focus is

---

50. R. and H. Lynd, *Middletown in Transition,* p. 358.

51. *Ibid.,* p. 329.

52. Gunnar Myrdal, *An American Dilemma* (New York: Harper, 1944), p. 493.

ostensibly upon the gains in efficiency and honesty brought about by the reforms, but who profit from the political apathy of the underdog.

Another goal for some reform groups, quite different from municipal reform, might be termed a "consensual ideal," the desire for a community where everyone is in basic agreement on the goals and purposes of life. R. C. Angell argues for this type of community in terms of moral integration, which he defines as "a set of common ends and values toward which all are oriented and in terms of which the life of the group is organized."[53] Sebastian de Grazia, who bases his case upon the conviction that the lack of a common ideology creates a burdensome anxiety in the members of a community, also argues (though for a different purpose) for a community with a common set of beliefs.

One of Angell's indices of moral integration is the crime rate in a community, a rough clue, he believes, to the general acceptance by the members of the community of common moral norms and, possibly, also to the proportion of people with antagonism toward society. Another index of moral integration is the rate of contributions to community chests in the several cities. Considering these two factors as indicative of one kind of community ideal, the morally integrated community, we may ask whether such communities include higher political interest and turnout among their virtues. A correlation of proportion of population voting in 1940 in nineteen non-Southern cities with these two indices of moral integration reveals virtually no relationship.[54] Indeed, what relationship there is between criminality and turnout is positive, indicating that high turnout is slightly less likely in a "morally integrated" city than in a community where there are more people with antagonisms and conflicts with society. On balance, it appears that the morally integrated city may draw upon motives of citizen duty and social adjustment to sustain its voting rates, to some marginal extent, while the morally unintegrated city may draw more upon motives of intergroup antagonism and loyalties to groups which are partially excluded from full social participation.

As may be seen in all of these cases, there is no necessary correspondence between various visions of community well-being and the motivations to be "political" or even "interested in public affairs." The means and the goals of politics remain obscurely entangled.

The relationship between certain civic ideals and political participation may be summarized as follows.

Because middle-and upper-status groups in the community fear the influence of lower-status groups, yet share the American belief that everyone should make his voice heard in democratic politics, these groups embody a dimly perceived ideo-

---

53. Robert C. Angell, "The Moral Integration of American Cities," *American Journal of Sociology,* 57 (1951), special supplement to July issue, p. 2.

54. For this correlation, Angell's indices of criminality and rate of welfare giving for predominantly pre-World War II years were related to proportion of total population voting for President in 1940. The data on voting were obtained through correspondence with registrars of voters in the several cities.

logical conflict. This conflict is partly resolved and concealed by the formula of municipal reform: non-partisan politics, city-wide elections, city-manager govern- ment—devices which improve the efficiency of administration while they weaken working-class and ethnic political ties.

Moral integration in a city, as measured by indices of crime rates and rates of contribution to community chests, is insignificantly related to turnout (what rela- tionship there is indicates that political participation is higher where crime is greater and community giving lower).

Part V

The Influence of Social Institutions on Political Life

CHAPTER 19

Mass Media and Mass Politics

MEDIA CONTENT—PUBLIC AFFAIRS

T HE MEDIA OFFER A varied menu for varied appetites. Some idea of the proportions of different kinds of political material offered in the daily press in middle size cities may be obtained from the data in Table 19.1.

TABLE 19.1.—Contents of 8 Wisconsin dailies and 4 Oregon dailies with circulations between 10,000 and 20,000 for the week October 23-November 1, 1948.

Type of Material	Per Cent of Non-Advertising Space Oregon Dailies	Wisconsin Dailies
State and Local Politics	5.1	2.3
News and Opinion on 1948 election	7.1	8.1
Domestic Governmental Affairs (excludes election and foreign affairs)	4.4	5.4
Foreign Affairs	5.8	8.5
All Governmental and Foreign Affairs	20.2	25.2
Opinion on Governmental and Foreign Affairs	4.6	5.8
Crime, Vice, Accidents	10.4	20.2
Social Events and Items about People	20.3	19.0
Sports	10.8	13.9
Comics and Humorous Cartoons	14.6	8.0
Other Pictorial	12.4	13.0

SOURCE: "Content of Selected U. S. Dailies," October 23-November 1, 1948, "Bulletin 16," Department of Agricultural Journalism, Univ. of Wisconsin, 1949 (mimeographed), pp. 1-25.

Advertising in these dailies occupied a little more than half of the total space, of which, in this period of a national election, political advertising represented

only a small proportion (12 per cent in Oregon, 2 per cent in Wisconsin).[1]
On this basis, one might estimate that, at least in an election period, the daily
press devotes from one-eighth to one-twelfth of its total space to news and
opinion on politics and governmental affairs.[2]

Since, as is well known, front page material is seen much more frequently
than other material, it is important to note that the material on governmental
and foreign affairs is much more likely to appear on the front page than is
other material; indeed, it comprises about half of the front page reading matter.[3] The apathetic need not seek politics; it greets his eye whenever he turns
to the newspaper.

Papers differ, of course, in their treatment of political and governmental
affairs: the larger the circulation, the *more* likely the paper is to devote attention to state and local political affairs and the *less* likely it is to devote attention to foreign affairs and to crime, vice, and accidents.[4] This suggests that the
metropolitan press is more politicized than the smaller urban press. On the
other hand, region is more important than size in determining treatment of
public affairs: the differences between Oregon and Wisconsin are larger than
the differences between papers with different circulations.

As for changes over time, so far as the evidence goes, the decline and rise
of interest in government and politics since 1900 does not seem to have been
paralleled by any changes in treatment of public affairs in the press. Over the
past fifty years there has been a moderate increase in the proportion of attention given to foreign affairs, (although the changes since 1920 have been
minimal) and an increase in interpretive comment by columnists and commentators, but national news from Washington, as a proportion of total content, has remained the same.[5]

The proportion of television broadcast time devoted to public affairs is
probably less than the comparable proportion space in the daily press; this
medium is more frankly regarded as a source of entertainment. Studies of
sample TV programs in three cities show that the programs dealing with
public policy and political or foreign affairs come under two headings: "general

---

1. See source for Table 19.1, p. 11. In this study similar analyses for eight metropolitan dailies and six other strategically located papers reveal similar uses of newspaper space. I wish to express my indebtedness to Wilbur Schramm for guiding me to
a number of relevant studies cited in this chapter.

2. Mott's analysis of newspaper content in 1940 confirms this general impression,
with the exception that it suggests a somewhat greater attention to foreign affairs. See
Frank Luther Mott, "Trends in Newspaper Content," reprinted in Wilbur Schramm, ed.,
Mass Communications (Urbana, Ill.: University of Illinois Press, 1949), p. 393.

3. *Content of Selected U. S. Dailies, op. cit.,* p. 17.

4. *Ibid.,* pp. 10-17.

5. F. L. Mott, *op. cit.* An examination of the editorial content of *The New York
Times* over the past fifty years shows growing attention to foreign affairs, war, disarmament, the United Nations, Communism, and atomic power; that is, the editorials
have appropriately reflected the issues of the time. For the same reason, they show declining attention to issues considered less pressing today, such as "trust busting" and
tariff reform. See Ithiel de Sola Pool, *The "Prestige Papers," A Survey of their Editorials* (Stanford, California: Stanford University Press, 1952).

news" and "public issues" (chiefly interviews with political leaders and panel discussions). Percentages of total time devoted to these two classes of broadcasting in three cities is shown in Table 19.2 (but note that the program analyses took place between elections).

TABLE 19.2.—Percentage of Total Broadcast Time Devoted to General News and Public Issues by TV Stations in Three Cities.

City	General News	Public Issues
Chicago (July 30-August 5, 1951)	4.0	1.6
New Haven (May 15-20, 1952)	4.1	1.4
New York (January 4-10, 1953)	6.6	1.5

SOURCES: Dallas W. Smythe, "Three Years of New York Television, 1951-1953" (Urbana, Ill.: National Association of Educational Broadcasters, 1953); Donald Horton, Hans O. Mauksch, and Kurt Lang, "Chicago Summer Television, 1951" (Chicago, Ill.: National Opinion Research Center and the University of Chicago, undated); Dallas W. Smythe, "New Haven Television, 1952" (Urbana, Ill.: National Association of Educational Broadcasters, 1953).

Although TV probably devotes less time to public affairs than the press devotes space to that subject, what little evidence we have suggests that television and radio are at least as influential as the daily papers. More people reported that television was their most important source of information and opinion in the 1952 campaign than reported this about any other medium.[6]

As for radio, about an eighth of the total broadcast time in a late November week in 1946 was devoted to news and commentators (about three times the proportion for television) and an additional 1 per cent was devoted to "forums and panels" which might have included a relatively high proportion of political or public affairs content.[7] Although news can focus upon accidents, society affairs, and local scandal as well as political and governmental affairs, one might tentatively estimate that the proportion of time and space devoted to these affairs in radio is closer to the newspaper pattern than it is to the television pattern. For all its impact at election time, television has increased the entertainment content and decreased the civic and political exposure of the American citizenry.

For those who are interested in public affairs, the media offer an abundant, but "thin" and repetitive supply of news, some opinion, but little serious analysis. The functions served by the British weeklies are but indifferently performed in America. For the majority of the people, those with only moderate interest in public affairs, the media offer "news" and topics of conversation, and sufficient benchmarks for a crudely differentiated political orientation. For the large number of disinterested persons, the media ensure a minimum awareness of events by reason of the juxtaposition of entertainment and human

6. Angus Campbell, Gerald Gurin, and Warren E. Miller, "Television and the Election," *Scientific American, 188* (1953), pp. 47, 48. Among other things, this study suggests that television is supplanting the radio but *not* the newspaper in audience exposure.

7. Kenneth Baker, "An Analysis of Radio's Programming," in Paul F. Lazarsfeld and Frank N. Stanton, *Communications Research 1948-1949* (New York: Harper, 1949), pp. 59-72.

interest material with material on public affairs. Whether this diet of entertainment and serious news is appropriately nourishing for the functioning of democracy is still unclear. But at least it is a sustaining diet in that it permits the electorate to make broad discriminations and, in one sense, encourages sufficient popular participation to operate the system.

MEDIA CONTENT—POLITICAL CAMPAIGNS

As may be noted in Table 19.1, during an election week election news comprises about a third of the news and opinion on public affairs, or, taking large and small dailies together, about 8 per cent of the non-advertising content of the press. In this treatment there is a general slighting of the policy issues in favor of other kinds of material.[8] For example, in the Connecticut and Wisconsin senatorial campaigns of 1952 between 25 and 31 per cent of the total newspaper treatment of these campaigns in these states dealt with policy issues, and, oddly enough, editorials were, compared to other types of matter, least likely to discuss such policy issues. Moreover, when this policy treatment is examined, we find that in both 1952 when the United States was engaged in a foreign war, and in 1940 when France had just fallen to the Axis powers, between two-thirds and three-fourths of the campaign policy treatment dealt with domestic affairs.[9] The responsibility for this, however, should not be laid at the door of the press alone. On the contrary, the emphasis in the news treatment reflects the emphasis in both the campaign speeches of the candidates and in the party's own advertisements in the newspapers.[10]

The media, like the candidates themselves, do not treat the campaign as an opportunity for debate, that is, for argument and rebuttal. Instead they reflect the competitive assertions of the candidates, each of whom stresses the points he regards as most likely to win approval for his side, ignoring the arguments of the opposition. In doing this, the press reflects the candidates' emphasis on goals rather than means, general promises rather than specific measures.[11] Furthermore, even when the media do deal with policy matters, there is usually no identification of the party positions on these policy stands, a factor which helps to explain the low level of public information on the policies advocated by the two major parties and their candidates.[12]

---

8. Except where otherwise indicated, the information on newspaper treatment of political campaigns is based on a study of the 1952 Senatorial campaigns in Connecticut and Wisconsin. See LeRoy C. Ferguson and Ralph H. Smuckler, *Politics in the Press, an Analysis of Press Content in 1952 Senatorial Campaigns* (East Lansing, Mich.: Michigan State College, 1954).

9. Paul F. Lazarsfeld, Bernard R. Berelson and Hazel Gaudet, *The People's Choice* (New York: Columbia University Press, 1948), p. 116.

10. Compare Ferguson and Smuckler, *op. cit.,* p. 33 and Bernard R. Berelson, Paul F. Lazarsfeld, and William N. McPhee, *Voting* (Chicago: University of Chicago Press, 1954), p. 236.

11. See especially analysis in P. F. Lazarsfeld and associates, *op. cit.,* p. 116.

12. See Angus Campbell, Gerald Gurin, and Warren E. Miller, *The Voter Decides* (Evanston: Row, Peterson, 1954), p. 128.

Of the roughly 70 per cent of the non-policy political material in the press at campaign time, the majority deals with the personalities of the candidates, their home life, business experiences, friendships with local favorites, and patriotism, here again often reflecting the candidates' own choice of topics. In 1952 Stevenson, partly because he was less well known than his opponent, employed these personal themes more than did Eisenhower,[13] and in the 1952 senatorial races in Connecticut the paid political advertisements of the two parties (particularly those dealing with William Benton) reflected this emphasis on "human interest" material. Appeals to special groups (farmers, labor, Negroes), in terms of friendship and identification, not policy, comprises another significant element of the press campaign treatment. And all of this treatment, both references to policy and references to other matters, is charged with emotional appeals, references to "democracy," "the American way," and particularly to tradition of one kind or another.

As to the political bias of the press, analysis of a substantial body of material reveals consistent but moderate bias in the news columns favoring the candidate given support in the editorial pages.[14] A careful analysis of the front page news treatment of four papers supporting Stevenson and four papers supporting Eisenhower in 1952 revealed that when the greater "newsworthiness" of Eisenhower was taken into account, this sample of the press tended to give favored treatment of their "own" candidates in terms of type of headlines used, placement of stories, use of pictures, and amount of space devoted to the two candidates. Furthermore, the contents of the stories themselves, in the use of non-neutral phrases, revealed bias in favor of their "own" candidates.[15] Other analyses have shown that headline treatment often is prejudicial to a favored candidate by amount of space and position of story, a factor which should be taken in conjunction with studies showing that the nature of the headline often affects what the reader perceives in the story.[16] One of the most significant areas of bias, moreover, the selection of features, columnists, and cartoons, rarely appears in studies of newspaper bias because these are included as legitimate areas of editorial expression.

Since the press is overwhelmingly Republican in its editorial preference (67.3 per cent of the papers in 1952, against 14.5 per cent Democratic—and the circulation of the Republican papers is proportionately much greater),[17] the biased presentation and interpretation of the news tends to elicit the con-

---

13. Malcom W. Klein and Nathan Maccoby, "Newspaper Objectivity in the 1952 Campaign," *Journalism Quarterly, 31* (1954), p. 294.

14. See *Ibid.*, pp. 285-96; Berelson and associates, *op. cit.*, pp. 234-52; P. F. Lazarsfeld and associates, *op. cit.*, pp. 120-36; Nathan B. Blumberg, *One Party Press?* (Lincoln: University of Nebraska Press, 1954); Robert Batlin, "San Francisco Newspapers' Campaign Coverage: 1896, 1952, *"Journalism Quarterly, 31* (1954), pp. 297-303; *Content of Selected U. S. Dailies, op. cit.;* Galen Rarick, *California Daily Newspaper Reporting of the 1950 U. S. Senatorial Campaign: A Content Analysis* (M.A. thesis, Stanford University Library, 1951: summarized in Stanford University News *Press Release,* January 26, 1951.

15. Klein and Maccoby, *op. cit.*

16. See Percy H. Tannenbaum, "The Effect of Headlines on the Interpretation of News Stories," *Journalism Quarterly, 30* (1953), pp. 189-97.

17. See Nathan B. Blumberg, *op. cit.*, p. 14.

fidence and reinforce the partisanship of the adherents of the Republican party and to discourage the Democrats. Here lies one of the more significant reasons for greater Republican than Democratic turnout at every educational and occupational level.

On the other hand, this bias has not prevented high visibility for the Democratic cause nor made it impossible for the public to hear and see the Democratic case. In Elmira in 1940, even though there was a two-to-one disproportion of content favoring the Republicans, the Democrats read and heard their own side about as much as the Republicans read and heard theirs.[18] Moreover, in allocating responsibility for this bias, we must observe that where people are given a choice, as in New York, only a fraction of the Democratic public selects a newspaper on the basis of ideological or party preference.[19] In this way they fail to bring market support as a counter pressure to the ownership and advertising pressures making for Republican bias in the media.

Over time, certain changes in the political content of the media are apparent. A study of the treatment of the 1896 and the 1952 presidential campaigns in three California papers (with continuity of ownership over this period) reveals that some sixty years ago the press devoted proportionately more space to a political campaign than is devoted today, focusing more on local political figures than is usual in modern treatments.[20] This corresponds to what is thought to be the net decline of political interest in the country during this period, both reflecting that fact and, in some small measure, accounting for it. On the other hand, it is also true that the 1952 treatment was less biased (as indicated by the complexion of unattributed statements in the news stories), and, even in 1952, devoted less attention to problems of corruption and vote coercion—a healthy sign of the maturation of American politics. Such evidence indicates that, over the past sixty years, American political interests may have waned, they have probably been "nationalized," and they have shifted in focus away from the problem of achieving a fair election.

Reviewing the previous two sections we may summarize the material as follows:

From a twelfth to an eighth of the total content of the daily press deals with public affairs but headline and position emphasis raise its visibility so that all newspaper readers are at least partially exposed to news, some receive opinion orientation (the proportion of space devoted to columnists has grown over the past fifty years), but few find serious political analysis.

Television devotes proportionately less attention than the press to public affairs, but has equal or greater political impact on its audiences.

Treatment of political campaigns in the press show the following tendencies:

---

18. Bernard R. Berelson calls this situation a "functional balance." See his "Communications and Public Opinion," in Wilbur Schramm, ed., *Communications in Modern Society* (Urbana, Ill.: University of Illinois Press, 1948), pp. 179-80.

19. Gerhart H. Saenger, "Social Status and Political Behavior," *American Journal of Sociology, 51* (1945), pp. 11-12.

20. R. Batlin, *loc. cit.*

(1) little emphasis on policy issues, particularly foreign policy; (2) more reporting of candidates' speeches as competitive assertion than as debate (statement and rebuttal); (3) emphasis upon vague goals rather than specific measures or means; (4) emphasis upon personal qualities of candidates; (5) emphasis upon emotional appeals, tradition, and social norms; (6) fairly close reflection of the content of candidate's speeches, appeals, and advertisement themes—as in the above emphases; (7) low emphasis on party label and poor association of party policy with campaign discussion.

Analysis of the Republican-Democratic "bias" in the daily press reveals the following: (1) A tendency for papers to favor the candidate supported in the editorial pages by: (a) headline treatment, (b) position of the stories (c) use of pictures, (d) amount of space devoted to the candidates, (e) the use of non-neutral phrases, (f) selection of quasi-editorial features such as columnists and cartoons. (2) Sufficient treatment of "opposition" news so that readers may learn the claims of the opposition party and gain some perspective on the campaign issues. (3) A twenty-five year trend toward the "Republicanization" of the daily press producing overwhelming Republican dominance combined with a growth of one-paper communities.

Political preferences of the press and general campaign treatment of the respective parties is a minor consideration in reader choice (where there is choice). This withdraws consumer sanctions as an influence on editorial policy.

Over a sixty-year period (or somewhat less) the press has shown the following trends: (1) a moderate increase in attention devoted to foreign policy; (2) a moderate increase in proportion of public affairs news devoted to national news and a corresponding decrease in local affairs; (3) a moderate decrease in attention devoted to political campaigns; (4) a moderate decrease in biased treatment of campaign news.

HOW DO THE MEDIA AFFECT THE POLITICAL
INTERESTS OF THE PUBLIC

What effect does exposure to this material have upon political behavior? However inadequately, in an election the media inform the public of the more salient issues, the names and public personalities of the candidates, and, to some extent, the nature of the supporting figures which each candidate has attracted to his side. In elections, the media provide orientation by associating the name of the candidate with a party label which has meaning for the individual (indeed in Britain, where the label is not put on the ballot, the central problem for each party is to make sure that this association is clarified for the public). In referenda, where the party label is absent, the media usually fail to give this kind of orientation and as a partial consequence, turnout falls off. Perhaps more important than anything else, however, is the communication of the simple message: "There will be an election next Tuesday." Like Mother's Day, election day must be heralded in the press so that the public will be prepared to do its duty.

There is a mutual influence between exposure to the media and participation. "The more people read politics, the more they talk politics; and the more they talk, the more they read." The Elmira study shows this relationship as follows:

TABLE 19.3.—Exposure to Political Content in Media and Political Discussion in June and October, 1948.

	Percentage Naming Last Person with Whom Politics Discussed (October)*	
	Higher Media Exposure	Lower Media Exposure
Had talked politics in June	96 (190)	86 (133)
Had not	89 (238)	73 (226)

* This table holds with an interest control.

SOURCE: Bernard R. Berelson, Paul F. Lazarsfeld, and William McPhee, "Voting" (Chicago: University of Chicago Press, 1954), p. 246n.

Among those who were talking politics in June those who exposed themselves to more political material in the media were more likely to be talking politics in October, and the same was true for those who did not talk politics in June. Exposure increases political discussion for both the June discussants and the June non-discussants. But it is also true that the June discussants were more likely to fall in the higher exposure group, while it was about a fifty-fifty proposition for the June non-discussants, as may be seen by looking at the "N" figures in parentheses. Obviously there are limits to this spiral effect, among which are the satiation of interest, and the demands of competing events,[21] what might be called the declining marginal utility of politics.

There may be marked differences in long-and short-term effects. We know that people who first reject a message from a discredited source tend over a period of time to forget the source and to look upon the message more favorably.[22] Also, some people who have initially rejected the attitudes suggested by a film tend to accept them after the passage of time.[23] It is therefore likely that political attitudes and behavior which show no relation to exposure in the short run may have such a relationship in the long run. Moreover, there are certain kinds of structuring of thinking and basic inarticulate premises which the media promote, but which are difficult to analyze comparatively because they are almost universal. It is in this way, for example, that the media set the stage for political debate through their emphasis on what is important and their acceptance of certain social goals as the proper criteria for a policy discussion.[24]

21. B. R. Berelson and associates, *op. cit.*, p. 248.

22. Carl I. Hovland and Walter Weiss, "The Influence of Source Credibility on Communication Effectiveness," *Public Opinion Quarterly*, 15 (1951), pp. 635-50.

23. Carl I. Hovland, Arthur A. Lumsdaine, and Fred D. Sheffield, *Experiments on Mass Communications*, Princeton, Princeton University Press, 1949 (Volume III of *Studies in Social Psychology in World War II*), pp. 182-200.

24. See B. Berelson, "Communications and Public Opinion," *op. cit.*, p. 182.

Finally, not only are there changes of attitudes (conversions), but also reinforcement of present attitudes, and the activation of new (or latent) attitudes. In view of the fact that only a small per cent of the sample interviewed in the 1940 Erie County study were converted from Democratic to Republican positions, or vice-versa, the latter two types of effect may be more important, at least in campaign situations.[25]

It may be argued that the most important political effect of the media is their creation of a set of general attitudes toward the field of politics, attitudes not attributable to any special message or medium but to the general characteristics of the media. Most of these general effects are said to discourage the public from active participation in political affairs. They deserve examination.

The first of these, put forward under the heading of "narcotizing dysfunction," develops the idea that reading and listening to politics serve as a substitute for action, partly because they occupy time that otherwise might be employed for political activity, partly because they salve the individual's social conscience by offering substitute means of showing his interest and concern in public matters.[26] The pattern of responses previously termed a "spectator interest" in politics suggests that in some small measure this effect has support in empirical evidence. The fact that reading and listening do not fit into a (Guttman) scale of participation lends additional support to this hypothesis. Yet it must be a rare effect: reading and listening are more often than not a preliminary stage for political action. The fact that people stop at this stage does not indicate that they have substituted the reading and listening for the action, but rather it indicates, in most instances, only that they are insufficiently motivated to go further.

A second argument deals with the possibility that the "media may increase political apathy simply through presentation of the magnitude, the diversity, and the complexity of the political issues on which the responsible citizen is supposed to be informed."[27] Under these circumstances readers and listeners may be overwhelmed or discouraged and simply give up. It is certainly true that persons who feel that "politics and government seem so complicated that a person like me can't really understand what's going on" tend to participate less than others. But is this feeling of confusion attributable to the media? Rather, is it not the case that politics and government are in fact complicated and that the media tend rather to over-simplify, to personalize, to stereotype so as to give a false impression of simplicity? Life, not the reporting of life, is the villain in this drama.

A third argument holds that the "diversionary content" of the mass media, the features, comics, sports pages, women's pages, advertisements, tend to distract people's attention from the substantial political problems which confront them.[28] Were it not for these aspects of the media, Americans would

25. P. F. Lazarsfeld and associates, *op. cit.*, pp. 94-103.
26. Paul F. Lazarsfeld and Robert K. Merton, "Mass Communication, Popular Taste, and Organized Social Action," in Lyman Bryson, ed., *The Communication of Ideas* (New York, Harper, 1948), pp. 105-106.
27. B. Berelson, "Communications and Public Opinion," *op. cit.*, p. 181.
28. *Ibid*, p. 182.

turn to the state of world affairs and their national destiny. Although marginally true, this argument, too, seems overstated. "Plausible as it may seem at first glance, the withdrawal and escapist theme that links . . . immersion in mass forms of divertisement with poverty of public opinion appears on closer inspection to be very far from persuasive."[29] In fact, as noted above, the mass media may have more political news and coverage than most people want or use. In balancing their escapist material with news, the press, radio, and television may be discouraging the more frivolous features of the American culture.[30] At least the extent of political content of the newspapers does not seem less than readers desire, according to the evidence in the Survey Research Center study of reading habits in Albany, New York, set forth in Table 19.4.

TABLE 19.4.—Newspaper Reading Habits in Albany, New York, 1949.

"What part of the paper are you most interested in?"

Part of paper	Per cent mentioning**
News*	44%
Funnies	20
Sports	18
Local news	17
Editorials	13
Ads, want ads	11
Society, births, obituaries	9
Women's section, fashions, personal advice	6
Other	13
Nothing special	4
Almost everything	8
Do not read newspapers	3
No answer	1

* An additional 40 per cent said they read the news when they were directly asked.
** The total is more than 100 per cent because some people named more than one part of the newspaper.

SOURCE: Survey Research Center, "Interest, Information, and Attitudes in The Field of Foreign Affairs, Ann Arbor, Mich., 1949 (mimeographed), p. 21.

And the quality of the reading of the news by the 44 per cent who volunteered this socially approved answer and the 40 per cent who, when asked, said they read the news, is further illuminated by the next question:

---

29. Herbert Goldhamer, "Public Opinion and Personality," *American Journal of Sociology,* 55 (1950), p. 351.

30. "It seems, therefore, that the mass media, among their highly complex and ambiguous effects, do help to prop up the prestige of the political sphere in the United States, and that within this sphere they have the effect of favoring the older, moralizing political styles." David Riesman, *The Lonely Crowd* (New Haven: Yale University Press, 1950), p. 227.

TABLE 19.5.—Newspaper Reading Habits in Albany, New York, 1949.

"Would you say you read national and international news rather
carefully or do you usually just read the headlines?"

Care in reading news	Per cent answering
Do not read news	4%
Just headlines, skim	47
More than headlines, not much	4
Sometimes carefully, sometimes not	14
Carefully, skip some things	19
Very carefully	6
National carefully, international not	3
International carefully, national not	1
No answer	2
	100%

SOURCE: Same as Table 19.4

Relating these data to their information about self-appraisal of interest in foreign affairs, the Survey Research Center found a "striking" correlation between degree of care in reading news and interest in foreign affairs.

What this suggests, therefore, is that the media are, at least in the short run, as much a product of public demands as a force which imposes these lighter interests upon the public at the expense of more serious political matters.[31] And, as a side-issue, it may be noted that when the complexion of public opinion on political matters is compared with the nature of the news treatment in the daily press, it appears that the news treatment is more sober and impartial than most of the popular opinions expressed. Therefore, it may be said that the actual function of the press is to expose the public to more political news and less emotional versions of the news than would be the public's natural selection if it could purchase news item by item.

A fourth argument on the over-all effect of the media in enlisting the public for the work of democracy deals with what might be called the "rapport" of the media with the public. Considerable evidence shows a working-class lack of confidence in the press, and this lack of confidence holds generally for Democrats as contrasted to Republicans.[32] Were there a substantial labor press, or were a substantial part of the press Democratic, the political messages of the press might easily find a more receptive audience. One would then find that kind of acceptance which today characterizes the special magazines which are received by their audiences as messengers of known and friendly disposi-

---

31. Walter Lippmann came to the same conclusion many years ago; see *Public Opinion* (New York: Macmillan 1922), p. 46. For a discussion of some differences in short and long run effects, see Douglas Waples, "Press, Radio, and Film: Some Papers on Current Research," *Public Opinion Quarterly*, 5 (1941), pp. 463-69.

32. See Arthur Kornhauser, Albert J. Mayer, and Harold L. Sheppard, *When Labor Votes* (New York: University Books, 1956), pp. 88-91.

tions. Under these circumstances, whatever other effects the arrangement might have, the total politicizing effect of the media would almost certainly be more substantial.

The media serve to confer status upon people, activities, and ideas.[33] A fifth effect, then, would be their conferral or denial of status to political figures. We have no data on the image of the public official or of the politician in the news and comment on the news; no doubt the images are multiple, varied, and incompatible, as they are in the public mind. Politician and mayor, bureaucrat and public servant, cookie-pusher and diplomat—all such phrases evoke stereotypes which contradict each other. Perhaps, however, in their eagerness for scandal the media may, on the whole, tend to denigrate these figures. But it should be recalled that only 3 per cent of the political content referring to the 1952 Wisconsin and Connecticut senatorial races dealt with corruption, a figure which may be compared to the 8 per cent of the public who, when asked an open-ended question on their perceptions of the two major parties in that year, mentioned corruption in Washington as a reason for not voting for the Democratic party.[34] On the other hand, the very prominence of public affairs and the names of public officials in the news does confer upon them a kind of status which has a positive civic effect. Apparently status is given with one hand and taken away with the other.

It would be an error to believe that only the serious or non-fictional material in the media confer status. The change in fictional hero types from titans of industry to the heroes of the consumption world is illustrative of this aspect of the problem. But one may ask, "where are the heroes of politics and government?" An analysis of the occupational distribution of heroes in the *Ladies' Home Journal, True Story, Atlantic, Saturday Evening Post,* and *Country Gentlemen* in the twenties and thirties, shows that public service heroes never represent (with one exception, *True Story* in the twenties) more than 9 per cent of the total hero population in any of these media in either decade.[35] (Most of the heroes, of course, were businessmen or professionals.) Nor was there any increase in public service heroes in the thirties, when government became a much more prominent feature of the news scene and government employment increased markedly. Perhaps, in its fiction, radio is a little more political, however, since about a fifth of the main characters in the "soap operas" of the early forties (war period) were "high officials."[36] On the whole, it appears that in fiction, with its rather more intense audience participation, there is little opportunity for identification with political or public figures; little status is conferred on political or governmental leaders and, in fact, they are paid little attention.

---

33. P. F. Lazarsfeld and R. K. Merton, *op. cit.,* p. 101.

34. L. C. Ferguson and R. H. Smuckler, *op. cit.,* p. 46; A. Campbell and associates, *The Voter Decides,* p. 45.

35. Patricke Johns-Heine and Hans H. Gerth, "Values in Mass Periodical Fiction, 1921-40," *Public Opinion Quarterly,* 13 (1949), pp. 103-13.

36. Rudolph Arnheim, "The World of the Daytime Serial," in Paul F. Lazarsfeld and Frank N. Stanton, eds., *Radio Research, 1942-1943* (New York: Duell, Sloan and Pearce, 1944), p. 43-85.

A closely related (sixth) argument, dealing again with the fictional content of the media, points to the nature of the solutions to the endless problems
which beset the characters in this mass of gelatinous material. While the
problems are largely interpersonal, they inevitably reflect the social circumstances of the actors: poverty and wealth, tension between members of different social classes, expenses of sickness, educational opportunities or lack
thereof, and related matters. But the causes of these problems inevitably are
treated as personal failure and matters of individual character and strength,
or, in a sense, as a destiny which overtakes a citizen without plan or reason.
And the solutions to the problems are also personal, not social; and never
governmental. Here, on the whole, the media distract attention from politics,
obfuscate political relations, and inhibit political participation.

In the seventh place, the media enforce social norms, that is, they close
"the gap between 'private attitudes' and 'public morality'."[37] Throughout
society there exist varieties of behavior (business practices, patronage matters
in government, sexual arrangements) which are contrary to approved social
norms and yet are tolerated and known "privately" but widely to exist. It is
only when knowledge of these deviations becomes public and they are pub-
licized through the media, that sanctions are invoked. "Publicity, exerts pressure for a single rather than a dual morality."[38] Not the least of these areas
is the morality of political participation—the good citizen votes, is moderately
well informed, and is vigilant against the evil forces of politics. The press
tends to place tension on the individual who is privately lax in these respects,
even though everyone else in his immediate social environment is lax, too.
But there is no public morality in favor of giving money to a political party,
or joining a political party, or caucusing with the party, or working for a
social movement (except civic "reform"), or developing a markedly independent view on a political issue. The social norms which the media enforce
are, if anything, negative in these areas.

Politics is the area of conflict and change, but (eighth) for several reasons
the media do not deal with many kinds of social conflict and change. The
media derive their income from their readers and their advertisers. Their
readers may be offended by references to certain issues which they regard as
sacred. Their advertisers are equally sensitive in other areas. But to be meaningful politics must deal with underlying structures and group status. To
handle this problem of readership and advertiser accommodation, the media
tend to strip politics of its meaning by failing to discuss such matters as class
structure and income distribution in America, differential conditions of life
among Negro and white groups, recent earnings in the medical profession, and
conflicts of religious groups over control of the schools.

Now all of these arguments pointing to ways in which the media tend to
depoliticize the public contain kernels of truth and are, in this sense, germin-
ally true. That is, for some people at some time on some topics, the media

37. P. F. Lazarsfeld and R. K. Merton, *op. cit.,* pp. 102-105.
38. *Ibid.,* p. 103.

operate in these diverting or inhibiting ways. For others, the media tend to encourage political participation and to raise the visibility of political figures and events to a high level. Without in any way denying the presence of any of these media effects in specific instances, we must, in some sense, strike a balance among the several tendencies—and the balance shows that the general effect of exposure to the media is a politicizing one. This is true across the board with reference to attitudes and behavior. Those who are more exposed to the media (sometimes with education held constant) are more likely to:[39]

be interested in politics
vote
discuss politics
belong to more organizations
have more opinions and more political information
have a firm party preference
adopt their party's views on current issues
have strong candidate preferences (but not to be "hero worshippers")

In review then, we may say of the effects of exposure to the media upon political behavior:

Exposure to the media increases political discussion and political discussion increases exposure to the media.

The reinforcement effect of the media is greater than the conversion effect.

While reading, listening, and viewing political material in the media are sometimes substitutes for civic or political action (narcotizing dysfunction), usually they are preliminary to such action.

While the media occasionally discourage political action by featuring the complexity of social problems, more frequently they oversimplify them giving a (false) impression that the members of the public can devise their own solutions.

The media present more news and comment on public affairs than most of the public demand, thus politicizing rather than apathizing the public.

Failure of the media to establish ideological rapport with large sections of the public tends to discourage participation.

While the news sections of the media tend to give prominence to political figures, and, in this sense, confer status upon them and upon political activity, the fiction in the media fails to cast its heroes in governmental or political roles.

Fictional presentations in the media attribute evil and suffering to personal, not social or political, solutions to the problems presented, thus distracting attention from the gains to be achieved through political participation.

Emphasis upon citizen duty in the media (to the extent that it is emphasized)

---

39. These findings are supported by evidence in the three voting studies cited above (*The People's Choice, The Voter Decides,* and *Voting*), plus data in Survey Research Center, *Interest, Information, and Attitudes in the Field of World Affairs;* Ralph O. Nafziger, Warren C. Engstrom, and Malcolm S. Maclean, Jr., "The Mass Media and an Informed Public," *Public Opinion Quarterly,* 15 (1951), p. 109; Bernard R. Berelson, "The Effects of Print upon Public Opinion," in Douglas Waples, ed., *Print, Radio, and Film in a Democracy* (Chicago: University of Chicago Press, 1942), pp. 41-65; and Morris Janowitz and Dwaine Marvick, *Competitive Pressure and Democratic Consent* (Ann Arbor, Mich.: Bureau of Government, University of Michigan, 1956).

serves to bring the widely recognized but private "do-nothing morality" closer to the official morality of the democratic dogma.

The tendency of media owners, advertisers, and segments of the media audience to dislike references to the roots of social conflict (class or ethnic) weakens the resonance of the media with the problems of the time, and hence weakens the power to stimulate political response.

On balance, however, exposure to the media is associated with: (a) interest in politics, (b) higher turnout, (c) joining community organizations, (d) superior information, (e) stronger views, (f) closeness to the party position, (g) strong candidate preferences.

WHEN DO THE MEDIA POLITICIZE THE PUBLIC?

To be effective, the political material in the media must, of course, be observed by the public. We have already examined the complexion of the observers, those who read, listen, and view political material, finding, as might be expected, a relative concentration of better educated, more prosperous, male, older, urban people in the political audience—with many differences among the media.[40] Here we inquire into the circumstances which make such exposure effective. When does the political content of the media "come through" and alter knowledge, attitudes, or behavior of the individual?

One feature of the media presentation of politics which serves to widen its influence, as mentioned above is the juxtaposition of political material and pictures and stories of greater audience appeal. "Some people actively go after political content. But there is another type to whom political content 'just comes,' "[41] and this heterogeneity of sports, crime, and politics, makes it easy for this latter "type" to pick up a kind of political orientation. The integration of politics with entertainment may be essential for democracy. In Riesman's words, "pictures are only the come-on for social-issues."[42]

Yet, in an important sense, the "come-on" often fails, for a person may "see" an item but decline to read it. A readership study of Minneapolis daily newspapers found that of all varieties of news and editorials (war, crime, arts, sports, etc.) with one exception, the stories on government and political activity were least likely to be read, even in part, by people who "saw" them.[43] This does not mean that most people who saw the material did not read it; three quarters of them did. But it does mean that the popular appeal of this material, the kind of appeal which would make people who notice an item want to read more about it, is lacking. Here again is evidence that rather than seducing the public from politics, the media flings its political and public affairs material at many people who only look away.

---

40. See Chapter 6.

41. B. R. Berelson and associates, *op. cit.*, p. 244.

42. D. Riesman, *op. cit.*, p. 227.

43. *Readership Dimensions of the Newspaper*, Research Division, University of Minnesota School of Journalism, March, 1948 (mimeographed), p. 11. Note, however, that the period examined, February 21-26, 1944, was not a campaign period.

What are the more effective means of presenting political material? Of course this varies with the audience, but in general it may be said that aural and pictorial means of communication are more effective than reading matter, particularly for the less well educated groups.[44] In the 1940 campaign, "to the extent that the formal media exerted any influence at all on vote intention or actual vote, radio proved more effective than newspapers."[45] There is some suggestion, however, that combined aural and pictorial communication such as movies (or film strips combined with lectures) are more effective than either taken separaetly—a fact which may account for the tendency of voters in 1952 to consider television their most important source of news and opinion.[46]

There are several reasons for the effectiveness of radio and television.[47] It is more "personalized" in the sense that it is a person-to-person communication with the possibility of identifying with the speaker who speaks to his unseen audience. There is an opportunity for group solidarity among listeners if more than òne is in the room at the time, and hence more discussion of the news. Less effort is required, hence an audience not reached by print is exposed. "For those interested in politics, whether middle class or working class, contact with other people is the typical way of keeping informed. For the uninterested in both classes it is radio"[48] and, it should be added, television. Finally, Democrats tend to be distrustful of the newspapers' treatment of politics, but not of the radio or television which they regard as more neutral.

Magazines have a special effectiveness among the better educated, and among opinion leaders generally.[49] Moreover, as mentioned earlier, if it is a specialized magazine (farm journal, professional magazine, labor weekly) it "already has a foot in the door, so to speak, because it is accepted by the reader as a reliable spokesman for some cause or group in which he is greatly interested and with which he identifies himself."[50]

As for the content of the material, it has sometimes been said that politics is given a bad name in comparison to business because political speeches tend to be devoted to attacking the opposition while advertising

---

44. See Joseph T. Klapper, "The Comparative Effects of the Various Media, in Wilbur Schramm, ed., *The Process and Effects of Mass Communications* (Urbana, Ill.: University of Illinois Press, 1954), p. 91-105.

45. P. F. Lazarsfeld and associates, *The People's Choice*, p. 128.

46. The evidence for the relative effectiveness of television cited above (p. 000), must be weighed against the apparent lack of support for this view in Janowitz and Marvick, *op. cit.*, pp. 66-71 and in Herbert A. Simon and Frederick Stern, "The Effect of Television upon Voting Behavior in Iowa in the 1952 Presidential Election, "*American Political Science Review, 49* (1955), pp. 470-77.

47. See J. T. Klapper, *op. cit.*, pp. 99-102.

48. Mark Benney, A. P. Gray, and R. H. Pear, *How People Vote* (London: Routledge & Kegan Paul, 1956), p. 137.

49. In addition to the tables in A. Campbell and associates, "Television and the Election," see Kenneth P. Adler and Davis Bobrow, "Interest and Influence in Foreign Affairs," *Public Opinion Quarterly, 20* (1956), pp. 89-101.

50. P. F. Lazarsfeld and associates, *The People's Choice*, p. 134.

is devoted to praising a business product. Political communication then adds up to a total unfavorable presentation while commercial communication adds up to a total favorable presentation. So far as media presentation of campaign material is concerned, this is not true. In one of the most bitter campaigns, the California senatorial contest between Richard Nixon and Helen Douglas in 1950, the California press devoted only 25 per cent of its total statements about the election to items unfavorable to either candidate, compared to 34 per cent neutral and 41 per cent favorable.[51] Furthermore, the press and the candidates themselves tend to stress the most appealing features of the campaign, the personalities of the candidates, the human interest stories, and the easy-to-understand versions of policy problems. Certainly many of the winning devices of the skillful propagandist—"glittering generalities," "just folks," "transfer"—are central features of political communication. On the other hand, the decline of bias and partisanship in the press noted earlier may take away some of the "reader interest." Apparently, in some sense the media have in fact become "tutors of tolerence,'" as Riesman says,[52] and political tolerance cannot be expected to have much audience appeal.

Another circumstance that contributes to the failure of influence proportionate to the effort put forward in presenting political and public affairs material is the lack of pictorial presentation. Pictures attract at least twice the "readership" that articles do (on inside pages almost four times as much), but in six daily issues of a Minneapolis paper (February 21-26, 1944), pictures and captions on "government and political activity" accounted for only 2.7 per cent of the total pictorial content of the paper.[53]

We are asking here about the circumstances which are associated with audience politicization by the media. Radio and television sell commodities, and change buying habits. Can they also change citizenship or political habits? Assuming that part of the audience, at least, has some predisposition to accept the civic or political messages put forth, how can the media convert these into such behavior as voting, writing to congressmen, or attending public discussions of public issues. In analyzing this problem, Wiebe points out that in commercial advertising, this *social mechanism* for facilitating the translation of impulse to act is as available as the corner drugstore or the supermarket.[54] But the social mechanisms for many kinds of civic acts are not always so available. In illustrating this, Wiebe remarks that Kate Smith's radio bond selling program was successful because the impulse could be translated into an act by a telephone call to the radio station. The appeal for civilian defense workers by WJZ-TV was equally effective because the mechanism (the Civilian Defense organization) was easily accessible and

---

51. See Galen Rarick, *loc. cit.*, and Stanford University *Press Release, loc. cit.*. The comparable proportions for three San Francisco papers in 1952 were: unfavorable, 26 per cent; neutral, 43 per cent, and favorable, 31 per cent. See Robert Batlin, *op. cit.*, p. 299.

52. D. Riesman, *op. cit.*, pp. 217-23.

53. *Readership Dimensions of the Newspaper*, p. 9.

54. G. D. Wiebe, "Merchandising Commodities and Citizenship on Television," *Public Opinion Quarterly, 15* (1951-52), pp. 679-91.

easily located. But appeals for establishing community councils to combat juvenile delinquency were ineffective because of the lack of available mechanisms to translate impulse to action, and the impulses generated by the televized Kefauver hearings on crime in politics were thwarted because most people didn't know who their local party committeemen were, and often, these committeemen were unsympathetic. In this sense the party was not an available social mechanism. The polling booth is an available social mechanism, and voting may be increased by moral suasion in the media, and sometimes by a mail campaign, as well by personal contact.[55] Writing letters to congressmen, since most urbanites don't know the names of their congressmen, is impeded by the lack of facilitating institutions, except, of course, when an interested advocate stands by with postcard, pencil, and information. Similarly, since most people don't know who their party committeemen are or where the registration office is (and it may be too far away in any case), joining "the political party of your choice" may be an act for which social facilities seem distant or unavailable. The political messages of the media which suggest some act beyond voting, then, are likely to be ineffective for lack of social mechanisms to facilitate such acts.

The social network of personal friends and acquaintances serves both as a supplement to the media and as a competitor. Each clique and friendship group has its own opinion leaders who retail what they have read in the media.[56] They tend to be of the same social class but to have slightly higher educational and occupational positions than the other members of the group. Even when persons of such higher status are less well informed (among women, but probably not among men), they continue to exercise their leadership functions. In politics the opinion leaders tend to be men; the flow of influence is from men to women, and, where status and age lines are crossed, from higher to lower and from older to younger even though most political guidance is given and received within, rather than between, age and status brackets.[57] Since there is a tendency for the opinion leaders' opinion leaders also to be of higher status than themselves, the progression of opinion leadership reaches by gradual stages from the highest status to the lowest status in society. The political messages in the media come across most effectively, then, when they become the topic of conversation in this chain of personal relationships and are conveyed by opinion leaders at each level to their followers.

This is true, in part, because this secondary chain of communication, the person-to-person network, may be more effective than direct contact with

---

55. See Harold F. Gosnell, *Getting Out The Vote* (Chicago: University of Chicago Press, 1927).

56. See Elihu Katz and Paul F. Lazarsfeld, *Personal Influence* (Glencoe, Ill.: Free Press, 1955).

57. *Ibid.*, pp. 271-95. Note, on this point, some contradiction in the evidence: in *The People's Choice*, (p. 150) Lazarsfeld and associates say that "the coverage is greater" in the network of personal relationships, but in *How People Vote*, (p. 137) Benney and associates say that radio reaches the disinterested people who do not talk about politics among themselves.

the media itself.[58] Thus personal conversation often seems less purposive, less designed to persuade, and hence the message slips past a person's defenses. The inadvertent approach, however, is also characteristic of much of the material on radio and in the press reducing this advantage of personal communication. More importantly, where there are subconscious barriers to "hearing" or "getting the point" of communication the message most often is misinterpreted or not perceived.[59] A more genuine advantage is the possibility in personal communication of adapting arguments to the particular situation of an individual and of avoiding issues which are known to be disliked. The arguments can be tailor-made to the individual. Then, too, the rewards which come from agreement or compliance with a live individual arc not availablc whcn the mcssage comes through print or over the air. It is said that a person is more likely to trust an intimate source than the radio or newspaper. Against this, however, one must weigh the prestige and authoritativeness of the radio and the newspaper. The gratifications in feeling that a person is interested in you, your opinions, and your welfare make the personal situation more persuasive, unless, of course, some ulterior motive is suspected. In personal contact a person can persuade another to adopt a point of view or perform a given act, such as voting, without providing the grouds for belief or creating conviction. And finally, people respond more readily and with greater emotion to persons than to issues; more readily to a living presence than to print or a shadow on a screen.

Considerations of this nature led Lazarsfeld and associates to conclude that "in comparison with the formal media of communication personal relationships are potentially more effective . . ."[60] On most issues this is probably true, but it should be noted that people's own estimates of whether they are more influenced by "what they read or hear on the air" or by "conversations with people" varies from topic to topic: on communism they are more influenced by the media; on whether "we are heading toward more unemployment" the personal testimony of friends seems relatively more important.[61]

On the question of the condition for effective media for political stimulation the following propositions seem relevant.

The integration of political material with entertainment in the media serves to sensitize the apolitical public and thus contributes to the more adequate functioning of the American democracy.

The politicizing effect of this integration of entertainment and politics is impeded by the fact that, compared to other material, the political and governmental material fails to invite further reading by those who see the items.

Although the newspaper audience is greater than that of any other medium

58. P. F. Lazarsfeld and associates, *The People's Choice*, pp. 150-58.

59. See Eunice Cooper and Marie Jahoda, "The Evasion of Propaganda: How Prejudiced People Respond to Anti-Prejudice Propaganda," *Journal of Psychology*, 23 (1947), pp. 15-25.

60. P. F. Lazarsfeld, *The People's Choice*, p. 150.

61. See Samuel A. Stouffer, *Communism, Conformity and Civil Liberties* (Garden City, N.Y.: Doubleday, 1955), pp. 226-27.

and the paper has more material on public affairs and politics than does television (and probably radio), the political impact of television and radio may be greater than the impact of newspapers. This is because (a) aural and pictorial means of communication are more effective with the less well educated, (b) the source is personalized and identification with the speaker may increase media influence, (c) the circumstances of listening increase "audience solidarity" and inter-communication among audience members, (d) listening and viewing require less effort than reading, (e) the broadcasting sources are more likely to be trusted than the daily press.

Specialized magazines derive some influence from their status as known and trusted in-group spokesmen.

The political content of the media achieves influence through its personalization and simplification of problems, and its use of such propaganda appeals as "transfer," "glittering generalities," "just folks," but loses reader appeal in neutral reporting and low pictorialization of public affairs.

The media lose effectiveness when the social mechanism for implementing their political messages is unfamiliar, "distant," or uninviting.

The media gain in political effectiveness when their messages are retailed through the network of personal relationships by opinion leaders. Such personal influence is effective because it is adaptable to particular views, it permits compliance without persuasion, there are personal rewards in agreement, and the present human person is for everyone the prime and original repository of trust and affection.

WHEN IS THE PUBLIC RECEPTIVE TO A

POLITICAL MESSAGE

The media may perform their part in translating events into "news" and offering alternative opinions for public consideration, but unless the public is ready to receive these messages, communication fails. Reception depends upon the needs, the mental set, and the moods of the public.[62] How shall these be characterized?

George Herbert Mead, Harry Stack Sullivan, and others have developed theories of selective attention and inattention which elevate these faculties into central psychological properties of life.[63] Schramm notes "we scan our communication environment like an index, selecting among cues and con-

---

62. See David Krech and Richard S. Crutchfield, *Theory and Problems of Social Psychology* (New York: McGraw Hill, 1948), pp. 87-88. In this analysis of predispositions affecting perception we are generally indebted to the Krech and Crutchfield approach and to Wilbur Schramm's discussion of "The Anatomy of Attention," in Schramm, ed., *The Process and Effects of Mass Communication*, pp. 29-32.

63. See George Herbert Mead, *Mind, Self, and Society* (Chicago: University of Chicago Press, 1934), Harry Stack Sullivan, *The Interpersonal Theory of Psychiatry* (New York: Norton, 1953). See also Elton Mayo, "Notes on Consciousness and Attention," in Hugh Cabot and Joseph A. Kahl, eds. *Human Relations, Concepts in Concrete Social Science* (Cambridge, Mass.: Harvard University Press, 1953), Vol. 1, pp. 196-202.

centrating our attention on the signs that specially attract us."[64] However explained, it is certainly important to note that a person will see in the media what he has been sensitized to see: he will see the reporting of Anglo-American relations if he is sensitized to foreign affairs; he will see news about corruption in politics if he has been taught that politics are corrupt. "The facts we see depend on where we are placed and the habits of our eyes."[65]

Attitudes toward the source, the medium, commentator, or columnist affect the reception of the message. In a study of attitudes of auto workers in the 1952 campaign, more respondents (42 per cent) distrusted the newspaper than any other medium and more people trusted television in contrast to other media. It is important to note that the order of frequency of expressed trust in a medium is precisely the same as the order in which respondents attribute importance in giving them information on the candidates.[66] From the earlier prestige studies we know that political views attributed to a prestigeful source are often accepted, while these same views are rejected if said to come from a disliked or low-status source.[67] Yet, over time, the messages from the less trusted source may have a growing importance, since sources are forgotten while the initially suspected message grows in plausibility.[68]

Beyond this, a person sees what is useful to him. People pay attention to political reporting when some issue which affects their careers, incomes, perquisites, or status is being discussed in the media.

A kind of second-order interest in politics occurs when political issues become associated with politically extrinsic symbols or groups or men with special appeal—much as the questions in quiz programs become invested with interest by the fact that the contenders stand to gain or lose fortunes in framing their answers. Foreign policy takes on interest for an individual when the diplomatic dramatis personae are familiar and interesting figures; municipal ownership of utilities becomes of interest to some when the phrase "creeping socialism" associates the issue with emotive symbols. In short, the political transfer value of words and men is considerable.

The political transfer value of reference groups is particularly strong. Ethnics scan lists of candidates, looking for cognate names: Jews look for

---

64. W. Schramm, "The Anatomy of Attention," p. 29.

65. Walter Lippmann, *Public Opinion* (New York: Macmillan, 1922), p. 80. "Thus when we perceive a politician, our perception of that particular politician is influenced by all our other precepts involving politicians." Krech and Crutchfield, *op. cit.,* p. 94.

66. A. Kornhauser and associates, *op. cit.,* pp. 89-90.

67. See, for example, T. E. Coffin, "Some Conditions of Suggestion and Suggestibility: A Study of Certain Attitudinal and Situational Factors Influencing the Process of Suggestion," *Psychological Monographs,* No. 241 (1941); I. Lorge, "Prestige, Suggestion, and Attitudes," *Journal of Social Psychology, 7* (1936), pp. 386-402.

68. See Herbert C. Kelman, and Carl I. Hovland, " 'Reinstatement' of the Communicator in Delayed Measurement of Opinion Change," *Journal of Abnormal and Social Psychology, 46* (1953), pp. 327-35; Carl I. Hovland and Walter Weiss, "The Influence of Source Credibility on Communication Effectiveness," *Public Opinion Quarterly, 15* (1951), pp. 635-50.

Jewish names, Italians for Italian names, Poles for Polish names. So ethnic-consciousness is politicized. The member of a fraternal order whose attention is drawn to a lodge brother in public affairs; the man who is excited when he finds a resident of his home town in the news; the nationalist whose concern with foreign affairs is based on the prestige of the flag abroad—all follow with close attention the leads given by their non-political group loyalties.

In general, it may be true that people follow political news when it tells them things they like to hear, that is, when political news is good news. But this has its limits, as is seen in the finding that "rosy headlines" did not help to sell newspapers during the war.[69]

People follow political news when it deals with figures with whom they can identify and whom they "understand." In noting reactions to the different characters in the drama of the 1952 political conventions, Lang and Lang, found that Dirksen was seen as a performer or showman, Dewey as a behind-the-scenes kingmaker, but Rayburn was seen as a whole personality doing a difficult job under trying circumstances.[70] This latter kind of identification occurs, say these authors, when a person sees a public figure in a situation where his personal reactions and feelings come across—a situation depending upon the lack of strong predispositions against the man or what he stands for and upon continuous exposure over a period of time in a proper setting. But empathy of this kind is only one source of interest; hate, fear, and love will serve as well.

People pay attention to political reporting and public events in the news if they can use the information in conversation with others to show how much they know or to avoid revealing ignorance, to advance a program, to support partisan arguments against opponents, to ingratiate themselves with partisan superiors, to fulfill prophecies, to denigrate disliked prominent men, to create heroes, to validate a theory, to flatter their self-image, to legitimize their hostilities, to rationalize their failures, to provide vicarious excitement, to distract them from personal troubles, and to satisfy their need for meaning and order in their environment.[71]

A more general way of stating the predispositions which influence people to pay attention to the political content of the media is to say that this content must have familiar elements, that is, it must fit into an appropriate frame of reference, and it must be functional, that is, it must somehow be rewarding to the individual. The most common of these rewards are said to be "(a) agreement with social norms or majority opinion, (b) various types of ingroup membership or 'belongingness,' and (c) release from tension."[72] Just as one must ask about opinions, "Of what use to a man are his opinions?" So one

---

69. See Elizabeth C. Winship and Gordon W. Allport, "Do Rosy Headlines Sell Newspapers?" *Public Opinion Quarterly*, 7 (1943), pp. 205-9.

70. Kurt Lang and Gladys E. Lang, "The Television Personality in Politics: Some Considerations," *Public Opinion Quarterly*, 20 (1956), pp. 103-12.

71. See Bernard R. Berelson, "What 'Missing the Newspaper' Means," in P. F. Lazarsfeld and F. Stanton, *Communications Research 1948-1949*, pp. 111-29.

72. See J. T. Klapper, "Mass Media and Persuasion," in W. Schramm, ed., *The Process and Effects of Mass Communication*, p. 319.

must inquire of the member of the media audience, "Of what use to a man is the news?"

Exposure to certain subjects is negatively rewarding or, put the other way around, inattention may serve to avoid tension-producing situations. Two of these punishing situations relate to what was thought for a time to be an amazing public indifference to the problems surrounding atomic defense and atomic policy in general. One explanation for this indifference lies in the tendency for people to avoid anxiety-provoking or fear-inducing situations, an avoidance which may be expressed in apathy or preoccupation with other things and rationalized in any number of ways.[73] The other explanation relies upon a theory of guilt over America's role in dropping the first atom bomb, and consequent popular dissociation with the implications of atomic warfare. "From the psychoanalytic viewpoint, such a tendency represents the defensive reaction to guilt—in this case, the American's guilt about his initiatory act (at Hiroshima) the implications of which he selectively ignores or inattends."[74]

A third form of psychic punishment occasioned by exposure to the media occurs when an individual is marked by "intolerance of ambiguity."[75] For some persons the tensions created by conflicting ideas, or opposing courses of action, are intolerable. Such persons, often authoritarian in their general personality constellation, must either expose themselves to a single area of the media where only a single and congenial point of view will be expressed, or, as may often be the case, avoid extended exposure altogether.

More generally, as Cooper and Jahoda have pointed out, material which violates views which serve important psychic functions for the individual —as ethnic prejudice may "bind" the aggressive feelings of the authoritarian personality—will be distorted or ignored.[76] In 1948 the Republicans who believed in rent control were less likely to "see" reports of Dewey's speeches against price control reported in the Elmira press.[77]

The predispositions which prepare audiences to receive messages or discourage their reception may be summarized as follows:

Perception of politics or specified political themes in the media is a function of a politically sensitized attention frame.

In the short run, the more trust people have in the source the more likely they are to attribute to that source importance in affecting their political attitudes; in the long run, the trustworthiness of the source becomes less significant in influencing views.

Politics is likely to become vested with borrowed significance for a person to

73. Irving L. Janis and Seymour Feshbach, "Effects of Fear-Arousing Communications," *Journal of Abnormal and Social Psychology, 48* (1953), pp. 78-92.

74. Helen Swick Perry, "Selective Inattention as an Explanatory Concept for U. S. Public Attitudes Toward the Atomic Bomb," *Psychiatry, 17* (1954), p. 236.

75. See Else Frenkel-Brunswik, "A Study of Prejudice in Children,"—*Human Relations, 1* (1949), pp. 295-306; and "Intolerance of Ambiguity, as an Emotional and Personality Variable," *Journal of Personality, 18* (1949), pp. 108-43.

76. See E. Cooper and M. Jahoda, *op. cit.*

77. B. Berelson and associates, *op. cit.*, pp. 220-23.

the extent that messages in the media link political issues to symbols, reference groups, or men for whom the person has evaluative predispositions.

Within limits, men are more likely to perceive politics in the media if the political material tells them what they want to hear and if the political leaders are presented so as to evoke love, hate, fear, or empathy.

More generally, political material is perceived and has an influence to the extent that it serves a need for the individual, i.e., if it provides (a) information useful in solving a career or other objective problem, (b) means of social adjustment to others, or (c) opportunity for the release of psychic tension.

Political material will be unperceived when its perception is punishing because it creates guilt feelings, or evokes anxiety, or poses conflicts difficult of resolution, or runs counter to views serving other psychic needs.

CHAPTER 20

How Political Institutions Affect Electoral Activity

THE AMERICAN GOVERNMENT rests upon a theory of consent, that is, a theory that popular beliefs and desires are the source of legitimacy in government. Political parties and interest groups are the vehicles for conveying to the government the wishes of the public. Thus parties, interest groups, and governmental institutions together should conspire to maximize popular participation and to elicit from every citizen some expression of his political views. How, and to what extent, do they do this?

POLITICAL PARTIES AS REFERENCE GROUPS

Political parties are tripartite institutions. First, they are legal institutions with a structure defined by law, custom, and by-laws. Second, they are associations of leaders seeking to capture the offices of government. And third, although it may be true that "Whatever else the parties may be, they are not associations of the voters who support the party candidates,"[1] nevertheless they are significant reference groups for these votors.[2]

What is the nature of this party image or group reference in the minds of the public? In the first place, the two major political parties are emotionally significant reference groups for almost 95 per cent of the population (even

---

1. E. E. Schattschneider, *Party Government* (New York: Rinehart, 1942), p. 53. For a discussion of party membership see Clarence A. Berdahl, "Party Membership in the United States, Parts I and II," *American Political Science Review, 36* (1942), pp. 16-50, 241-62.

2. Berelson and associates define parties as constituting national leadership, local organization, and "the symbol in the minds of men." This latter part of the definition corresponds to the party as "reference group" above. See Bernard R. Berelson, Paul F. Lazarsfeld, and William N. McPhee, *Voting* (Chicago: University of Chicago Press, 1954), p. 179.

though this is barely acknowledged by about 20 per cent of the people) in the sense that people have a "pro" or "anti" feeling about the two parties. At election time about a third of the population feels a "strong" identification with their party.[3] It is, perhaps, of this group that Merriam speaks when he says "at times the party spirit seems almost a form of general intoxication."[4] It is strongest among the older voters, whose loyalties have been hardened by experience, and among Protestants, who seem more certain of their party loyalties than do Catholics and Jews; but strong party identification is no more likely to be found in the city than in the country, and neither sex nor race seems to make much difference in modifying the strength of party loyalty. People who have more education have a very slight tendency to feel *less* strongly about their party loyalties; perhaps because education frees them to look at issues and men as well as party. (It is not because they prefer the term "independent.") And, interestingly enough, the middle income groups are, to a small extent, less emotional about their party feelings than either the more prosperous or the less prosperous who may have clearer orientation on "which side their bread is buttered."[5]

In the general scheme of group loyalties, party loyalties probably do not rate very high; at least in Elmira, when respondents were asked which of their group identifications were important to them, "only 18 per cent of all respondents named a political party (as against 65 per cent for a religious group, 45 per cent for a work group or profession, or 42 per cent for a nationality)."[6] And in another sample, only a quarter of the population said that they would take the advice of their party, as contrasted to other groups, in an election.[7] But even if, contrasted to other institutions, parties are not considered generally salient, they may be central forces in organizing political attitudes and behavior. Over the long run party identification has more influence over a person's vote decision than any other single factor, although in any one election this may not be true. Moreover, in general, party identifiers tend to vote more than those with no party loyalties at all; and those with strong identifications tend, in each party, to participate more in the election campaign than those with weak identifications.[8] As for their attitudes on

---

3. See Angus Campbell, Gerald Gurin, and Warren E. Miller, *The Voter Decides* (Evanston, Ill.: Row, Peterson, 1954), p. 93. The stability of these popular identifications is shown in *ibid.*, p. 94.

4. Charles E. Merriam, *The Making of Citizens* (Chicago: University of Chicago Press, 1931), p. 113.

5. Angus Campbell and Homer C. Cooper, *Group Differences in Attitudes and Votes, A Study of the 1954 Congressional Election* (Ann Arbor, Mich.: Survey Research Center, 1956), pp. 38-61.

6. Berelson and associates, *op. cit.*, p. 168.

7. Howard E. Freeman and Morris Showel, "Differential Political Influence of Voluntary Associations," *Public Opinion Quarterly, 15* (1951-52), pp. 703-14.

8. Although Campbell, Gurin, and Miller (*op. cit.*, pp. 107-108) do not find a close association between party identification and turnout, Campbell and Cooper (*op. cit.*, p. 41) show such an association, and Samuel Eldersveld finds "the less an individual is committed to one of the major parties and the more his political predisposition is uncrystallized, the less likelihood there is of his voting." ("The Independent Vote: Measurement, Characteristics, and Implications for Party Strategy," *American Political Science Review, 46* (1952), pp. 752-53.

policy matters, party identifiers "not only vote the party line; within limits they also think the party line,"[9] and they do this regardless of socio-economic status. In foreign policy, when the rival party leaders adopt positions similar to each other, party loyalty naturally doesn't affect a person's views on American policy; but when the party leaders take different stands, as in the firing of General MacArthur by President Truman in 1951 and in the party attitudes toward our Korean policy in the election of 1952, then party loyalty seems to have a very strong effect on public opinion regarding foreign policy.[10]

It isn't always the case that attitudes on policies, candidates, and parties are congruent, although the tendency of party loyalty to serve as a central organizing attitude encourages such congruence. When the most important of these attitudes are in harmony with each other, a person is much more likely to go to the polls and be otherwise active in a campaign.[11] Conflicts, on the other hand, as when the same person has an attachment to the Republican party and a "liberal" New Deal view of policy, tend to discourage participation.[12] When the party position on an issue is not known, or when there is none, the party obviously does not serve as a reference group in opinion formation. Furthermore, when the party leaders are found performing acts which are generally disapproved of, such as engaging in graft, but when these do not affect the satisfactions which flow from party membership, membership in the party does not influence behavior or belief; members behave in no way different from non-members.[13] Party identification, then, is broadly distributed in the population, important in many, although not all, political situations, but, unlike its European equivalent, unimportant as a general scheme or orientation in social life. Moreover, also unlike European situations, American political parties are more likely to serve as positive referents (I will go along with my party position), than negative referents (I will oppose the views of the "other" party).[14]

Whether this party spirit and party reference has gained or lost over the years is uncertain. Evidence covering the past fifteen or twenty years shows no trend in the number of persons who associate themselves with a party label or, alternatively, who call themselves independents,[15] although specific groups, like the farmers and the Negroes, have, in the 1950's, loosened their party ties. Election campaigns vary in their powers to evoke party loyalty. There are at least two principles at work here: (1) the influence of party identification upon electoral decisions is inversely proportionate

---

9. Campbell and Cooper, *op. cit.*, p. 93.

10. George Belknap and Angus Campbell, "Political Party Identification and Attitudes Toward Foreign Policy," *Public Opinion Quarterly, 15* (1951-52), pp. 601-23.

11. Campbell, Gurin, and Miller, *op. cit.*, p. 158.

12. Erwin L. Linn, "The Influence of Liberalism and Conservatism on Voting Behavior," *Public Opinion Quarterly, 13* (1949), pp. 299-309.

13. On the corruption issue see G. D. Wiebe, "Responses to the Televised Kefauver Hearings: Some Social Psychological Implications," *Public Opinion Quarterly, 16* (1952), pp. 179-200.

14. Freeman and Showel, *loc. cit.*

15. Eldersveld, *op. cit.*, p. 753.

to the "charisma" of the candidates;[16] (2) the influence of party identification upon electoral decisions is inversely proportionate to the salience of the issues in the elections. Thus party identification, although always important, is maximally operative in the least exciting, least colorful, and least significant campaigns.

The satisfactions to be derived from an appropriate use of political parties as reference groups include, among others, a sense of orientation in a confused situation, identification with the symbols of higher status, legitimization of aggression against other ethnic or class groups and a sense of solidarity with other people in a family, neighborhood, or factory. Much has been made of the last of these motives for joining parties. Fifty years ago, Ostrogorski wrote that a force "which impelled the American to herd together with his fellows in the party fold is one of the primordial facts of American social existence—the isolation of the individual."[17] And more recently this theme has been reinforced by those who believe that modern man "loves the party because it loves him; it provides him with the personal attention, friendliness, and affection he needs and does not receive in the competitive, rational, and impersonal world of business."[18] Yet this is hyperbolic; for less than 2 per cent of the population belong to political clubs, and fewer than 8 per cent of the Elmira population, for example, were contacted by party workers in 1948.[19] The search for social solidarity is expressed in politics in much less dramatic form, namely, in the adjustment of opinions and party preferences so as to avoid offense and to receive the rewards of social unity against an opposing group.

Love of party may be reinforced by the expectation of economic rewards such as tax relief or parity payments, but for most of the population the relation between personal gain and party action is obscure. It is true that the stronger the party attachment, the more likely a person is to think that he and his family will get along better financially if his party wins; but it is also true that the vast majority of the people think they would get along in the same way no matter which party won.[20] Economic support for love of party is clearly present among volunteers with government jobs or with spouses with government jobs at election time (about a third of the Elmira

16. For a comparison between the motives in the 1948 "party election" and the 1952 "personality election" see Angus Campbell, Gerald Gurin, and Warren E. Miller, "Political Issues and the Vote: November, 1952," *American Political Science Review, 48* (1953), pp. 359-85; also Philip Hastings, "The Independent Voter in 1952: A Study of Pittsfield, Massachusetts," *American Political Science Review, 47* (1953), pp. 805-10. On the volatility of the farm vote, see Leon D. Epstein, "Size of Place and the Division of the Two-Party Vote in Wisconsin," *Western Political Quarterly, 9* (1956), pp. 148-49.

17. M. Ostrogorski, *Democracy and the Party System in the United States* (New York: Macmillan, 1910), p. 409.

18. Sebastian de Grazia, *The Political Community* (Chicago: University of Chicago Press, 1948), p. 152. A somewhat similar theme may be found in Thomas North Whitehead, *Leadership in a Free Society* (Cambridge, Mass.; Harvard University Press, 1936), pp. 86, 228-31, 254-59.

19. Campbell, Gurin, and Miller, *The Voter Decides,* p. 29; Berelson and associates, *op. cit.,* p. 168.

party workers in 1948), and among the odd dollars workers, and the "bought" vote, although this latter exchange is said to be more often interpreted as a "token of esteem or gratitude" for a vote which would have been given in any case.[21] On the whole, the economic basis for party identification operates indirectly and tenuously, rather than directly through an appreciation of cash rewards of party support.

In summary, therefore, political parties are relevant reference groups for most people; this relevance may be characterized as follows:

The older a person is, the more salient are party references for him. The more socially (ethnically) secure a person is in his own stratum of society, the stronger are his party loyalties likely to be. The more education a person has, the weaker are his party loyalties. The less clear a person's class status, the weaker are his party loyalties.

Among various group references, political parties assume relatively low priorities; even on political issues other reference groups (such as business and union groups) are often more salient.

In the absence of important competing group references on political issues (and this is the most frequent case), political parties serve to organize political attitudes and behavior with the following exceptions: (a) when political leaders of the opposing parties agree, (b) when political parties fail to take clear stands or when these stands are unknown; and (c) when disagreement with party leaders is conventionally demanded but irrelevant to the personal satisfaction flowing from party identification (i.e., in cases of corruption).

The more congruent are a person's attitudes toward issues, candidates, and party preference, the more likely he is to vote, talk about politics, and electioneer.

Party identification is reinforced by adjustment needs, but fails substantially to ameliorate feelings of anomie or isolation. Party identification is only rarely reinforced by direct economic rewards or by anticipation of such rewards.

POLITICAL PARTIES ENLIST THE ELECTORATE

When we speak of organized effort by political parties to enlist the electorate in their causes we revert to discussing an organization of leaders, dropping temporarily the reference group meaning of the term. The purposeful activity of these leaders in mobilizing the electorate is directed toward two ends: (a) mobilizing as many of the voters as will vote for their ticket, and (b) retaining control of the organization. These purposes lead to a somewhat selective "enlistment of the electorate" both in terms of populations approached and in terms of activities encouraged.

Since a person must be legally qualified to vote, party officers seek to qualify those who they believe will vote their way by helping immigrants to become naturalized, persuading and assisting citizens to register, and mak-

---

20. Campbell and Cooper, op. cit., p. 88.
21. See Alfred de Grazia, "The Limits of External Leadership over a Minority Electorate," Public Opinion Quarterly, 20 (1956), pp. 122-123.

ing sure that the official registers include all of their partisans who can in any way be included.[22]

Having established the base group from which they must draw their voters, the party leaders must then mobilize them at election time, persuading them to go to the polls, and/or facilitating their movement there. Part of the job is done through the mass media in the course of the normal processes of campaigning. One of the chain of events arising from such campaigning, as Lazarsfeld and his associates have noted, may be characterized as follows: campaigning increases exposure; exposure then arouses latent predispositions composed of group or ideological referents; predispositions arouse partisan sentiments; and so the emotional basis is laid for participation.[23]

Although there have been some successful efforts to enlarge the turnout through mailing literature to citizens' homes,[24] the most effective way of getting the electorate to go to the polls is for an interested person to make a personal visit. In a small Detroit area study, personal visits by representatives of a "civic organization" more than doubled the turnout in an election.[25] Contact by a party worker has an effect both in maintaining a previous intention to vote and in inducing those to vote who had not intended to do so. In Elmira, however, the net change was small, leading the authors to conclude, "Party contact makes a difference, but the controlling variable was whether or not—far in advance of that party contact—the person himself wants to vote. The party organization only supplements the efforts of voters themselves. . . ."[26] Moreover, visits of this nature have virtually no effect on the direction of a person's vote, in some small part because party workers are themselves so little concerned with issues.

Instead of supplying that small extra margin of inducement needed in groups already imbued with a sense of civic duty, the party contact has a higher rate of effectiveness among those groups in the population least likely to vote: the least well educated, the younger citizens, those who belong to

---

22. See Sonya Forthal, *Cogwheels of Democracy, A Study of the Precinct Captain* (New York: William-Frederick Press, 1946); D. H. Kurtzman, *Methods of Controlling Votes in Philadelphia* (Philadelphia: University of Pennsylvania, Ph.D. dissertation, 1935 (publisher unknown)); William F. Whyte, *Street Corner Society* (Chicago: University of Chicago Press, 1943), pp. 192-252.

23. Paul F. Lazarsfeld, Bernhard Berelson, and Hazel Gaudet, *The People's Choice* (New York: Columbia University Press, 1948), pp. 75-76.

24. The "get out the vote" propaganda appeals sent out in Gosnell's experiment in Chicago in the 1920's were distinctly influential, but experiments in Detroit and Ann Arbor show virtually no influence for mailed propaganda. Clearly the nature of the propaganda is crucial. See Harold F. Gosnell, *Getting out the Vote* (Chicago: University of Chicago Press, 1927); Samuel J. Eldersveld and Richard W. Dodge, "Personal Contact or Mail Propaganda? An Experiment in Voting Turnout and Attitude Change," in Daniel Katz and associates, eds., *Public Opinion and Propaganda* (New York: Dryden, 1954), pp. 532-42; Samuel J. Eldersveld, "Experimental Propaganda Techniques and Voting Behavior," *American Political Science Review*, 50 (1956), pp. 154-65.

25. Eldersveld and Dodge, *op. cit., p.* 507.

26. Berelson and associates, *op. cit.,* p. 175.

fewer organizations and those less interested in the campaign.[27] In line with these findings, other studies show that personal contacts can induce people with a very low level of political information to vote.[28] Moreover, neither in cities nor in the country does it make much difference whether the proselytizing person is a professional or a volunteer.[29] Here we find, as in studies of factory workers, that the very fact that someone is interested in how you feel and what you do is important in altering the motives of people—as workers or voters.

Yet the scope of the effort is by no means proportional to the task. A survey by the American Institute of Public Opinion in 1954, showed that Democratic party workers called upon approximately 20 per cent of the electorate while Republican party workers called upon approximately 16 per cent. The proportion of households telephoned by representatives of each of the two parties was nearer in each case to 6 per cent.[30]

There are cogent reasons why the party effort to "get out the vote" is not more forceful. A recent gubernatorial election in Connecticut was conducted by the Democrats so as to minimize citizen interest, on the grounds that the party stood a better chance if the vote, at least in certain areas, was light. In Chicago in the 1924 and 1925 elections "Precinct captains of the most efficient type are not necessarily interested in getting out a full registration or a full vote." Persons of whose loyalties they were not certain were unlikely to be approached—and La Follette supporters, in 1924, were studiously avoided.[31] And often, in primaries, the contacts of party officers at the precinct or county level may be highly selective and of minimal scope. Sometimes, indeed, it better serves the interests of party officers to do nothing at all in such contests, waiting to see which candidate will be their party nominees before supporting anyone.

Because raising money is easier when effort is concentrated among people with higher income, party leaders have seldom attempted to enlist a large part of the electorate in this form of commitment. In 1954, although 15.8 million families stood ready to give $5.00 each to the party of their choice, only 2.7 million actually contributed, and only 4.9 million were asked to make a contribution.[32] Similarly, only about a quarter of those who claimed

27. *Ibid.*, p. 176. Eldersveld finds the same kind of relationship—except that personal contacts are more effective with men than women. "Experimental Propaganda Techniques," p. 162.

28. Eldersveld, "Experimental Propaganda Techniques," p. 163.

29. *Ibid.*, p. 161; Leon Weaver, "Some Soundings in the Party System: Rural Precinct Committeemen," *American Political Science Review*, 34 (1940), pp. 76-84.

30. AIPO release dated March 2, 1955. In Elmira, in a presidential campaign (1948), less than half as many people (8 per cent) were visited by party workers as were visited nationally. This suggests that the party organizations in Elmira were unusually weak.

31. Gosnell, *op. cit.*, pp. 74, 75.

32. AIPO release, March 3, 1955. It should be observed, however, that there is a substantial difference between stating a hypothetical willingness to give to a man who is not asking for the money and turning over the money to a man with his hand out.

to be willing to electioneer had been invited by the party leaders to do this kind of work.[33] As for really embracing a substantial part of the electorate in the party organization, the party leaders in general are reluctant to do this—at least this is true of the grass roots party leaders. Nor is this exclusiveness hard to maintain, since most people have shown no active desire to become intimately involved in the party processes of their communities.

Whether one regards this restricted participation as damaging to the democratic process or not depends to some extent on whether or not one believes, along with Schattschneider, that the central feature of democracy lies in choosing *between* competing candidates rather than in participating in the selection of one of the rival candidates.[34] Since it is probably true that exclusiveness by party leaders is inversely proportionate to their ethnic, social-class, or ideological congruence with their constituencies, there are certainly grounds for challenging this view. At least one might maintain the position that a constant pressure to enlarge the group admitted to party councils is a healthy force, even if (or because?) only partially successful.

Bryce believed that in American political life the proportions between those who made politics the main concern of their life (Inner Circle) and those who did not (Outer Circle) was "a sort of ozonometer by which the purity and healthiness of the political atmosphere may be tested."[35] A high proportion of professionals indicated corruption, a high proportion of amateurs indicated policies more likely to be in the public interest. Although an American scholar investigating rural politics in Illinois states "the wish-thought of some students who dream of 'local parties dedicated to the ideal of voluntary precinct work' . . . may not be as fantastic as might appear at first blush,"[36] political *control* is usually retained by Bryce's disliked professionals.

Yet someone must do the organizing work of the parties and if this is left to amateurs it may not get done, participation may fall off, the elections may be less meaningful. If only those who can afford to do this on a part-time basis engage in this work, a selective class factor has been introduced which distorts the party mechanisms in favor of the more prosperous citizens. Who will organize the lower classes if the professional boss who gets his cut from "honest graft" leaves the field? He may not serve disinterestedly, his motives may be "bad," but he mobilizes a stratum of society which might otherwise remain totally apathetic. The result of amateur politics in this area may be the turning over of the political loyalties of the lower income voters to the unions and, as in England, the more rigid economic stratification of political parties. On the other hand, perhaps "the influence which counter-works that of professionals is the influence of public opinion"[37] rather than the political

33. AIPO release, February 27, 1955.
34. "Democracy is not to be found *in* the parties but between the parties," E. E. Schattschneider, *op. cit.*, p. 60.
35. James Bryce, *The American Commonwealth* rev. ed. (New York: Macmillan, 1910), p. 64.
36. Weaver, *op. cit.*, p. 83.
37. Bryce, *op. cit.*, p. 68.

amateur, an influence which Bryce regards as a stronger force here than abroad. The experience of the last fifty years, and the changing nature of the professional politician (sometimes called "the decline of the boss"), have generally borne out this view of American political leaders as especially sensitive to public opinion.

Party organizations enlist the interest and support of the electorate according to the following principles.

Party leaders seek to (a) mobilize as many voters as will vote for their candidates, and (b) retain control of the party organization. The extent of party effort to get out the vote is a function of the interaction of these sometimes conflicting principles.

The effort of party leaders to increase turnout among "their" voters is channeled through three processes: (1) impersonal campaigning, chiefly through the media, a social process which increases exposure and evokes partisan sentiments, and so lays the emotional basis for voter action, (2) impersonal but direct mailings (and distributions) of literature, a process with only moderate effect on turnout, and (3) direct personal contact by a party worker. The effect on turnout of personal contact is (a) greater than the effect of impersonal contact, (b) much less important than precontest predisposition, and (c) more effective among those least likely to vote.

The effect of party contacts on electoral turnout is minimized by the small proportion of people contacted (in national elections)—a proportion accountable by (a) the small effect achieved by such contact, (b) poor party organization and failure to enlist those ready to electioneer for the party, (c) occasional restrictionist tendencies of party leaders, and (d) low issue orientation among party workers.

The effort of party leaders to enlist the electorate in caucusing and policy making at the grass roots level is proportionate to the restrictionist tendencies of the party leaders, which, in turn, may be related to their misrepresentativeness in ethnic, social class, or ideological terms and to the strength of their position in the party organization.

Although a higher ratio of amateurs to professionals in political life tends to make for "cleaner" politics and enhances middle-class values, reducing the influence of the ward politician reduces a meaningful political contact for lower-status groups, weakens their tie with politics outside of class-bound institutions, and increases the probable political role of unions.

A public opinion increasingly hostile to the "corrupt" behavioral norms of professional politicians imposes limits on these norms similar to those imposed by amateurs in politics.

THE NATURE OF THE ELECTION

Although elections differ in their formal aspects (non-partisan and partisan, primaries, and so forth) they also differ in their style and content, particularly in the image of the candidates which gets across to the electorate. The history of elections in America reveals that the elections featuring the most colorful candidates, those with charismatic qualities, consistently attracted the most voters to the polls, suggesting that the most important single factor in affecting turnout is the color and appeal of the candidates.[38] In 1952, President Eisenhower seemed to have these qualities, and it was indeed true that, unlike the situation in 1948, a number of voters whose beliefs were close to the Democratic voters' beliefs on campaign topics, repressed or ignored this fact and voted for "Ike."[39] Although by the more rigorous definitions of charisma, less than 1 per cent of the electorate saw Eisenhower in a manner which could be described as charismatic[40] his capacity to attract the support of people who called themselves Democrats and disbelieved in the policies of the Republican party was a measure of his considerable drawing power. The nature of candidate imagery conveyed to the electorate is a central factor in accounting for differences in turnout.

Closeness of Contest. Certainly the common-sense view of the causes of high or low participation in an election would hold that a close election, where the issue was in doubt, would bring more people to the polls than one in which the result was determined from the beginning. People invest their energy and interest in matters where they feel they can affect the result. Furthermore, the excitement of a close contest, even for those who do not care greatly about the result, is a stimulant. And, of course, it is harder to find good candidates for a party sure to lose; just as it is harder to raise money (and so to campaign effectively) for such a party. As for the institutional effort and the campaign the party is capable of putting on, only in two-party areas, characterized by frequent doubt regarding the winner, will substantial party efforts be forthcoming on both sides. There is both European and American testimony to support this view.[41]

But in the United States, when we eliminate regional factors by dropping the South (as a region with a special sub-culture) and examine counties instead of states, the relationship between turnout and closeness of vote disappears, as shown in Table 20.1. Moreover, in Britain, there is only the slightest connection between these two factors.[42] One reason for this lack of relationship is that the population characteristics of counties with habitually close elections often differ substantially from counties with habitually one-

---

38. See above, pp. 24-25.

39. Campbell, Gurin, and Miller, "Political Issues and the Vote," *op. cit.*

40. See James C. Davies, "Charisma in the 1952 Campaign," *American Political Science Review*, 48 (1954), pp. 1083-1102. Incidentally Davies finds that of the thirty-one persons with charismatic responses to candidates thirty were for Eisenhower.

41. Herbert Tingsten says, "On the whole popular participation stands in direct relation to the narrowness of the absolute or relative majority." *Political Behavior, Studies in Election Statistics* (London: P. S. King, 1937), p. 216. Harold Gosnell provides evidence that this relationship has recently prevailed in England (1924), France (1914), and other countries; see his *Why Europe Votes* (Chicago: University of Chicago Press, 1930), pp. 14, 50 *ff*. On the basis of a study of turnout in the forty-eight states in 1920 and 1924 Gosnell concludes about elections in the United States, "as the proportion of the vote received by the winning party in a given state approaches one-half, the greater is the per cent of the eligible vote cast in that state," *ibid.*, p. 199.

42. See H. G. Nicholas, *The British General Election of 1951* (London: Macmillan, 1951), p. 318.

TABLE 20.1.—Per cent Non-Voters in Random Selection of Non-Southern Counties, by Closeness of Election (1952).

Democratic per cent of two-party vote by county	Per cent non-voters in classified counties
20%—30% (Most Republican)	13%
31%—40%	18
41 —50	18
51 —60	17

SOURCE: Computed from data in Warren E. Miller, "One-Party Politics and the Voter," "American Political Science Review, 50" (1956), p. 711.

sided elections.[43] Second, there may be a tendency for one-party areas to develop around a given socio-economic or ethnic difference (the German counties of Texas, the cut-over regions of Michigan, the concentration of Irish in Boston, etc.), and hence to develop both the concentration and enclave mentalities described above.[44] If this were true, this would lead to higher levels of political interest counteracting the lack of intra-area competition. But third, the presumption that people vote predominantly because they seek some policy change which might be affected by an electoral decision again needs examination. Those who participate from sentiments of citizen duty are unaffected by the closeness of the election. Seven out of eight persons in a national sample disagreed with the statement, "It isn't so important to vote when you know your party doesn't have any chance to win."[45] One can satisfy his conscience as easily by a non-significant vote as by a significant vote. Furthermore, those who vote to show their solidarity with the dominant group can do so equally well in ritualistic elections; those who need to express their feelings of dependence or admiration for a strong figure can employ one-sided elections as well as close contests for their purposes; those who must register their protest against the dominant group can find satisfaction in voting in one-sided elections—perhaps even greater satisfaction because of the certainty that they need have no concern lest their party win. Many of the motives which politicize a person are, in fact, independent of the outcome of an election, and therefore independent of whether the outcome is ever in doubt.

43. See Samuel P. Huntington, "A Revised Theory of American Party Politics," *American Political Science Review*, 44 (1950), pp. 675-7.

44. See pp. 262-63. This seems to be true of the mining districts of England. Nicholas observes, "It is remarkable that the very highest median turnout is found in the 48 seats where the Labour majority was more than 40% of the poll (i.e. 70% of the vote). Of these 48, 33 are essentially mining seats; perhaps in them there is a unique sense of working-class solidarity which has to be demonstrated at the polls." H. G. Nicholas, *loc. cit.*

45. From unpublished data gathered by the Survey Research Center in their 1952 election study.

Since political acts are so heavily influenced by group interaction in a community, what is it that both sustains minority views and leads members of the minority party to express such views? In an ingenious investigation of this problem, Warren Miller has found that it is the party identification which probably sustains a member of the minority party in his minority vote decision, rather than his ideas on issues or his candidate preferences.[46] This means that anything which weakens the political parties (such as a non-partisan movement) may have disastrous effects on the minority parties in predominently one-party areas. One of these effects would be that their membership might simply lose interest in politics and public affairs.

These considerations modify the view that the unit-vote system in the electoral college (whereby all the state's electoral votes go to the majority candidate) "discourages voting in those states where one party has a clear ascendency, as that party is sure of securing all the electoral votes for that state."[47] Although there is some merit to this position we must also account for the lower turnout in the southern one-party states in terms of the weak non-policy motives discussed above.

Reviewing these data and interpretations, we may set forth the following hypotheses:

Although closeness of contest tends to enlist certain politicizing motives and, where habitual, to create stronger parties, the relationship between closeness of contest and turnout in the United States and Britain is small.

Among the factors preventing a stronger relationship are: (a) demographic differences between one party and two-party areas, (b) the colonization and enclave effects in many one-party areas, (c) the capacity of political participation to satisfy many needs which are independent of the outcome of an election, (d) the strong force of party-identification among the members of the subordinate party, (e) the generalization effect whereby habits and motives established in close elections are carried over to non-class elections.

Non-partisan Elections. Some fifty years ago Ostrogorski, speaking for a substantial body of opinion, held that parties had captured political responsibility away from the people, where it rightfully belonged, and turned politics to party rather than public ends. In particular, it was argued that the national focus [sic] of parties "made the electors lose their interest in local public life," and hence it would be better to do away with parties entirely at this level.[48]

In line with this philosophy, reformers sought, in the wake of the agrarian movements, "to give politics back to the people" by establishing non-partisan

---

46. Warren E. Miller, "One-Party Politics and the Voter," *American Political Science Review*, 50 (1956), pp. 707-25. This article employs closeness to a 50/50 ratio in a single election as a test for "one-partyness." When this is expanded to include the problems of duration of one-party dominance and the distribution of the vote over the electoral district, the conclusions may be somewhat modified.

47. Gosnell, *Why Europe Votes, op cit.,* p. 199.

48. Ostrogorski, *op. cit.,* p. 379. Even today in England one explanation of local political apathy is "that the growth of political parties has stifled genuine debate." See an analysis of this position in Douglas V. Verney, "The Great City," *Town Planning Review*, 26 (1955), p. 177.

elections. In Minnesota and Nebraska substantial success toward this objective was achieved, and since 1913 Minnesota has not only removed party labels from county and municipal ballots, but has also extended the principle to elections for state legislators. Some of the political results of this arrangement are:[49]

1. Non-partisanship serves to weaken the political parties in those areas where it is in effect.

2. Facilities for fund raising by candidates for non-partisan offices are restricted by non-partisanship.

3. Non-partisanship tends to frustrate protest voting.

4. Non-partisanship encourages the avoidance of issues of policy in campaigns.

Whether or not these effects are the costs necessary to achieve other gains, they do not represent a contribution toward enlarging the role of the electorate in public affairs. Perhaps, moreover, nonparticipant habits developed in non-partisan elections tend to be extended to other areas where the party label is permitted. Or, on the other hand, perhaps there is a kind of homeostatic principle at work here such that parties weakened in one area find compensation in another. One could test this hypothesis, in a highly tentative fashion, by comparing the electoral turnout in congressional elections in Minnesota, where non-partisanship has been carried further than any other state, with the electoral turnout in neighboring states. The evidence in Table 20.2 suggests that there is no process of generalization at work such that the effects of non-partisanship on participation in local elections are carried over to national or other partisan elections. Political parties have adapted to the situation and are able to get out the vote in national elections without difficulty.

TABLE 20.2.—Per cent Total Congressional Vote of Total Population in Three States 1946, 1950*

State	1946	1950
Minnesota	30	41
Wisconsin	26	56
Michigan	25	28

* There was a gubernatorial election in each state in each of these two years.

SOURCE: George Gallup and associates, "The Political Almanac" (New York: Forbes, 1952).

In summary, then, one might state:

Non-partisan elections tend to weaken electoral participation (in several forms) but this weakening effect does not extend to partisan elections in areas where non-partisanship is otherwise practiced.

49. These are taken from Charles R. Adrian, "Some General Characteristics of Nonpartisan Elections," *American Political Science Review, 46* (1952), pp. 766-76.

Primaries. Political primaries originated in Crawford County, Pennsylvania in 1842 in an effort to enlarge the opportunities for political expression by the rank and file members of the Democratic party in that county, as well as to reduce "intrigue and corruption" thought to be fostered by the convention system.[50] Today, as a consequence of dissatisfaction with "machine politics" and the persistent view that the electorate can shoulder an indefinite burden of political responsibility, every state has some form of primary, although in a few states, such as Connecticut, it has very limited applicability.

In this effort to enlarge citizenship participation the primary device has partially failed. The general participation in primaries is low.[51] In gubernatorial primaries in fifteen non-Southern states, for the period 1926-1952, "In three out of four primaries not more than 35 per cent of the potential electorate voted in the primaries of one or the other of the major parties. That is, the total Democratic primary vote plus the total Republican primary vote did not exceed 35 per cent of the number of citizens 21 and over."[52] This was, of course, much lower than the participation in the general gubernatorial elections.

The turnout in primaries is larger in those states where the turnout in general elections is larger; over time it follows the same pattern of rising and declining interest exhibited by national electoral patterns; and turnout especially tends to increase when strong factional interests are engaged in an intra-party conflict, as when the Mine Workers fought the regular Democratic organization in Pennsylvania in 1938. On the other hand, contrary to many beliefs, it is not true that the total participation in primaries is higher in relatively sure one-party states than in competitive states. Although in "sure" states a higher proportion of the members of the dominant party vote than of the subordinate, the electorate in the competitive states make up for this by turning out for the primaries of both parties.[53]

In almost all states, persons who live in districts where their party is especially strong tend to turn out for primaries more than those where it is in a weak or competitive position. This distribution means that areas of relative strength in a party preserve their strength, which may be functional for the majority party, but often tends to be disastrous for the minority party, where certain controlling ethnic or sectional or ideological groups are never forced, in the primaries, to broaden their appeal. Thus the primary system may, through differential participation, often preserve the dominant-subordinate party relationships in many states.[54]

As for the effect of primaries on turnout in the elections following the primaries, two forces seem prevalent. On the one hand, the primaries increase voter familiarity with issues and candidates, increase exposure to political

---

50. See James. H. Booser, "Origin of the Direct Primary," *National Municipal Review*, 24 (1935), pp. 222-23.
51. V. O. Key, Jr., *American State Politics: An Introduction* (New York: Knopf, 1956), pp. 133-68.
52. *Ibid., p.* 134.
53. *Ibid.,* pp. 136-139.
54. *Ibid.,* pp. 145-63.

propaganda, and generally politicize the electorate. The public controversy of Stevenson and Kefauver in the presidential primaries of 1956 seem to have had that result. A local "boss" of Connecticut has stated privately that under certain circumstances he positively encourages local intra-party contests for that reason. On the other hand, there is some evidence to show that, if the fight is a heated one, there is a tendency for persons whose candidates were defeated in the primary to reflect their displeasure by failing to vote in the subsequent election (or run-off primary, where that is the election). A brief glance at the record of one state, Mississippi, suggests that this principle of disaffection and defection is of very limited applicability. For the period 1919 through 1943, out of the seven Mississippi gubernatorial primary + run-off sequences, in only three was there a decline greater than 1 per cent in the rate of turnout in the second electoral contest, and in only one (1945) was the decline as great as 6 per cent.[55]

The primary system of nominations represents a supreme effort to enlarge the responsibilities of the electorate, yet by weakening party organizations, primaries may generally undermine the very institutions which, both as institutions and as "symbols in men's minds," must be counted upon to enlist the average man in the political causes of the times. The biased "sample" in the primary turnout may tend to perpetuate a misrepresentative selection of candidates with minimal appeal to marginal voters. Selection of minority party candidates through primaries has tended to produce candidates less distinguished than those produced by a convention system, partly because a convention can offer a candidacy to a person in such a way as to make it hard for him to refuse.[56] Thus the intentions of the sponsors of the primary system and the results may be quite divergent.

In the primaries of the majority party in one-party areas, that is, in the effective elections in these areas, party loyalty fails to be a significant motive for voting or electioneering. Attachments, at least in the South, are instead to "friends and neighbors," to cliques and factions which are generally more ephemeral.[57] Nor are the facilitative effects of party organizations present in primaries. In most such elections, the party machinery is less generally available to get out the vote, partly because of the official neutrality of the party officers. The absence of party organization, in both psychological and institutional respects, is a major factor in lower Southern participation.

One may hypothesize, then, the following tentative conclusions:

Primary elections tend to enlist larger numbers of participants when (1) the primaries are held in competitive two-party states; although the usually dominant

55. Based on data in Alexander Heard and Donald S. Strong, *Southern Primaries and Elections 1926-1949* (University of Alabama: University of Alabama Press, 1950), pp. 79-83.

56. See V. O. Key, "The Direct Primary and Party Structure," *American Political Science Review*, 48 (1954), pp. 1-26.

57. See V. O. Key, Jr., *Southern Politics* (New York: Knopf, 1949), pp. 298-511. However there are indications that, in some instances, the conflict of personal factions may conceal basic and enduring differences on policy. See Allan P. Sindler, "Bifactional Rivalry as an Alternative to Two-Party Competition in Louisiana," *American Political Science Review*, 49 (1955), pp. 641-662.

party has a bigger turnout than the subordinate party wherever the primary is held. (2) The primary contest reflects a contest between sociologically cohesive and organized groups (rather than merely friends and neighbors). (3) The primary is held (a) in an area with generally high interest in elections, and/or (b) at at time when the nation is experiencing some major politicizing influence.

In any electoral district those who live in the more "solid" partisan areas tend to turn out for "their" primary more than those who live in competitive areas or in areas where their party is subordinate.

Selection of candidates through a primary system, as contrasted to a convention system, may tend to weaken party organization, particularly the organization of the minority party, and, under certain circumstances, to make more difficult broader appeals to independent groups.

Primaries may enlarge the size of the electorate in a subsequent inter-party election in a two-party district or state by making the candidates and issues more salient to the electorate; but primaries may reduce the size of the electorate in subsequent elections by alienating those whose candidates were defeated in the primary.

Primaries are less effective than inter-party elections in inducing turnout because: (1) They do not have the benefit of motives based on party identification, and effective factional substitute is seldom possible because of the shifting nature of the factions. (2) The party machinery is less available to facilitate getting out the vote or mobilizing other forms of participation. (3) Assigning responsibility to a controlling group based on a continuing group identification is rendered difficult.

A Note on Proportional Representation. On balance, neither a system of proportional representation nor a plurality (or majority) system, such as is more usual in America, has the advantage in calling forth electoral enthusiasm or activity, although the two systems represent different ways of evoking such enthusiasm. P. R. holds out a guarantee that each person's vote will be effective; it stimulates factional loyalties (of which the most important is ethnic solidarity). On the other hand, it weakens the political parties (under the Hare system) and often leads to coalition governments where political responsibility is lost from view. (The alternative P. R. system, the list system which is rarely used in America, may strengthen parties, but then tends to lose the candidates in a party list.) As a consequence of these mixed effects, we find that in New York, where (Hare system) P. R. was tried for ten years, the system made little difference in the rate of turnout, and its record of voter enlistment in Europe is inconsistent and varied.[58]

Therefore:

Neither proportional representation nor plurality (or majority) electoral systems have a consistent advantage in enlisting the electorate in a democracy.

---

58. See Belle Zeller and Hugh A. Bone, "The Repeal of P.R. in New York City —Ten Years in Retrospect," *American Political Science Review,* 42 (1948), pp. 1127-48; Tingsten, *op. cit.,* pp. 223-25. Merriam (*op. cit.,* p. 107) argues that multi-party systems may be more "'provocative of civic interest" in the way they conduct election campaigns, but that they dissipate civic interest in the obscurities of coalition governments.

ELECTION ADMINISTRATION

In order to vote in an election, all states require that every elector must have resided in the state and in a given locality within the state for a given period of time. The reason for this is clear enough—but the net result is that a considerable portion of the population is disfranchised, often only because they have moved across on urban boundary from city to suburb without in any way lessening their comprehension of the issues in the state, certainly, and probably in the locality, too. In Chicago in 1924, 5.2 per cent of the non-voting was attributed to frustration because of legal residence requirements,[59] while a national study in 1952 found that about 12 per cent of the non-voters reported that they were disfranchised because of their failure to meet residence requirements.[60] These findings suggest that the increased mobility of the population from the 1920's to the 1950's has reduced the proportion of the population legally eligible to vote.

Other limitations on the franchise include: citizenship requirements, once a quantitatively more important obstacle than it is today; a minimum age requirement, twenty-one in every state except Georgia and Kentucky where the minimum age is now eighteen; the capacity to pass a literacy test in sixteen states, and the poll tax, to be discussed later. Furthermore, a person may be disqualified from voting if he becomes a pauper (in twelve states), or is convicted of certain crimes, or is adjudged mentally unsound.[61] If the state requires one to go in person to a specified place either at City Hall or in the neighborhood and register some time before every election, one further impediment to voting has been put in the way of the potential voter. Permanent registration, where the responsibility for keeping a proper roll is placed on city officials rather than primarily on the voters themselves, has been found to be helpful in enlarging participation; one set of data shows an average difference of turnout between cities with these different registration schemes of 9 per cent.[62] The hours of the opening and closing of the polls; the placing of the polls for greatest convenience, ensuring sufficient polling places or voting machines so that there is a minimum of waiting; proper provision for absentee voting and other matters of this sort, also affect the turnout. Merriam and Gosnell found that .8 per cent of the reasons for non-voting referred to congestion at the polls and another .8 per cent dealt with inconvenient location of the polling place.[63] It is possible that holding elections on Sunday, as in France, would have more effect on turnout than any other reform.

By sanctioning the fiction that the primary is a private non-governmental

---

59. Charles E. Merriam and Harold F. Gosnell, *Non-Voting* (Chicago: University of Chicago Press, 1924), p. 34.

60. Campbell, Gurin, and Miller, *The Voter Decides*, p. 37.

61. Bertram Bernard, *Election Laws of the Forty-Eight States* (New York: Oceana Publications, 1950), pp. 9-16.

62. Computed from National Municipal League data reported in Hugh Bone, *American Politics and the Party System*, 2nd ed. (New York: McGraw Hill, 1955), p. 518.

63. C. E. Merriam and H. F. Gosnell, *op. cit.*, p. 34

process and therefore not subject to the restrictions of the powers of the state to limit the franchise provided in the Fifteenth Amendment, the Court permitted the dominant white community to limit the Negro vote.[64] But in Smith v. Allwright (321 U.S. 649, 1944), the Supreme Court said:

> The United States is a constitutional democracy. Its organic law grants to all citizens a right to participate in the choice of elected officials without restriction by any State because of race. This grant to the people of the opportunity for choice is not to be nullified by a State through casting its electoral process in a form which permits a private organization to practice racial discrimination in the election. Constitutional rights would be of little value if they could be thus indirectly denied.

And primaries were declared to be public elections where discrimination is illegal. Now, although Negroes in the South are beginning to vote in somewhat larger numbers,[65] particularly in border states and in the big southern cities, the social pressures which produced the white primary are still at work and other legal, non-legal, and illegal devices for discouraging Negro voting have been expanded. Among these are the requirements that voters must understand the constitution, which opens the door to administrative discretion in interpreting whether an answer on, say, the double jeopardy clause reveals sufficient "understanding." Related to such provisions are the requirements dealing with literacy and certificates of education, which, although they often serve the purpose of preventing illiterate voters from being used as the tools of political interest, also lend themselves to discretionary abuse. Some of the other informal ways of preventing Negroes (and others) from voting are:[66]

1. Requiring Negro applicants to produce one or more white character witnesses.

2. Demanding severe property qualifications.

3. Putting "unreasonable" questions to Negro applicants on literacy tests.

4. Rejecting Negro applicants on technical mistakes in filling out registration blanks.

5. Making Negro applicants wait long hours in line.

6. Making Negro applicants fill out their own blanks while white applicants receive help from officials.

7. Informing Negro applicants that cards have run out, closing time has been reached, or that notification of application filing will be given at a future date.

8. Threatening by hangers on.

---

64. *Grovey v. Townsend*, 295 U.S. 45 (1933).

65. See recent copies of *The Negro Handbook;* Donald S. Strong, "The Rise of Negro Voting in Texas," *American Political Science Review, 42* (1948), pp. 510-22; O. Douglas Weeks, "The White Primary: 1944-1948," *American Political Science Review, 42* (1948), 500-509; Hugh D. Price, "The Negro and Florida Politics, 1944-1954," *Journal of Politics, 17* (1955), pp. 198-220; John H. Fenton and Kenneth N. Vines, "Negro Registration in Louisiana," *American Political Science Review, 51* (1957), pp. 704-13.

66. Report of the Committee on Registration and Voting in the Alabama Unit of the National Association of Colored People, *New York Times,* May 10, 1953.

Finally, of course, there is the question of the poll tax. Although a number of states have recently yielded to growing pressure to abolish the poll tax, four states still retain it: Mississippi, South Carolina, Virginia and Alkansas. The record shows clearly enough that when a state repeals its poll taxes the rate of participation in elections increases, but as V. O. Key points out, it is possible that the same forces which made for the repeal also made for greater participation. On the whole, it appears to Key that the effect of the poll tax is only moderately restrictive although still important. He says:[67]

The chances are that, if other things remain equal (and they rarely do), elimination of the poll tax alone would increase voting in most southern states by no more than from 5 to 10 per cent of the potential number of white voters. The evidence suggests, however, that the disfranchising effect of the tax is greater at the trough of the business cycle and that taxes cumulative over long periods of time—as the Alabama tax [repealed in 1954—R.E.L.] and the now repealed Georgia tax—have more severe effects than does a noncumulative tax.

As for disfranchising the Negro, the other more selective devices created for this purpose may continue in the absence of the poll tax. In review, therefore:

Certain kinds of legal and administrative impediments to registering and voting may be seen to have discouraged political participation at the polls. Whether such discouragement tends to be associated with generally lower political activity, or with a substitute political activity not dependent on voting, depends upon particular circumstances, but for most of the population, discouragement and apathy is the usual response. The impediments to the exercise of the franchise, at least, may be listed as follows: (1) Requirements dealing with: residence, citizenship, age, literacy, payment of poll tax. (2) Legal deprivation of the franchise to paupers, those convicted of committing a crime, and to those judged insane. (3) Extra-legal restrictions through (a) declaring primaries to be private non-governmental processes (now illegal), and (b) administrative discrimination in elections against persons of a disliked group. (4) Requiring periodic registration, as contrasted to permanent registration.

PARTICIPATION IN THE AMERICAN SYSTEM
OF GOVERNMENT

The Constitution, and the American system of government generally, serve, in certain respects, to discourage the electorate from voting. This is not by accident; it is by design of the framers who feared factions and uninhibited majority rule.[68] In arranging for a federal system, staggered elections, a bicameral system, a President independent of Congress, and (so they thought) an indirect presidential election, the members of the Constitutional Convention of 1787 were, in effect, depriving the electorate of the opportunity to cast a single ballot with concentrated significance. The significance is dis-

---

67. V. O. Key, *Southern Politics*, p. 617.
68. See *The Federalist*, especially Numbers 9, 10, 17, 45-51, 68.

sipated over several offices and over several elections; the stakes of any one election are thereby reduced.

Yet in arranging for the election of a single chief executive—America's major, though disputed, contribution to political practice—another set of forces was put in motion. In national, state, and local elections, electoral interest in the executive office is almost always greater than in the legislative offices. For example, in 1950, in twenty of the twenty-one states where there were simultaneous gubernatorial and senatorial elections, the vote for governor was larger than the vote for Senator (Vermont alone was the exception to this rule).[69] And the discrepancy is even greater when the elections for Governor and for Senator are held in different years.[70] The causes for this electoral focus lie in the command over publicity available to an executive but not usually available to a legislator, the greater influence he, as a single individual, appears to have in contrast to a member of a deliberative group, his control over matters of administrative policy, including appointment, not equalled by any single legislator and probably not even by the body as a whole, and other functions and roles available to his office. In addition, and perhaps as important as any of these more objective factors, there is the influence of sentiments aroused by a single paternal figure in whose custody each citizen is placed, sentiments which are an echo of the childish emotions residual in all men.[71]

The Constitution distributes the powers of government among the national government, the state governments, and the people, erecting a federal system. The special circumstances of creating a single nation out of many separate colonies, account in large part for this arrangement, but the rationale associated with it include a belief that people take a greater interest in, and are more competent to control the exercise of power closer to home. The decentralization involved in a federal arrangement places the functions of government, in some sense, nearer to the people, although not so near as the local community or municipality.

Although the data on electoral turnout in various kinds of elections have long indicated that, contrary to this theory, people are more interested in national than in local affairs, survey evidence now confirms this and indicates that of all levels of government, the state level is least interesting to the voter.[72] Thus a curious dissonance between investiture of power and public

---

69. From data in George Gallup and staff, *The Political Almanac, 1952* (New York: Forbes, 1952), p. 16. Charles Titus finds this relationship to be quite general. See his *Voting Behavior in the United States* (Berkeley: University of California Press, 1935), p. 50.

70. In Kentucky, for example, in the three elections from 1942 to 1951, gubernatorial turnout exceeded senatorial turnout the preceding year by: 2 per cent, 16 per cent, and 30 per cent.

71. See, for example, Filmore H. Sanford, "Public Orientation to Roosevelt," *Public Opinion Quarterly, 15* (1951), pp. 189-216.

72. See George Belknap and Ralph Smuckler, "Political Power Relations in a Mid-West City," *Public Opinion Quarterly, 20* (1956), p. 80. These differences are, as might be expected, least in the South and greatest in New England, where state elections are of minimal concern to most people. See Alfred de Grazia, *The Western Public, 1952 and Beyond* (Stanford: Stanford University Press, 1954), p. 172.

interest is established and one of the rationales for the American federal system—the grass roots argument which Bryce mentions in his commentary —is undermined.[73]

The reasons for greater interest in national than in state or local matters are not far to seek, although some erroneous notions have had some currency. It is not, as has been said, that political parties have focused attention on national as contrasted to local affairs. Nor is it that there is a lower level of integrity in local, as contrasted to national, government—this might better serve as a stimulus for action. Nor is it the lack of available leadership, although, of course, more able people generally seek national as contrasted to local posts. The reasons lie elsewhere. The local functions of government are more often managerial and custodial while the national functions are policy-making in a broad sense.[74] More important is the fact that the community which is invested with most emotion in this century is the national community (patriotism)—the stage of history features national events and leaders. Also, the magazines and network broadcasts are national in scope, hence they devote attention to national events, persons, and issues depriving state and local leaders of the "build up" which is necessary for full popular stature in a mass society. Finally, of course, there is no state or local equivalent for foreign affairs, war, and diplomacy—all of which represent an important focus of attention.

The multiplicity of levels and the election of executives as well as legislators have tended to multiply the burdens of the electorate, but beyond that there has been a tendency to have short terms of office and to elect a variety of public officials: judges, minor administrators, sheriffs, school officials, board members of quasi-independent commissions. In short, the doctrine of frequent elections to ensure "responsibility to the people" and the practice of the long ballot have so overburdened the electorate that it has wilted in the face of the imposing task. Although, over a four-year period, there are probably more votes per capita cast in the United States than in any other country (suggesting one sense in which it may be said that Americans participate more than others in elections and electioneering), the demands upon the electorate have reduced the political interests of the marginally concerned and dissipated the activity of the others. As a partial consequence, in neither national nor local elections do as large a percentage of Americans vote as vote in other countries.

This diffusion of responsibility in the national system, and the decentralization of political power throughout the federal system, has contributed to the weakening of political parties in the United States. This has had the effect of opening the way for the growth of interest groups, a development which provides an alternative vehicle for political participation by the public. In associating himself with these groups a person can learn about public issues, elect significant officials who represent his interests in the state and national

73. Bryce, *op. cit.*, pp. 350-54.
74. Verney (*op. cit.*) discusses these arguments in an analysis of the lack of interest in local political affairs in England where, without the federal problem, the same focus upon national affairs prevails.

capitals, contribute money, and petition the officials of government. Thus it may be argued that the American citizen's political life is not so impoverished as the electoral indices suggest; it has only undergone a change of venue.

This argument has some merit, but it suffers from the same defects which affect all reliance upon interest groups for policy formation. Many interests cannot be organized; the wealthy and the cohesive groups have too much influence among the interest groups (they have a plural ballot here as in the market place); the interest groups are no less oligarchical than the parties; and interest groups tend to fractionate a person so that he cannot, through these narrower vehicles, find representation as a whole man.

Looking, then, at the relation of these more general problems of government to popular interest and activity in a democracy we may say:

The provisions of the Constitution intended to impede direct and immediate majority rule, lessen the significance of each election, and thereby dissipate the interest of the electorate in electoral choices.

Provisions for the election of chief executives at each level of government increase popular participation in democratic processes.

The assignment of power and responsibilities to the states in the American federal system has the effect of vesting functions in the governmental units which are least interesting to the electorate, thereby creating disharmony between the location of power and the focus of popular attention.

Among the significant reasons for superior popular interest in national, as contrasted to both state and local, affairs are: (1) Local affairs are more "managerial" in character while national affairs deal with more controversial policy problems. (2) The community to which most popular emotion is attached is the national community. (3) The national circulation of much of the media leads them to focus attention on national leaders and events. (4) The drama of war, diplomacy, and foreign affairs (invested with strong feelings of in-group versus out-group) is national in character.

The greater the burden placed upon an electorate by frequent elections of many officials, the lower will be the rate of electoral participation in elections for the more important political offices.

CHAPTER 21

How Economic Life Affects Political Life

INDUSTRY AND POLITICS

"WITH THE DEVELOPMENT of industry," said Marx and Engels, "the proletariat not only increases in numbers; it becomes concentrated in greater masses, its strength grows, and it feels its strength more." Moreover, "this organization of the proletarians into a class, and consequently into a political party . . . compels legislative recognition of particular interests of workers."[1] In spite of this "recognition," in the Marxian view the worsening of the workers' situation eventually leads them to revolt against the owning classes and to organize a communist state under their own control.

The industrialization of society, according to this prognosis, should lead to an ever more intense political conflict. We know that for the United States, this has in fact been an erroneous prediction, largely because Marx's estimate of the effect of technological advance on the distribution of income was wrong. But there are other reasons. The factory system has failed to provide warm and unifying social relations for its employees. It has divorced work life from community life, atomized social life, and contributed generally to the lack of those close interpersonal ties which lead to greater social participation of all kinds.[2] The growth of unions, moreover, first took place not in the factory but among the skilled trades and even today unions have greater proportional strength among carpenters and others in the building trades and among barbers and musicians than among factory workers. Thus, although it

---

1. Karl Marx and Friedrich Engels, *The Communist Manifesto*, reprinted in *Capital, The Communist Manifesto and other Writings*, edited by Max Eastman (New York: Random House, 1932), pp. 330, 331.

2. See Elton Mayo, *The Social Problems of an Industrial Civilization* (Boston: Harvard Graduate School of Business Administration, 1945); Thomas N. Whitehead, *Leadership in a Free Society* (Cambridge, Mass.: Harvard University Press, 1936); F. J. Roethlisberger and William Dickson, *Management and the Worker* (Cambridge, Mass.: Harvard University Press, 1939).

is clear enough that membership in a union tends to be associated with higher political participation (and activity or office in a union increases this association), neither the spirit nor the organization of those who work in factories makes them more likely to assume political responsibilities more than those in similar occupations outside of factories.[3] In America, industrialization and the factory system has not had the immediate effect of increasing political interests or concern among the working class.

The economy is characterized by large units, both in terms of financial aggregations and units of production. With many exceptions this is true of both manufacturing and commercial enterprises. The political results of this concentration are substantial. It has created a "salariat," a large propertyless middle class, often termed the "new middle class" to distinguish it from the rentier, entrepreneurial, and shop-keeping "old middle class."[4] The salaried middle-class, as distinct from the rentiers and shop keepers, are politically less motivated and less active. This is partly because the ownership of real property stimulates political interest and partly because of the effect of the mobility of the salariat compared to the old middle classes. As a consequence, one finds, for example, that managers of absentee-owned corporations in California (in the thirties) had exceptionally low rates of registration.[5] These and other reasons also explain the generally lower rate of political giving and other political activity which characterized the managers of absentee-owned corporations in Elmira, as contrasted to the owner-management of local firms.[6] This lower political interest of the salaried middle class (as contrasted

---

3. In Delaware, Ohio, in both 1924 and 1948, carpenters and painters had a higher rate of turnout than laborers in manufacturing and mechanical industries and machinists and mechanics. Ben A. Arneson and William H. Eells, "Voting Behavior in 1948 as Compared with 1924 in a Typical Ohio Community," *American Political Science Review, 44* (1950), p. 434. European data, less explicit in their designation of occupation, fail to show any consistent relationship between the rates of voting of those designated "independent in trade and craft" and those simply classified as "workers." See Herbert Tingsten, *Political Behavior, Studies in Election Statistics* (London: P. S. King, 1937), p. 145.

4. See C. Wright Mills, *White Collar* (New York: Oxford University Press, 1951), especially pp. 324-54.

5. "Here [in a California sample] is a heterogeneous group of salaried business personnel and proprietors, 7 per cent of all male workers, who register only 53 per cent of their potential voting strength. As large-scale business enterprise develops, taking over an increasing proportion of the community's business, operated by paid managers who are moved from community to community at will, there is little incentive for these people to send down roots firmly into the life of any one city. This explains in part at least the low proportion who register." Dewey Anderson and Percy E. Davidson, *Ballots and the Democratic Class Struggle* (Stanford, Cal.: Stanford University Press, 1943), pp. 115-16.

6. Bernard R. Berelson, Paul F. Lazarsfeld, and William N. McPhee, *Voting* (Chicago: University of Chicago Press, 1954), pp. 157-60. We know of no systematic studies of the political behavior of the "old" as contrasted to the "new" middle classes in the United States. On the basis of somewhat unclearly defined European classifications, Tingsten found that in the 1907 elections in Austria-Hungary, nine out of twelve comparisons between an "independent" and a "salaried" group revealed higher turnout for the independent group. Calculation of the means of these percentage turnouts showed: independent 84 per cent, salaried 81 per cent. H. Tingsten, *op. cit.*, p. 152.

to small-property middle class) does not, of course, mean that concentration of economic power tends to weaken the political strength of business (although in certain instances this is no doubt true—see the record of the druggists' association),[7] it only means that the intensity of political concern in this middle stratum of society has been weakened by the concentration of ownership. Nor is there any indication that owning shares in a distant concern is as politicizing as owning personally supervised productive property.

The working-class operatives, on the other hand, are not deprived of property by the concentration of industry in large units, and are withdrawn from an intimate cross-class relation with their owner-managers, just such a relation as tends to depoliticize a member of a community. And they are more likely to work within the politicizing influence of larger cities. As a consequence, workers in larger plants are more likely to be leftist, which, in this context, probably means more likely to be politically active.[8]

In spite of the large scale units, the economy is competitive—not monopolistic nor governed by cartels. Brady has presented a thesis stating that this is a transient condition and that the rise of the business associations and their interlocking directorships in *"spitzenverbande,"* or peak associations, has set in motion a train of events here, as well as abroad, which will lead to the control of government by business.[9] This trend, he says, has politicized the business structure. This view is open to criticism on the grounds that the organization of business in trade associations is less significant than Brady supposes,[10] but the thesis has the merit of pointing to a relationship between organization of business in trade associations and an increase in political effort. The fact that a substantial portion of the allocations of markets and pricing policies are still determined by competitive action, rather than by centralized decisions by trusts, cartels, or trade associations, is a feature of the economy which weakens the political interests of the ruling business group. Competitive business leads to an atomization of conflict which, in this form, tends to be waged upon non-political grounds.

Yet there are also features of a competitive economy, which tend to awaken political interests and motivations among the competitors. Those businesses which persons can enter with little or no capital, like trucking and dry cleaning, often become most interested in governmental protection, licensing, rate regulation, and protective intervention of this kind.[11] Perhaps, as in so

7. See C. C. Regier, "The Struggle for Federal Food and Drugs Legislation," and David Cavers, "The Food, Drug, and Cosmetic Act of 1938: 'Its Legislative History and Its Substantive Provisions,'" *Law and Contemporary Problems, 1,* No. 1 (1933), and *6,* No. 1 (1939).

8. Seymour M. Lipset and associates, "The Psychology of Voting: An Analysis of Political Behavior," in Gardner Lindzey, ed. *Handbook of Social Psychology* (Cambridge, Mass.: Addison-Wesley, 1954), Vol. 2, pp. 1136-41.

9. Robert A. Brady, *Business as a System of Power* (New York: Columbia University Press, 1943).

10. Robert E. Lane, *The Regulation of Businessmen,* Ph.d. dissertation, Harvard University Library, 1949, pp. 181-94. Ohtre portions of this study appears under the same title (New Haven: Yale University Press, 1954).

11. See Donald Blaisdell, *Economic Power and Political Pressure,* Temporary National Economic Committee Monograph No. 26 (Washington, D. C., 1941).

many other areas, the relationship between competition and resort to political action for economic advantage is curvilinear—either too much (and hence the creation of what is sometimes called a "sick industry") or too little competition create situations where politics becomes salient.

One other feature of the bearing of economic structure on political action might be termed the "commercial tenuousness" of the society. A substantial portion of the population depend for a living upon commercial transactions with persons who are free to trade with others for equivalent goods and services. What is determinative in such situations is often a small quantity of friendliness, a minor ethnic identification, or some mutual friend.[12] This interwoven network of commercial and personal relationships may tend to increase people's partisanship in communities where there is substantial agreement on political matters, as is the case with regional political alignments. But in politically heterogeneous communities, where class and ethnic alignments create for each seller a politically mixed clientele, it may be economically hazardous to become publicly partisan and to seek to advance the cause of the party opposed by even a fraction of one's patrons.[13] This is an important difference between political loyalties with geographic boundaries, and political loyalties with economic or ethnic or ideological boundaries.

Like "commercial tenuousness" and the factory system, the openness of the labor market may have important influence upon the intensity of political sentiment in the United States. A labor market which provides fluid channels for men of ability to rise in the occupational scale discourages the search for political means of expression. This is Pareto's concept of the necessity for a circulating elite in a stable polity. The apparent concomitant of such an open elite structure, however, is the descent of the displaced, whose attitudes toward their challengers may lead them into intensely political defensive movements.

These tendencies are illuminated by a study of the nature of American occupational mobility in the 1910 to 1940 period. The author of this study concludes that the white collar group of occupations (professionals, semi-professionals, proprietors, and clerks) are relatively "isolated" from the blue collar and farming groups. "With almost no exceptions, the white collar classes were closer to one another (as measured by the relative ease of movement between them) than to all other classes."[14] On the other hand, there was an open class system in the sense that it was about half as likely for the son of a blue collar man to get into the white collar class as for the son of a white collar man to stay there (with the classes so broadly defined). Moreover, there has been no tendency for the opportunities for upward mobility

---

12. See Erich Fromm's discussion of "the marketing orientation" and the "personality market" in his *Man for Himself* (New York: Rinehart, 1947), pp. 67-82.

13. "Well, its a personal subject. . . . You see, in my field, there is no harm in avoiding unnecessary conflicts, and politics are subject to strong sentiments. . . . I have to maintain relations among employees and management, and I try to avoid trouble points. I've always felt it wise politics to be quiet about how I vote." Respondent quoted in Morris Rosenberg, "Some Determinants of Political Apathy," *Public Opinion Quarterly*, 18 (1954-55), p. 353.

14. Natalie Rogoff, *Recent Trends in Occupational Mobility* (Glencoe, Ill.: Free Press, 1953), p. 61.

to decrease in this thirty-year period, and, at the same time, the amount of *downward* mobility is smaller in 1940 than it was in 1910.[15] Thus, in spite of the obstacles in the way of movement into the white collar class, such movement is both substantial and persistent over time, and continues in the face of a decrease in downward mobility. These features of the labor market deprive society of certain sources of political bitterness and so contribute to the emotionally low-pitched "politics of happiness."

Like inter-occupational mobility, geographic mobility of labor tends to reduce political pressures; not only because it reduces the pockets of persistent unemployment in the country but because a population on the move runs into local residence laws and for about five years lacks the accumulated interest in local politics held by residents of longer duration.

Men in industries which either come under governmental regulation or receive governmental favors are more likely to be interested in politics and public affairs than those who do not. This is certainly true in terms of the support given to national lobbies, as is indicated by the fact that the industries with the largest number of registered lobbyists in Washington in the first quarter of 1948 are: railroads (twenty-eight), utilities (eighteen), real estate (the housing lobby considered by the Buchanan Committee to be the most successful of them all), insurance, air transportation, oil, sugar, shipping.[16] This is also suggested by the sources of revenue of the major political parties.[17] It would follow from this, therefore, that any factor which makes an industry dependent upon governmental policy tends to politicize the members of that industry—or at least its leaders. At an earlier period we might have said that "business affected with the public interest" represented the category of business particularly dependent on governmental policy, but today it is conceded that there is no exclusive category of business so affected.[18] Instead we may list a few of the considerations which tend to bring some industries under the influence of government more than others:

1. The industry is a natural monopoly (transportation, utilities).

2. The industry deals with matters critical to the defense of a nation (atomic energy, shipping, aircraft production).

3. The industry receives a substantial share of its patronage from the government (road building, munitions).

4. The industry is particularly subject to foreign competition (copper, wool, meat).

5. The industry depends upon natural resources under governmental control (lumber, hydro-electric, and all extractive industries).

6. The industry is "sick," i.e., cannot achieve conditions of competition in which a substantial portion of the industry operate profitably (dry cleaning, coal mining).

---

15. *Ibid.*, pp. 61-63.

16. Robert E. Lane, "Notes on the Theory of the Lobby," *Western Political Quarterly*, 2 (1949), pp. 156-57.

17. See pp. 56-62.

18. See Mr. Justice Roberts' discussion of this principle in *Nebbia v. New York*, 291 U.S. 502 (1933).

7. The industry is composed of some large efficient firms considered threatening by many small independent firms (drug and grocery stores).

The increased regulatory role of government, the increased proportion of governmental services covered by the term "welfare state," will broaden the number of industries coming under the above classifications and hence will increase the number of persons with visible economic stakes in governmental policy decisions. In review, then, the following hypotheses seem justified.

The factory system has not greatly increased working-class solidarity nor provided a basis for union organization superior to the craft system and therefore has not intensified political emotion as the Marxists have predicted.

The organization of industry and commerce in large units has created a "new middle class" of salaried white collar workers who are more mobile, less integrated in their communities, and who see fewer stakes in political decisions than the old middle class of small rentiers, shop-keepers, and other property owners.

"Healthy" competition among business firms reduces the forces leading to political activity; rise of centralized trade-association control over economic decisions leads to attempts at business control of government; overcompetition leads to demands for governmental control in favor of the established concerns.

"Commercial tenuousness," the network of economic relations which underlie social relationships, tends to inhibit free political expression lest some offended person invoke economic sanctions. The change from regional to class and ethnic politics increases the inhibiting force of commercial tenuousness.

Although there are moderate impediments to the movement of farm and blue collar workers into white collar occupations (upward mobility), these impediments do not prevent such movement on a broad scale. The white collar middle class is as open to outsiders now as it was thirty years ago while the amount of downward mobility is less now than it was thirty years ago.

The more business is affected by governmental policy, for whatever reasons (monopolistic inclinations, national defense implications, conservation), the more likely are its leaders to be engaged in political activity of various kinds. (This probably does not hold true for subordinate employees except where unions and management enter a compact for political purposes.)

INCOME AND POLITICAL ACTIVITY

As mentioned earlier, it is almost universally true throughout the West that the more prosperous people are more likely to be active in politics and to vote proportionately more frequently than the less prosperous.[19] That this is generally true in the United States is shown in Table 21.1. But does every dollar increment have the same effect or is there a kind of declining marginal productivity of income for voting? On the basis of these crude data, we find that (a) every increased thousand dollars of income increases turnout by a progressively smaller percentage, and (b) any given rate of increase in income from one level to another is likely to bring a smaller *rate* of increase in turnout as one ascends the income scale. Evidently when a man has a

19. See Tingsten, *op. cit.*, pp. 120-80.

TABLE 21.1.—Per cent and Rate of Increase of Groups Voting by Income Groups, 1948 and 1952.

Income Classes	$ Increase over Lower Bracket	Rate of Increase Over Lower Bracket	% of Group Voting	Absolute % Increase Over Lower Bracket	Rate of Increase Over Lower Bracket
1948					
Under $2,000			46		
$2,000—2,999	$1,000	50%	61	15	33%
$3,000—3,999	$1,000	33	74	13	21
$4,000—4,999	$1,000	25	75	1	1
$5,000 & over	$1,000	20	82	7	9
1952					
Under $2.000			53		
$2,000—2,999	$1,000	50%	68	15	28%
$3,000—3,999	$1,000	33%	76	8	12
$4,000—4,999	$1,000	25%	83	7	9
$5,000 & over	$1,000	20%	88	5	6

SOURCE: Angus Campbell, Gerald Gurin, and Warren E. Miller, "The Voter Decides" (Evanston, Ill.: Row, Peterson, 1954), p. 73.

smaller income new increments of income have a greater effect upon his attitudes and create more situational pressures than equal amounts (or rates) of increased income at a higher economic level.

On a second point, these data offer some suggestive evidence: What is the economic threshold of political involvement? Is there an income level below which participation is markedly less likely than it is for persons just above that level—a kind of political plimsoll line? This would only be true if the income-voting relationship were marked by one or two clear discontinuities. The data suggest that the economic threshold of political action is close to the minimum for survival, probably in the bottom income bracket presented in these data. Evidently very few people will vote at the subsistence level and a minimum of $2,000 (1948, 1952) is necessary for a majority of the income group to vote.

How does the pattern of the distribution of income affect the politicization of various groups? Is there a normal distribution, deviations from which are disturbing to the body politic? Although the material is speculative, some proposals on this point by Harold Davis are worth inspecting.[20] Davis takes a modified version of Pareto's original law of income distribution and by the examination of Roman and American history derives a "concentration ratio"

20. The following discussion is based on data in Harold T. Davis, *Political Statistics* (Evanston, Ill.: Principia Press, 1954), pp. 219-65. "The formula for the law of income distribution is $N_x = \dfrac{A}{x^a}$, where N_x is the number of people having the income x or greater, A is a constant depending on the size of the economy, and a is approximately 1.5" (p. 189). The concentration ratio (p) is expresses as $p = \dfrac{1}{2a-1}$ (p. 194).

such that "revolution is likely in any economy where the concentration ratio exceeds a certain critical value . . . and a civil war is likely in any economy where the concentration ratio falls below a certain critical value. . . ."[21] He argues that there was a low concentration of wealth (chiefly slaves) in the South prior to the Civil War which, because of the lack of a few really powerful individuals, aggravated the situation leading to conflict; and that a low concentration ratio in France during the Popular Front period contributed to their political and economic difficulties of that period. Two periods of low concentration in the United States, 1920 and 1932, were associated with major shifts in power between the two parties.

Setting aside the many questions about the illustrations given, we may use Davis' indices of income inequality to look more closely at the relation between the concentration of income in the United States and the state of political ferment indicated by voter turnout. During the period 1914 to 1948 on which Davis has coefficients of concentration, we see a range of values from a low of 0.317 (1943) to a high of 0.595 (1916). As Davis points out, the United States has experienced these fluctuations "without an undue amount of political unrest."[22] Our own calculations confirm this: there is almost no correlation ($r = -.18$) between turnout in presidential elections during this 1920-48 period and income distribution. Although a decline in concentration of income and a rise in rate of women voting introduce trend factors in this period, a comparison of adjacent voting years (to minimize trend factors) also shows only minimal relationships. On the whole one cannot, at least by these measures, support any view that the concentration or distribution of income, within the ranges indicated, has any relationship to the level of political activity or concern of the American public. In this period the ostentatious display of wealth had lost its vogue and changes in the inequalities of income distribution were probably not visible.

We have been speaking of certain electoral influences of a given position in the income scale, and of the pattern of income distribution both from the point of the individual and the economic system. Now we focus upon the level of income for the economy as a whole, a prosperous economy contrasted to an unprosperous one. As is often the case, this contrast may be done between two different economies at the same time, or between the same economy at two different times. If we were to take different nations at roughly the same time, we would find that, in the Western world, the nation with the highest per capita income (United States) had the lowest rate of voting, and the country with the third lowest per capita income (Italy) had the highest rate of voting—but the cultural features of different nations are so great that a pursuit of this line is unprofitable. Turning, instead, to a comparative analysis among the American states, and examining the relationship between per capita income and electoral turnout in nonSouthern areas of the United States, we find only a minimum correlation ($r = -.11$ for fourteen New England and Middle Western states), suggesting a most tenuous relationship

---

21. *Ibid.*, p. 211.
22. Davis, *op. cit.*, p. 211.

indeed.[23] Cross-cultural and cross-state data do not at all support the view that national or state wealth and electoral participation are related in the same way as individual wealth and participation in the United States and throughout the world.[24]

As for the relationship between increase and decline of national income over time, the data are somewhat clearer. It has long been assumed that depressions bring out a protest vote. But who protests? By and large it appears that those who take the trouble to protest are those who have been voting all along. Economic disaster does not mobilize the electorate in larger numbers. Table 21.2 compares the state of the economy with the change (from the previous presidential election) in the index of eligible voters voting in a given year, and gives the percentage change from the previous election:

TABLE 21.2.—Relation of Change of Business Activity to Change of Electoral Turnout, 1884-1944.

Year	Index of Business Activity: Per cent Deviation from Normal (October)	Index of Participation: Change from Previous Election in Votes Cast Per Thousand Eligible Voters	Per Cent Change in Turnout Between Election Years
1884	−10	−17	− 2.2
1888	+ 6	+20	+ 2.6
1892	+ 5	−23	− 2.9
1896	−17	+28	+ 3.7
1900	− 5	−57	− 7.2
1904	− 5	−77	−10.5
1908	−10	+05	+ .8
1912	+ 8	−63	− 9.5
1916	+16	+37	+ 6.2
1920	− 4	−144	−22.6
1924	—	−02	− .4
1928	+ 9	+83	+16.9
1932	−41	+04	+ .7
1936	− 7	+41	+ 7.1
1940	+10	+02	+ .3
1944	+32	−70	−11.3

SOURCE: Index of Business Activity is taken from Louis Bean, "How to Predict Elections" (New York: Knopf, 1948), p. 193. Bean's data are from The Cleveland Trust Company, Cleveland, Ohio.

---

23. Department of Commerce, *Survey of Current Business*, 1952; Congressional Quarterly, *Weekly Report, 14* (1956), pp. 416-21.

24. H. Tingsten, *op. cit.*, pp. 120-80.

A brief examination of these figures shows the following relationships between economic activity and political participation:

Direction of Economic Change	Direction of Change of Political Participation	
	Decline in Political Participation	Increase in Political Participation
8 election years showing a decline in economic activity in October	4	4
7 election years showing an increase of economic activity in October	3	4
1 election year showing no change in business activity in October	Decrease in Index of Participation of 02.	

From these data it appears that electoral participation over the years is not related to increase or decline in business activity. Men do not respond to depression by increased turnout at the polls, nor do they respond to prosperity by indifference or preoccupation with other things. Of course, the direction of the vote is another matter, and does, to some extent, lend support to an economic interpretation of politics, but economic interpretations of politics receive no comfort from the above historical analysis of rates of turnout.

If, as appears to be the case, it is generally true that depressions do not increase electoral turnout, what accounts for the public impression that deflationary periods, such as the thirties, or the earlier depressions starting in '73 and '93, politicized the country? Apparently this is due to an increase of other kinds of political activities, those discussed above under the heading "social movements." Small groups of what might be called "latent agitators," finding the milieu favorable, increase their output, multiply their followers (who still represent a small fraction of the population), and give the illusion of size and importance. Their voices, relatively unheard in prosperity, become suddenly magnified as through an amplifier, and they speak as though for millions. It was in such a way as this that the "youth movement" on the campuses in the thirties, with a membership of less than one-half of 1 per cent of the student body, became a portent and gave the illusion of massiveness when there was little there but a core of dedicated persons with a small periphery of supporters.[25]

On the basis of these considerations, the following hypotheses may be put forward.

There is a declining marginal productivity of income for voting, in the sense that for each dollar increase in income or each percentage increase in income, there is a smaller increase in proportion of persons voting and a smaller rate of increase in proportion of persons voting.

The economic threshold of voting, in the sense of a major discontinuity in the relationship between income and voting, is (if there is such) close to the bottom of the income scale.

25. See, for example, Dixon Wecter, *The Age of the Great Depression, 1929-1941* (New York: Macmillan, 1948).

The distribution and concentration of income, in gross terms and within the range experienced in the United States in the last thirty odd years, is not related to changes in popular political involvement.

Intercultural and inter-state comparisons do not reveal the same relationship between high income and greater electoral participation revealed by data on individuals in the American culture.

A decline in national income (in the United States), and therefore in average per capita income, is not related to greater popular political involvement as indicated by greater electoral turnout, but may be related to expansion of vocal social movements giving the impression (perhaps, an accurate one) of increased political concern in the society.

OCCUPATIONS AND POLITICAL ACTIVITY

A person's work life is certain to color his outlook on society, to structure his attitudes, and affect his behavior. The type of work he does, his occupation, will influence his political behavior chiefly through affecting (1) his skills and capacities, (2) the people with whom he associates, (3) his perceived stakes in political decisions, and (4) the social roles which the occupation imposes upon him. At the same time, the occupation will serve as a screening device to select from among the population persons with certain skills, friendship and status memberships, and role preferences. Selection and influence are thus intertwined in the relationships observed between occupation and political activity.

By and large the professional classes, especially lawyers, teachers, and journalists, are engaged in pursuits where skills in handling the abstractions implicit in much public policy are most readily developed. Moreover, the professions attract persons with the highest intelligence.[26] For the professional person, too, the civic role is especially emphasized; it goes along with the job. As for the stakes involved in political decisions, the lawyer and the doctor both find professional interests in much legislation (judicial appointments, public health, etc.), and most teachers are public servants, with the stakes that go with government employment.

Other public servants also find support for their political interests in the white collar skills which their work requires and develops. Possibly, too, a political network which facilitated his getting the job in the first place may enhance a public servant's political involvement. It is for reasons such as these that professional people, teachers, and public servants everywhere have voting rates among the highest in the country.[27] But it should be noted that

---

26. See C. T. Pihlblad and C. L. Gregory, "Occupational Selection and Intelligence in Rural Communities and Small Towns in Missouri," *American Sociological Review, 21* (1956) pp. 63-70.

27. These are general relationships with occasional deviations. The four highest occupational groups in Austin, Texas were (in order of turnout): public service, trade, professional service, and pedagogy. In Delaware, Ohio: college teachers, public school teachers, public service including public officials, with bankers, merchants and clerks tied for fourth place. See Roscoe C. Martin, "The Municipal Electorate: A Case Study," *Southwestern Social Science Quarterly, 14* (1933), p. 215; Arneson and Eells, *op. cit.*, p. 434.

both teachers and public servants (the latter by law) are often restricted in the kind of political electioneering they may engage in. In their official roles teachers may be, and usually are, "civic," but not partisan.

Businessmen, according to the nature of their jobs, may develop political skills, as is seen in the high number of "opinion leaders" among salesmen.[28] Their network of communications, frequencies of contact with like-minded persons, and exposure to politicized media is high. Again, depending upon their occupation, their stakes in public decisions may be vital. It may be that some businessmen are restrained from asking for help by their ideology "that the government should have only limited powers and be restrained in their use is a fundamental and ever-recurring proposition in the business creed."[29] But this only adds fuel to their desire to prevent labor and other interests from receiving favorable intervention by government and hence hardly takes them out of the political arena. In any event this ideology is easily rationalized or circumvented in situations where the government can perform acts business-men want performed.

The working man neither develops skills on the job nor is selected for skills which make politics understandable or meaningful to him. Although his interaction with other working men may be high, as noted earlier, it is often of a superficial nature and does not weld the men into unifying groups with a sense of common needs. Political decisions seem remote from the immediate needs in their lives and they avoid the impact of the civic pressures which surround those higher in the hierarchy of occupation. On the other hand, persons in this occupational group may be enlisted in union work which does develop political interests and skills.

Within this group certain occupations are notable for their deviant rates of political activity. The domestic servant, surrounded as he is by persons with different political interests to whom he is often personally loyal, has a low rate of voting both in Europe and the United States.[30] It is said that certain occupations such as mining and seafaring, where the contact is close and reinforced by mutual interdependence in the face of danger, are characterized by higher than average rates of political activity.[31] They are often, for example, in the vanguard of radical movements, and are among the best organized of all occupations. A recent study compared the rates of turnout in seventeen elections for three mining counties and three industrial counties in

---

28. Paul F. Lazarsfeld, Bernard Berelson, and Hazel Gaudet, *The People's Choice,* 2nd ed. (New York: Columbia University Press, 1948), p. 50.

29. Francis X. Sutton, Seymour E. Harris, Carl Kaysen, and James Tobin, *The American Business Creed* (Cambridge, Mass.: Harvard University Press, 1956), p. 184. The theoretical rationale behind such a minimum government viewpoint has found expression in the classical economists and in Herbert Spencer's *The Man versus the State,* but has been weakened by such welfare economists as Pigou, Lerner, and Baumol, as well as by the Keynsian doctrines on fiscal policy. Conversations with British and American businessmen confirm the view that the Americans are governed rather more by their heritage of laissez faire doctrine than are the British.

30. H. Tingsten, *op. cit.,* pp. 166-68; Arneson and Eells, *op. cit.,* p. 434. But it appears that domestic service has a more depressing effect on voting in Europe (where domestic servants may be torn between socialist inclinations and loyalties to their traditional, perhaps hereditary, employers) than in the United States.

31. See S. Lipset and associates, *op. cit.,* pp. 1,135.

Pennsylvania and found that, even when the size of community was controlled, there was a significantly greater turnout in the mining communities.[32]

As for agriculture, the skills involved and the selective factors which account for the lower intelligence of the farming population,[33] tend to depress the level of political understanding in the group. Interaction with others is relatively lower in farming due to the isolated condition of work. Today, indeed, the stakes of farmers in political decisions are higher than ever before, and made visible by competitive bidding by both parties, but this is a recent phenomenon and is vital only for some farmers—those, as Lipset points out, with certain "supported" cash crops for sale.[34] It is for reasons of this sort that nationally, at least throughout the nonSouth, the rural and farming rate of electoral participation is low.

Thus political activity may be encouraged or discouraged by the cumulation of these factors, or by the salience of any one: salesmen, whose verbal skills are expressed in their opinion leader capacity; public servants who are, in a sense, electing their employers; miners whose community of purpose and solidarity is reinforced by the conditions of their work; and teachers and lawyers who occupy "civic" roles, all reveal the force of one or more of these factors.

The rise and fall of popular concern with political affairs reflects the changes in the ways men earn their living. Between 1940 and 1950 the following shifts in proportion of the labor force engaged in various occupations have taken place.[35]

Declining Proportion of the Labor Force	*Increasing Proportion of the Labor Force*
farm management	professional and technical managers, officials, proprietors (other than farm)
farm labor	
unskilled labor (other than farm)	clerical
	sales
domestic service	craftsmen and foremen service (other than private household)

Numerically the most important shifts deal with the decline of farming and the rise of operatives, craftsmen and foremen, and clerical workers (but not salesmen). All of the declining occupations are those whose members usually have had relatively low political interests, while many of the growing occupations, particularly the white collar jobs (professional, managerial, clerical and sales), are those traditionally associated with higher political interests. In addition there have been shifts in industry which also suggest changes in political motivation. The decline in mining, where political interests are high, is more than compensated for by the rise in governmental employment and

---

32. Howard E. Davis, "Turnout and Leftism: A Comparison Between Miners and Industrial Workers in Pennsylvania," (Yale University, manuscript, 1956). The reported differences were significant at the 1 per cent level.

33. Pihlblad and Gregory, *op. cit.,* p. 65.

34. S. Lipset and associates, *op. cit.,* p. 1135.

35. Department of Commerce, Bureau of the Census, *Statistical Abstract of the United States, 1955* (Washington, D. C., 1955), p. 199, Table No. 240.

construction (both politically active occupations), together with the more politically neutral areas of trade and manufacturing.[36] The recent increase in electoral participation, then, is partly attributable to changes in men's occupations.

Taking a longer view, several sweeping movements command attention. The industrial revolution brought men together in common postures of opposition to the "owning classes"; it increased the interaction of like-minded persons, if not in the factories at least in the cities built up around the factories. A "commercial revolution," following hard on the heels of industry, enlarged the demand for people with education, and created many more jobs which increased facility with words and abstractions. These skills, too, are useful in politics. The rise of the welfare state enlarged the number of jobs offered by the government (as well as the number of other occupations affected by governmental decisions), greatly increasing the number of people whose stakes in public policy are made immediately visible. The dramatic decline in the percentage of the population engaged in agriculture, a process still in full swing, has diminished the proportion of people who are, or think they are, socially autonomous, divorced from the major currents of life. As for the changing nature of housekeeping, two forces are evident: the decline of the domestic servant has reduced those whose occupations led them to refrain from political expression; and the automation of the home has released the housewife so that she can, if she chooses to, find the leisure for casting a ballot or joining the League of Women Voters. Among other things, the automatic washing machine has, by proxy, cast a lot of ballots in recent elections. Lying behind the revival of political interest in the second quarter of the century, these occupational trends may account for a substantial portion of the change.

In review the following tentative conclusions are in order.

The occupations which facilitate political expression are those which select people with, or which develop on the job, the following: (1) intellectual or social skills helpful in political understanding and expression; (2) patterns of social interaction with like-minded others or with politically minded others; (3) higher than average stakes in governmental policy; (4) occupational roles congenial to "civic-mindedness," "ward-heeling," "agitation" or some other socially recognized types of political behavior.

Occupational trends increasing political expression in recent times include: (1) The second phase of the industrial revolution, decreasing the number of unskilled laborers and increasing the number of white collar jobs. (2) The commercial revolution, increasing educational requirements and expanding the middle classes. (3) Expanded welfare and regulatory state functions, increasing the number of public servants and others affected by governmental decisions. (4) An agricultural revolution (not agrarian revolt), decreasing the number of (relatively unpoliticized) farmers, and, combined with number (3) above, raising the political stakes of the remaining farmers. (5) The housekeeping revolution, decreasing the number of domestic servants and increasing housewife leisure at the same time.

---

36. *Ibid.*, Table No. 239.

Part VI

Popular Government and the Good Society

CHAPTER 22

Popular Participation in Government:

How Much? What Kinds? By Whom?

U NIVERSAL MANHOOD suffrage is not yet one hundred years old, even in America, and universal adult suffrage is scarcely forty years old. The discussion of political participation has barely emerged from an era when the focus of the argument was not the use of a privilege, but the extension of a right. Equalitarian sentiment, crucial to the question of the right to vote, is marginal with respect to the exercise of that right.

We start, then, with the premise that legal exclusion of any adult group from the right to vote (except for certain tests of competence or residence) is an evil. As Justice Warren noted in the Brown desegregation case, legal discrimination is the worst form of discrimination because it carries the implication of a mature and considered social judgment and is vested with the reverence given to the law.[1] Exclusion from the right to participate in political parties, or to exercise the right of petition, is of the same evil nature. Such rights must be secure. What of the use of the right?

INDIVIDUAL GAINS AND LOSSES

Shall we adopt the principle that, given the right to participate in democratic processes, all should participate? Underlying this view is some belief in the natural harmony of nature and society such that when each seeks to achieve his ends in politics the good of all is somehow achieved. As in economic life, these ends may be some material reward, but, also as in economic

---

1. *Brown, et al. v. Board of Education of Topeka, et al.,* 347 U.S. 483 (1954).

life, they may be increments of power, or friendship, or self-esteem, or the relief of intra-psychic tensions. Neither in politics nor in economics is there any assurance that the values of society will be maximized through such a universal individual effort.

Both society and the individual gain in the widespread exercise of the right to participate in democratic processes—and both experience some loss. How shall these be assayed? The individual gains in the expression of some need—catharsis—if nothing more. But does he generally satisfy his needs expressed in this way? Lasswell says: "The findings of personality research show that the individual is a poor judge of his own interest. The individual who chooses a political policy as a symbol of his wants is usually trying to relieve his own disorders by irrelevant palliatives."[2] And David Riesman argues:[3]

When . . . the incomprehensibility of politics makes self-interest obscure and when feelings of impotence make self-interest pointless even when clear, we must ask whether self-interest alone, in its traditional senses, is enough to arouse people to a state of concern or action. . . . May not the danger be that they will become sold, if at all, on a spurious self-interest?

People do attempt to relieve their disorders by "irrelevant palliatives" and they do become sold on "spurious self-interests"; but they also achieve individual and group gains through political expression. The record of the treatment of Negroes in areas where they can vote, compared to their treatment where they cannot, reveals the nature of the gains which may be achieved. Where they have no political power, they are treated better by the police, and where they achieve substantial political power, public housing, schools, and civil rights legislation are made available.[4] "The most plausible assumption is that if certain groups or classes of citizens habitually do not vote, their interest will be neglected in the actions and policies of governments."[5] Where rural areas are overrepresented, as they are in most state legislatures, the benefits of government are distributed unequally in the interests of farmers.

The individual gains from his participation in other ways. From participating in a social movement—even if it is only a movement to elect an admired candidate—he gains a variety of satisfactions including the deceptively ambiguous concept of "a sense of purpose." Something outside himself becomes important. This is in no way to be confused with nationalist or "groupist" fallacies: "To be a socialist is to submit the I to the thou: socialism is sacrificing the individual to the whole."[6] Rather it has to do with the mental

---

2. Harold D. Lasswell, *Psychopathology and Politics*, reprinted in *The Political Writings of Harold D. Lasswell* (Glencoe, Ill.: Free Press, 1951), p. 194.

3. David Riesman, *Faces in the Crowd* (New Haven: Yale University Press, 1952), p. 37.

4. See Gunnar Myrdal, *An American Dilemma, The Negro Problem and Modern Democracy* (New York: Harper, 1944), pp. 497-504.

5. V. O. Key, Jr., *Southern Politics in State and Nation.*(New York: Knopf, 1949), p. 508.

6. Joseph Goebbels, *Michael* (Munich: F. Eher, 1936), p. 57; quoted in Erich Fromm, *Escape from Freedom* (New York: Rinehart, 1941), p. 223.

health of the individual which is enhanced by what are called "outside interests."

The risks in submitting the "I" to the "thou," the self to the group, cannot be ignored. Such a course of action sacrifices the individual so that he abandons his legitimate claims upon society, flees from choice, and abdicates his responsibilities. A society where this is encouraged is inevitably unstable because of the repression of the self demanded of the individual. One is reminded of Riesman's definition of an appropriate involvement in politics as one which includes "self *and* others," but neither self nor others alone.[7] Furthermore, most persons who are asked to give up their individuality in some political cause will experience the privatization drives which Kris and Leites noted in totalitarian societies.[8] What seems at first like a solution to group conflict becomes, because it is based upon a psychological contradiction, ephemeral, and in the long run will probably be productive of intra-national as well as inter-national conflict.

A person's self-image is affected not only by the knowledge that he possesses a legal right, but also by the exercise of that right. In the first instance, this is how he *knows* that he does in fact have the right. But also people take their self-images from their social situations, from the reflection of themselves they see in such cues as forms of address, minor courtesies, and postures of attention accorded to them by others. The police, the civil servants, the court house politicians are very likely to reflect in these cues, as well as in formal policy, the political power of the persons with whom they are dealing. Officials know who is a "constituent" and who is not. And others in the community know and respond to who has power and uses it.

Politics has a therapeutic value in many ways. Extremist politics helps a person to legitimize and rationalize his aggression and to reduce the load of guilt he might otherwise bear. It has been said of one sample of cases that being a Communist helped to strengthen their egos and develop the powers of self-assertion of a number of timid people.[9] To the extent that radical politics achieves therapeutic results of a lasting order, the individual no longer needs his political crutch and becomes free to adopt more conventional beliefs.[10] Just as political therapy is possible in extreme political situations, it is also possible for those who need the support of conventional ideas, moral acts, and the satisfactions of performing civic duties.

In these several ways, the person who takes part in the processes of democratic government receives a personal reward. But he also loses something. Participation may be costly in terms of the time and energy involved, and what he gives up may be of more use to society as well as to himself than

7. David Riesman and Nathan Glazer, "Criteria for Political Apathy," in Alvin W. Gouldner, ed., *Studies in Leadership* (New York: Harper, 1950), pp. 551-53.

8. Ernst Kris and Nathan Leites, "Trends in Twentieth Century Propaganda," in Geza Róheim, ed., *Psychoanalysis and the Social Sciences* (New York: International Universities Press, 1947), pp. 393-410.

9. See Solomon Diamond, "A Study of the Influence of Political Radicalism on Personality Development," *Archives of Psychology, 29*, No. 203 (1936).

10. See Gabriel Almond, *The Appeals of Communism* (Princeton: Princeton University Press, 1954), pp. 297-369.

his political work. The immediate gains from electoral decisions are usually few; the larger gains are remote and contingent upon the confluence of many uncontrollable forces. Political participation as a form of leisure activity is less relaxing and amusing than other forms of entertainment. Society typically rewards occupational success more than civic duty and regards devotion to the family as a prior claim upon a man's loyalties—at least at the level of the grass roots participant.

In many situations, indeed in most, the individual can believe with justice that his vote, or his letter, or his contribution will not affect the outcome of an electoral or legislative decision. This may be the case because that particular decision is a foregone conclusion or because of a plausible belief that certain authorities are not responsive to what "people like me" say or do.

By withdrawal the citizen may avoid a painful choice. He does not have to choose between two reference groups with different policies; he does not have to bring together in his own mind mutually incompatible ideas which are all dear to him; he does not have to risk alienating friends, customers, superiors, or in-laws; he does not have to expose himself to ego-deflating revelations of ignorance or incompetence. All around him are people who are also apathetic who give him reassurance that he is not too derelict in his duties in this behavior. Because the culture is ambiguous, contradictory, or overly subtle in its demands in the political field, he can rationalize and find support for many aspects of his political withdrawal.[11]

In short, there is a balance of advantages and disadvantages, of rewards and punishments in each decision to take part in the political processes of nation and community.

SOCIAL GAINS AND LOSSES IN BROAD PARTICIPATION

Of course, society gains something when any one of its individual members becomes happier, richer, and more satisfied with a situation he cannot change; but social gains and individual gains bear a complex relationship, a complexity never dreamed of in Bentham's philosophy. Social gains, roughly speaking, are the increase in productivity of the nation, the removal of sources of inter-group and inter-personal tension, the "equitable" distribution of the nation's goods and services, the preservation of a well-ordered but flexible society, the enhancement of human dignity, the enrichment of the culture, and the broadening of opportunity for each to develop his capacities as best he can. Are these values jeopardized or supported by a broader, rather than a narrower, popular participation in democratic processes?

This question has always been answered partly, at least, in terms of the nature of the new groups to be included. Chancellor Kent alleged that the broadening of the franchise would include the covetous poor, the evasive

---

11. See Morris Rosenberg, "The Meaning of Politics in Mass Society," *Public Opinion Quarterly*, 15 (1951), pp. 5-15; and Rosenberg, "Some Determinants of Political Apathy," *Public Opinion Quarterly*, 18 (1954-55), pp. 349-66.

debtors, and the indolent shirkers.[12] Admission of Negroes was opposed on the grounds of their venality; women suffrage has been opposed on grounds of impracticality and lack of interest in public affairs; even democratically inclined youth have said to be without fixed principles, resembling "a ship in a tempestuous sea without a rudder."[13] Who, today, are the non-participants?

They are the young, and the young, as we know, are somewhat better informed on civic issues, somewhat more internationalist and more tolerant of heterodoxy. They are more likely to be in less homogeneous personal environments where they receive conflicting viewpoints; they are somewhat more flexible in their party allegiances, but not greatly so.[14] In short, voters drawn from this group, in spite of the fear of "rudderless youth," seems to offer no cause for alarm.

Non-voters (and non-participants generally) are more likely to be of lower education, lower income, and lower occupational status than voters. These groups are the carriers of economic (welfare state) liberalism, but also of intolerance, ignorance of political issues and background information, xenophobia, unwillingness to sacrifice for long range goals, and authoritarianism.[15]

Non-participants are, proportionate to the population, more likely to be found in the South, and Southerners are more likely to be intolerant of heterodoxy, somewhat higher than the rest of the country in authoritarian attitudes (but, at least until recently, more internationalist—partly for party-linked reasons), less well informed on political issues, and, incidentally, more inclined to have feelings of apathy in presidential elections than in state and local elections.[16]

Non-participants are, proportionate to population, more likely to be rural, and hence share the characteristics of rural groups as contrasted to the rest of the population: lower level of education, somewhat lower intelligence, less tolerance for heterodoxy, greater likelihood of being parochial in attitudes and xenophobic toward strangers, less well informed on public issues (but not on identification of persons).[17] Again there is no available evidence that rural non-voters are more heavily endowed with these characteristics than rural voters, although, marginally, this is probably the case.

Non-participants are more likely to be women than men, and hence to be less tolerant of heterodoxy, less well informed about issues and less able

12. *Reports of the Proceedings and Debates of the {New York} Convention of 1821*, edited by N. H. Carter, W. L. Stone, and M. T. C. Gould (Albany, 1821), p. 219.

13. Quoted in Eugene P. Link, *Democratic-Republican Societies, 1790-1800* (New York: Columbia University Press, 1942), p. 203.

14. See pp. 216-19; Samuel A. Stouffer, *Communism, Conformity, and Civil Liberties* (Garden City, N. Y.: Doubleday, 1955), pp. 89-108.

15. In addition to the discussion above in Chapter 16, see Stouffer, *op. cit.*, p. 93, David Riesman, "Orbits of Tolerance, Interviewers, and Elites," *Public Opinion Quarterly, 20* (1956), p. 53.

16. See Stouffer, *op. cit.*, 109-30; Alfred de Grazia, *The Western Public, 1952 and Beyond* (Stanford: Stanford University Press, 1954), pp. 172, 178.

17. Stouffer, *op. cit.*, p. 112; Ralph O. Nafziger, Warren C. Engstrom, and Malcom S. MacLean, Jr., "The Mass Media and an Informed Public," *Public Opinion Quarterly, 15* (1951), pp. 105-14.

to identify public figures, less likely to be exposed to several points of view, less likely to be exposed to political communication, more likely to be concerned with candidates as contrasted to issues in elections, more likely to be influenced by church policy in politics.[18]

Further studies which focus upon the attitudinal characteristics of the non-voters, without, however, controlling for class or group memberships, show that low participants are more likely to oppose any "change" ever in the Constitution, to feel that newspapers should not be allowed to criticize the government, to oppose the United Nations, to be ignorant of the Bill of Rights, and (but?) to be relatively more satisfied with the present state of politics.[19] These views, however, are more likely to be due to the lower educational level of non-voters than to any particular selective factor within a given social stratum. On the other hand, when relevant group memberships are held constant, the non-voter is less likely to have feelings of political effectiveness, more likely to regard civic duties casually, and is more likely to be dissatisfied with the community in which he lives and with his occupational life.[20]

Finally, to the extent that political participation on a college campus and in the larger society are comparable, one may apply the findings of a deeper probe into the personality of non-participants. It will be recalled that in the Mussen and Wyszynski study of Wisconsin campus political activity, the apathetics were, in many ways, not those who would be likely to make a positive contribution to the politics of the nation or the community. These authors stated:[21]

The politically apathetic individual . . . seems to be generally passive, dissatisfied, and generally threatened. Although he gives evidence that he is fundamentally hostile he cannot accept his hostile impulses. Instead he appears to be completely submissive and unchallenging to authority. . . .

What do people with little experience in or information about politics do when, at a late stage, they feel impelled to take an interest in it? Allport suggests that participation without appropriate emotional commitments is likely to lead to reactive responses, unhealthy for the individual and the community.[22] Voting under these circumstances is either conventional and without meaning for the individual, or else irritated and blind. Adorno and asso-

---

18. See Chapter 15; Stouffer, *op. cit.*, pp. 131-55; Nafziger and associates, *op. cit.*

19. Gordon M. Connelly and Harry M. Field, "The Non-Voter—Who He Is, What He Thinks," *Public Opinion Quarterly*, 8 (1944), pp. 175-87.

20. Angus Campbell, Gerald Gurin, and Warren E. Miller, *The Voter Decides* (Evanston, Illinois: Row Peterson, 1954), pp. 191, 197; Alice S. Kitt and David B. Gleicher, "Determinants of Voting Behavior," *Public Opinion Quarterly*, 14 (1950), pp. 408-409; Elizabeth Douvan and Alan M. Walker, "The Sense of Effectiveness in Public Affairs" (Ann Arbor, Michigan, Survey Research Center, 1954, processed).

21. Paul H. Mussen and Anne B. Wyszynski, "Personality and Political Participation," *Human Relations*, 5 (1952), p. 80. It should be noted, however, that these findings apply to a group selected for their marked disinterest in politics; they may not at all apply to a middle group of only mildly interested persons.

22. Gordon W. Allport, "The Psychology of Participation," *Psychological Review*, 52 (1945), pp. 117-32.

ciates find that people who "feel somehow obliged to have political opinions, because of some vague idea about the requirements of democracy, help themselves with scurrilous ways of thinking and sometimes with forthright bluff."[23] Riesman and Glazer conclude that the divorce between influence and "opinionation" leads to irresponsible and insalubrious political expression.[24] And the new voters who voted for Eisenhower in 1952, held policy positions more like those of Democrats than Republicans[25]—a situation suggesting at least some disorientation among these less experienced voters. It certainly is not clear that increased participation without an appropriate background of interest and involvement benefits either the participant himself or the society of which he is a member.

Yet certain cautions are necessary. One of these is that the forces increasing participation by people in this reserve may select those who are more like the present group of participants, attitudinally and sociologically. Also, the same arguments which may now be made to reduce the pressure for larger participation, might have been made (and probably, in modified form, were made) to prevent enlarging the franchise at an earlier time. Few regret the establishment of the universal adult franchise. The predicted alarming consequences did not materialize. One should note, moreover, that the party loyalties of some of these groups—lower income and Southern—act as restraining forces upon certain of their attitudes. As Riesman (and Lipset) point out, "The lower classes tend to vote Democratic . . . because of underdog attitudes toward government spending, control of business, and like matters; this links them by organizational and rhetorical ties to a party which has historically stood for free trade and which has been pulled and pushed by events and leadership into favoring civil liberties and restricting xenophobia."[26] Furthermore, in the infinitely complex series of events which cause a society to move toward even mildly authoritarian patterns, the failure of these groups to exercise political power may be more dangerous than any political success they might have. If their economic needs are overlooked, they may become alienated from the society and their latent anti-social impulses given new impetus. Finally, there are important moral questions in discouraging, or even failing to encourage, the free exercise of the franchise by all men of whatever persuasion.

An additional consideration occurs with respect to local elections, where the non-participants are much more numerous and of a somewhat different complexion. In these elections there may be some substance to the commonly expressed view that the highest participant group is a machine-dominated clique working for its own advantage. In such elections the particularized interest in jobs, favors, contracts, and protection is an important considera-

---

23. T. W. Adorno, Else Frenkel-Brunswik, Daniel J. Levinson, and R. Nevitt Sanford, *The Authoritarian Personality* (New York: Harper, 1950), p. 659.

24. David Riesman and Nathan Glazer, "The Meaning of Opinion," *Public Opinion Quarterly, 12* (1948), pp. 631-48.

25. Angus Campbell, Gerald Gurin, and Warren E. Miller, "Political Issues and the Vote: November, 1952," *American Political Science Review, 47* (1953), pp. 359-85.

26. Riesman, "Orbits of Tolerance, Interviewers, and Elites," p. 56.

tion, and where the turnout is low those who stand to gain in these ways may determine the course of an election or council decision. Here, then, is a situation where the political reserve consists of a different group, including more middle-class, better educated, "civic minded" individuals. Enlarging this electorate, then, promises a different range of voting patterns and electoral choices.

Although the attitudes and interests of the groups from which the newcomers to national politics may come are out of harmony with the general values of a tolerant democratic society, the risks to society of withdrawal by these members of the political reserve is greater than the risks of participation. The very act of participation tends to create bonds of identification between the participant and the society. As Tocqueville says:[27]

> . . . I maintain that the most powerful and perhaps the only means that we still possess of interesting men in the welfare of their country is to make them partakers in the Government. At the present time civic zeal seems to me to be inseparable from the exercise of political rights. . . .

Just as participation in small group activities, and particularly in the policy-making processes of these small groups, has been shown to enhance consensus, so participation in national or community processes tends to enhance the loyalty and sense of identification of participants with nation and community. One of the ironies of history may have been the psychological effect upon the Continental Communists and Socialists of their decision to assume parliamentary responsibilities. Once they became partakers in the government, their alienation from society was mitigated, and their class interests weakened in some measure by an interest in the welfare of their country.

Dissonance between democratic values and practices imposes a burden upon the integrity and conscience of a people. Just as disproportionate influence among various social groups leaves something to be explained, so do autocratic tendencies in political life. These tendencies are present everywhere, but where they have achieved the dimensions of certain urban political machines, they, too, impose a moral burden upon those who seek to reconcile democratic values and practices. "For the sake of its emotional health," says Erikson, "a democracy cannot afford to let matters develop to a point where intelligent youth, proud in its independence and burning with initiative, must leave matters of legislation, law and general policy to 'insiders' and 'bosses.' "[28] To avoid cynicism, youth, and also age, must in a democratic society experience the sense that they can in some small measure influence the nation's destinies.

Intelligence on "where the shoe pinches," in Lord Lindsay's phrase, is provided by political participants. If democracy is to perform the function it is said to perform best—the communication of a source of dissatisfaction to policy makers so that they (the policy-makers, not the communicants) can devise a solution—all persons must send messages to the government about

---

27. Alexis de Tocqueville, *Democracy in America,* translated by Henry Reeve and edited by Phillips Bradley (New York: Knopf, 1945), Vol. I, p. 243.
28. Erik H. Erikson, *Childhood and Society* (New York: Norton, 1950), p. 282.

the condition of their metaphorical shoes. At the same time, or later when the policies are being debated, it is important to know what the public is willing to do, what sacrifices they are willing to make, whether they are willing to bear arms, support heavier taxes, or tighten their belts for further rationing.[29] Since these sacrifices will be imposed generally on voters and nonvoters alike, it is useful to have the information from as broad a sample as possible.

Other forms of communication between elite and public are valuable. It has been argued that foreign policy toward Europe at the end of World War II was wiser and more fruitful than policy toward Asia because there was an informed "attentive public" for European policy but not for Asiatic policy. Morgenthau's views on the post-war treatment of Germany were subject to informed criticism "from the floor"; Marshall and Knowland addressed empty halls on the China question.[30]

The communities that men live in assume a character consonant with the distribution of influence among the residents. Where there is the equivalent of a "lord of the manor," say, an "X family" as in Middletown or a group of dominant families who operate with minimal restraint, the community is marked by a kind of uxorious relationship between man and lord, failure of nerve on the part of the working class, middle-class obsequeiousness. In the studies of small towns and Southern cities, these stigmata are laid bare. But where the "lower orders" of the community, through unions and violence as in Akron, or through a "back of the yards movement," or through ethnic associations, achieve organizations with their own leadership and assert their influence, the community assumes a different character. Part of this character is the undercurrent of conflict, but associated with the conflict is a spirit of independence and dignity.

But it is also true that society accrues certain disadvantages from universal and intense popular interest in politics. Berelson and associates find utility in the division of labor in politics, as elsewhere, attacking the assumption that there must be an average man endowed with all the qualities useful to the political process. Once this is recognized, it follows that one can assign different political roles to the political activists and the indifferents and that a balance between the two can achieve beneficent results. Among these are the following:

Since it is the indifferent voters who are the most likely to change their minds between or during campaigns, they offer a kind of flexibility to the system, permitting a moderate degree of alternation between administrations. Unencumbered by very strong party loyalties, they are more responsive to the situation of the moment, although also less well informed.

The low level of intensity of the indifferents permits the two-party system to continue without a tendency for splinter parties to develop. The activists on either side are thus permitted to organize and structure a party machine

29. A. D. Lindsay, *The Modern Democratic State* (London: Oxford University Press, 1943).

30. Gabriel A. Almond, *The American People and Foreign Policy* (New York: Harcourt, Brace, 1950), pp. 139-46.

to which the indifferents can repair in election time for their political nutriment.

The relatively low level of intensity of concern among many people (including some activists, oddly enough) permits a rapid and harmonious adjustment to the verdict of the electorate or the decision of Congress. In this atmosphere of acceptance—because it didn't matter very much anyway—the emotional intensity of the dedicated ideologue is certain to appear inappropriate.[31]

But Berelson and his associates' analysis, while illuminating, fails to account for the concentration of indifferents and non-participants in lower-status groups. Their discussion proceeds as though the indifferents were randomly selected, like their sample. It is in fact a matter of great significance that non-voting is a function of income and occupation everywhere, and of race in the South. Whatever stability is achieved through the withdrawal of low-status groups is achieved at the cost of fair representation and a just distribution of governmental goods and services.

One must ask, also, whether the kind of flexibility achieved through the changeability of the indifferents is a fruitful one. The waverers and changers during an election, as Lazarsfeld and associates have pointed out, "show a limited range of community contacts and interests in their personality ratings . . . and suffer somewhat more from emotional maladjustment as evidenced in more unhappiness and lack of self-assurance."[32] Berelson recognizes this problem; it is not clear that he faces it squarely. Certainly one can say that the socially marginal, the persons at the focus of several cross pressures, may be in the best position to influence the course of an election, however painful it may be for them. But to say that the psychologically marginal are also to be entrusted with this responsibility is to raise anxieties about the rationality of a system that invests the paraneurotic with a form of temporary sovereignty.

Along somewhat similar lines it has been argued that a high political consciousness among the people and concern over the nature of electoral decisions represents a threat to the stability of a government. Tingsten reports:[33]

An exceptionally high voting frequency may indicate an intensification of political controversy which may involve a danger to the democratic system. The enormous election figures in Austria 1923-1930 and in Germany 1930-1933 were symptoms of a political tension heightened in the extreme, and foreshadowed the fall of the democratic regimes.

This is also the view of F. G. Wilson, who argued that when voting approached 90 per cent of the possible electorate electoral tension tended to destroy the "will toward the constitutional."[34] Under these circumstances, it was claimed,

31. Bernard R. Berelson, Paul F. Lazarsfeld, and William N. McPhee, *Voting* (Chicago: University of Chicago Press, 1954), pp. 314-17.

32. Paul F. Lazarsfeld, Bernard Berelson, and Hazel Gaudet, *The People's Choice*, 2nd ed. (New York: Columbia University Press, 1948), p. 70.

33. Herbert Tingsten, *Political Behavior, Studies in Election Statistics* (London: P. S. King, 1937), p. 225.

34. Francis G. Wilson, "The Inactive Electorate and Social Revolution," *Southwestern Social Science Quarterly, 16* (1936), pp. 73-84.

the intensity of concern over the results of the election were likely to make acceptance of the victory of the other side almost impossible of attainment.

While these considerations are useful caveats, the illogicality of arguing from such evidence (which Tingsten does not do), that one should be content with low participation, or even discourage participation if it should rise above a given point, is clear enough from the theoretical premises of this discussion. Participation is a product of multiple factors; it is embedded in an area of multiple causation. Because high participation under the stimulus of one set of conditions is associated with revolutionary pressures, or does create dangerous electoral tension, it does not follow that high participation caused by other factors has the same meaning. As Powell says, comparing German and American experience:[35]

The crucial question is not whether or not a group has a high number of non-voters, but rather concerns the reasons for not voting. Is it caused by a sense of impotence stemming from confusion and dissatisfaction with existing political channels? Or does it result from a lack of awareness of the political sphere? The latter explanation and its implications seem to be more applicable to the United States.

This is the import of Key's argument against Wilson, pointing out that while West Virginia sometimes shows a rate of participation close to 90 per cent and Virginia shows a general rate closer to 35 per cent, there is no evidence that there is any less respect for the constitution in West Virginia than in Virginia.[36] Austria (1923-30) and Germany (1930-33) show an etiology of electoral participation wholly different from West Virginia in the thirties, or Utah in 1952.

Finally, some merit may be found in a system which gives to those groups which are now relatively apathetic enough representation to have their cases heard, but not so much that they can employ their strength to society's disadvantage. It is true that these under-represented groups do, in fact, achieve considerable influence. Taking Woodward and Roper's figures as representative of the way in which the political elite, "politists" in Alfred de Grazia's term, are concentrated among the better income, better occupation, urban group, Ithiel Pool nevertheless finds that these figures "do not show a closed elite."[37] On the contrary, "the third of the population at the lowest economic level is still able to provide a certain number of political activists, roughly 7½ per cent of the politists. The Negro population of the United States seems to provide some 4 per cent of the politists, a number considerably below its

---

35. Inge B. Powell, "The Non-Voter: Some Questions and Hypotheses," *Berkeley Publications in Society and Institutions, 1* (1955), p. 30.

36. V. O. Key, Jr., *Politics, Parties, and Pressure Groups,* 3rd ed. (New York: Crowell, 1952), p. 581.

37. Ithiel de S. Pool, "Oligarchy and Mobility in Political Parties," paper delivered at the American Political Science Association Meeting, Washington, D. C., 1953 (processed); Pool's basic data come from Julian L. Woodward and Elmo Roper, "Political Activity of American Citizens," *American Political Science Review, 44* (1950), pp. 872-85. The term "politists" and some discussion of their nature occur in Alfred de Grazia, *The Elements of Political Science* (New York: Knopf, 1952), pp. 82-94.

portion in the population, but yet a significant representation."[38] And on the other hand the group that is most over-represented among the highly active politists (2.3 per cent of the population), comprises only about half of that elite. V. O. Key, working over a special tabulation of the same basic data, concludes: "According to this analysis about 64 per cent of the most politically active 10 per cent of the adult population consists of persons of C and D economic levels,"[39] which is less than their proportionate share, but still significant. As is evident from these figures, the degree of distortion of group representation among the political activists depends upon how one defines "activitists"—the more is required of a person before he can be so classified, the greater the class distortion in representation.

It would not, of course, be fair to say that these authors fail to recognize, or even minimize, the significance of the distorted picture of participation which their analyses present. But by contrasting this picture with the nature of other elites, or by a realistic appraisal of the distribution of skills in society, there is no escape from their judgment that our political activists are distributed among social groups in such a way as to open up channels of influence for every group.

WHAT SHOULD BE DONE?

When the arguments on both sides have been duly recorded, and the balance has been weighed, we conclude that, true to its spirit, a democracy must encourage all its members to speak up and make themselves heard. Yet because the risks are considerable, perhaps certain precautions should be taken to modify the way this is done. First, can the irrational, projective nature of political expression be reduced in some manner so that fewer members of the public seek to relieve unconscious psychic tensions in political life? To this end Lasswell suggests a "politics of prevention" employing clinicians to help relieve politicians of their projective tendencies.[40] Such a plan would not greatly affect the electorate, however, although the use in educational institutions of some form of political self-analysis might help a number of people to become rid of their projective political beliefs.

If it is hard to devise a means of modifying the projective nature of political expression among the larger public, perhaps the influence of popular opinion upon officials should be limited. Walter Lippmann argues for this view of representation (as Burke did before him) suggesting that the President in particular (since Congress is still too close to the people) should consider himself the custodian of the public good and disregard the importuning of the petitioners who seek to influence him on matters of current policy. Furthermore, since the voters in any one election represent only a part of the public, and do not at all represent future publics, he must con-

38. Pool, *op. cit.*, pp. 24-25.
39. Key, V. O., Jr., *Politics, Parties, and Pressure Groups*, p. 579.
40. Lasswell, *op. cit.*, pp. 173-203.

sider that his mandate is not to follow the platform or set of policies discussed in the election, but rather to use his judgment in the public interest.[41] Lippmann's view, however, fails to solve the age-old problem of the philosopher king: What if he is a weak, wrong-headed, or mean man? "What is the public interest?" *"Quis custodiet ipsos custodes?"*

Perhaps the solution is self-selection of the participants, with minimal exhortation by civic leaders: the divorce of participation from concepts of civic duty. This is Riesman's solution. If those who elect to vote or to follow public affairs in the press is a small proportion of the population, this is a matter of no concern, for self-selection, according to this view, implies that the interested, the informed, and the people with political responsibilities will perform the civic duties which must be done.[42] But in point of fact, moralizing the acts of participation tends to bring out the responsible, dutiful, and humane who might not otherwise participate. Demoralizing participation may vest too much influence in the special pleaders, the persons with the most obvious interests in public policy, a situation which, as we have seen in our urban "machine" elections, is not conducive to civic health. In reality there are no short cuts to the adequate expression of the public interest and there are no firm guarantees that this will be used responsibly.

WAYS TO HIGHER PARTICIPATION

If one rejects the arguments for the individual and social utility of political apathy, and concludes that on balance the society is more likely to give "liberty and justice for all" if some approximation of "all" participate in politics, there are still a host of questions to be answered: How? At what cost? With what side effects? The social engineer who undertakes to increase political participation cannot ignore his responsibility to look at all the important consequences, not just the ones the culture or his employer selects for his immediate attention.[43]

As a means of achieving an understanding of high participation situations, and the risks that are run by those who focus on the goal of participation rather than the means of achieving it, we may examine a few model situations with high participation.

In recent years, Italy has had one of the highest electoral participation rates in Europe, due, in part at least, to the dramatic and polarized choice between parties with dogmatic (Marxist and Christian) cores.

---

41. Walter Lippmann, *Essays in the Public Philosophy* (Boston: Little, Brown, 1955). Compare John Adams: "All Projects of government, formed upon a supposition of continual vigilance, sagacity, virtue and firmness of the people, when possessed of supreme power, are cheats and delusions." *Works,* Vol. VI, p. 166.

42. Riesman, *Faces in the Crowd,* pp. 34-54.

43. For a penetrating discussion of the social scientist's responsibility for examining *all* the important consequences of his advice in industry, advertising, or government, see Robert K. Merton, *Mass Persuasion: the Social Psychology of a War Bond Drive* (New York: Harper, 1946).

Germany, 1930-33, had an exceptionally high rate of participation because of the challenge of two revolutionary parties of right and left and the threatened collapse of a weak republican regime.

The rate of participation in Belgium and Australia was markedly increased by a system of fines for non-voting.

In Louisiana, from 1928, when Huey Long became Governor, to 1936, when the battle for succession to his machine became most intense, electoral participation rose steadily from about 42 per cent to about 65 per cent of the adult white population. Some of this was due to controversy over the administration, some due to electoral fraud, but much of it was due to the "charisma" of the man Huey Long.[44]

Intensity of participation among Communists in the Anglo-Saxon countries may be overwhelming. As Almond says, the party may require its own members to "sacrifice their own individuality, give themselves up fully to the party's purposes."[45] It may be completely all-absorbing. With many exceptions, the high participation of party members in the United States and Britain generally revealed a search for the legitimization of aggression, for solidarity in a lonely world, for the assuagement of guilt, in short, for social channels of displaced emotion.[46]

High participation in Holland is associated with the tense religious conflict of that country; high participation in Utah is associated with the religious deviance of the residents of that state, high participation in a labor district in the United States is related to the saliency of group (class) consciousness as conveyed by unions; high participation in the agrarian protest movements of the nineties was associated with relative depression and clear and suitable targets—the railroads, the trusts, and the creditor banks.

On the other hand, the relatively high participation in the suburbs of Eastern United States today is associated with the greater education, higher income, and higher occupational status present in those communities—just as these qualities are everywhere (in the United States) associated with higher participation.

Even accepting this picture of the possible "high participation models" (and one could do the same thing for low participation areas) one may still desire to increase participation "the right way" in any given area. What would be at stake in such a proposal?

1. *Increase cultural pressure to participate by manipulation of the moral content of civic norms.* This is no doubt the least effective of all methods of increasing attention and understanding of public affairs and politics. Although, as is well understood, a sense of civic duty is one route to higher participation, reliance upon this one factor is hardly adequate. In any event, this has a selective appeal to the middle classes, and the working class is the area of lowest participation. Whether "norm-conformity" is a general tendency to be encouraged in an area of thought where we are said to be overly sensitive to peer group opinion is a larger question which would also require analysis.

44. V. O. Key, Jr., *Southern Politics*, pp. 523-24.
45. Gabriel Almond, *The Appeals of Communism*, p. 305.
46. See above, Chapter 9.

Beyond this, one must ask: Duty to whom? and Duty for what? As Herring says:[47]

Unless participation without regard to aims is deemed desirable in itself, the good citizen cannot act without allying himself with various interests. The question of ends and hence of values is here inescapable. Interest and participation by the good citizen mean little in themselves. Rather ask: What pattern of interests emerges in a given instance from citizen activity?

Momentous values are at stake when political conflict is posed in terms of Marxist and Christian ideologies, but in the absence of such a conflict, the values at stake do not evoke such a strong sense of duty. Relativistic and incrementalist politics in a consenual atmosphere is uncongenial to strong moral appeals. If it is said that the duty is to oneself, one must be shown how one suffers a moral loss if he fails to vote or engage in politics. If it is a duty to one's group, what group? And how has the individual let that group down by his withdrawal from politics?

2. *Encourage the search for political understanding.* The concept of enlightenment as a motive is dear to the heart of Western democracy; its advocates were instrumental in launching the democratic movement two hundred years ago. Clearly, as part of a general understanding of the world we live in, popular understanding of politics and public policy is desirable. But one cannot be sure of the effects of mere widespread distribution of information of certain kinds. A day by day tabulation of the number of Negroes moving into a community; an increment of information on the percentage of "liberals" among teachers; a clear perception of the compromises made in foreign policy for some future gain may all play into popular prejudices so that partial enlightenment, so to speak, is a shallow draught from the Pierian spring and disastrous to the harmony and progress of the community. No longer is the theme "open covenants openly arrived at" considered the key to a democratic foreign policy.

There are areas where the corrosive forces of rational understanding will diminish political interests as fast as the implication of the new enlightenment is comprehended. If, as has been supposed, the political controversy between what are taken to be moral absolutes embedded in theological doctrines, or the challenge to some cathected religious symbol posed in a political context, induces participation, the treatment of morality or religion as comparative cultural norms to be studied scientifically will deprive people of their political intensity. The mythology of their causes is a political stimulus for the McCarthyite, the Know Nothing, the Ku-Klux-Klan member, and the Communist; if the myths dissolve, that stimulus, although not others, of course, loses its force.

3. *Increase the general level of education.* Hardly under the banner of political reform, but nevertheless with growing force, the average school-leaving age is rapidly increasing in the United States. As we know, education is clearly associated with active participation, and of all educational experi-

---

47. E. Pendleton Herring, *The Politics of Democracy* (New York: Rinehart, 1940), p. 34.

ences, college education is most effective in this regard. Since college education is being extended even more rapidly than other forms, some of the recent
trends toward greater political participation may be accounted for by this
factor. On the other hand, the fact that the longer a student stays in college
the more he expresses (while in college) cynical views of politics and a dis-
inclination to take part in civic or political affairs should caution one to
examine in detail the political meaning of educational experiences.

4. *Increase group identification.* There can be no doubt that the atomized
individualism of the American leads away from political action and that a
reversal of this individual focus of attention is a move toward greater political
involvement all around. But does the type of participation where every man
thinks of himself primarily in group terms come to a fruitful end? If men
conceive of themselves politically chiefly as Catholics or Protestants; as working class, bourgeoisie, or upper class; as Southerners or Westerners; as
Yankees or Italian-Americans, and so forth, political action will serve where
private action now suffices. Intransigeance, however, is a function of such
status identification because status is less easily changed than party loyalty,
or issue preference.

There are strong and sometimes fruitful forces in American culture which
discourage strong group identification and encourage men to seek the solution to their problems in individual terms. Four such forces are notable.
Provision for vertical social mobility is one, for it tends to open up for each
person avenues of advancement which he can travel alone. It suggests to the
working man that he need not rely on the union or the labor movement for
his economic gains; on the contrary he can achieve these gains for himself by
identifying with a superior status group and seeking to achieve membership
in that group. Likewise, a competitive economy tends to discourage group
identifications for business men. An economy where businessmen are under
legal and other pressure not to "combine in restraint of trade," where the
firm and not the trade association is most important in economic conflict, and
where businessmen are led to compete in the marketplace for their advantages
is an economy which tends to depoliticize business.

A third force for atomizing conflict and reducing group loyalties is represented in the formal separation of church and state. Because the relationship
among Catholics, Protestants, and Jews is, in this country, largely an interpersonal affair and not made a matter for group conflict, each person can
accommodate to persons of other faiths as he wishes without politicizing his
religious feelings. The absence in the United States of religious parties is both
a product and a cause of this personalization of inter-faith relations. It has
brought enormous benefits in the terms of conflict in American politics.

Finally, the doctrine of the melting pot, individual assimilation among
ethnic groups, has weakened group identifications and atomized our social
conflicts. It is, like the belief in individual vertical mobility, only partly operative, but it too is embodied in law. The recent decision of the courts not to
enforce restrictive covenants will have the effect of discouraging Ghettos and
their associated ethnic politics, just as the desegregation order of the Supreme
Court will have an increasing effect on the interpenetration of racial groups in

school. These four culturally encouraged beliefs and practices, partially reinforced by law, make clear not only why it is difficult to increase group identifications in America, but also why it may be undesirable.

5. *Politicize social organizations.* When the Protestant churches assume a political posture, as they did in the fight for Prohibition,[48] or when the Catholic Church becomes exercised over an issue, as was the case with the child-labor amendment;[49] when unions develop political auxiliaries such as the Political Action Committee or the League for Political Education;[50] and when trade associations discover some augmented interest in politics, as did the Cement Institution in the controversy over basing point legislation[51]—when these things happen formerly inactive segments of the public enter the arena with what might be called a vengeance. Whether one views this as the kind of enlarged participation which is socially beneficial depends, no doubt, on where one stands with respect to the issues which aroused these organizations. But a general policy which would encourage all the organized segments of American life, all of the interest groups and other interests still unorganized, to attempt to exercise even more influence, issue more literature, exert more pressure, spend more money on behalf of their causes, seems like a doubtful expedient. A policy tailored in this form would most probably elicit the criticism of those who even now consider that "special interests" means "special privilege," and of those others who view participation of the Church in politics as subversive to both.

6. *Change the electoral situation so that every vote has the same weight.* Both logic and substantial evidence show that where constitutional provisions and gerrymandered districts make electoral contests a "sure thing," one of the forces making for greater participation is eliminated. A fairer system of apportionment, in particular, would create the political environment where participation would be nourished. As Gosnell says:[52]

It has been argued that a fair system of representation would increase interest in voting, since the voters would feel that their votes would count in determining the result. In Switzerland [after reforming the scheme of apportionment] there was such an increase in participation, and this increase has been sustained.

7. *Raise the stakes in electoral contests.* Participation increases with popular perception of the stakes in political decisions. Where two cohesive groups are contesting some policy of agreed significance the public becomes politicized, at least to some extent. But where there are consensual politics,

48. See Peter H. Odegard, *Pressure Politics, the Story of the Anti-Saloon League* (New York: Columbia University Press, 1928).

49. See Grace Abbot, "Federal Regulation of Child Labor, 1906-1938," *The Social Service Review, 13* (1939), pp. 409-30; Tom Ireland, *Child Labor as a Relic of the Dark Ages* (New York: Putnam, 1937), pp. 207-39.

50. See, in addition to the *CIO News* and the AF of L *League Reporter,* Fay Calkins, *The CIO and The Democratic Party* (Chicago: University of Chicago Press, 1952).

51. See Earl Latham, *The Group Basis of Politics* (Ithaca, N. Y.: Cornell University Press, 1952).

52. Harold F. Gosnell, *Democracy, The Threshold of Freedom* (New York: Ronald, 1948), p. 192.

the homogenization of the parties, and the appeal to the middle voter as the marginal man, the tendency is in the other direction. The vehicle for increasing the individual's sense of having something at stake in an election might be a drift away from relativism and tolerance; polarization of opinion; or the emergence of issues of confiscation of property, dissolution of unions, restriction of a church—which, like the present desegregation issue in the South, would seem "total" in their impact. The enhanced stakes would have the effect of making the acceptance by the defeated of the victors and their policies a more difficult matter. If the stakes were great enough, that tension which Francis Wilson described as depriving the constitution of its value might develop into a reality and, in any event, might spill over into ancillary areas of group conflict such that community harmony all up and down the line would be jeopardized.

8. *Strengthen political parties.* If the party "symbol in men's minds" loomed larger and gained in attraction; if the local party organizations were better organized and, say, as active between elections as the British party agent; and if the party discipline were strong enough in the legislatures of the nation to make "party program" a more vital feature of politics—if all these things took place no doubt the electorate would be more active and public affairs would take on a new life. Yet when party labels become even more cathected, the number of flexible minds at election time becomes smaller and party politics (like Church politics) may settle down to a matter of birth rates in different groups. And if the party discipline meant that each party became ideologically more homogeneous, the discouragement of individual variation within the parties would tend to build up one-party areas. Solid areas are never attractive stamping grounds for canvassers of either party—particularly the minority party which not only fails to be persuasive in such areas but has no vote to get out.

9. *Raise the prestige and rewards of government and politics.* A culture which rewards its political and civil servants with indifferent regard and comparatively low economic return is a poor place for the sense of civic duty to flower into anything more than a voting complex. It is possible, at least, that the civic leader who deplores politicians and insinuates that the government is a poor thing at best does more to depress than to increase an interest in politics.

10. *Increase the self-esteem of the depressed groups.* Voting is an act of assertion and is more frequent among people who feel that their assertion is meaningful. While the reduction of discrimination and social slights may tend to lesson group solidarity and hence to work toward lower participation, it will help to build a self-esteem among such groups whereby the individual, spontaneously and as an individual rather than a group member, may come to politics with the necessary confidence.

11. *Politicize the female role.* Since the rate of political interest, knowledge, and activity of women is generally lower than that of men, it is appropriate to consider how to relieve this depressed area of politics. Broadly speaking, political affairs are considered by the culture to be somewhat

peripheral to the female sphere of competence and proper concern. Would it be wise to reinforce the feminist movement, emphasizing politics on the women's page along with the garden club and bridge club news, and making ward politics something like volunteer work for the Red Cross or the hospital auxiliary? No doubt something along this line could be done, but it is too seldom remembered in the American society that working girls and career women, and women who insistently serve the community in volunteer capacities, and women with extra-curricular interests of an absorbing kind are often borrowing their time and attention and capacity for relaxed play and love from their children to whom it rightfully belongs. As Kardiner points out, the rise in juvenile delinquency (and, he says, homosexuality) is partly to be attributed to the feminist movement and what it did to the American mother.[53]

12. *Raise the level of social skills and information in the population.* Like every other area of life, political participation is impeded by a failure to "know the ropes." As Thomas and Doris Reed say, "If a citizen is to play the 'game' of politics, he must first learn the rules of the game and its more commonly used techniques."[54]

13. *Increase the "color," "strength," and "charisma" of the candidates.* There is substantial evidence that major differences in the rate of turnout in different elections are in part attributable to the personalities of the candidates. It is easier to "libidinize" a man than a policy, and the strong dependency needs, needs for orientation, and needs for relief from responsibility characteristic of our time as well as of other times make leadership appeal a crucial feature of electoral behavior.[55] This may be even more true for types of participation over and beyond voting, where motivations of a duty nature are not so likely to be determinative.

The risks in such an appeal are obvious. They indulge the citizenry in the gratification of immediate psychological needs at the expense of any long-run improvements in their situation. They confuse the import of elections and virtually eliminate the meaning of an electoral "mandate"—not a very clear meaning under the best of circumstances. They impose the gratification of intra-psychic needs of a marginally rational group in the population as a condition for election. In short, pursuit of this method of increasing participation so weakens the rationale of democracy that the defense of this form of government has little but sentiment left.

---

53. Abram Kardiner, *Sex and Morality* (Indianapolis, Ind.: Bobbs-Merrill, 1954), pp. 216-45.

54. Thomas H. and Doris D. Reed, *Evaluation of Citizenship Training and Incentive in American Colleges and Universities,* pamphlet published by the Citizenship Clearing House, Law Center of New York University, 1950, p. 9. It should be noted that the Falk Foundation effort in the mid-fifties to train college students in practical politics tended to emphasize practical skills and overcome resistances due to lack of familiarity with politics, rather than to exhort students to be better citizens on civic grounds.

55. John Bowlby, "Psychology and Democracy," *Political Quarterly, 17* (1946), pp. 63-64.

CONCLUSION

The conclusions which emerge from this analysis of methods of increasing participation suggest that, in a larger sense, the target for social reform is not the degree of participation by the electorate, but rather the nature of the society in which political life takes place. If the values inherent in a democratic orientation are cultivated in all areas of the society a healthy political life will follow as a matter of course. Political life is an expression of the values, the institutions, and the tensions of a society; political symptoms which appear pathological from the standpoint of the democratic model are reflections of the malfunctioning of social institutions.

We must accept realistic standards of performance for the electorate, standards which are in line with the evidence on how people do in fact think and act in the political arena. What institutional failures account for the fact that many people fall below these standards? In these global terms, why do people withdraw, over-moralize, endow their politics with venom, sacrifice long-range to short-range political goals, and displace their personal disorders onto political objects? Several major institutionalized defects are apparent. The failure of family life adequately to socialize the child leads to political expressions of dependency and an associated search for a charismatic leader, to hostility and attacks on out-groups, and authoritarianism. The failure of the social order to provide the economic security, status, and opportunities for advancement which the culture promises, leads to a politics of class warfare (not merely the conflict of economic interest groupps) and alienation. The failure of society to bring its practices of ethnic assimilation into line with the doctrine of the equality of man leads also to alienated political beliefs and movements, and to the use of the political machine to provide rewards denied in the marketplace. The failure of the society to provide educational opportunities such that rural and working-class youth profit from the experience, and are made welcome in the urban middle-class high school classroom, leads to political ignorance and withdrawal, short-sighted interpretation of individual and group interest, and manipulation by political leaders skilled in influencing the mass mind. Community domination by a few central leaders and families, and the associated lack of independent organs of expression for others, leads to political apathy, lack of communication on "where the shoe pinches," and the possibilities of alienated, destructive, and unpredictable political expression in a stress situation. The failure of the media to represent the interests of Democrats and the working class encourages trivial, irrelevant, and half-hearted political expression among these groups. The failure of the political and governmental machinery to provide fewer but more crucial elections (because the founders were afraid of popular choices) dissipates the interest and energy of the public and encourages political withdrawal.

The sins of society, when a failure to live up to the values of democracy is a sin, emerge in political life as symptoms of disorder. It is better to attack the sin and not the system. In doing this we cannot rest on concepts of equalitarianism grown to fruition in the struggle for universal franchise. We cannot abandon the field to the individual conscience unguided by social norms of duty. We cannot resist the expression of emotion in politics because of the frightening experience of historical parallels. We cannot abandon the issue on the grounds that all politics is irrational anyway. We cannot blink our eyes to the fact that the nonparticipant today is likely to be endowed with only a tenuous grip on democratic attitudes; but we cannot forget that he must have political expression for the satisfaction of his own legitimate needs. In good conscience we cannot do these things. Instead we must create the social patterns and the conditions of personality growth from which a democratic and humane political expression will flow. Only in this way will there develop a public capable of assuming the responsibilities of democracy, bringing to fruition the promise of an ancient dream.

Author Index

Subject Index

A

Activity, political, 92-94; and group membership, 188, 190; latent structure of, 93-94; as life style, 197; and partisanship, 177; passive v. active involvement in, 94; *see also* Discussion, Exposure, Financial contributions, Petitioning, Voting, Writing letters

Affection, need for, 302; *see also* Social adjustment

Age groups in politics, 40, 48; and anomie, 168; characteristics of youth, 341; childhood influences, 204-08; and citizen duty, 159; and joining organizations, 77-78; life phases, 216-19; and media exposure, 83; and party identification, 300; and sense of political effectiveness, 151; *see also* Youth, Generations, Family

Aggression, feelings of, 118-20; external expression of, 119

Agreement, strain toward, 108

Agriculture, 333, 334; *see also* Rural

Alienation, 232, 344

Anomie, 166-69

Anxiety, and selective inattention, 297

Apathy, 108, 114, 116-18, 126; of Democrats, 144; and isolation, 187; and low sense of effectiveness, 153; and the media, 283-89; and municipal reform, 270-71; Negro, 252; and personality, 342; and rearing, 205; representation of, 347-48; *see also* Involvement, Non-Participants, Voting, Withdrawal

Apportionment, 41; and turnout, 353

Ascendance: see Dominance

Associations, voluntary, 191-95; church connected, 245; and concentration of power, 259-60; ethnic isolation of, 261; politicization of, 353; programs of, 260; *see also* Groups, Political organizations, Reference groups

Atomization, 352-53

Attention, shapelessness of, 140

Attentive public, and foreign policy, 345

Audiences: receptivity of, 294-98; attitudes toward the source, 295; scanning process of, 294; uses of symbolic attachment, 295; *see also* Exposure, Media

Authoritarianism, 126-27

Automation, 334

Awareness, political, 232; *see also* Interest, Involvement

B

Band-wagon: see Expectations

Bicameralism, 317

Bosses: see Machines, political

British: electoral reform, 40-42; amateur in politics, 306

Bryan, W. J., 22, 24, 25

Burke-Wadsworth bill, 71

Business cycle and turnout, 328-30

C

Campaigns, political, 23-26, 278-81, 304; *see also* Electioneering

Candidate appeal, 24-25, 138, 139; and

331-32; and voting patterns, 48, 331-34; and writing letters, 68; *see also* Education, Income, Social class

Oligarchy: see Elite, Power

One-party areas: characteristics of, 308-09; primaries in, 312, 313

Opinion leaders, 53-54; and gregariousness, 165; and the media, 292; and occupations, 331-32; *see also* Influence

Opinion, public, control by, 306-07; limitation of, 348-49

Other-directed personality, 109; *see also* Social adjustment

"Outer Circle," 306

Overdetermination of political participation, 131-32

Ozonometer, political, 306

P

Paradigm of electoral behavior, 6

Pareto's law, 327-28

Participation: degree desired, 340-48; gains and losses for the individual, 337-40; *see also* Activity, and the specific forms of participation

Parties, political: competition between, 306; contact of and turnout, 304-05; discouragement of turnout, 305-06; financing of, 52-56, 305-06; leadership needs, 303; nature of, 299; and nonpartisan elections, 311; and partisanship, 175-80; and primaries, 312-14; as reference groups, 299-301; strengthening of, 354; weakening of, 319; *see also* Party-identification

Partisanship, 175-80; and cross pressures, 201; *see also* Party-identification

Party-identification, 138, 139, 175; and candidate charisma, 301-02; demography of, 299-300; and economic rewards, 302-03; ethnic tradition of, 242; as limitation on ethnocentrism, 343; in one-party areas, 310; as organizing force, 300-01; positive-negative balance, 301; satisfactions of, 302

Patronage, 105, 239, 240; *see also* Favors

Perception: and electoral behavior, 6; of economic gain in politics, 103

Personality: of independents, 346; political views and, 97-100; and 1948-1952 elections, 98; *see also* Political man

Petitioning public officials, 63-77; bureaucratic-legislative targets, 66; local-national differences, 64-65; qualities required to petition, 63-64; social class differences, 64-65; *see also* Writing letters to officials

Policy, pursuit of, 169-75; increased polarization of, 353-54

Polish-Americans in politics, 243, 247, 248, 262-63

Political efficacy: see Effectiveness

Political man: argument on the nature of, 27, 28; conscious needs, 101-114; emphasis on power, 124-25; evasion of choice, 36; political significance of, 97-100; political involvement, 133 ff; social attitudes of, 163 ff; unconscious needs, 101-114; *see also* Aggression, Conflict, Neurosis, Personality, Self-interest

Political organizations, 74-79; *see also* Associations

"Politists," 52, 347

Polls, hours of closing, 315

Popular government, defense of, 27-37

Position in group, effect on political interests, 195-97

Power: concentration of, 256-61; pursuit of, 124-28, 132

Precinct leaders, 52-53; and economic gain, 107

Primaries, 312-14

Privatizing: ignorance, 114; needs, 359; *see also* Withdrawal

Progressive movement, 229-30

Property-ownership, 322-23

Proportion effect, 262-63

Proportional representation, 314-15

Prosperity, and turnout, 328-30

Proximity, social, principle of, 229

Public interest, business affected with, 325

Puritanism: effect on businessmen, 229; effect on Norwegian-Lutherans, 244; *see also* Morality

R

Race: see Negro

Radicalism, and sense of political effectiveness, 154; *see also* Communism, Deviance

Radio, and politics, 277, 290, 291; *see also* Exposure, Media

Randolph, A. P., 237

Rationality: and apathy, 351; and vote decision, 338

Reading habits, 283-85; *see also* Exposure

Rebellion, youthful, 207

Reference groups: definition of, 188-89; intensity of public identification, 352; and media attention, 295; and perception of economic needs, 105; political